D0475829

Hannibal's Last Battle
Zama and the Fall of Carthage

Hannibal's Last Battle
Zama and the Fall of Carthage

Brian Todd Carey

Joshua B. Allfree
Tactical Map Illustrator

John Cairns
Regional Map Illustrator

Pen & Sword
MILITARY

First published in Great Britain in 2007 by
Pen & Sword Military
an imprint of
Pen & Sword Books Ltd
47 Church Street
Barnsley
South Yorkshire
S70 2AS

ISBN: 978-1-84415-635-1

A CIP catalogue record for this book is
available from the British Library.

Typeset in 11/13pt Ehrhardt by Concept, Huddersfield
Printed and bound in England by CPI UK

Pen & Sword Books Ltd incorporates the imprints of Pen & Sword Aviation, Pen & Sword Maritime, Pen & Sword Military, Wharncliffe Local History, Pen & Sword Select, Pen and Sword Military Classics and Leo Cooper.

For a complete list of Pen & Sword titles please contact
PEN & SWORD BOOKS LIMITED
47 Church Street, Barnsley, South Yorkshire, S70 2AS, England
E-mail: enquiries@pen-and-sword.co.uk
Website: www.pen-and-sword.co.uk

Contents

Preface and Acknowledgements

Few historical figures in western civilization have commanded as much attention from historians, generals and military theorists as Hannibal Barca. Born into a well-placed Carthaginian military dynasty, Hannibal and his brothers Hasdrubal and Mago, followed in their father Hamilcar's footsteps and dedicated their lives to battling the Romans in Spain, Italy and North Africa. Hannibal's epic journey across the Alps and numerous victories over Roman armies during the Second Punic War have been studied for millennia, while his destruction of the Roman host at Cannae in a double-envelopment has often been considered the perfect engagement. Nearly always fighting at a disadvantage in manpower and resources, Hannibal rose to the ranks of legend within his own lifetime, becoming the most feared man in the Mediterranean. It is even said his reputation was so fierce that Roman parents merely had to utter '*Hannibal ad portas*' ('Hannibal is at the gates') when their children misbehaved.

In the twentieth century more attention has been paid to the generalship and campaigns of Hannibal's arch-enemy and eventual nemesis, Publius Cornelius Scipio 'Africanus'. This scrutiny has given rise to a new appreciation of this Roman commander, with many historians proclaiming Scipio to be 'greater than Hannibal' as either tactician, strategist, or both. Like Hannibal, Scipio was from a well-established noble family, but, unlike his Punic adversary, Scipio had the advantage of fighting for a civilization with extraordinary resources and a growing desire for imperium. The struggle between these two giants of their age is emblematic of conflicts between antagonists and civilizations in any age, which is probably why historians have spent so much effort studying these two extraordinary generals.

As the title of this study suggests, this monograph concentrates on the campaigns of Hannibal and Scipio Africanus during the Second Punic War, emphasizing the events leading up to the Battle of Zama in 202 BCE. In order to put this campaign in perspective, time is spent exploring the origins, course and outcome of the First Punic War and the events leading to the eventual destruction of Carthage in the Third Punic War. It is hoped that this work will serve as a brief introduction to the Punic wars and to the personalities and campaigns of two of military history's most compelling figures.

When I began research on this book, Joshua B. Allfree and John Cairns, my illustrators for *Warfare in the Ancient World* and *Warfare in the Medieval World*, came on board again and provided outstanding tactical and regional map illustrations. Their efforts give this book its uniqueness. We could not have completed this project without the collaboration and support of a few notable people. We would like to first and foremost thank Pen and Sword Books, especially our managing editor Rupert Harding. Mr Harding's wisdom and guidance throughout the process of publishing three books in three years has proved invaluable, as has the adroit copy editing of Philip Sidnell, whose knowledge of, and passion for, ancient military history is evident in his support of this project. Without these gentlemen's generous assistance this book would simply not have been possible. Special thanks is also extended to Dr Jon Carleton, Chair of History and Military Studies at the American Public University System, for his encouragement while writing this book. Finally, we would like to thank our family and friends whose unwavering support over the process of creating these three books has been instrumental to our success.

Brian Todd Carey
Loveland, Colorado

List of Maps

Key to Maps

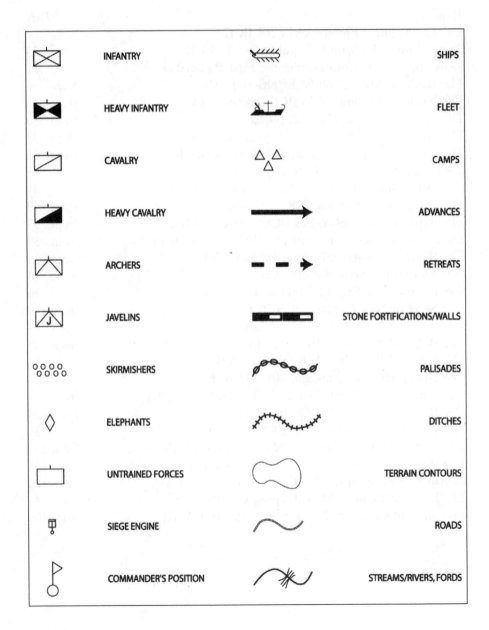

INFANTRY		SHIPS
HEAVY INFANTRY		FLEET
CAVALRY		CAMPS
HEAVY CAVALRY		ADVANCES
ARCHERS		RETREATS
JAVELINS		STONE FORTIFICATIONS/WALLS
SKIRMISHERS		PALISADES
ELEPHANTS		DITCHES
UNTRAINED FORCES		TERRAIN CONTOURS
SIEGE ENGINE		ROADS
COMMANDER'S POSITION		STREAMS/RIVERS, FORDS

List of Illustrations

Chronology of the Punic Wars (264–146 BCE)

264
Carthage seizes the city of Messana in northeastern Sicily and control over the strategically important Strait of Messina between Sicily and Italy. Rome declares war and sends a relief army from Italy under the command of consul Appius Claudius Caudex. The First Punic War between Rome and Carthage (264–241) begins.

260
The Romans build a navy from scratch and, under the command of consul Gaius Duilius, win a decisive naval engagement against Carthage near Mylae in northern Sicily.

256
A Roman navy under the command of the consul Marcus Atilius Regulus defeats a Carthaginian fleet near Sicily's Cape Ecnomus in the largest naval engagement of the ancient world.

255
Rome lands an invasion force in North Africa under the command of consul Marcus Atilius Regulus. Carthage hires the Spartan mercenary commander Xanthippus, who defeats the Roman army at Tunis and captures the consul. Rome also loses over two hundred warships in a storm off the coast of Sicily.

249
Carthage defeats a large Roman fleet off the western coast of Sicily in the Battle of Drepana.

247
Carthaginian general Hamilcar Barca is sent to Sicily to take command of the defence of the island.

241
A Roman navy under the command of consul Gaius Lutatius Catulus defeats a large Punic fleet at the Battle of Aegates Islands. Hamilcar sues for peace. End of the First Punic War

240
Hamilcar Barca's army returns to North Africa and rebels against Carthage, initiating the Mercenary War (240–237).

238

Rome intervenes in Sardinia, removing Punic influence and annexing island.

237

Mercenary War ends. Hamilcar Barca arrives in Spain and begins consolidating Carthaginian control over the southern peninsula.

229

Hamilcar Barca is killed by the Oretani tribe in Spain. He is replaced by his son-in-law Hasdrubal. Hasdrubal founds the city of New Carthage as the capital of Carthaginian Spain and continues to campaign in Iberia.

225–220

Rome defeats Insubres and other Gallic tribes in the Po Valley, expanding its influence in northern Italy (Cisalpine Gaul).

221

Hasdrubal assassinated and succeeded by Hannibal Barca as governor and commanding general of Spain.

219–218

Hannibal attacks the Spanish city of Saguntum, taking the city after an eight-month siege. The loss of this Roman ally forces the Senate to declare war on Carthage.

218

Second Punic War between Rome and Carthage begins (218-201). Hannibal leaves New Carthage with large army, crosses Pyrenees, and evades Roman army at the Rhone River. Hannibal crosses the Alps, defeats Roman armies at Ticinus and Trebia. Roman general Gnaeus Cornelius Scipio arrives in Spain.

217

Hannibal pushes south toward Rome, evading two Roman armies sent to intercept him, and ambushes consul Gaius Flaminius at the Battle of Lake Trasimene. Quintus Fabius Maximus elected dictator in Rome and enacts policy of harassing Hannibal's forces. Hannibal skirts Rome and winters in Apulia. Publius Cornelius Scipio (the Elder) joins brother in Spain.

216

Rome abandons delaying strategy and moves to engage Hannibal Barca. Hannibal defeats an enormous Roman army at Cannae. Capua and other members of the Roman Confederation defect to Punic cause.

215

Hannibal captures the strategically important city of Casilinum in Campania. Hannibal and Philip V of Macedon enter alliance against Rome. First Macedonian War begins (215–205).

214

Romans retake Casilinum. The Hellenistic city-state of Syracuse defects to Carthage. Rome sends an army to Sicily under the command of Marcus Claudius Marcellus. A Roman army under the command of proconsul Marcus Valerius Laevinus defeats the Macedonians near Apollonia.

213

Roman attack on Syracuse fails. Romans settle into siege of the city. A Carthaginian relief army lands in Sicily.

212

Romans reduce Syracuse, ending the Greek city-state's independence on the island. Hannibal takes Tarentum in Apulia, while Rome besieges the rebel city of Capua.

211

Hannibal marches on Rome, while the Romans take Capua and sell the population into slavery. In Spain, Gnaeus Cornelius Scipio and Publius Cornelius Scipio (the Elder) are killed.

210

Hannibal continues to have military success in Italy. Publius Cornelius Scipio (the Younger) appointed by Senate to command in Spain. Romans raid the coast of North Africa.

209

Quintus Fabius Maximus elected to fifth consulship and recaptures Tarentum. Scipio the Younger storms New Carthage.

208

Scipio defeats Punic forces at Baecula in Spain. Hasdrubal Barca (brother of Hannibal) leads relief army out of Spain. Romans under the command of proconsul Marcus Valerius Laevinus raid coast of North Africa.

207

Hasdrubal Barca invades Italy and attempts to rendezvous with Hannibal. Roman armies under the command of consuls Gaius Claudius Nero and Marcus Livius Salinator defeat and kill Hasdrubal at Metaurus River. Laevinus raids coast of North Africa.

206

Scipio defeats Carthaginian forces at Battle of Ilipa in Spain. Later, Scipio suppresses a rebellion led by the Spanish chief Indibilis of the Ilergetes.

205

First Macedonian War ends. Scipio elected consul and prepares invasion of North Africa from headquarters in Sicily. Scipio's legate Gaius Laelius raids North Africa. Romans recapture Locri and Scipio weathers Pleminius scandal. Mago Barca (brother of Hannibal) invades Italy, landing near Genoa.

204

Scipio invades North Africa, landing near Utica. Scipio sets up camp (*castra Cornelia*) outside of city.

203

Scipio destroys enemy winter camps and defeats Carthaginians at Battle of the Great Plains. Hannibal and Mago recalled from Italy. Mago killed in retreat, but his army returns to North Africa.

202

Scipio defeats Hannibal at the Battle of Zama.

201

Peace treaty ratified by Roman Senate. End of Second Punic War. Scipio returns to Rome, given triumph and takes cognomen 'Africanus'. Hannibal elected as chief magistrate of Carthage and reconstructs the Carthaginian economy in order to pay the high reparations demanded by Rome.

200

Second Macedonian War between Rome and Macedon begins (200–196).

197

Consul Titus Quinctius Flamininus defeats King Philip V of Macedon at the Battle of Cynoscephalae.

196

Second Macedonian War ends.

195

Hannibal Barca exiled from Carthage, travels to the court of Antiochus III of Syria.

193

Scipio Africanus and Hannibal meet at the court of Antiochus III in Ephesus.

192

Syrian War between Rome and Syria begins (192–189).

190

Consul Laelius Cornelius Scipio (Africanus' brother) defeats Antiochus at Magnesia in Anatolia. Syrian War ends.

184

Scipio Africanus dies in exile at Liternum in northern Campania.

183

Hannibal Barca commits suicide at his villa in Bithynia.

172

Third Macedonian War (172–167) begins between Rome and King Perseus of Macedon.

168

Consul Lucius Aemilius Paullus (later 'Macedonicus') takes over command of Roman forces in Macedon.

167

Paullus defeats Perseus at Pydna, ending the Third Punic War. Kingdom of Macedon dissolved, replaced by four republics.

151

Carthage declares war on King Masinissa of Numidia.

149

Third Punic War begins between Rome and Carthage (149–146). Both Roman consuls, Lucius Marcius Censorinus and Marcus Manilius, invade North Africa and besiege Carthage. Siege bogs down. Fourth Macedonian War (149–148) begins between Rome and Macedon when Andriscus invades Macedon.

148

Roman siege of Carthage continues. Fourth Macedonian War ends.

147

Consul Publius Cornelius Scipio Aemilianus (Africanus' grandson) elected consul and given command in North Africa. Arrives at Carthage with new army and tightens siege.

146

Scipio Aemilianus captures Carthage. Carthage is destroyed, along with allied cities in region. Third Punic War ends. Roman province of Africa established.

Introduction: A Clash of Civilizations

The Battle of Zama as Turning Point

> *[T]here are times when Fortune thwarts the plans of the valiant, and others when ... a brave man meets one stronger than himself.* – Polybius on Hannibal's loss to Scipio Africanus at the Battle of Zama.

On a spring morning in 202 BCE, two of history's greatest generals reviewed their troops on the dusty plain of Zama, located five days march southwest from the ancient capital of Carthage in North Africa. On one side, the great Carthaginian general Hannibal Barca (247–183 BCE) arranged his multi-national army in three long lines and prepared to meet an experienced Roman army commanded by his rival and equal, Publius Cornelius Scipio (c.236–184 BCE). Rarely in history do generals of similar military genius meet on a battlefield to decide the fate of their own civilization. The Battle of Zama would be such an engagement, a turning point in the history of western civilization, for to the victor would go the riches of the western Mediterranean and the resources to build an enduring empire, and to the vanquished a diminished state and eventual eradication.

The Battle of Zama was the climax of the Second Punic War (218–202 BCE), a seventeen-year struggle between the Roman Republic and the maritime power of Carthage and the second conflict in a generation. The First Punic War (264–241) witnessed a Roman victory and the expansion of Roman imperium into Sicily (and later Sardinia) and the reduction of Carthaginian territorial and economic hegemony in an area with very old Punic ties. Although Rome was able to enforce an unequal peace, Carthage bounced back by investing Spain, putting itself again into the path of Roman expansion. A second Punic war was inevitable.

A year before, in 203, Hannibal Barca was called home by his government to lead the defence of his homeland after spending fifteen of the seventeen years of the war ravaging the Italian countryside, a feat unrivalled in the annals of military history. His decision in the late autumn of 218 to cross the Alps and bring the war directly to Italy put the Romans immediately on the defensive, while his early string of victories at Ticinus, Trebia, Trasimene and Cannae in the space of just two years (218–216) brought Rome to the brink of collapse. Hannibal had killed or captured between 80,000 and 100,000 legionaries and their commanders, robbing Rome of a third of its standing military force and most of their experienced officer class.[1] Hannibal's success was so complete that after the debacle at Cannae in 216 the Romans refused to meet him in a set-piece battle on Italian soil.

Down, but not out, the Romans entrusted a young general named Publius Cornelius Scipio (later 'Africanus') with the task of rebuilding an army. Scipio did so, and then used a mirror strategy of attacking Carthaginian Spain to harass the Punic lines of communication while giving his legionaries valuable military experience. Now commanding veteran legions, Scipio prepared his expeditionary force in Sicily and then brought the war to North Africa to threaten Carthage itself. Once in Africa, the Roman general was joined by fierce Numidian mercenaries, the very same mercenaries that had served his foe so well in recent years against Rome. Scipio's army now swelled to 29,000 infantry and over 6,100 cavalry, smaller than Hannibal's 36,000 infantry, 4,000 horse and eighty war elephants.

Confident in his ability to match a numerically-superior army due to the quality of his cavalry, Scipio rode up and down the Roman ranks, encouraging his men to fight. Across the field Hannibal gave his own battle speech. What was at stake was more than the lives of the tens of thousands of men and beasts gathered on the killing field, but the course of western civilization itself. The Battle of Zama was a watershed event in the history of two very different civilizations, one a Semitic *thalassocracy* or maritime power, the other an Indo-European land power with deep agricultural roots. These differences not only informed the political and economic development of Carthaginian civilization in North Africa and Roman civilization on the Italian Peninsula, but also moulded the way each culture made war.

Phoenicia's heir: The Rise of Carthage

According to legend, the Phoenician princess Dido first set foot on the northeast coast of ancient Tunisia and named it Carthage in 814 BCE. She picked this spot to found a new city because of the presence of fine natural harbours near coastal hills suitable for defence and arable land nearby. Carthage's placement on a hammerheaded promontory jutting out from the Tunisian mainland was an ideal location for a capital of a sea-borne civilization, reminiscent of the Phoenician city of Tyre in Lebanon.

Since the founding of Carthage by Phoenician colonists, this Semitic civilization put most of its energy into creating a maritime empire. The

Phoenicians were linguistic cousins of the Hebrews who settled along the Lebanese coast of the Levant just north of ancient Palestine. The end of the Bronze Age around 1000 BCE freed this entrepreneurial people from the grasp of their powerful Egyptian and Hittite neighbours, allowing them to use the valuable cedar trees found in their territory to construct a merchant navy consisting of sleek *bireme* war galleys and high-decked round ships. From their chief cities of Byblos, Sidon and Tyre, Phoenician sailors carried the famous Tyrian purple dye, glass, wine and lumber to markets in Egypt, Syria, and the Aegean coastline. Eventually these ships sailed into the western Mediterranean, past the Straits of Gibraltar and onward into the Atlantic, reaching Britain and the west coast of Africa.

In the eighth century BCE, the Phoenicians were conquered by the Assyrians, and later, in the sixth century, by the Chaldean and Persian empires. With Phoenicia absorbed into regional Iron Age empires, Carthage inherited the Phoenician settlements on the coasts of western Sicily, southern Spain and on the adjoining isles. These islands were valuable possessions – Malta as a cotton plantation, Elba as an iron mine, and the Balearic Islands of Majorca and Minorca as a recruiting ground for light infantry slingers. They also served as naval stations to preserve Carthage's monopoly of the sea-lanes.

As Carthage's population grew and outstripped its local resources, it expanded along the littoral of North Africa into a region called the *Maghreb* (modern Morocco, Algeria, Tunisia, and Libya), creating a substantial empire by the late third century BCE. The Carthaginians first traded with, and later subdued, many of the indigenous Berber tribes there, building colonies and intermarrying freely with these subject peoples. Those tribes which would not assimilate were pushed to the fringes, where they either raided Punic territory or offered their services as allies or mercenaries. The light horsemen from Numidia are perhaps the most famous of these warriors, serving in the Carthaginian army for generations.

By 500 BCE Carthage was the largest and richest city in the western Mediterranean, famous for its fine public buildings and luxurious villas. By the third century BCE Carthage's most impressive and imposing features were its city walls and its complex of docks. The city was built on a naturally-defensible position and then heavily fortified, and it was protected by two restricted land approaches. The northern approach was along a 3,000 yard-wide isthmus protected by three massive defence works towering one above the other. The southern approach was narrower and terminated at the foot of the city walls. The two isthmuses were separated by Lake Tunis, an unfordable body of water, and washed by the sea on their outer shores. A twenty-two mile wall enclosed the great city, the entrance of which lay to the east of the southern sandbar, as well as the citadel which was constructed on the Byrsa hill, overlooking the city.[2] The great complex consisted of a rectangular commercial port near

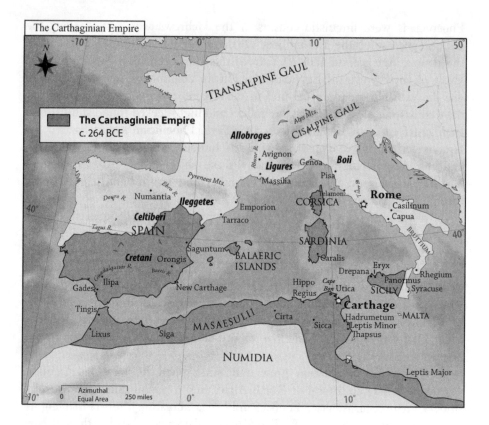

The Carthaginian Empire

the entrance and a circular military harbour protected by a double-set of walls. According to Appian, a second century Graeco–Egyptian writer living in the Roman Empire:

> The harbours had communications with each other, and a common entrance from the sea, 70 feet wide, which could be closed with iron chains. The first port was for merchant vessels, and here were collected all kinds of ships' tackle. Within the second port was an island, and great quays [docks] were set at intervals round both the harbour and the island. The embankments were full of shipyards which had capacity for 220 vessels. In addition to them were magazines for their tackle and furniture. Two Ionic columns stood in front of each dock, giving the appearance of a continuous portico to both the harbour and the island. On the island was built the admiral's house, from which the trumpeter gave signals, the herald delivered orders, and the admiral himself oversaw everything.... Not even incoming merchants could see the docks at once, for a double wall enclosed them, and there were gates by which the merchant ships could pass from the first port to the city without traversing the dockyards. Such was the appearance of Carthage at that time.[3]

Modern excavations reveal the depth of the original military harbour at only five feet, custom made for Punic warships that only had a four-foot draft.[4]

Like city-states in Italy and Greece during the Archaic period (c.750-c.500 BCE), Carthage was ruled by kings with divine right to rule and broad powers in war making, religion and governance. In parallel developments similar to the cities of Rome and Athens, Carthage went through a gradual transformation from monarchy to a bi-cameral legislature consisting of an aristocratic Council of Elders and Assembly of the People very similar to that of Rome, with political power concentrated in the hands of a few very wealthy merchant families.[5] Even the Greek philosopher and statesman Aristotle (384-322 BCE) was pleasantly surprised by the democratic nature of the Carthaginian political system.[6] Two leaders called *suffetes* were elected annually from the oligarchy, holding an executive position similar to the position of *consul* in Roman government, except that suffetes did not normally act as commanding generals. The Carthaginian government hired professional soldiers to fill that responsibility, giving rise to military dynasties whose fortunes rose and fell based on their success in war, the Barca family being the most famous.

Carthaginian religion was Semitic in origin, being transplanted with the original Phoenician colonists. Prayers were offered to such familiar Near Eastern deities as Baal Hammon, Tanit and Melqart, harsh gods and goddesses who demanded dramatic and severe forms of sacrifices, including child sacrifice. This ritual was condemned by Roman and Greek observers, who thought the practice was barbaric.[7] But over time, the Carthaginians gathered other deities into their religious pantheon from wherever they settled, with Greek and Egyptian gods and goddesses being favoured. Though the addition of foreign gods had a moderating effect on Carthaginian religious practices, human and child sacrifice continued in times of national crisis.

After independence from Phoenicia, Carthage's main foreign policy concern was the Greek city-state of Syracuse located on the eastern coast of Sicily just across from the toe of Italy. In an attempt to take over the entire island, the Syracusan tyrant Agathocles (r.317-289 BCE) made war against Carthage in the fourth and early third centuries, eventually giving up his claim to western Sicily. His death in 289 inspired Carthaginian expansion on the island, but this came at a time when the region was faced with a new and powerful political player – the Roman Republic.

Rome: From City-State to Master of Italy
About the same time Phoenician colonists from Tyre were founding Carthage in the eighth century BCE, villagers along the Tiber River in central Italy were consolidating their distinctive round-hutted villages into a small city-state called Rome. According to tradition, Rome was founded in 753 BCE by Romulus, who became the first of seven Roman and Etruscan kings in what is known as the Regal Period (753–509 BCE). Practical, innovative, and very hard working,

these first Romans were religiously conservative agriculturalists, praying to indigenous deities and to those borrowed from contacts with Etruscans to the north and Greeks to the south. Contacts with the Etruscans led to invasion and occupation around 620 by Lucius Tarquinius Priscus. Etruscan kings ruled Rome until about 509 when the last of these monarchs, Lucius Tarquinius Superbus ('the Proud'), was removed by the Romans.

The origins of the Etruscans are not clear, but after 650 BCE they became the dominant cultural and economic force in north-central Italy and founded settlements as far south as Capua, giving them direct contact with the Greek colonists living in southern Italy. The Etruscans contributed a great deal to Roman engineering and culture during this century of occupation. They introduced the arch to the Romans, constructed the first road through central Rome – the Sacred Way – and oversaw the development of temples, markets, shops, streets and houses using a grid pattern. The Etruscan toga and short cloak were also adopted by the Romans, with the Roman aristocracy favouring Tyrian purple-dyed clothing as a status symbol. Even the Latin alphabet is of Etruscan origin, a modification of one derived from the Greeks.

In religious matters, the Romans in the Regal Period were very conservative and pragmatic. They practiced a type of ancestor worship. The gods were viewed as disembodied spirits or powers which could be won over by the right prayers and sacrifices and whose will was revealed in the flight of birds and in thunder. This superstitious belief was so strong that it could determine if or when a battle took place. The Romans viewed their relations with the gods as contractual – if the state did its duty to the gods, then it hoped the gods would be pleased and cooperative. If things went awry, then great pains were taken by appointed officials to restore the gods' favour through sacrifice and extra-ordinary vows at public temples. As the Roman kingdom evolved into the Roman Republic, the aristocratic class, known as the *patricians*, maintained their monopoly of religion over the lower or *plebeian* class. Roman religion became increasingly a centralized and state-guided endeavour.

Around 509 BCE, the Romans overthrew Etruscan rule. Newly-independent Rome replaced the Etruscan monarchy with a republic governed by a council of elders drawn from the wealthy class. This council, or Senate, annually elected two *consuls* as chief magistrates of the Roman state. From 362 BCE, *imperium*, or the authority to command the Roman army, was entrusted to the consuls, or to their junior colleagues, the *praetors*. Though the election of co-rulers ensured a balance of political power, it had serious military drawbacks. The two consuls shared responsibilities for military operations, alternating command privileges every other day. Recognizing the inefficiency of this system, Roman law provided for the appointment in times of national crisis of a *dictator*, for the duration of six months.

After expelling their Etruscan overlords, the early Roman Republic expanded from a tiny area of Latium in the Tiber River valley using their well-organized and highly-disciplined army and adopting a tolerant policy toward the people they conquered. But the Roman military were not always certain of success. In the fifth century the Romans and their allies the Latins barely held their own against the local mountain tribes. Over the next century the Romans survived and even thrived, pushing north against the Etruscans, conquering Veii in 396, and south against the tribes of central Italy, besting them one by one. They even endured a whirlwind invasion of Celtic tribes in the early fourth century (c.390). Their generally lenient treatment of the vanquished and their tolerance of native traditions and practices made them acceptable occupiers, though the Campanians and Samnites fought for decades against Roman expansion, eventually succumbing to the relentless Roman military machine.

As they advanced the Romans built roads along strategic routes and established colonies of retired Roman and Latin soldiers as permanent garrisons at key points. These newly-conquered regions entered into a Roman confederation, yielding control of their foreign affairs and perhaps a third of their territory in return for local autonomy and exemption from taxes. They also became an important source of military manpower, enabling Rome to not only continue its conquest of new regions, but also to recover from seemingly disastrous battlefield debacles.

As Carthaginian warships plied the western seas and skirmished with Syracuse in the fourth century, Rome, which had no navy of its own, was using its powerful army to expand southward into what was known as *Magna Graecia* or 'Greater Greece', the area south of modern Naples encompassing the toe and heel of Italy that had been colonized by the Greeks. Once the Romans had secured this area at the beginning of the third century BCE, their focus turned to Sicily. Here, Rome competed with two other regional powers – Carthage and Syracuse – for control of this economically-important island. Friction between these three players would eventually lead to the First Punic War (264–241 BCE), with Syracuse siding with Rome in the conflict.

For twenty-three years Rome and Carthage battled each other for control of Sicily, an endeavour that required Rome to build a navy from scratch to challenge Punic control of the sea. Despite losing fleets to both Carthaginian naval acumen and Mediterranean storms, the Romans persevered and eventually won the First Punic War in 241, forcing Carthage to except a punitive peace stripping away Sicily and a high financial indemnity. Demanding blood, Rome continued the pressure on Carthage over the next two decades, until friction over territory in Spain precipitated a Second Punic War in 218 BCE.

Nearly seventeen years later, the war was not going as Hannibal Barca had planned. His early string of seemingly-decisive victories over Rome in Roman territory had not produced what he had hoped for – the unravelling of the Roman confederation and destruction of Rome as a regional competitor. Instead, Rome had persevered and, under the inspired generalship of Publius

Rome During the Middle Republic

Rome
The Middle Republic
c. 218 BCE

Cornelius Scipio, brought the war directly to Carthaginian territory to threaten the capital itself.

The story of Hannibal's last battle is more than the story of how men and animals manoeuvred on a battlefield on that dusty plain in ancient Tunisia some twenty-two centuries ago. The Battle of Zama was the climax of two generations of warfare involving two generations of warriors. Both Hannibal and Scipio were members of military dynasties and sons of prominent generals who had fought the enemy and failed. Hamilcar Barca failed to defend Sicily in the final stages of the First Punic War, while the first Publius Cornelius Scipio (known to history as Scipio the Elder) was unsuccessful in intercepting Hannibal in southern Gaul before he crossed the Alps in 218 and was defeated at Ticinus a year later. Both sons wanted to avenge the spoiled reputations of their fathers, and a victory on the field of Zama would provide this opportunity. Interestingly, the Battle of Zama would be the third time Hannibal and Scipio the Younger would face each other, but the first time that Scipio would hold overall command of Roman forces in the engagement. Hannibal had won the day at Ticinus (218) and Cannae (216) early in the Second Punic War, but after honing his skills campaigning in Spain, the pupil Scipio was now in North Africa to test the master.

This work is intended to be a history of the Second Punic War (218–202 BCE) with an emphasis on the climactic battle between Rome and Carthage at Zama in 202 BCE. Zama witnessed the generalship of two extraordinary commanders, Hannibal Barca and Scipio Africanus, in a battle which at once sealed the doom of one civilization (Carthage) and launched the other (Rome) into preeminence in the Mediterranean. Background will be provided on the Carthaginian and Roman civilizations and military institutions, followed by a discussion of the origins, course and outcome of the First Punic War. Next, the lives, generalship and campaigns of Hannibal Barca and Scipio Africanus will be explored during the first years of the Second Punic War. All of this will lead up to an exhaustive discussion of the Battle of Zama itself, one which will include a detailed account of Carthaginian and Roman military organizations and tactics utilized, and ending with an appraisal of both Hannibal and Scipio as generals. The aftermath of the battle will be explored, specifically the life of Hannibal as political exile and Scipio as political genius. Finally, the rise of Rome as a Mediterranean power in the first half of the second century will be discussed, culminating in the destruction of Carthage in the Third Punic War. This monograph is intended to be a short history aimed at both the undergraduate university student and armchair historian. Our story begins with a discussion of the military organization and tactics of the Carthaginians and the Romans and the origins of the First Punic War.

N.B. All dates in this book are BCE, unless otherwise stated.

Chapter 1

The First Punic War (264–241 BCE)

The Organization and Tactics of the Carthaginian Army
The military traditions inherited by Hannibal Barca and Scipio Africanus during the Second Punic War (218–202 BCE) reflect the character of Carthaginian and Roman civilization as a whole. The Roman military machine began exclusively as a land army and grew out of the experience of wars of expansion in Italy, while the Carthaginians, as a thalassocracy, built a powerful navy to protect their sea-lanes and colonial possessions in the western Mediterranean, and supplemented their navy with a land force relying heavily on subject peoples and mercenaries. Although both traditions originally drew heavily from the Greek way of war, each modified their armies to meet their specific needs. For the most part, the military organization and tactics used by both generals were already in place by the First Punic War (264–241 BCE).

Unfortunately for modern historians, Rome's destruction of Carthaginian civilization after the Third Punic War (149–146 BCE) was so complete that we are left with no contemporary Punic chronicler to explain the organizational and tactical elements of their military in the way the Romans did. What we can piece together about the Carthaginian way of war comes from Roman sources, primarily Polybius and Livy.

By birth and education Greek, Polybius (c.200–118 BCE) was a distinguished official from the city of Megalopolis in Arcadia. This city became the seat of power for the Achaean League, a Hellenic group noted for its pro-Macedonian and anti-Roman sentiments. After the Romans defeated King Perseus of Macedon (reigned 179–168) in 168 BCE, Polybius became one of the thousands of leading Greeks brought to Rome as war captives. He was fortunate enough to befriend and tutor Publius Cornelius Scipio Aemilianus, the adopted grandson of Scipio Africanus. This connection, and a deep-seated interest in the testimony of eyewitnesses, letters, lost treaties, and Punic inscriptions, provided Polybius with a wealth of information about the Second Punic War.[8]

Livy (Titus Livius) was the outstanding Roman historian of the Augustan age. He lived from 59 BCE to 17 CE and wrote a history of Rome in Latin filling 142 books. Livy covers the periods 753–243 and 219–167 BCE with great detail. He is particularly strong in his comparisons of Hannibal Barca and Scipio Africanus after the Battle of Zama.[9] But Polybius and Livy, along with Plutarch, Appian, and Cassio Dio, were also pro-Roman in their accounts, and this bias combined with the thorough razing of Carthage after the Third Punic War severely hampered these historians in their reconstruction of the three wars between Rome and Carthage.

By the time of the First Punic War, Carthage's citizens had for the most part ceased to fight as foot soldiers, though they did command the army and serve in a professional officer class.[10] Polybius does make certain references to 'the phalanx of the Carthaginians' at the end of the First Punic War when referring to the defence of Carthage itself, so historians do believe that an indigenous Punic army of perhaps 1,500 men did exist to defend the homeland.[11] As a wealthy maritime empire, Carthage had the luxury of using its subject peoples and mercenaries to fight its wars. North Africans of mixed Libyan and Phoenician descent made up a quarter of the army, though Celts, Spaniards, Numidians and Greeks also served, as did soldiers from the various islands in the western Mediterranean.[12]

Each of these subject peoples or mercenaries brought their own tactical specialization to the battlefield, and when coordinated by a general of the calibre of Hamilcar Barca or his son Hannibal, the multinational Carthaginian army was a force to be reckoned with. The backbone of the Punic heavy infantry was made up of Liby-Phoenicians who fought in a Greek-style phalanx. There is some debate concerning how these troops were armed, either with long pikes in the Macedonian fashion, or with the shorter thrusting spears favoured by hoplites.[13] However they were armed, their armour consisted of helmets, greaves, and linen or leather corslets and a round shield. These soldiers made up the main shock component of the army.

Barbarian heavy infantry included Spanish and Celtic contingents. Spanish warriors fought with either a cut-and-slash sword known as a *falcata*, a curved, single-edged weapon derived from the Greek *kopis*, or a short double-edged thrusting sword from which the Roman *gladius hispaniensis* was patterned.[14] Like the Romans, they discharged two short javelins, a light one made entirely of iron, and a heavier, weighted one made of wood and iron right before entering hand-to-hand combat. In fact some historians believe that the Romans adopted the use of weighted javelins (*pila*) from the Iberians.[15] Spanish warriors were protected by a flat oval shield or *scutum*, similar to that carried by the Romans.[16] These *scutarii*, so named because of these shields, were some of Hannibal's best troops in the Second Punic War and a match for Roman infantry.[17] Polybius described the Spanish soldiers' national dress as short purple-bordered tunics.[18]

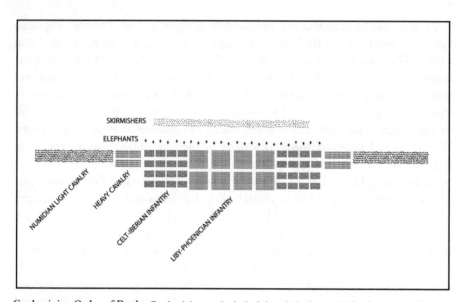

SKIRMISHERS

ELEPHANTS

NUMIDIAN LIGHT CAVALRY

HEAVY CAVALRY

CELT-IBERIAN INFANTRY

LIBY-PHOENICIAN INFANTRY

Carthaginian Order of Battle. Carthaginian armies lacked the relatively standardized approach of Roman organizations. A typical Carthaginian pre-battle deployment often consisted of infantry formations flanked by cavalry and screened by skirmishers. Notable amongst these light troops were the deadly slingers from the Balearic Islands. Elephants were also deployed in front of the army, spaced 15 to 45 metres apart. The beasts could prove highly effective against infantry, and also helped protect the army against enemy cavalry, as horeses shied from contact with the pachyderms unless they had been trained together. However, elephants posed almost as great a danger to their own infantry as they did to the enemy, as they could often be stampeded by missile fire, trumpet blasts, or spikes sown on the ground. Carthaginian armies were composed of a number of different tribes, complicating communications, though this was offset by allowing troops to fight using their native methods under their own leadership. The Carthaginian heavy infantry, mainly Liby-Phoenician in composition, were often described as deployed in phalanx formations. The phalanx had the advantage of mass and was difficult to stop, but was far more unwieldy than the Roman legion and could often be outflanked if caught without cavalry support. Carthaginian cavalry was Hannibal's true arm of decision and was normally far superior in number and quality to the Romans. Numidian light cavalry was particularly skilled and presented a significant danger to Roman formations.

Celtic infantry were recruited from the Gallic tribes north of the Po River. The Celts (or Gauls as they were sometimes referred to) were an Indo-European people who inhabited an area of Western Europe including modern France, southern Holland, Switzerland, and Germany west of the Rhine. Most of the Celts were settled farmers like the Greeks and Romans. They were organized into tribes and capable of fielding very large armies. Like other Indo-European peoples, these tribal warriors were organized into clans and lived for war, glory, plunder and, peculiar to Celtic tribes, headhunting. The Celts usually fought with a long slashing sword and without body armour and were protected only by their oval, leather-covered shields. Polybius tells us that the Celts fought naked, while Livy recounts that they fought wearing only trousers.[19] Although individually brave, Celtic warriors could be unreliable in mass warfare. Hannibal often used these undisciplined warriors as shock troops to attack the enemy centre before committing his better trained and more reliable cavalry.

The Carthaginians benefited from light infantry of a superior quality than those that served the Romans. We know that Greek *peltasts* (javelin throwers), so named because of the light wicker shield or *pelta* carried by the skirmishers, were employed by Punic commanders. The most famous of these light troops were the slingers from the Balearic Islands, who served as mercenaries for various armies for almost six hundred years.[20] Armed with different kinds of slings made from black-tufted rush, hair or sinew depending on range and target, the Balearic slingers had a fast rate of fire and were extremely accurate even at long range.[21] The heavy sling could fire a stone the size of a tennis ball over three hundred yards.[22] Balearic warriors also served as javelin throwers and spearmen.

Unlike the Romans who emphasized infantry as their decisive arm, the Carthaginian art of war held a special place for cavalry, which evolved into the dominant tactical system in Punic warfare. The core contingents were comprised of a small number of elite Carthaginian and Liby-Phoenician heavy cavalry made up of upper-class professional soldiers. Carthaginian commanders also utilized Celtic and Spanish cavalry. Celtic cavalry were recruited from the nobility and were protected by expensive mail armour, metal helmets, and a round or oval shield. They were normally armed with a long sword and heavy thrusting spear or lance.[23] Celts were natural fighters, and their hatred of the Romans made them natural allies for the Carthaginians. Spanish light cavalry, like their infantry, were not armoured, but wore the same purple-bordered tunics. Each horseman was armed with a cut-and-thrust *falcata* and two javelins or light spears with butt-spikes. There is some evidence that some Spanish horse were heavy cavalry, armed with heavier spears or lances, and may well have been armoured.[24]

The finest light cavalry was supplied by the Numidians, a fierce nomadic people from the remoter parts of what is now Tunisia and Algeria. These accomplished equestrians of Berber stock began as enemies of Carthage, but were eventually turned into allies or mercenaries. Contemporary chroniclers have them fighting under either Punic commanders or their own captains, of whom Masinissa and Syphax are the most famous. Numidian soldiers developed a special relationship with the Barca family, serving Hannibal and his younger brothers Hasdrubal and Mago in Spain during the Second Punic War.[25] Numidian horsemen rode without armour, protected only by a small buckler shield or leopard skin draped over their arm. They also rode without reins, controlling their mounts by a rope around the neck, the pressure of their knees and a small riding stick. Like other barbarian light cavalry throughout the ancient world, these mounted warriors utilized hit-and-run tactics, riding close to the enemy, discharging their javelins, and then riding away.[26] Hannibal used these specialists in manoeuvre warfare with great effect against the Romans at Trebia in 218 BCE, taunting the legionaries into action at a time of the Carthaginian commander's choosing.

Organizationally and tactically, Carthaginian warfare owed much to the Hellenistic combined-arms system exemplified by the campaigns of the Macedonian Alexander the Great (356–323) and modified over the next century by the Hellenistic Successor kingdoms. Alexander's unprecedented successes at Granicus River (334), Issus (333) and Gaugamela (331) cast a long shadow on the conduct of warfare throughout the classical world, and Carthaginian commanders in the third century were well schooled in how to orchestrate infantry and cavalry on the battlefield. And like the Macedonians, cavalry, not infantry, was the decisive arm in Carthaginian warfare. Punic warfare even utilized elephants in war which they had first encountered in their war with King Pyrrhus (319–272 BCE), a brilliant general from the Hellenized region of Epirus northwest of Greece, in what is now roughly modern Albania.

War elephants provided Hellenistic generals with a new weapon system, one that fused shock and missile elements. Each beast usually carried a driver or *mahout* seated on its neck and a turret containing a spearman, for shock combat, and an archer or javelin thrower for missile fire. Although slow and vulnerable to enemy missile attack, the war elephant's main advantages in combat were its size and the terror it inspired in troops and enemy horses unused to fighting the pachyderm. Moreover, war elephants were sometimes used as living siege engines, forcing the entrance to cities.[27] Normally, larger Indian elephants were used in Hellenistic warfare, though Carthage preferred the smaller African forest elephants because they were easier to acquire and train.[28]

On the battlefield, war elephants were placed in the forward ranks of the formation and spaced fifty to 150 feet apart to discourage enemy cavalry charges because horses that were not trained around elephants were frightened of their size, smell, and sound. But using elephants in a combat setting was also fraught with danger. If struck by too many arrows or javelins, an elephant might become uncontrollable and stampede through its own ranks (the mahout carried a hammer and large iron spike to dispatch the animal if it turned on its own troops).[29] In order to protect the pachyderm cavalry, later Successor generals added a permanent detachment of light troops (usually archers) and dressed the elephant in leather or metal barding to protect the animal from missiles and hamstringing.[30]

As war elephants became more common in Hellenistic warfare, special anti-elephant devices were adopted by their foes. The most common defence was planting the ground with sharpened spikes, thereby targeting the animal's soft foot tissue. Wounded in this manner, a war elephant was nearly impossible to control and often trampled its own troops. By the time of the Second Punic War the novelty of elephant warfare had mostly worn off, and the civilizations around the Mediterranean basin knew how to manage the threat of these large beasts. The sight of an elephant in full panoply did inspire awe and fear in the barbarian peoples of Europe (the Roman emperor Claudius used them in his conquest of Britain in 43 CE), and it is for this reason that Hannibal might have included thirty-seven of these creatures in his train.[31]

What is perhaps most surprising is the amount of battlefield success the Carthaginian army had despite its multinational composition. Coordinating such an exotic mix of warriors, with their different languages and weapons, is difficult in any age, and even more so in classical warfare with the limited command, control and communication devices available to commanders. The sounds of drums, trumpets and flutes which commanders used to orchestrate troop movements could easily be drowned out by the din of combat, while standard bearers could be cut down or lose their will to fight.[32]

But, like great commanders of any age, Hannibal was known for his personal courage in battle which endeared him to his troops. He demanded absolute obedience, sometimes disciplining his troops with beatings and death sentences by crucifixion. These challenges were further exacerbated during his campaigns when he had to replace so many of his troops after crossing the Alps in late 218 with new, barbarian recruits. It is testimony to the brilliance of Carthaginian commanders who, over the course of the third century and two Punic Wars, fielded these kinds of armies with great success against the rising power of a new and formidable enemy, the Roman Republic.[33]

The Organization and Tactics of the Roman Army

When Rome appeared as a city-state in the Tiber valley sometime in the middle of the eighth century BCE, its first army differed little from those of other small communities in Latium. It is believed that Rome's first military organization was based on the tribal system, reflecting the three original Roman tribes (the Ramnes, the Tities, and the Luceres).[34] Each tribe provided 1,000 infantry towards the army, made up of ten *centuries* consisting of 100 men each. The tribal contingent was under the command of a *tribunus* or tribal officer. Together, these 3,000 men made up a *legio* or levy. This infantry force was supplemented by a small body of 300 *equites* or 'knights', aristocratic cavalry drawn equally from the three tribes.[35] Thus, from the very beginning of Roman military tradition cavalry was not held in high regard and would remain a subordinate arm to infantry during the Archaic and Republican periods (c.750–31 BCE). As we shall see, inferior cavalry units will hinder Roman efforts against Hannibal in the Second Punic War.

Initially, the organization of the early Roman army was heavily influenced by their powerful neighbours to the north, the Etruscans. Etruscan civilization emerged in Etruria around 900 BCE as a confederation of city-states. By 650 BCE, they had expanded in central Italy and became the dominant cultural and economic force in the region, trading widely with Greeks and Carthaginians on the Italian peninsula. Under direct occupation by the Etruscans between c.620–509 BCE, Rome benefited greatly from this cultural exchange, with Roman villages transformed into a thriving city-state.[36] And although these

Etruscan city-states were united in a league of usually twelve cities, they seldom operated together unless faced with an outside threat. Like the Greek *poleis* to the east, the Etruscan cities spent most of their energy fighting each other.

Sometime in the sixth century BCE, the Etruscans adopted the Greek method of fighting and organized their militia-armies into phalanxes. After conquering the Roman city-state in the late sixth century BCE, the newly created Etrusco-Roman army was composed of two parts: the Etruscans, and their subjects the Romans and Latins. The Etruscans fought in the centre as heavy infantry hoplites, while the Romans and Latins fought in their native style with spears, axes and javelins on either wing.[37] The army was divided into five classes depending on nationality.[38] The largest contingent, or first class, was composed of Etruscan heavy infantry armed in Greek fashion with heavy thrusting spear and long sword and protected by breastplate, helmet, greaves and a heavy round shield. The second class were spearmen conscripted from subject peoples and armed in Italian fashion with spear, sword, helmet, greaves, and the oval shield or *scutum*, probably of Samnite origin. The third class was lightly-armoured heavy infantry spearmen with the *scutum*, while the fourth and fifth classes were light infantry javelin throwers and slingers.[39]

The second of the Etruscan overlords in Rome, Servius Tullius (578–535), is credited in the middle of the sixth century BCE with attempting to integrate the population by reorganizing the army according to wealth and not nationality.[40] The Servian reforms reflected an old Indo-European custom where citizenship depended on property and the ability to maintain a panoply and serve in the militia. The reforms segregated Etrusco-Roman society into seven groups.[41] The wealthiest group formed the cavalry or *equites*, made up of Etruscan nobles and members of the Roman upper class. The *equites* did not act in the capacity of heavy or light cavalry, but served as mounted infantry and scouts.[42]

The second wealthiest group acted as heavy infantry, fighting in the phalangeal formation and armed as before in the Greek manner. The third through sixth groups were armed in native Italian fashion identical to the pre-Servian period. The seventh class, or *capite censi*, were too poor to qualify for military service.[43] Tactically, the Servian army fought as before, with heavy infantry in the central phalanx, protected by lightly-armoured heavy infantry on the wings and light infantry skirmishers in the front until the phalanx engaged. There is no mention of archers in the Servian reforms. Like the Greeks, the Romans seemed to disdain the bow and arrow as a weapon of war, preferring it for hunting.[44]

The early Republican army was a citizen army. In fact, the original meaning for the word *legio* (derived from *legere*, Latin for 'to gather together') was a draft or levy of heavy infantry drawn from the property owning citizen-farmers living around Rome.[45] The army continued to adhere organizationally to the Servian reforms and consisted of three legions, each of a thousand men, supplemented by light infantry provided by the poorer citizens and cavalry by the wealthy class.[46] Divided into ten centuries of a hundred men, each legion was commanded by a military tribune appointed from the senatorial class, while each century was commanded by a *centurion* promoted or elected from the ranks of the legionaries.[47]

During the first century of Republican rule, the Roman army continued to utilize the phalanx-based tactical system. But the battle square proved less effective against opponents unaccustomed to the stylized hoplite warfare favoured by the Mediterranean classical civilizations. When, in 390 BCE, 30,000 Gauls crossed the Apennines in search of plunder, the defending Roman legions were pushed against the Allia River.[48] The Roman phalanxes, outnumbered two-to-one and overwhelmed by the ferocity and physical size of the Celtic marauders, were defeated, unable to cope with the barbarians' open formation and oblique attacks.[49] The sack of the 'Eternal City' in 390 BCE left a lasting impression on the psyche of Roman civilization. The surviving Romans who witnessed the violation of their city from a nearby hill vowed never again to fight unprepared. The military reforms of the early fourth century BCE are associated with the leader Marcus Furius Camillus, a man credited with saving the city from the Gauls and remembered as a second founder of Rome.[50] Although history cannot precisely answer if Camillus himself was responsible for the Camillian military reforms, the changes that bear his name dramatically altered the character of the Roman legion in the fourth century BCE.

The Roman army's experience against Gauls in the north and campaigns against the Samnites (343–290 BCE) in the rough, hilly terrain of central Italy forced a change in tactical organization, with Roman commanders altering the panoply and tactical formation of the legions to meet the different fighting styles of their opponents, whether barbarian or civilized, giving individual legionaries more responsibility and greater tactical freedom. This is sometimes referred to as the 'Polybian' legion, so named because the historian Polybius gives us the most detailed description of its workings. During this time the Roman army expanded from three to four legions, and the number of legionaries per legion grew to 4,200 infantry, supported by 300 Roman cavalry.[51] As before, the wealthiest men made up the cavalry (*equites*), divided into ten groups or *turmae*, commanded by *decurions*. These men were armed and armoured in Hellenistic fashion with spear and sword and protected by helmet, cuirass and small circular shield.[52]

As part of the reorganization of the 'Polybian' legion, the Roman century had been reduced from one hundred to sixty men apiece.[53] Each of these centuries was commanded by a centurion and a hand-picked assistant, or *optio*, members of a professional veteran officer class who drilled the legionaries and commanded them in battle. The centurion led his troops from the front, while the *optio* stood at the rear of the formation to maintain order. Centurions also administered discipline to the troops when necessary. Roman discipline was usually corporate in nature, though extraordinary circumstances could require a capital punishment known as *decimation*. It was inflicted on legionaries who had given ground without cause in combat or exposed their neighbours to flank attack. The process of decimation took place after the engagement, when a tenth of the offending unit was chosen by lot, then clubbed to death by their own comrades.[54]

During this time the Roman army abandoned the phalanx altogether in favour of a new linear formation organized around four classes of soldiers defined not only by wealth, but also by age and experience.[55] The Greek-style battle square was replaced by three lines of heavy infantry, the first two-thirds were each armed in an innovative manner with two weighted javelins, or *pila*, and a sword and were protected by helmet, breastplate, greaves and the traditional oval *scutum* favoured by the lower classes. The ranks of the foremost of these two lines, the *hastati*, were filled with young adult males in their twenties, while the centre formation, or *principes*, was comprised of veterans in their thirties. The third and last line, or *triarii* were armoured as above but armed in the older fashion with thrusting spear and *scutum*. The *triarii* consisted of the oldest veterans and acted as a reserve. The first line (*hastati*) and second line (*principes*) consisted of 1,200 legionaries each, while the third line (*triarii*) was made up of only 600 soldiers.[56] The poorest and youngest men served as *velites* or light infantry skirmishers. Armed with light javelins and swords and unprotected except for helmet and hide-covered wicker shields, the *velites* acted as a screen for their heavier-armed and less-mobile comrades. Each legionary was still responsible for supplying his own panoply, but in order to maintain uniformity within each century, the weapons were frequently purchased from the state.[57]

Before battle, the *hastati*, *principes* and *triarii* formed up in homogeneous rectangular units or *maniples* of 120 men (two centuries probably deployed side-by-side), protected by the *velite* light infantry. Each maniple was commanded by the centurion from the right-hand century and organized around a *signum* or standard kept by the *signifer*, who led the way on the march and in combat. Each maniple deployed as a small independent unit, typically with a twenty-man front and six-man depth and may have been separated from its lateral neighbour by the width of its own frontage, though this is still a matter of some debate.[58] Livy tells us that the maniples were 'a small distance apart'.[59] Moreover, the *hastate*, *principes* and *triarii* maniples were staggered, with the *principes* covering the gaps of the *hastati* in front, and the *triarii* covering the gaps of the *principes*. This checkerboard, or *quincunx*, formation provided maximum tactical flexibility for the maniple, allowing it to deliver or meet an attack from any direction.[60] As Polybius describes:

> The order of battle used by the Roman army is very difficult to break through, since it allows every man to fight both individually and collectively; the effect is to offer a formation which can present a front in

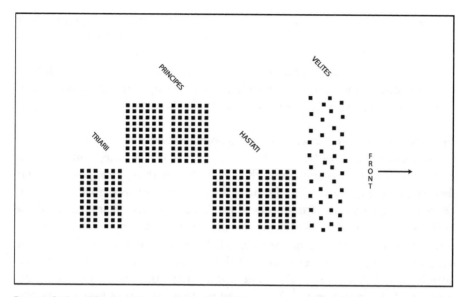

Roman Order of Battle. A Roman cohort, organised into three maniples of two centuries each, deployed for battle. The front centuries are comprised of *hastati*, the middle of *principes*, and the third of *triarii*. Maniples of *hastati* and *principes* are made up of 120 infantrymen, while the veteran *triarii* are 60 men strong. Each maniple also has 40 *velites* who deploy in front of the cohort as a skirmishing and screening element. The checkerboard deployment provdes flexibility and manoeuvre room needed for manipular tactics.

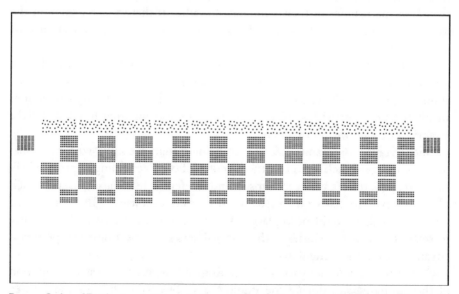

Roman Order of Battle. A typical Roman legion, consisting of thirty maniples, flanked on the left and right by ten *turmae* of cavalry, made up of thirty horsemen each. The strength of the legion lay in its flexibility, highly trained legionaries, and the support each element provides to the others by their deployment. The weaknesses of the Roman formation are its lack of shock power compared to a phalanx-type formation and its extremely weak cavalry element, as can readily be seen in this illustration. An enemy army with a robust cavalry arm, such as the Carthaginians, was difficult to pursue with such an undersized mounted force.

any direction, since the maniples which are nearest to a point where danger threatens wheel in order to meet it. The arms that they carry both give protection and also instil great confidence into the men, because of the size of the shields and the strength of the swords which can withstand repeated blows. All these factors make the Romans formidable antagonists in battle and very hard to overcome.[61]

In battle, the maniple legion presented a double threat to its adversaries. After the screening *velites* withdrew through the ranks of the heavy infantry, the *hastati* moved forward and threw their light *pila* at thirty-five yards, quickly followed by their heavy *pila*.[62] Drawing their short thrusting Spanish swords, or *gladii hispaniensis*, the front ranks of the *hastati* charged their enemy, whose ranks were presumably broken up by the javelin discharge. When the two formations joined, the legionaries exploited the tears and stepped inside the spears of the enemy front rank into the densely-packed mass and wielded their swords with much greater speed and control than the closely packed spearmen could defend against.[63] As the leading Romans thrust into the enemy, the succeeding *hastati* threw their *pila* and engaged with swords. The battle became a series of furious combats with both sides periodically drawing apart to recover. During one of these pauses, the *hastati* would retreat back through the open ranks of the battle-tested and fresh *principes* and *triarii*. The *principes* then closed ranks and moved forward, discharging their *pila* and engaging with swords in the manner of their younger comrades. If there was a breach in the Roman line, the veteran *triarii* acted as true heavy infantry and moved forward to fill the tear with their spears.

The new Roman system had many strengths. By merging heavy and light infantry into the *pila*-carrying legionary, the Roman army gave its soldiers the ability to break up the enemy formation with missile fire just moments before weighing into them with sword and shield, in effect merging heavy and light infantry into one weapon system.[64]

Once engaged, the maniple's relatively open formation emphasized individual prowess and gave each legionary the responsibility of defending approximately thirty-six square feet between himself and his fellow legionaries, a fact which placed special emphasis on swordplay in training exercises.[65] But even if the maniple failed, it could be replaced by a fresh one in the rear. This ability to rotate fatigued legionaries with fresh soldiers gave the Romans a powerful advantage over their enemies.

One of the keys to the success of the Roman war machine was the adoption of the deadly *gladius* during the Punic Wars. Twenty inches long and three inches wide, the *gladius* was primarily a stabbing weapon, and legionaries were trained not to use it for cut-and-slash attacks, the preferred method of their enemies. Instead, Roman soldiers would employ a shield parry, followed by a sharp under-thrust with the *gladius* into the enemy's torso, creating the killing trademark of the Roman infantry.[66] This tactic was especially effective against poorly-armoured barbarians.

The 'Polybian' legion served the Republic well in its expansion against the Samnites, Etruscans and Gauls in northern and central Italy during the fourth century BCE. But Rome faced new challenges in the third century BCE from the Greeks in southern Italy, the Carthaginians in Spain and North Africa and the Hellenistic Successor States in the Levant. Rome's martial contacts with these other regional powers would test the effectiveness of the maniple legion against combined-arms tactical systems inspired by the success of the Macedonian art of war.

The first significant test of the maniple legion came against the Greeks in *Magna Graecia*, southern Italy, in the Tarentine Wars (281–267 BCE). Rome's expansion into the lower peninsula forced the Greeks living there to forge an alliance with King Pyrrhus of Epirus (r.297–272), an ambitious Greek king seeking to emulate the conquests of Alexander the Great. Rome's struggle against Pyrrhus proved to be a difficult one, and over the course of the war, Rome suffered two major defeats. But poor generalship, rather than an inferior fighting force, was the cause of the failures at Heraclea in 280 and Asculum in 279 BCE. But even while Pyrrhus' forces were victorious over the Romans, his battles, especially at Asculum, cost him dearly, giving modern historians the term 'pyrrhic victory' to symbolize a costly victory. The Romans finally decisively defeated Pyrrhus' army at Beneventum in 275 BCE, and by 265 BCE southern Italy was under Roman hegemony.[67] Rome now controlled *Magna Graecia* and its many Greek cities, but this victory also brought it into very close proximity with the island of Sicily and Carthage's economic and territorial interests.

The First Punic War: The War at Sea and on Land
The origins of the First Punic War (264–241 BCE) lay in the growing competition between Rome and Carthage for control of the islands and sea-lanes of the western Mediterranean. This war witnessed the maturation of Rome as a regional sea power and the defeat of Carthage on land and at sea. It would also have a profound impact on the conduct of the Second Punic War (218–201 BCE) and the Carthaginian strategy envisioned by Hamilcar Barca and implemented by his son Hannibal when hostilities broke out a second time between Carthage and Rome in 218.

In the decades leading up to the beginning of the First Punic War both regional powers had agreed to stay out of each other's spheres of influence. Treaties in 348 and again in 279 clearly gave Rome control over the Italian Peninsula and Carthage dominion over the western seas and islands. But as the third century wore on, both sides knew that competing economic interests would create friction and eventually war.

The First Punic War's *casus belli* would be control of the Straits of Messina between Sicily and Italy. In 265, a powerful Greek army from the city of Syracuse launched an attack on Messana, a rival city to the north located on the northeast corner of Sicily. Years earlier a band of mercenaries and pirates called Mamertines (from the war god Mamers or Mars whom they worshipped) had seized Messana and used it as a base of operations against Syracuse.[68] Rival factions within the besieged city sent embassies to both Rome and Carthage offering the city in return for military assistance. Rome dispatched an army under the command of consul Appius Claudius Caudex, but he arrived too late. Carthaginian forces had already invested the city and taken control of the strategic strait. Unwilling to tolerate a Carthaginian presence in what was perceived as Rome's sphere of influence, the Senate accused Carthage of violating the long-standing treaty and declared war in 264. The first of three Punic wars was on.

Rome immediately found itself presented with a strategic problem – how to prosecute a war against Carthage's thalassocracy without a navy of its own. A North African fleet patrolled the Straits of Messina and the Carthaginian commander, Hanno, felt confident his navy would keep the Romans at bay. He would be proved wrong. Claudius' army of perhaps two legions and support troops (perhaps 20,000 men) garrisoned the Italian city of Rhegium, an important port facing Messana across the straits.[69] Under cover of darkness and using commandeered fishing boats and merchant ships, Claudius boldly ferried his troops across the waterway and surrounded Messana. Outmanned and outwitted, Hanno was forced to retreat, leaving Messana to the Romans.

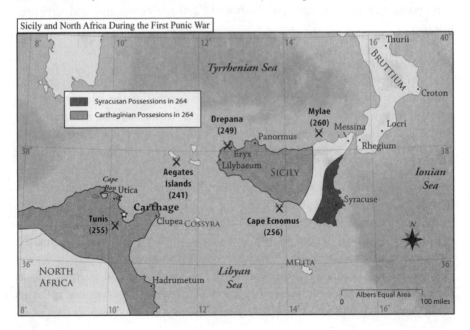

Sicily and North Africa During the First Punic War

Sicily remained the main theatre of operations for the entire First Punic War.

After seizing Messana, the Romans threatened Syracuse itself in 263. Despite the lack of sophisticated siege techniques, Rome was able to compel the Syracusans into an alliance, but not even the presence of a powerful ally in Sicily could keep the war going well for Rome and most of the warfare which took place on the island consisted of siege warfare. Roman siege techniques were still rather simplistic at the beginning of the Punic wars. Rome had learned how to organize and sustain long sieges in its wars of Italian expansion, while also developing such skills as the escalade (when soldiers attack enemy walls with scaling ladders), battering, and sapping (tunnelling under walls). In fact, it was during this period that the Romans perfected the deployment of the *testudo* (a formation where legionaries create a protective, interlocking canopy with their shields to protect them from missile fire). The Romans also became proficient at protecting their siege lines with elaborate field fortifications. Despite these developments, Roman warfare remained seriously deficient in the use of artillery, specifically catapults, when the First Punic War began. Roman siegecraft did mature during the conflict with Carthage, with Romans eventually mastering the use of artillery. Our knowledge of Roman siege warfare also increases due to the detailed accounts of Polybius, who was an expert on siege warfare and who gave very detailed accounts of the Roman sieges of this period.[70]

The Carthaginians used their superior navy to raid the Italian coast and blockade Sicilian ports, denying Roman troops the supplies needed to secure the island completely. Unable to lure their adversary into a decisive engagement on land, the Romans made a fateful decision to seek battle on the open water. In 260 Roman engineers and carpenters constructed over 120 large naval vessels (reportedly one hundred *quinqueremes* and twenty *triremes*) in only two months, using a Carthaginian galley that ran aground as a template.[71] Fortunately for the Romans, the Italian Peninsula was blessed with great forests of fir, the preferred wood for warship construction.[72] The commanding admiral, consul Gnaeus Cornelius Scipio, then assembled crews and drilled them on benches on the beach before putting them to sea. Polybius tells us that the ships were launched as soon as they were finished.[73] By creating a navy literally from scratch the Romans exhibited the resourcefulness and adaptability that were hallmarks of their civilization.

But even the Romans recognized that ships built and manned in haste would have problems matching the Carthaginian fleet in open water. To compensate for inexperience, an unnamed Roman shipwright fitted an unknown number of quinqueremes with a boarding device known as a *corvus* (Latin for crow or raven).[74] Four feet wide and thirty-six feet in length and fitted with an iron spike on the end, the *corvus* was pivoted from a mast by a topping lift, then dropped onto the adjacent ship's prow or deck, securing it in place as Roman marines crossed the plank and engaged in hand-to-hand combat with enemy sailors. The application of the *corvus* in naval warfare allowed Rome to fight as a land power at sea, evening the odds against an accomplished naval power.

Though the quality of the ships and crews no doubt differed, both Carthaginian and Roman quinqueremes and triremes were narrow war galleys whose chief offensive tactic was to ram an opposing ship with its bronze 'beak'. In combat, a fully-equipped Carthaginian or Roman quinquereme had a complement of 300 sailors, of which 250 to 270 were rowers and the remainder manned the rigging, masts, and rudders.[75] These vessels also carried a detachment of between 80 and 120 fighting troops, including archers and catapult operators for offensive missile fire and swordsmen and spearmen to defend the deck from boarding. There was one notable difference between Punic and Roman warships. The *corvus* made Roman ships very top-heavy, much less manoeuvrable, and extremely vulnerable to bad weather.

Armed with a novice navy, the Romans sought battle with the Carthaginians in the summer of 460 in the waters off Mylae, on Sicily's northeastern coast. The Roman flotilla, led by the consul Gaius Duilius, watched as the Carthaginian fleet of 131 galleys sailed right toward them, probably in a single line abeam, the standard formation a superior fleet took when meeting an inferior one.[76] Polybius maintains that the Carthaginians were not concerned by the strange superstructures fitted to the Roman ships.[77] When they tried to ram the Roman ships, the Romans dropped their *corvi* onto the unsuspecting Punic ships, catching thirty vessels immediately off guard. Unable to escape the falling

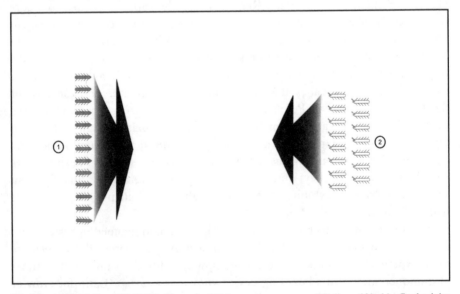

The Battle of Mylae, 260 BCE, Phase I. Off the northwest coast of Sicily, a 131-ship Carthaginian fleet (1) closes with a 145-ship Roman fleet (2). The Carthaginians sail in line abreast, counting on their superior seamanship to offset the slight numerical superiority enjoyed by the less-skilful Romans. The Carthaginians pay no heed to the odd structures mounted on the bows of the Roman vessels.

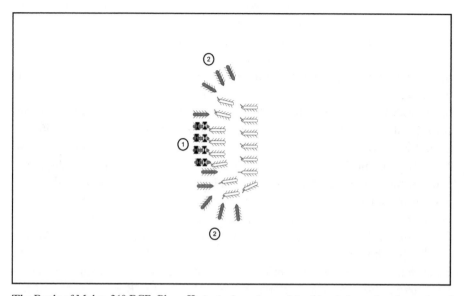

The Battle of Mylae, 260 BCE, Phase II. As the fleets close and the ships clash together, the purpose of the odd structures on the Roman vessels becomes clear. The *corvus* provides a ready-made gangplank for Roman infantry to board enemy vessels. Upon closing with the Carthaginian vessels, the *corvi* are released, their steel beaks slamming into the enemy decks and locking the ships fast. Roman marines swiftly cross the bridges and overwhelm the startled Carthaginian sailors (1). The Carthaginians attempt to envelop the Roman flanks (2) but the *corvi* rotate to face the oncoming ships.

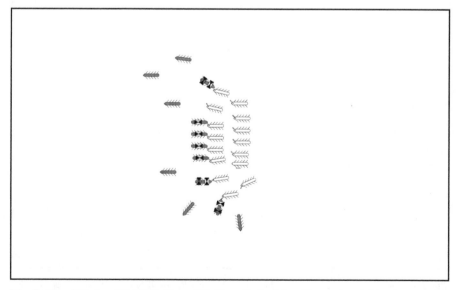

The Battle of Mylae, 260 BCE, Phase III. More Carthaginian ships are impaled by the *corvi*. The Romans capture or sink around fifty ships, causing the rest of the enemy to flee. The defeat sends a shock wave through Carthaginian naval circles.

gangplanks, the North African sailors watched as the Roman marines swept onto their decks. Altogether, the Romans sank or captured as many as fifty enemy ships, stunning the Carthaginian sea power.[78]

The victory at Mylae gave the Romans local command of the sea around Sicily and allowed the Italians to broaden the theatre of operations to include Sardinia, Corsica and Malta. Confident in their newfound abilities as sailors, the Romans continued to build ships and engage the Carthaginians in large-scale naval battles. The most significant of these victories took place in 256 near Cape Ecnomus in south-central Sicily. Here, a Roman flotilla of 330 ships and 140,000 men met and defeated a Carthaginian fleet of some 350 ships and 150,000 men in one of the greatest naval battles of the classical period.[79] The Roman objective was simple – the destruction of the enemy navy in order to establish command of the sea and strike directly at Carthage itself. With the Carthaginian fleet in flight, the Romans refitted and sailed for North Africa.

The Romans landed at the city of Aspis just south of Cape Hermaia (modern Cape Bon), some seventy-five miles east of Carthage. After beaching their ships and surrounding them with a trench and palisade, the Romans ventured out and captured Aspis. But with winter approaching, Rome sent word recalling one consul and the fleet to friendly waters, leaving Regulus with forty ships and two under strength legions and auxiliaries (15,000 foot and 500 horse) to ravage the countryside.[80]

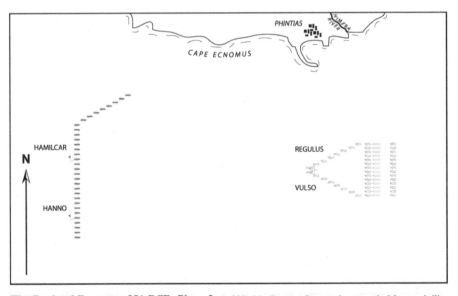

The Battle of Ecnomus, 256 BCE, Phase I. A 330-ship Roman fleet under consuls Marcus Atilius Regulus and Lucius Manlius Vulso and a 350-ship Carthaginian fleet under Hamilcar and Hanno approach each other off the southern coast of Sicily. One Roman squadron tows transports containing an expeditionary force, shielded by a fourth squadron to their rear. Three Carthaginian squadrons are in line, while the landward squadron positions itself to outflank the Romans as the forces close.

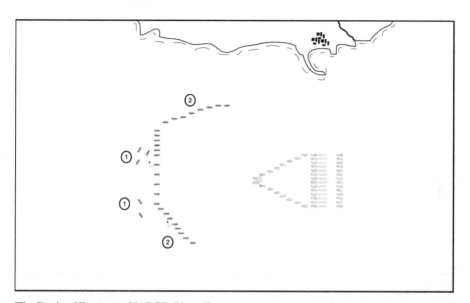

The Battle of Ecnomus, 256 BCE, Phase II. Hamilcar signals the fleet, ordering his centre squadrons to thin their rank by sending ships to the flanks (1), hoping to entice the aggressive Romans into concentrating on this weak point while ignoring their flanks. The Carthaginian flank squadrons begin to manoeuvre for a flank attack against the Roman formation (2).

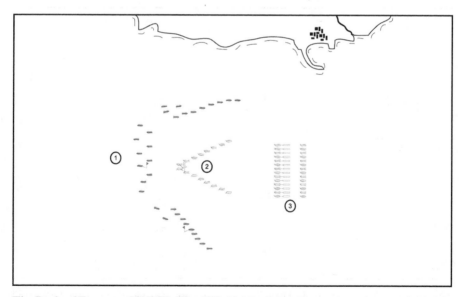

The Battle of Ecnomus, 256 BCE, Phase III. The Carthaginian centre comes about and feigns flight from the Roman wedge (1). Regulus and Vulso take the bait and pursue (2), but the ships towing the transports and their covering force cannot keep pace and fall behind (3).

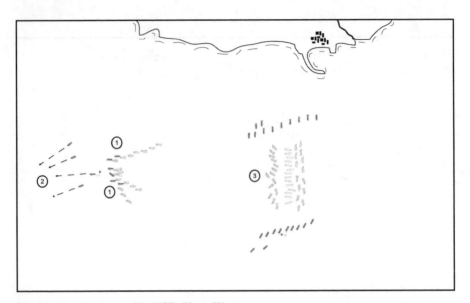

The Battle of Ecnomus, 256 BCE, Phase IV. The Roman vanguard engages the main Carthaginian squadrons (1). the corvi prove highly effective, locking the opposing vessels together and allowing the Roman marines to rapidly assault the grappled Carthaginian ships. The remaining Punic ships flee, this time in earnest (2). The Roman's third line cuts the towed troop transports free and joins the fourth line in engaging the Carthaginian squadrons approaching from the north and south (3).

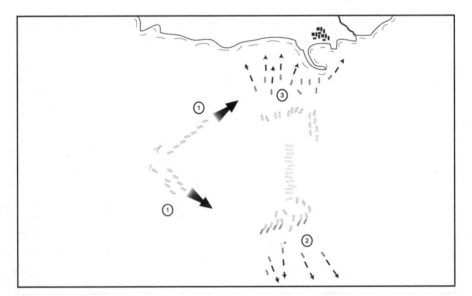

The Battle of Ecnomus, 256 BCE, Phase V. Rather than pursue the fleeing Carthaginians, Regulus and Vulso order their squadrons to come about and sail to the aid of their comrades (1). Meanwhile, the Roman's third and fourth squadrons succeed in driving off the Punic ships approaching from seaward (2) and trap the landward element against the coastline (3). At a cost of only twenty-four ships lost, the Romans capture sixty-four galleys and sink thirty. After refitting, the Roman fleet and expeditionary force sails for North Africa.

The Carthaginian authorities quickly put their wealth to use and hired an experienced Greek general named Xanthippus to lead their defence. Brought up in the Spartan military system, Xanthippus was a capable and charismatic leader who quickly hired an army of mercenaries to supplement the native garrison, raising a substantial force of 15,000 infantry, 4,000 cavalry and 100 war elephants.[81] In the spring of 255 (most probably May) Xanthippus took the initiative and led his force against the invading Romans. When the two hosts made contact somewhere in the flat country southwest of Tunis, near the town of Adys, the Romans encamped a little more than a mile away and waited. The following day the Carthaginians held a war council and decided to attack while their soldiers were in good spirits.[82]

Xanthippus ordered the war elephants forward and stationed them in a line to screen the forming army. The Carthaginian heavy infantry assembled behind the pachyderms, with the cavalry on the wings. He placed some additional mercenary forces on the right wing and light infantry in front of both cavalry detachments. The Romans moved eagerly to accept battle, screening their forming legionaries with *velites*, ever wary of an elephant charge. Polybius tells us that Regulus positioned his forces 'shorter and deeper than usual' as a defence against the elephants, but it also shortened the frontage of the entire army, making it more vulnerable to the Carthaginian cavalry, which already far outnumbered the Roman horse.[83]

The Battle of Tunis opened just as the Roman's expected, with Xanthippus ordering the Punic war elephants and cavalry on both wings forward. The Romans immediately met this attack, 'clashing their shields and spears together, as is their custom, and shouting their battle-cry'.[84] The Roman cavalry, outmatched and outnumbered, was immediately routed on both wings. The Roman legionaries on the left faired much better, avoiding the elephant charge and driving the Carthaginians and mercenaries back, pursuing their enemy as far as the Punic camp. In the Roman centre, the forward maniples tried in vain to meet the elephant charge, but were trampled underfoot. Still, the formation held, owing to its increased depth. Despite this modest success, the remainder of the Roman line found itself pressed between the charging elephants in front and encircling enemy horse behind. Even those legionaries which managed to fight their way through the elephants now faced a fresh Carthaginian phalanx bearing down on them. Surrounded on all sides, the Roman centre was annihilated. Retreating early, Regulus was captured along with about 500 of his troops. Only the 2,000 Roman legionaries who sacked the Carthaginian camp managed to escape back to Aspis. Polybius states Carthaginian casualties at 800 mercenaries.[85]

The victory at Tunis would serve the Carthaginian cause for generations. A composite Punic army made up of local North African militia and mercenaries could defeat Rome, a perennial land power, as long as the population remained safe behind the long walls of Carthage, safely resupplied by sea from its far-flung

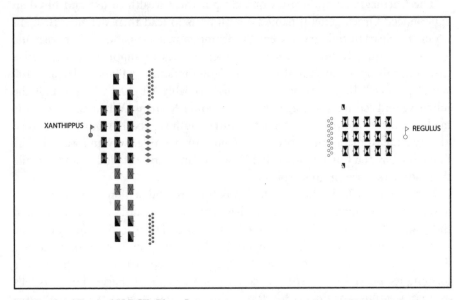

The Battle of Tunis, 255 BCE, Phase I. Somewhere on the plains southwest of Tunis, the Greek general Xanthippus deploys his army behind a protective line of 100 elephants to face a smaller Roman force led by consul Marcus Atilius Regulus. The Roman deployment is deeper than normal in an attempt to counter the danger posed by the enemy's pachyderms.

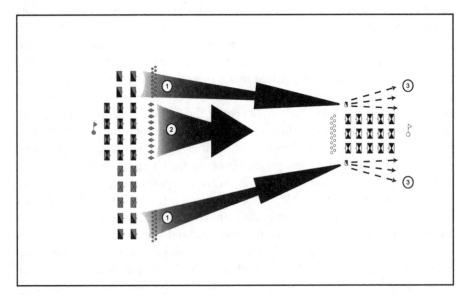

The Battle of Tunis, 255 BCE, Phase II. Xanthippus opens the action as expected, ordering his cavalry wings (1) and elephants forward against the Romans. Outnumbered eight-to-one, the Roman horseman have no hope of success and are driven quickly from the field (3). The legionaries clash spears and shields together, shouting their battle cry as they watch the line of elephants lumbering towards them.

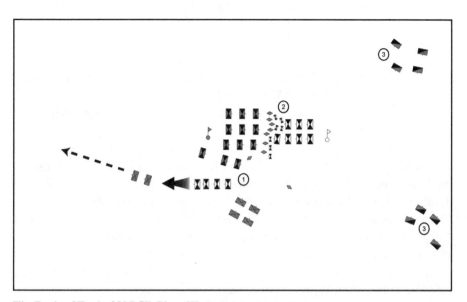

The Battle of Tunis, 255 BCE, Phase III. The Roman left drive off many of the attacking elephants and infantry, pursuing some of them back to their camp (1). The Roman right fares less well, as men are trampled underfoot and pressed hard by the enemy phalanx (3). Meanwhile, the Punic cavalry breaks off its pursuit of the inferior Roman horse and begins to reform in the Roman's rear (4).

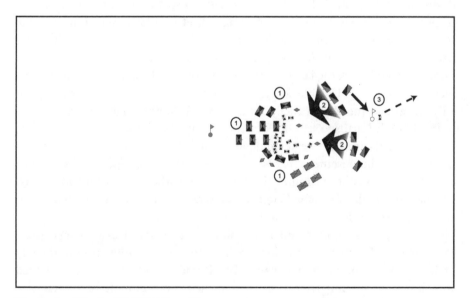

The Battle of Tunis, 255 BCE, Phase IV. Pressed on all sides by Carthaginian infantry and elephants (1) and the advance of the Punic cavalry to their rear, the Roman army is annihilated. Attempting to escape the fate of his men, Regulus flees the field with 500 men but is quickly captured (3). Only the 2,000 men that had sacked the Punic camp managed to avoid their comrades' fate.

maritime empire. Xanthippus' strategy at Tunis would also inspire Hannibal Barca at Zama half a century later. The loss at Tunis also left an indelible mark on the Roman psyche. It illustrated the difficulty of outfitting, deploying and maintaining a Roman army in North Africa. The defeat not only inflamed Roman enmity towards Carthage, its lessons would be remembered by older Romans in the Second Punic War, men like the influential Fabius Maximus, who understood all too well the value of a Punic victory on North African soil to the Carthaginians.

The Romans sent a fleet to rescue the remaining legionaries, who managed a spirited defence of Aspis. This Roman fleet secured a major victory against the Punic fleet in 255 off Cape Hermaia. But on the return home, the Roman flotilla was struck by a massive storm, destroying 184 of the 264 ships.[86] The Carthaginian army did not fare much better. After defeating Rome's 'Army of Africa', Carthage faced an even more dangerous enemy when the Numidians attacked and ravished its territory. After a ruthless campaign, the Carthaginians exacted a terrible tribute of 10,000 talents and 20,000 head of cattle from the rebelling tribes, even capturing and crucifying the chiefs.[87]

Over the next six years (255–249) the main theatre of operations returned to the island of Sicily centred around the Punic fortress at Lilybaeum and its harbour city of Drepana, though Romans did occasionally raid Carthaginian territory in North Africa. Storms continued to wreak havoc with Rome, destroying a fleet in 254 and again in 249. Also in 249 the Carthaginians enjoyed a major naval victory, defeating a fleet of 123 quinqueremes at the Battle of Drepana off the west coast of Sicily, near the harbour of the same name. Rome lost ninety-three ships, while Carthage did not lose a single vessel. Drepana would mark the last time the North African thalassocracy would win a major naval victory. Despite success, Carthage could not raise the land siege of Lilybaeum and the war in Sicily ground on for another eight years.

In 247 BCE Carthage sent one of their best and brightest generals, Hamilcar Barca, to Sicily to take over command, though there is evidence that he was never given the resources necessary to win the campaign.[88] His famous son Hannibal was born around the time of his father's departure for Sicily. Polybius has high praise for Hamilcar, calling him 'the general who must be acknowledged as the greatest on either side, both in daring and in genius'.[89] He was an aggressive commander, defending Sicily from bases at Heirkte (near Panormus) and Eryx while raiding southern Italy in Bruttium around the city of Locri on the toe of the peninsula. But Rome's steady pressure, combined with lessening support from Carthage, spelled the beginning of the end for Hamilcar in Sicily. In 242 the Romans finally captured the harbour at Drepana, cutting off Lilybaeum from resupply by sea. Polybius makes it clear that the Roman strategy was to provoke a major naval engagement to land a 'mortal blow' against Carthage.[90]

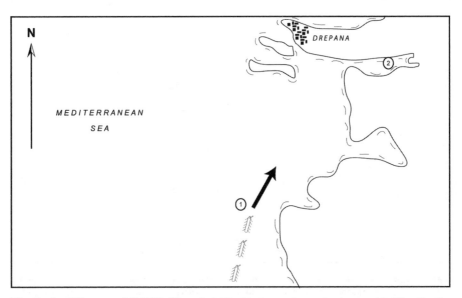

The Battle of Drepana, 249 BCE, Phase I. A 123-ship Roman fleet under the consul Publius Claudius Pulcher attempts a surprise attack (1) against the main Punic fleet's anchorage in the harbour (2) near Drepana on the west coast of Sicily. The Roman quinqueremes are spotted by Carthaginian lookouts and the Punic admiral, Adherbal, gives orders for the fleet to sortie.

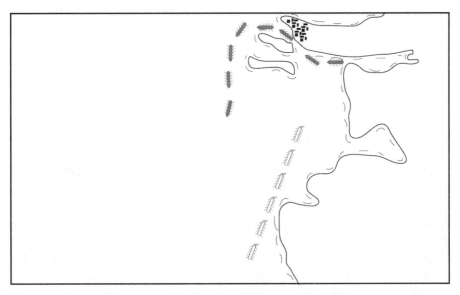

The Battle of Drepana, 249 BCE, Phase II. Claudius's fleet nears the southern harbour entrance but they are too late to prevent the Punic force, roughly equal in size, from slipping out to the north, coming about, and forming a line of battle to engage the Romans.

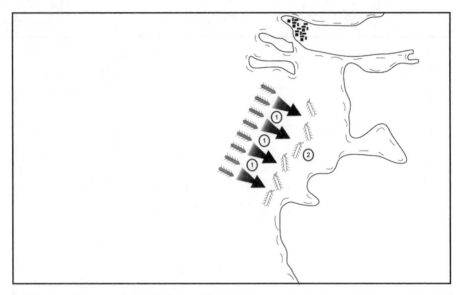

The Battle of Drepana, 249 BCE, Phase III. Adherbal orders his fleet forward (1). Inexpertly handled and pinned against the shore, the Roman fleet fails to form a cohesive line and loses ninety-three ships (2). The Carthaginians lose no ships in what would prove to be their last major naval victory.

It seems the Senate had been preparing for this *coup de grace* by rebuilding the Roman navy, slipping 200 quinquereme hulls into the water for the upcoming campaign. The new Roman consul Gaius Lutatius Catulus kept his sailors well drilled and provided with the best food and drink in anticipation for the battle to come.[91] By the spring of 241 the Roman fleet was in excellent condition. The Carthaginians, on the other hand, did not use the military capital won after the victory at Drepana and the Roman losses to weather. In fact, it took Carthage some time to muster the 250 ships and crews to send to Sicily and for the first time in the First Punic War the Roman sailors were probably better trained and equipped than their North African counterparts.[92] This became evident when the two fleets made contact on March 10 near the Aegates Islands just west of Sicily.

The Carthaginian fleet, laden with supplies and lacking a large contingent of marines, was blessed with a strong westerly wind, and made a run for the port city of Eryx. Seeing this action, the Roman consul and commanding admiral Catulus had to make a difficult decision – move to intercept the Punic fleet despite the heavy swells facing his rowers, or risk a successful running of the blockade and resupply of his enemy. Catulus chose to fight. He ordered his ships to take on more legionaries and, to make space, remove their masts. Catulus then formed his quinqueremes into a line in the high seas and rowed toward the Punic fleet. In response the Carthaginians lowered their sails and unstepped their masts in preparation for ramming. The Romans faired very well at the beginning of the battle, sinking fifty enemy ships and capturing

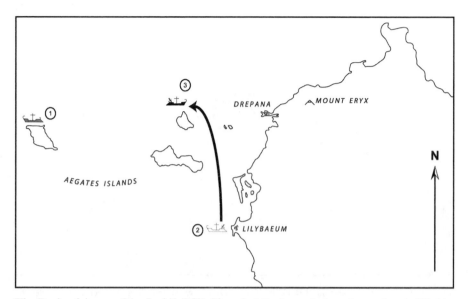

The Battle of Aegates Islands, 241 BCE, Phase I. A Punic supply fleet of approximately 250 ships arrives at the westernmost of the Aegates Islands and awaits a favourable wind to take it to the vicinity of Mount Eryx. There the Carthaginians intend to resupply their land forces, embark a large marine force, and engage the Roman fleet. The Roman consul, Caius Lutatius Catulus, receives word of the Punic force and orders fleet to sail from Lilybaeum (2) to another of the islands to intercept the enemy (3).

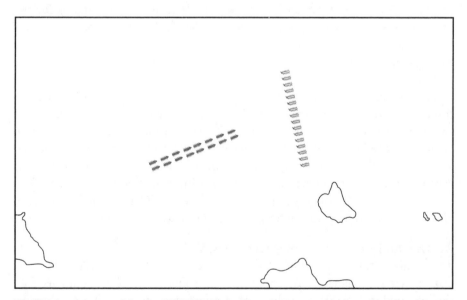

The Battle of Aegates Islands, 241 BCE, Phase II. A westerly wind springs up and the Punic fleet begins their run towards Eryx (1). Catulus orders his captains to unstep their masts to make room for more marines and the Romans deploy to engage the approaching ships (2). Hanno, the Carthaginian admiral, orders his ships to lower sail and unstep masts to prepare for combat.

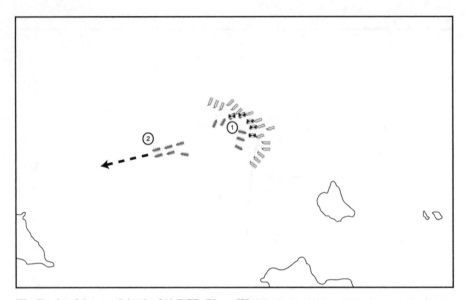

The Battle of Aegates Islands, 241 BCE, Phase III. The constant drilling imposed upon the fleet by Catulus pays off in the rough waters as Roman seamanship proves superior to Carthaginian. The quinqueremes, packed with marines, engage and board the poorly-handled Punic vessels, overwhelming the undermanned crews (1). An easterly shift of the wind manages to save some of the Punic fleet, as they re-step their masts and escape (2). Without masts, the Romans are unable to pursue. Carthaginian losses total 117 ships versus around thirty Roman vessels sunk. The battle proves decisive, destroying much of the Punic fleet and preventing the resupply of Hamilcar's hard-pressed army in western Sicily.

another seventy. Contemporary authors provide relatively low figures for the Punic prisoners captured considering the number of ships taken, perhaps owing to how many sailors drowned in the rough seas.[93] Luckily for the Carthaginians, a change in the direction of the wind allowed many of their ships to raise mast and sail away.

The Roman victory at the Aegates Islands decided the war. After twenty-three years of campaigning, Rome's pursuit of an aggressive strategy of attrition and exhaustion finally bore fruit. The Carthaginians were either unable or unwilling to build another fleet to challenge Rome for command of the sea, and without adequate resupply from North Africa, Hamilcar Barca could not continue the defence of western Sicily. Wanting to disassociate themselves with the disaster at the Aegates, the Carthaginian Council of Elders gave Hamilcar full authority to sue for peace in 241. The First Punic War was over.

An Unequal Peace and the Mercenary War

The costs of the First Punic War were enormous for both sides. Polybius claims that the Romans lost about 700 warships to the Carthaginians 500, though modern historians believe this number is inflated.[94] The Romans defeated the Carthaginians using the same strategy which won them the Italian peninsula – ruthless determination and a willingness to accept a high price in men and materiel. Rome continued the war despite heavy losses suffered in the storms of 255–254, the defeat at Drepana and devastating storm of 249. Rome's wealth and seemingly bottomless manpower reserves allowed it to continue to fight when other nations would have sued for peace. The Romans were also masters of exploiting the weaknesses of their defeated enemies. Carthage was no exception.

The Romans initially asked for the surrender of Hamilcar's Sicilian army and the punishment of all Roman and Italian deserters, but this demand was quickly rejected. The mercenary army was able to leave Sicily, their arms and honour both intact.[95] In all other areas the Romans were able to dictate an unequal peace. Rome demanded:

- The Carthaginian evacuation of Sicily and all islands between Sicily and North Africa
- Neither side was to make war on the other's allies, nor were they to recruit soldiers or raise money for the construction of public buildings in the other's territory.
- The Carthaginians were to give up all Roman prisoners freely, while paying a ransom for their own.
- The Carthaginians were to pay an indemnity to the Romans of 3,200 talents, 1,000 payable immediately, and the rest over a ten-year period.[96]

Rome had broken Punic naval mastery of the western Mediterranean, while acquiring a substantial navy of its own. The western half of Sicily was absorbed into the Roman sphere of influence and became in essence Rome's first province outside of Italy. Soon it would be providing the city of Rome itself with grain, making many in the equestrian class very wealthy. Yet despite securing Sicily and forcing war reparations, Carthage remained a major power and strategic counterweight to the rise of Rome, possessing sizable possessions in Africa and Spain and, for the moment, Sardinia.

Carthage's power was further weakened by what came to be known as the Mercenary War (240–237) in Africa.[97] When Hamilcar's army of 20,000 men prepared to return to Africa, he organized them into smaller detachments and sent them to Carthage to receive their arrears of several years' back pay. This scheme was designed to lesson the burden on the Carthaginian treasury and prevent the presence of so many mercenaries in the capital. But the Punic authorities ignored this arrangement and refused to pay anyone until all of the troops had arrived on African soil, probably hoping the soldiers would eventually accept a lower payment. The increasingly unruly mercenaries were finally sent to the city of Sicca, where they encamped and began to negotiate with Carthage. This well-equipped veteran army of Libyans, Gauls, Spaniards, Greeks, and runaway slaves soon realized their own strength and increased their demands. The army broke down along ethnic lines and the largest contingent, the Libyans, turned mutiny into open revolt. Many Libyan and Numidian towns joined in rebellion against their Punic masters, their young men swelling the ranks of the mercenaries. The revolt was principally led by three men – the Libyan Mathos, an escaped Italian slave named Spendius, and the Gallic chieftain Autariatus. Fortunately for the Carthaginians, none of the rebel commanders had experience commanding large armies, whereas the Punic command, shared by experienced generals of Hamilcar and Hanno (later 'the Great'), consistently outmanoeuvred the larger rebel armies. Finally, in 237, the mercenaries were defeated, but not before the war brought Carthage to the brink of destruction, further reducing its treasury and weakening its ability to deal with Rome as it transgressed on Punic territory on Sardinia, nearly starting another war.

Sardinia would be brought under Roman hegemony in 238 when Punic mercenaries mutinied and seized the island, only to be expelled two years later by the native population. The mercenaries then went to Rome for assistance much like the Mamertines had at the beginning of the First Punic War. Similarly, the Romans used this cry for help as reason to send an expedition to occupy the island. When the Carthaginians objected, Rome threatened them with a conflict they were in no position to fight. Adding insult to injury, the Senate demanded and received another indemnity of 1,200 talents, further spoiling the already poisoned relations between Rome and Carthage. Polybius maintains the Sardinian revolt was the 'greatest cause' of the Second Punic War.[98]

With Sicily and Sardinia now lost and Punic possessions in Africa unstable after the Mercenary War, Carthage decided to move west and expand further into Spain. The Carthaginian government picked the greatest general of the day, Hamilcar Barca, to take over operations in Iberia.[99] Hamilcar crossed the straits near the Pillars of Hercules (modern Gibraltar) and arrived in 237. As military governor of Spain, Hamilcar enriched himself and his allies and secured Punic control of the coastal strip of southern Spain while pushing up into the ancient Baetis (modern Guadalquivir) River valley and the fertile territory of the Contestani, in what is now Murcia. For nine years Hamilcar campaigned continuously until he was ambushed and killed while fording a river by a Celtiberian tribe known as the Oretani in 229.

Hasdrubal, his son-in-law and second-in-command, succeeded him as commanding general and governor, his position seconded by his army and then again by the authorities in Carthage. Hasdrubal seems to have accomplished more through diplomacy than through war, going so far as to marry a Spanish princess to cement an alliance.[100] Hasdrubal is also noted for founding the city of New Carthage (modern Cartagena) on the coast of southeastern Spain, a well-fortified location with a deep harbour that would serve as the Punic capital in Iberia. Hasdrubal was assassinated by a Celtic slave in the late summer or early autumn of 221, with his brother-in-law Hannibal Barca (the oldest son of Hamilcar) assuming command.

Chapter 2

The Early Campaigns of Hannibal

Hannibal's Early Life and the Origins of the Second Punic War
Hannibal Barca was twenty-six years old when he took command of the Carthaginian forces in Spain. Hannibal had grown up on the Iberian Peninsula near his father and learned the family business from the greatest Punic and mercenary leaders his father's wealth could buy. What Hannibal remembered of the towering temples, gardens and harbours of Carthage is conjecture, but we can assume that he claimed Spain as his homeland, having been raised there in his father's military camps since his childhood. Like other adolescent Punic aristocrats, Hannibal was taught Greek by a Greek tutor, and he would keep two Greek secretaries with him on his staff throughout his campaigns.[101]

Though a young general by modern standards, he already had years of invaluable practical experience fighting against various Iberian tribes, experience which would pay great dividends in the war with Rome. Like his father, Hannibal also possessed an amazing knack for commanding diverse peoples and their tactical systems. He understood how to manipulate the motivations of each of the nationalities in his army and exploit their military strengths on the battlefield, leading to spectacular victories against difficult odds.[102] Like Alexander the Great before him and Julius Caesar after, he also shared in the physical privations of his soldiers on campaign, endearing him to his men. Hannibal was intimately familiar with not only the Carthaginian art of war, but also the machinations of Punic politics. He realized that military success generated political currency, and he wasted little time securing his political position and building a military reputation.

Polybius informs us that Hannibal inherited his father's master plan for the recovery of Carthage as a regional power and that the conquest of Spain was central to this plan. By controlling Spain, Hannibal could build up trade, pay off the heavy Roman indemnity, augment his army and set up a staging area for an invasion of Italy. But there was more to this plan than securing Carthage's future. Hannibal possessed a deep-seated personal hatred for Rome that dated back to his childhood. In a rare glimpse of Hannibal's private motivations, Polybius relates a story the Punic general told near the end of his life at the court of a fellow Rome-hater, King Antiochus III of Syria:

> At the time when his father was about to set off with his army on his expedition to Spain, Hannibal, who was then about nine years old, was standing by the altar where his father was sacrificing to Zeus [Ba'al Hammon?]. The omens proved favourable, Hamilcar poured a libation to the gods and performed the customary ceremonies, after which he ordered all those who were present at the sacrifice to stand back a little way from the altar. Then he called Hannibal to him and asked him affectionately whether he wished to accompany the expedition. Hannibal was overjoyed to accept and, like a boy, begged to be allowed to go. His father then took him by the hand, led him up to the altar and commanded him to lay his hand upon the victim and swear that he would never be a friend to the Romans.[103]

This famous anecdote cuts to the heart of Hannibal's life-long hatred of Rome and illustrates an unwavering devotion to his father's cause of warring with the Romans.

Within months of Hasdrubal's assassination, Hannibal consolidated his power base, attacking the Olkades tribe of the upper Guadiana River, the Vaccei of north-central Spain (around Salamanca), and the Carpetani near the modern city of Toledo.[104] After putting his Spanish house in order, he returned to New Carthage for the winter of 220–219, only to find a Roman embassy waiting there with a warning – do not push farther north and threaten territories north of the Ebro. The Romans were there on behalf of their ally Massalia (modern Marseilles).

The Massaliotes were Greeks who founded Massalia in the seventh century BCE. Over the centuries their influence spread along the littoral of southern Gaul westward into Iberia, where they founded numerous colonies, most prominently Emporion near modern Barcelona. Massalia had long sparred with Carthage over trading rights in the western Mediterranean, and this friction forced the Greeks into an alliance with Rome. Hannibal's recent campaigns worried the Massaliotes, who already had to abandon some of their trading centres because of aggressive Punic expansion.

The Romans were also concerned with a powerful Carthaginian presence in eastern Spain. It was no secret to the Senate that domination of Iberia was part of Carthage's revitalization strategy, and a resurgent Carthage could threaten not only Roman hegemony in southern Gaul, but Italy directly. The Romans were also aware that an invasion by Hannibal coordinated with a Gallic insurrection could precipitate open revolt among Rome's allies throughout the Italian Peninsula. Forest tribes like the Boii, Insubres and Taurini in Cisalpine

Gaul (northern Italy) had threatened Rome's new northern border, periodically raiding across the Apennines and striking Roman colonies. Their last foray was only defeated in 225 BCE, having reached Telamon, halfway between Pisae (modern Pisa) and Rome.[105]

Friction increased when Rome interfered in 220 on behalf of Saguntum, a Spanish town south of the Ebro and a recent ally of Rome. From the time of Hasdrubal's command, Rome had sought a counterbalance to the growing Punic presence in eastern Spain, courting Saguntum into an alliance in 226. But because this city was clearly within Carthage's sphere of influence, Hannibal disregarded the Roman threat and laid siege to the city. Saguntum, initially divided between those who supported Rome and those who supported Carthage, eventually sided firmly with Rome and put to death pro-Carthaginian citizens, while threatening local tribes in league with Hannibal. Seeing these injustices as a pretext for war, Hannibal reduced the city after a bloody eight-month siege lasting probably from May 219 to late December or early January 218.[106]

Hannibal was seriously wounded in the thigh manning a battering ram while attacking the city's walls.[107] Like Alexander the Great before him, Hannibal

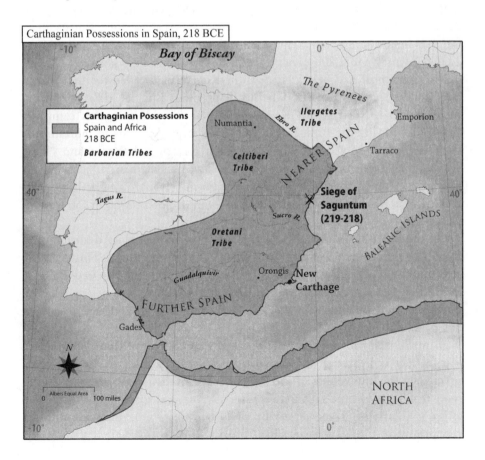

Carthaginian Possessions in Spain, 218 BCE

shared in the personal dangers of combat, actions that endeared him to his men. But warfare was changing in the third century BCE, and generals were embracing a more managerial style of command, one where heroic leadership from the frontlines was being replaced by giving orders from the rear, allowing for adjustments to strategy and tactics once the battle was joined.[108]

Rome, for its part, was very slow in its response to the attack on Saguntum, delaying any decision until after the election of new consuls in March of 218 (the first month of the republican Roman calendar), some time after the fall of the city. Rome finally sent an embassy to Carthage itself demanding the surrender of Hannibal and his advisors. The ultimatum was rejected and the Roman Senate declared war.

The Second Punic War: Initial Strategies

Roman troop placements in 218 indicate that the Senate was going to pursue a two-pronged strategy against Carthage, with one army sent against Spain and the other against North Africa itself.[109] Commanding the Spanish army was the newly-elected consul, Publius Cornelius Scipio (also referred to as Scipio the Elder, father of Scipio Africanus), charged with intercepting and defeating Hannibal's army before launching an attack against Carthaginian interests in northern Spain. Scipio commanded a substantial army consisting of 22,000 infantry and 2,200 cavalry, supported by some sixty ships.[110]

Once Hannibal had been defeated, the Roman plan called for the African army, under the command of Tiberius Sempronius Longus and staging from Sicily, to invade North Africa in a movement reminiscent of Regulus' campaign (255 BCE) during the First Punic War. This strategy seems to indicate that the Romans intended on fighting a war on foreign soil (Spain and North Africa), probably with the assistance of rebellious Carthaginian subjects in both regions.[111] Rome would not be satisfied with merely putting Carthage in its place, Rome was out to break the back of its most potent rival in the western Mediterranean.

On the other hand, Hannibal's aim was not the complete destruction of Rome but the reduction of its effectiveness as a regional power. This is clearly seen in the text of the treaty Hannibal made with the Macedonian king Philip V in 215 to help Carthage in its war with Rome.[112] With Roman power reduced, Carthage could regain lost territory in Sicily and Sardinia and have free reign in Spain and southern Gaul.

As mentioned above, Hannibal's strategy was a mirror of Rome's: bring the war to Italy and through the destruction of Roman armies on the battlefield precipitate the unravelling of the Roman confederation. Since allies made up more than half of Rome's manpower reserves, this strategy would have the dual effect of depriving Rome of troops while boosting Punic numbers through recruitment of former Roman allies.[113] According to Livy:

Hannibal's opinion never varied; the war should be fought in Italy. Italy, [Hannibal] said, would provide both food and supplies and troops for a foreign enemy; whereas if no movement was made in Italy, and the Roman people were allowed to use the manpower and resources of Italy for a war in foreign parts, then neither king nor any nation would be a match for the Romans.[114]

To test the theory that the war should be fought in Italy, Hannibal sent agents to Cisalpine Gaul to see if the barbarians there were sympathetic to the idea of direct Punic assistance in making war against the Romans. When the envoys returned to New Carthage in May they carried the answer Hannibal was seeking: the Celts would support Carthage with supplies and troops.[115]

The obvious drawbacks of this strategy were the problems that campaigning in enemy territory always conjured: maintaining secure lines of communication while fighting in a hostile environment. To further complicate Hannibal's plans, to implement his strategy of a war on Italian soil he needed to elude a Roman army sent to intercept him and then bring his invading Carthaginian host across the Alps in winter because the Romans controlled all the coastal approaches to Italy.[116]

Historians have long speculated whether this plan was based on sound strategic principles or whether it was influenced by internal feuding within the Carthaginian government. Both Hamilcar and his son Hannibal enjoyed support from some powerful members of the Punic aristocracy, but their political rival Hanno (who had commanded with Hamilcar during the Mercenary War) also exerted substantial influence in Carthage. This may explain why Hannibal never had great support from the Punic navy.[117] Unlike the First Punic War where Carthaginian sea power played a decisive role in Punic strategy, the Second Punic War would be a war fought on land in Italy, Spain and finally, North Africa. Confident he now had the allies necessary to pursue a war against Rome in Italy, Hannibal assembled and trained an army in the early spring and considered his land route across the Alps.

Dangerous Journey: Hannibal Crosses the Alps
Hannibal left the friendly gates of New Carthage probably some time in mid-June 219 at the head of a very large army by classical standards, consisting of 90,000 infantry, 12,000 cavalry and thirty-seven war elephants.[118] After a six-week march north along the eastern coast of Spain, Hannibal crossed the Ebro River, the traditional frontier between Carthaginian territory in the south and the wild north. Contemporary sources do not give us very much concrete information about this phase of Hannibal's march, but we do know the Punic commander did move against a number of pro-Roman tribes living between the Ebro and the Pyrenees. Hannibal lost a lot of troops during this fighting

(precise numbers are unknown), but the sacrifices were required in order to secure his line of communication from Italy back to Spain. Without this lifeline, the Italian campaign would be stillborn. Once the Spanish tribes were pacified, Hannibal gave one of his trusted officers a contingent of 10,000 foot soldiers and 1,000 horse to keep an eye on the pro-Roman Massaliote city of Emporion on the coast and guard the mountain passes between Spain and Gaul.[119] By the time Hannibal left Emporion in late August his army had contracted significantly due to garrisoning and some desertions. He also released a further 10,000 Spaniards, perhaps as a conciliatory gesture or perhaps to cover up his own troop evaporation.[120] Polybius tells us that the Punic general had no more than 50,000 infantry and 9,000 cavalry by the time he began crossing the Pyrenees.[121]

Hannibal decided on an interior route because the Romans controlled the coastline between Spain and Italy. Pushing through the tribal resistance in the mountain passes and descending into Gaul, Hannibal negotiated an agreement with many of the Celtic tribes for safe passage, allowing the Carthaginian forces to arrive at the Rhone River relatively unmolested. Hannibal shed another 12,000 infantry and 1,000 cavalry on this trek, losing some to war, but most to garrisoning, as recent archaeological finds along this route suggests.[122]

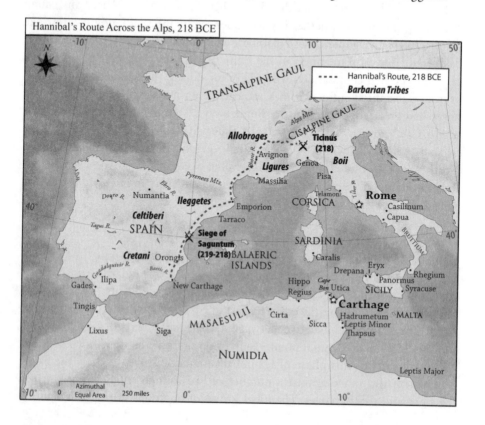

Hannibal arrived at his first major geographical barrier, the Rhone River, in late September. The precise place where the Punic army crossed the Rhone has been a subject of great debate among scholars, but Polybius states that Hannibal began crossing the Rhone some four days' march from the sea, perhaps at the site of the modern French city of Beaucaire.[123] There is some suspicion that Hannibal marched along an ancient route that would later be named by the Romans *via Domitia*.[124] To prepare for the crossing, the Punic commander bribed the locals living along the bank of the river and purchased their canoes and boats, even purchasing logs to make their own barges. Within just two days, Hannibal had enough vessels for crossing. But as the Carthaginians readied their boats, the other bank of the Rhone filled with barbarians preparing to contest the crossing. Recognizing the need for a diversion to weaken the barbarians' resolve, Hannibal sent a detachment of troops (most likely cavalry) north to cross the Rhone upstream, probably across from where Avignon is today.[125] There, the Punic horse waited and hid for a few days until the main crossing was ready.

On the fifth day since reaching the Rhone, Hannibal ordered a full-scale crossing. The first Punic assault rapidly established a foothold on the farther bank, and when the Gauls pored out of their position to attack the invaders, the once-hidden Carthaginian cavalry struck the rear of the tribal warriors with complete surprise, routing the barbarians. Hannibal could now bring the rest of his troops across safely, and the crossing was completed by nightfall. Only his thirty-seven elephants remained on the west bank.

The next morning Hannibal learned that Scipio the Elder's Roman fleet had anchored at the mouth of the Rhone River. He immediately dispatched 500 of his finest Numidian cavalry south to investigate, then went about bringing the pachyderms across the river.[126] He also met with an envoy of chieftains from the Po Valley, first among them a powerful man named Magilos. These men had crossed the Alps to meet with Hannibal and cement their alliance against the Romans. Livy even points out that when the Carthaginian troops, tired from their march and apprehensive about crossing the Alps, seemed dispirited, Hannibal attempted to raise their spirits by pointing to the visiting chieftains and said, 'How do you think these envoys got here, on wings?'[127]

After carefully bringing his elephants across the Rhone on large rafts, Hannibal began his march upriver when his Numidian cavalry returned from a clash with Scipio's reconnaissance force of 300 Roman horse, supported by Gallic cavalry and led by local guides. The scouting Roman cavalry had bumped into the Numidian cavalry, and after a short and bloody fight, chased the African cavalry back to their camp, then turned and bolted back to the mouth of the Rhone.[128] Contemporary sources claim that 200 of the 500 Numidian horsemen were killed in this skirmish, with a loss of only 140 Roman horse.[129] Scipio immediately broke camp and began rowing up the river in an attempt to catch the Punic army. Unfortunately for the Romans, Hannibal was now many days ahead of them and, after a four-day march north along the east bank of the river, putting more space between himself and his adversary. After resupplying his troops for the winter passage, Hannibal led his men east into the foothills which lay beneath the snow-capped Alps. At the head of the column were the cavalry and elephants, followed by infantry and the supply train. Hannibal himself, with his best infantry, brought up the rear.[130] It was mid–October.

Historians have long debated about what path Hannibal took to cross the mountains, though Polybius clearly indicates that it was a high pass.[131] A few days into the march, the Carthaginians encountered the hostile Allobroge tribe holding the high ground dominating a pass ahead. Hannibal sent forward a scouting party made up of Gauls, who reported that the Allobroge warriors had abandoned the high ground during the night. Hannibal then seized the heights and the march was resumed. But the danger was not over, and the barbarians attacked the packed Punic column as it wound along the mountainside, frightening pack animals and men alike, plunging some to their deaths in the gorge below. According to Livy,

> the natives, springing from their places of concealment, fiercely assaulted front and rear, leaping into the fray, hurling missiles, rolling down rocks from the heights above.[132]

The barbarians were finally put to flight by Carthaginian soldiers who managed to seize the high ground and attack the tribesmen from behind.[133] Hannibal's troops would be ambushed again by tribesmen a few days later while in a deep ravine. After fierce fighting, the Carthaginians finally forced the enemy warriors to withdraw.

Hannibal reached the main watershed nine days into the march. Here he rested for two days to allow stragglers to catch up before starting his descent. It was now snowing in the high country, and according to Polybius,

> The track which led down the mountain was both narrow and steep, and since neither the men nor the animals could be sure of their footing on account of the snow, any who stepped wide of the path or stumbled overbalanced and fell down the precipices.[134]

Almost as many men and animals were lost over the cliffs as had been killed in the fighting.[135] Hannibal faced another setback when his passage was blocked by a massive landslide, so severe it required the reconstruction of the path. Finally, after a reported fifteen-day march (one modern estimate puts it at a more reasonable twenty-four), Hannibal reached the fertile expanses of the Po Valley somewhere near Turin no later than mid–November.[136] He arrived with only 12,000 African and 8,000 Spanish infantry and 6,000 cavalry, or about a quarter of the number of troops that set out originally from New Carthage five months earlier.[137]

Seizing the Initiative: Early Punic Victories at the Ticinus and the Trebia (218 BCE)

Hannibal arrived in northern Italy with an army of 26,000 hungry and exhausted men and immediately prepared to enact his strategy to make war against the Romans in Roman territory. An army of 26,000 men seemed 'pitifully small to challenge the might of Rome' in the words of one leading authority on Hannibal, yet with the assistance of his Gallic allies, he not only rebuilt his army quickly, he went on to defeat the Romans on two occasions before the end of 218 BCE.[138]

Hannibal certainly recognized that his bold crossing of the Alps had given him the initiative in the war against Rome, but he also realized that he needed to quickly resupply his army and replace the fallen troops if he was to push forward with his plans.[139] Hannibal's numbers could only be replaced by Celtic contingents. Unfortunately the first Gauls he dealt with were not the same barbarians he had made a pact with earlier, so his first attempt to recruit troops from the Taurini was met with resistance, forcing him into a demonstration of his army's might. The chief city of the Taurini was attacked and, after a three-day siege, reduced, its population massacred in a coldly calculated display of Punic military strength intended to overawe the local tribes.[140] The demonstration worked. As the Carthaginians helped themselves to the Taurini's winter stores, barbarians flocked to join the Punic effort. Rested, Hannibal marched down the Po Valley toward his Gallic allies the Insubres and Boii and toward Roman territory.

When Scipio realized he would be unable to catch Hannibal on the Rhone in southern Gaul, he made a decisive and fateful decision to transfer command of his Roman army to his brother Gnaeus and ordered them westward to Spain to protect old allies and secure new ones. No doubt Scipio understood that Hannibal would need a secure line of communication to conduct a war in Italy, and this army's presence in northern Iberia could disrupt that lifeline. Scipio returned to the Roman port city of Pisae in Italy and sent word to the Roman Senate of Hannibal's intentions. The Senate immediately recalled Sempronius Longus from Sicily where he had been preparing his army for an invasion of North Africa. After a Herculean effort, Sempronius was able to transfer his army to the Adriatic port of Ariminum (modern Rimini) by early December.[141]

Meanwhile, Scipio took command of two Roman legions operating in the Po River. These legions had been placed there to protect the two new Roman colonies of Placentia and Cremona whose 6,000 colonists were barely established when the Celts in the region revolted earlier. It was very uncommon for a consul to abandon one army and take command of another, and it is possible that when Hannibal learned of the existence of a Roman army at Placentia he assumed it was the same army he had evaded in southern Gaul.[142] When Scipio discovered the Punic army was now across the Alps and operating in the same area, he marched out to confront the invaders.

After crossing the Po River with a makeshift pontoon bridge made of boats, Scipio and his two legions marched along its north bank toward where his scouts believed Hannibal's army was located. Scipio bridged a second river, this time the Ticinus River (a tributary of the Po), somewhere near the modern city of Pavia. The Romans were now marching through the territory of the Insubres, and though the Insubres were allies of Carthage, the presence of Roman legionaries had a chilling effect on Hannibal's ability to recruit from the local tribes. What was needed was a battlefield victory over the Romans to both boost Punic morale and persuade the Gauls into joining Hannibal. This opportunity took place near the Ticinus River in late November, 218.

When the two armies' scouts first made contact with each other, both Hannibal and Scipio ordered their forces to make camp.[143] The next day both commanders led a large reconnaissance force on a fact-finding mission. Hannibal brought most of his 6,000 cavalry with him, outnumbering Scipio and his Roman, Latin and Gallic horse, though we are unsure by how much. The Roman consul also had a number of light infantry *velites* with him. When the two forces finally met, they each deployed ready to fight. Scipio placed his *velites* as a screen for his Gallic cavalry, keeping his Italian horse in reserve. Hannibal placed his Spanish heavy cavalry in the centre and his Numidian light cavalry on both wings.

The Battle of the Ticinus opened in typical fashion with Scipio ordering his *velites* forward to harass the Punic lines with their javelins, but before these light troops could throw their missiles, both sides' heavy cavalry surged forward in a charge, meeting in the centre of the battlefield in a general melee as the *velites* retreated back through the galloping Gallic horse. For a while neither side held an advantage until the Numidian light cavalry swept around the Roman flanks, cutting down first the disorganized *velites* before wheeling and striking the reserve Roman horse in the rear. During this stage of the battle Scipio was gravely wounded. Tradition states that the consul was only saved by his seventeen-year old son, also named Publius Cornelius Scipio. This younger Scipio would later become Scipio 'Africanus', Rome's greatest general, conqueror of Spain, and the ultimate victor over Hannibal at the Battle of Zama in 202 BCE. Their commanding general and consul wounded, the Romans were routed. And although the Battle of the Ticinus was more of a large cavalry skirmish than a set-piece battle, with Hannibal's Spanish and Numidian cavalry proving decisive over the Roman and allied horse, it served as a harbinger of the battles to come.

Demoralized, Scipio and his army broke camp and retreated back over the Ticinus River, and though Hannibal did pursue, he was unable to seize the makeshift bridge before it was dismantled, forcing the Punic commander to march two days westward along the Po before a suitable spot was found to build a bridge. Meanwhile, Scipio retreated back to his base at Placentia, camping west of the River Trebia on the opposite bank to the city. Two days after crossing

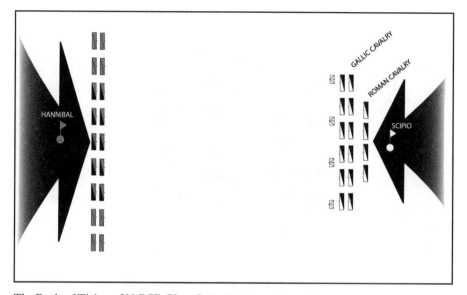

The Battle of Ticinus, 218 BCE, Phase I. Carthaginian and Roman forces deploy into fighting order as they close with each other near the Ticinus River. Hannibal's Spanish heavy cavalry is flanked by his Numidian light horse. Opposing them are Scipio's Gallic cavalry screened by javelin-wielding velites and backed by a reserve of Roman horsemen.

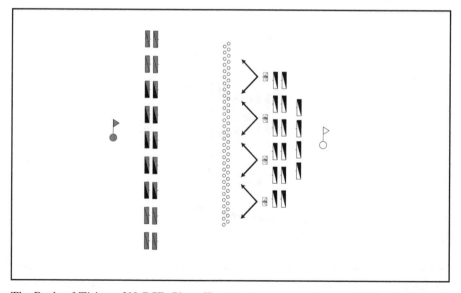

The Battle of Ticinus, 218 BCE, Phase II. As the forces near each other, Scipio orders his velites forward, javelins at the ready.

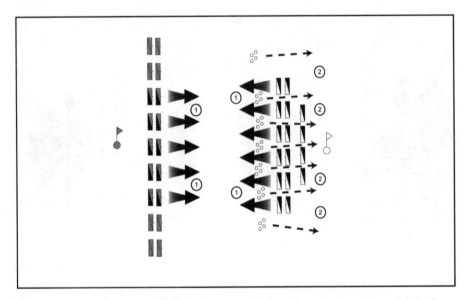

The Battle of Ticinus, 218 BCE, Phase III. Before the Roman skirmishers can throw their javelins at the approaching Carthaginian host, the heavy cavalry on both sides charge (1). The velites retreat through gaps in the Gallic formations (2) as the horsemen rapidly close with each other.

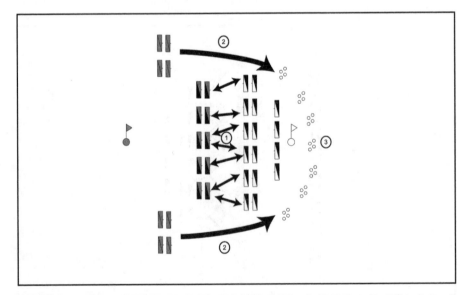

The Battle of Ticinus, 218 BCE, Phase IV. As the cavalry battle swirls in the centre (1), Hannibal sends his Numidian light cavalry arcing around the flanks (2), cutting down the velites in their path as they sweep into the Roman rear (3).

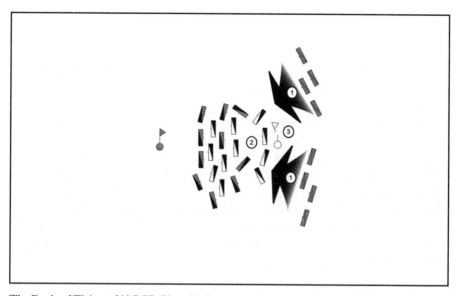

The Battle of Ticinus, 218 BCE, Phase V. The Numidian cavalry wheels and charges (1), smashing into the rear of the Roman cavalry reserve (2). During the ensuing action, Scipio is badly wounded (3). The attack on their rear and wounding of their general and consul prove too much and the Romans are routed from the battlefield.

the Po, Hannibal caught up to Scipio at his base at Placentia and formed up on the flat plain in front of the Roman camp about five or six miles away.

That night, Gauls in the service of Rome murdered and beheaded a number of sleeping legionaries and then deserted to Hannibal. The Carthaginian commander welcomed the 2,000 Celtic infantry and 200 cavalry that came over, promising rich rewards and sending them back to their tribes to raise support for the Punic cause.[144] Soon, Hannibal's ranks began to swell as more local Gauls joined his army. Recognizing his strategic position was becoming more untenable each day, Scipio ordered his army to withdraw across the Trebia under cover of darkness. Moving troops when your enemy is in close proximity is one of the most difficult military actions, and Scipio no doubt understood the risks of such an operation. When Hannibal learned his enemy was attempting to withdraw, he ordered first his Numidian cavalry, then the rest of his army, against the Romans. The Numidian horse paused to sack and burn the abandoned camp, allowing Scipio to bring most of his army across the river, though he did lose some of his stragglers to the Carthaginians.

Scipio set up camp again near the modern village of Rivergaro in a much more defensible position and awaited reinforcements. He did not have to wait long. Sempronius Longus arrived from the Adriatic port of Ariminum at the head of a consular army made up of another two legions. Confident in his ability to defeat the invading host, he took sole command of the combined consular army due to Scipio's injury.[145] Hannibal watched patiently as the new army formed. The presence of two Roman consuls and four legions presented Hannibal with an ideal opportunity to beat a substantial Roman army in a set-piece battle and put his master plan in motion. But as he prepared to offer battle on his terms, a Carthaginian raid against a nearby Gallic ally of Rome nearly precipitated a full-blown engagement.

Hannibal had sent a force of 2,000 infantry and 1,000 Gallic and Numidian cavalry to forage and plunder the camp of a duplicitous Celtic chieftain. Already spoiling for a fight, Sempronius came to the barbarians' aid with a strong cavalry force and 1,000 light infantry *velites*.[146] Laden with loot, the Carthaginian raiders were chased back into their own camp. The Punic picket repulsed the Romans, but instead of feeding more troops into a fight not of his own choosing, Hannibal held his men back. The Romans refused to press their attack against the fortified Carthaginian camp, and the Italians returned to their own camp in high spirits and claiming victory. Polybius showered praise on Hannibal's generalship:

> In this situation [Hannibal] acted as a good general should: he checked the troops that were in retreat and compelled them to halt and face about as they approached their own camp. He would not allow them to pursue and engage the enemy, however, he sent out his officers and buglers to recall them.[147]

Sensing that his adversary Sempronius was eager for a fight, Hannibal began to prepare the battlefield to his advantage. He recognized that the Romans would only offer battle in open terrain, so he decided to fight in an open treeless area near his camp that was bisected by the River Trebia and its high, overgrown banks. There, he would place his youngest brother Mago with an equal force of 1,000 infantry and cavalry, setting up an ambush to be sprung at a precise time.

The Battle of the Trebia began at dawn on a frost-encrusted morning in late December 218, when Hannibal sent his Numidian light cavalry across the Trebia to attack the Roman camp. The action was designed to precipitate a general engagement and Sempronius did not let Hannibal down. The Roman consul ordered out his cavalry to meet the Numidians, followed closely by his skirmishers and legionaries. Polybius tells us that the Roman soldiers and their mounts left their camp without eating breakfast.[148] Matters worsened quickly for the Italian soldiers and their allies as they marched into a snowstorm and crossed the Trebia in high flood, wading through water chest deep. When the Romans finally forded the river and formed up for battle across from the Punic army, they were a wet and freezing lot. Time and cold temperatures now favoured Hannibal and his army.

Hannibal's troops had eaten, groomed their horses and donned their armour around campfires. As the Roman army approached, Hannibal ordered 8,000 pikemen and slingers forward to screen his army as they deployed to the open field prepared earlier, about 1,400 yards in front of his camp.[149] The Carthaginian general's army had swollen since crossing the Alps to 20,000 infantry (Spaniards, Celts and Africans) and 10,000 cavalry equally divided on both wings, including the Numidian light horse which had returned. He formed his infantry in one line with his most unreliable troops, the Celts, in the centre. Finally, he placed his elephants in front of his infantry to deter Roman cavalry charges.

The Roman army formed up in standard fashion with 16,000 heavy infantry legionaries and 20,000 allied infantry in the centre and 2,000 Roman cavalry on both wings. Sempronius drew up his infantry in three lines with the legions in the middle and their allied foot on each side. About 4,000 *velites* and allied skirmishers screened the Roman army.[150]

The main battle opened with a general exchange of missile weapons by skirmishers on both sides. Polybius maintains that the Romans came off worse in this phase of the battle because they were suffering from the cold and had used up many of their javelins when pursuing the Numidian light horse.[151] With no advantage gained, Sempronius recalled his light troops. It was at this moment of transition that Hannibal ordered his own numerically superior cavalry to attack the Roman cavalry on each wing, sweeping the Italian horse from the field and stripping the legionaries of their protection. Both infantry lines in the centre advanced and engaged in a vicious melee. Hannibal now launched his reformed Numidian light cavalry and his light troops against the exposed Roman flanks. The allied infantry, already pinned against the legionaries in the centre by the advancing Punic elephants and infantry, broke

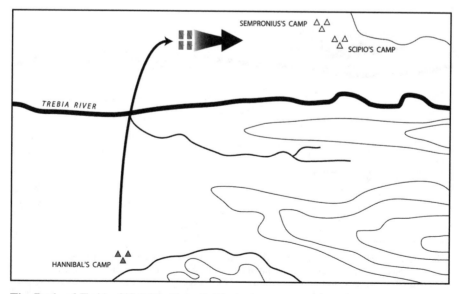

The Battle of Trebia, 218 BCE, Phase I. The battle opens at dawn as Hannibal, hoping to goad Sempronius into action, despatches his Numidian light cavalry across the Trebia to strike the Roman camps.

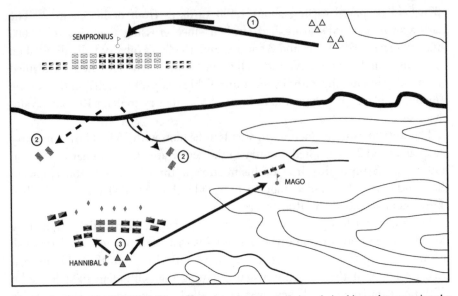

The Battle of Trebia, 218 BCE, Phase II. Sempronius takes the bait, ordering his cavalry out against the Numidians, who turn back towards the Trebia. The Roman consul orders his legions and allied infantry out as well, and they form facing the icy river (1). In their haste, the men and horses deploy before breakfast can be served. The Numidian riders re-cross the Trebia (2) to join the deploying Carthaginian force (3). The Carthaginian forces have breakfasted and their horse have been fed and groomed.

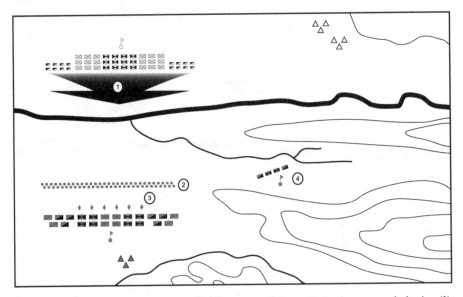

The Battle of Trebia, 218 BCE, Phase III. As Sempronius's forces slowly advance towards the river (1), the Carthaginians deploy behind a screen of pikemen and slingers (2). Hannibal places his elephants forward to deter cavalry charges against his infantrymen (3). His less-reliable Celtic infantry is in the centre where they can best be controlled, and the cavalry is formed into two equal forces on each wing. Hannibal's youngest brother, Mago, is sent to the right to prepare an ambush (4).

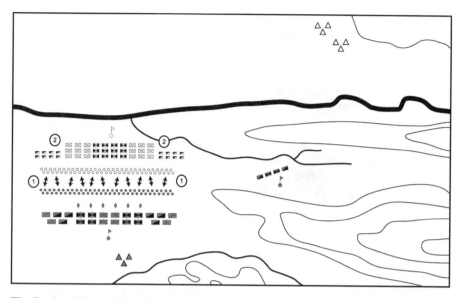

The Battle of Trebia, 218 BCE, Phase IV. Wading chest-deep waters of the Trebia in a snow storm, Sempronius's army throws out a screen of javelin-wielding *velites* to enage their opposite numbers in missile combat (1) as the Romans realign their formations (2).

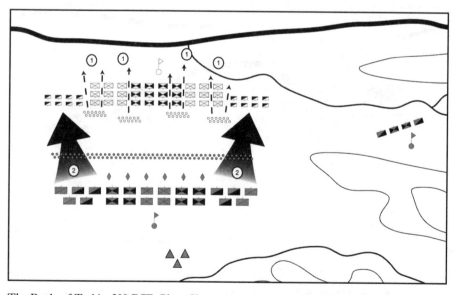

The Battle of Trebia, 218 BCE, Phase V. Sempronius recalls his skirmishers (1) who have expended most of their javelins and are suffering from the cold. The disorder created by the *velites* return through the lines presents Hannibal with a golden opportunity and he orders his cavalry to charge the numerically inferior Roman horse (2).

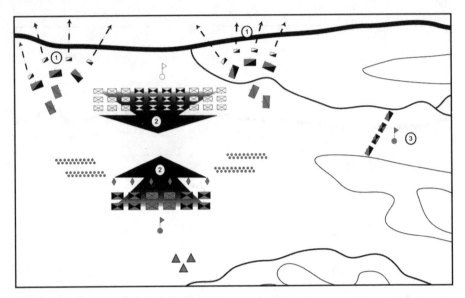

The Battle of Trebia, 218 BCE, Phase VI. The Roman cavalry is routed from the field by the Carthaginian horse (1), exposing the flanks of Sempronius's main body. The infantry of both sides advance towards each other, intent on battle (2). Meanwhile, Mago bides his time, undetected on the Roman's left flank (3).

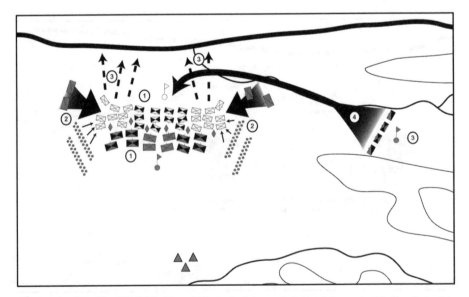

The Battle of Trebia, 218 BCE, Phase VII. As the infantry clash in a violent melee (1), Hannibal orders his reformed light cavalry and skirmishers to attack the Roman flanks (2). Already pressed from the front by Carthaginian infantry and elephants, the flank attack proves too much, and Sempronius's allied infantry routs (3). Mago seizes the moment and launches his force against the rear of the Roman legionaries in the centre (4).

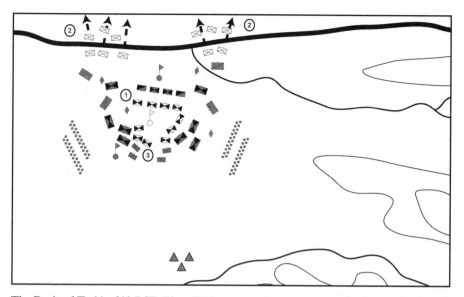

The Battle of Trebia, 218 BCE, Phase VIII. Even though the veteran *triarii* manage to face about to meet Mago's attack (1), their disciplined stand is not enough to save the day. The fleeing allied infantry are pushed into and across the Trebia (2), and the solitary Roman success against the Celtic infantry (3) merely delays the inevitable. Sempronius and around 10,000 legionaries manage to fight their way out, abandoning the camps and retreating to Placentia.

and ran. Sensing the moment was finally right, Mago led his 2,000 troops from their hiding place and fell on the rear of the legionaries. The veteran *triarii* in the third line turned around to face this unexpected threat, but to no avail. Their allied infantry were now being pushed backwards toward the banks of the Trebia. Only the legionaries in the centre had any success, cutting through their Celtic adversaries. But this success was not enough to save the day. With his army disintegrating all around him, Sempronius and about 10,000 of his troops (mostly legionaries) fought their way out of harm's way and, abandoning their camp, back directly to Placentia in a cold, driving sleet.[152]

Roman casualties at Trebia were extraordinary, with perhaps as many 20,000 Roman legionaries and their allies killed.[153] But despite the loss of so many allied troops, the Roman legionaries fared well against their opponents, a fact not lost on Roman commanders. Legionaries would figure prominently two years later in the Roman planning at the battle of Cannae. Punic losses were light and confined mostly to the Celts in the centre of the fray. But Polybius tells us that the cold and violence also took the lives of all but one of the elephants, robbing Hannibal of a tried and true weapon in the Carthaginian art of war.[154] Sempronius would winter in Placentia and then move back to Ariminum in the early spring of 217. Now master of northern Italy, Hannibal Barca released his non-Roman captives and sent them home in an attempt to undermine the Roman Confederation. He then wintered in the Po Valley and prepared for his march south into central Italy and the heart of Roman territory.

Ambush at Lake Trasimene and Rome's 'Fabian' Strategy (217 BCE)
In March 217 the Roman Senate picked two new consuls, Gaius Flaminius and Gnaeus Servilius Geminus, to lead the effort against the Punic invaders. The new consuls marched north in early spring, Flaminius to Arretium and Servilius to Ariminum, in an attempt to cut Hannibal off from the most obvious routes south into central Italy.[155] What route Hannibal took is not precisely known for certain, though he probably crossed the Apennines from east to west through the Colline Pass before navigating the dangerous Arno swamps.[156] Here, most of the pack animals faltered and died while many of the horses became lame due to the prolonged march through the mud. Both Livy and Polybius comment that Hannibal developed opthalmia while crossing these wetlands, leading to the loss of sight in one eye.[157]

Leading his beleaguered army out of the swamp riding the lone surviving elephant, Hannibal found Flaminius encamped in Etruria (modern Tuscany) in front of the city of Arretium. Hannibal boldly marched past the Roman army of 30,000 Roman soldiers and allies and pushed south toward Rome itself, burning Roman settlements as he marched, baiting the consul into pursuit.[158] Flaminius quickly broke camp and haphazardly began to track down the Punic army, despite the warnings from his officers concerning the importance of an orderly march to defend against Hannibal's superiority in cavalry. Flaminius wanted to defeat the Punic invaders before they reached the gates of Rome, and was willing to brave combat without the aid of Servilius' consular army at Ariminum.

Hannibal continued to march south toward the capital keeping the city of Cortona and its hills on his left and Lake Trasimene on his right. The ancient road itself ran along the northern shore of Lake Trasimene between the hills and the water, an ideal place to ambush the trailing Roman army. On June 20, Hannibal entered the valley and peeled off some elements of his army to hide in the hills and defiles, then established a camp on one of the hills above the lake.[159] Shadowing the Punic army, Flaminius stopped and rested his troops a few miles to the west on a defensible plain.

That night Hannibal set the rest of his ambush, quietly deploying the rest of his troops along the ridge and in the defiles next to the road, their progress aided by a bright moon. The following morning, according to Polybius, 'a thick mist still hung over the lakeside'.[160] Impatient to overtake his enemy, Flaminius broke camp early and marched along the shore of the lake, entering both the valley and the fog of war. As soon as the greater part of the Roman army was in the defile, Hannibal sprung the trap.[161] Polybius recounts:

> The sudden appearance of the enemy took Flaminius completely by surprise. The mist blotted out all visibility, and with the attack being launched from higher ground and from so many points at once, the [Roman] centurions and military tribunes were not only not able to issue

any of the necessary orders but even to grasp what was happening. They found themselves attacked from the front, the flanks and the rear. In consequence most of the troops were cut down while still in marching order and without the least chance of defending themselves, delivered up to slaughter ... by a complete lack of judgment on the part of their commander.[162]

The Roman column was attacked along its entire length by Hannibal's cavalry, who rode down many of the legionaries and their allies were they stood. The rest were pushed back into the lake where many were either killed or lost their footing in the mud and drowned under the weight of their armour. The only Roman troops to escape the ambush were the 6,000 members of the vanguard who hacked their way through Punic light troops blocking their path, seizing a nearby hill. Flaminius himself was killed by the leader of the Insubrian cavalry after the latter cut his way through the consul's veteran *triarii* bodyguard and ran him through with his spear.[163] Livy tells us that it took Hannibal's men three hours to destroy the Roman army.[164] By the time the noon sun had burned off the morning mist, 15,000 Roman soldiers lay dead and another 10,000 captured.[165]

As before, Hannibal released the allied troops, instructing them that his quarrel was with Rome, not her subjects. The following day, even the 6,000 Romans in the vanguard surrendered. Punic losses were 1,500 men, most of these Celts.[166] Adding insult to injury, a Roman cavalry force of 4,000 men

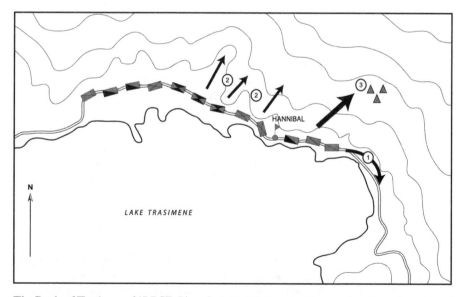

The Battle of Trasimene, 217 BCE, Phase I. As Hannibal marches his army along the northern shore of Lake Trasimene (1) he directs some of his forces into ambush positions overlooking the road (2). The remainder of the Carthaginians make camp in the hills overlooking the lake (3). Hannibal knows he is being followed by a Roman army under Flaminius, and intends to turn the tables on his pursuers.

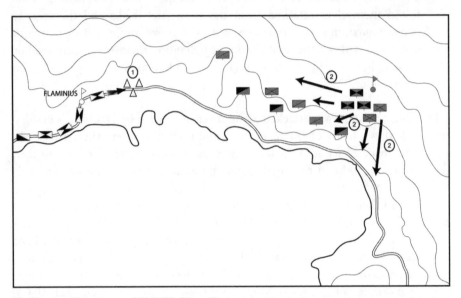

The Battle of Trasimene, 217 BCE, Phase II. As night falls, the Romans make camp on a plain along the shore (1). Aided by a bright moon, Hannibal deploys his remaining soldiers in concealed positions along the road (2).

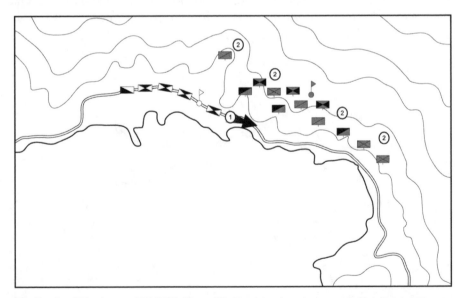

The Battle of Trasimene, 217 BCE, Phase III. Flaminius, impatient to catch Hannibal and his army before they can reach Rome, rushes his troops onto the road the next morning, heedless of the early morning fog (1). Shrouded by the mist and concealed in the hills and defiles overlooking the lake, Hannibal's army awaits their commander's signal to attack (2).

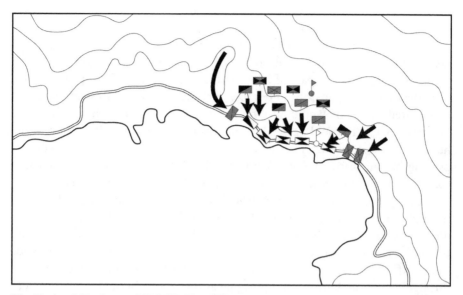

The Battle of Trasimene, 217 BCE, Phase IV. Hannibal springs his ambush, trapping the Romans between his charging forces and the lake. Flaminius and his soldiers are taken completely by surprise as the Punic forces burst out of the fog from the high ground on their left.

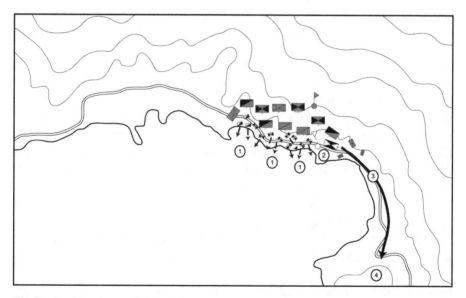

The Battle of Trasimene, 217 BCE, Phase V. Most of the Roman army is ridden down by Hannibal's cavalry or drowned in the lake (1) and Flaminius himself is killed by the leader of Hannibal's Insubrian cavalry (2). The Roman vanguard manages to cut its way through the light troops blocking its path (3) and takes up a position on a nearby hill (4), but the stand proves hopeless and they surrender the following day.

sent by Servilius to assist Flaminius was intercepted and defeated by one of Hannibal's most trusted cavalry officers, Maharbal, killing half the Roman force and capturing the other half.[167]

Hannibal continued south but did not march on Rome itself. He did not possess the necessary siege train required to take such a formidable city, and seizing the city was not part of his overall strategy of breaking up the Roman confederation. Ancient sieges often took months to successfully complete. Had he invested Rome, he would not only have had to contend with an impressive fortification which would have taken months to reduce with a large siege train, he would also have had to deal with large Roman relief armies capable of pinning him in place. Wisely, Hannibal skirted the capital and headed south, confident in his ability to beat the armies of Rome on the battlefield.

Crossing the Apennines again from west to east, Hannibal led his army through Umbria and by way of Picenum to the Adriatic Sea, collecting so much plunder along the way that 'they could neither drive it or carry it with them'.[168] The Carthaginian army arrived on the coast in late July and made camp. After resting and taking on supplies, the Punic army marched south through Samnium, burning and pillaging as they went. In the Roman province of Apulia Hannibal was once again challenged by a substantial Roman army, but this time, the Romans had adopted a new emergency strategy to deal with the Carthaginian invaders.

When news of the overwhelming defeat at Lake Trasimene reached the streets of Rome weeks earlier, the Senate took the drastic step of appointing as military dictator Quintus Fabius Maximus, a well-respected consul in the years 233–232, when he won fame defeating the Ligurians in northwest Italy, and again in 228–227. The election of Fabius as dictator in the summer of 217 was by popular vote, breaking from the tradition of choosing a man nominated by an active consul on Roman soil. Flaminius was dead and Servilius was cut off from the capital by Hannibal's march, forcing the Roman people to take matters in their own hands. But Roman politics even influenced this vote. Fabius was not allowed to pick his own second-in-command (known as the *Magister Equitum* or 'Master of the Horse'), instead, the Senate pressed upon him Marcus Minucius Rufus, a former consul and aggressive commander.

By nature a cautious general, Fabius would refuse to meet the Carthaginian army in battle, preferring instead a strategy of delay and harassment, earning him the nickname *Cunctator* or 'the Delayer'. Rome's 'Fabian' strategy was designed to force Hannibal to keep moving in order not to exhaust local food and forage.[169] Fabius based his strategy on a combination of factors: his ability to refuse battle; on the tactical power of the defence; on his control of walled cities faithful to Rome, and on his excellent logistics.[170] This seemed like a prudent strategy considering the Roman losses at the Ticinus, the Trebia and Lake Trasimene over the previous two years, but it was not widely popular. There did exist Roman factions that wanted to defeat Hannibal in a set-piece battle, and Fabius' lieutenant, Minucius, was among them. After raising new legions to replace the losses sustained at the Trebia and Trasimene, Fabius took command of six legions and set out after Hannibal.

When Fabius caught up with Hannibal in Apulia, the Carthaginian general drew up his army for battle. But Fabius refused to engage, instead taking and holding the high ground above Hannibal's line of march and attacking Punic foraging parties. By attacking foragers and stragglers, Fabius was using small raids to whittle away at Hannibal's forces.[171] Hannibal understood this strategy of attrition would eventually bleed his army white while simultaneously emboldening the Romans, so he decided to provoke Fabius into a battle by ravaging the countryside. He marched west, crossing the Apennines again, and descended into the fertile plains of Campania, burning and looting one of the agricultural crown jewels of southern Italy – the *ager Falernus*. But try as Hannibal might, the Roman dictator would not be pulled into a set-piece battle. Moreover, many of Rome's key allies in southern Italy did not immediately abandon the confederation as Hannibal had hoped.

Unwilling to winter in the devastated *ager Falernus*, Hannibal sought to return to Apulia. To do so, he needed to cross a pass occupied by 4,000 of Fabius' legionaries, sent there to ambush the Carthaginians. Hannibal, in a masterful ruse, gathered 2,000 head of cattle and tied bundles of wood to their horns. Setting the wood ablaze, he herded the beasts up a spur near the pass at night. When the Romans guarding the pass saw the line of ascending torches, they mistakenly believed the Punic army was outflanking them, and abandoned the pass. Hannibal led his army across the pass and back into northern Apulia to winter in the city of Gerunium.

Meanwhile, Fabius had been recalled to Rome to stand before the Senate and defend his strategy of delay and harassment. His second-in-command, Minucius, was left to shadow the Punic army. While foraging outside of Gerunium, Hannibal was drawn into a substantial skirmish with the Roman Master of the Horse, a skirmish the Carthaginian commander lost. Though not strategically decisive, when news of this minor victory reached Rome, the Senate, growing tired of the 'Fabian' strategy, rewarded Minucius with half of the dictator's army. Overconfident, Minucius engaged Hannibal again near Gerunium, but this time his army would have been destroyed had it not been for the timely arrival of Fabius. With the campaigning season now drawing to a close, a contrite Minucius rejoined Fabius and the Roman and Carthaginian armies returned to their winter quarters.

Cannae: Hannibal's 'Killing Field' (216 BCE)

In December 217 Fabius' six-month dictatorship expired and the Roman Senate opted to return to the selection of consuls to run Roman military affairs. Hannibal's swath of destruction in Campania left a bad taste in Rome's mouth, and many prominent Roman citizens were calling once again for a military solution to the Punic menace. Abandoning the Fabian strategy, the Senate decided to seek out and crush Hannibal once and for all in a decisive military engagement at a time when Rome had overwhelming numbers on its side. To accomplish this, the Senate elected Lucius Aemilius Paullus and Gaius Terentius Varro as consuls in March 216 and began an emergency levy to put two new legions in the field. Four legions were already encamped outside of Gerunium watching Hannibal, and Paullus and Varro would march two new legions to buttress the 60,000 infantry and 4,500 cavalry already shadowing the Punic army. Hannibal broke camp in early June and marched south to the ruined citadel at Cannae, the location of a Roman magazine and plenty of forage for the Carthaginian army. Hannibal took this strategically important site to provoke a battle with Rome, and he was not disappointed.

Marching from Rome at the head of more than 20,000 troops, Paullus and Varro rendezvoused with the Roman army and set out with a massive force consisting of eight legions and an equal number of allies to track down and finally defeat Hannibal's forces. In the August of 216 BCE, the Romans caught up with Hannibal near the village of Cannae in Apulia. The resulting battle of Cannae pitted a Roman army of 80,000 infantry and 6,400 cavalry against Hannibal's Punic army of 45,000 infantry and 10,000 cavalry in one of the most famous battles in military history.[172]

Hannibal camped west of the Aufidius River, while the Romans camped two-thirds of their army opposite the invading army, the remainder staying on the opposite side of the river to limit Carthaginian foraging. Varro, whose day it was to command the Roman army, lined up for battle on the east side of the river, placing his legionaries in the centre in an extra deep formation (in places, between thirty-five and fifty men deep) because of the narrowness of the plain. No more than 2,000 legionaries could engage the enemy at one time.[173] Moreover, many of the legionaries were fresh recruits recently added to make up for the horrendous loses suffered at Trebia and Trasimene.[174] Varro's strategy was simple: overwhelm the Carthaginian centre with the sheer weight of his legionaries. Betting on his heavy infantry to win the day, he then placed his inferior Roman cavalry on both wings to check the advance of the more numerous Carthaginian horse.

Understanding the threat to his centre, Hannibal arranged his troops south of the Romans, placing his Celtic and Spanish infantry in the centre in a convex formation and making the centre deeper than the flanks in order to match the Roman frontage and delay the legions' advance. Hannibal kept his more reliable African infantry in reserve behind each flank of the crescent, and placed his cavalry on the flanks opposite the Roman horsemen. Hannibal, assisted by his youngest brother Mago, would command the centre. His staff officer Hasdrubal Gisgo led the Carthaginian left, while Hanno commanded the right, with the brilliant Maharbal leading the Numidian light horse. Outnumbered two-to-one in total numbers, the Carthaginian general placed his hope on his cavalry that was superior to the Romans in both numbers and quality.

As was typical of classical engagements, the battle opened with skirmishing, then Varro ordered the weighted Roman centre to close with the Carthaginians. At this moment, Hannibal ordered the cavalry on his wings to strike the weaker Roman cavalry opposite them. As the Romans engaged with the leading edge of the Carthaginian infantry, the centre yielded to the Roman advance, slowly transforming from a convex to a concave formation. On the wings, the Carthaginian cavalry routed the Roman horse on both sides. As tens of thousands of legionaries were sucked into the centre of this rapidly developing 'killing field', Hannibal's African cavalry ran past the Roman flank and swung into the rear of the Roman army. 'The result', according to Polybius, 'was exactly what Hannibal had planned':

> The Romans by pressing too far ahead in pursuit of the Celts were trapped between the two divisions of Africans. They could no longer hold their maniple formation, but were compelled to turn singly or rank by rank to defend themselves against the enemy who were attacking their flanks.[175]

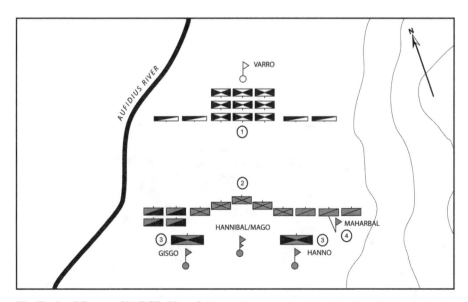

The Battle of Cannae, 216 BCE, Phase I. Due to the narrowness of the plain, Varro is forced to deploy his legionary infantry in a very deep formation (1). The infantry, many of whom are raw recruits, are flanked by poor quality Roman cavalry. Hannibal, assisted by his brother Mago, deploys his Spanish and Celtic infantry in a convex formation in the centre (2). His reliable African infantry, commanded by Hasdrubal Gisgo on the left and Hanno on the right, is in reserve at each infantry flank (3), and his strong cavalry formations form the wings, with his elite Numidian light horse led by Maharbal (4).

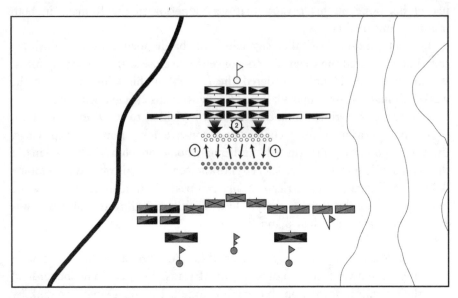

The Battle of Cannae, 216 BCE, Phase II. The action begins with skirmishing by both sides (1). As the light troops trade blows between the two armies, Varro orders his infantry forward (2) towards the Carthaginian line.

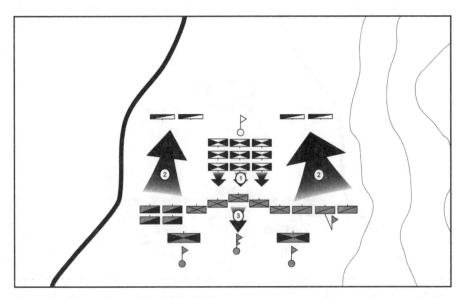

The Battle of Cannae, 216 BCE, Phase III. As the Roman infantry closes with the Punic centre (1), Hannibal orders his cavalry to charge the Roman horse (2). As Varro's legionaries engage the enemy, the Carthaginian centre begins a controlled withdrawal (3).

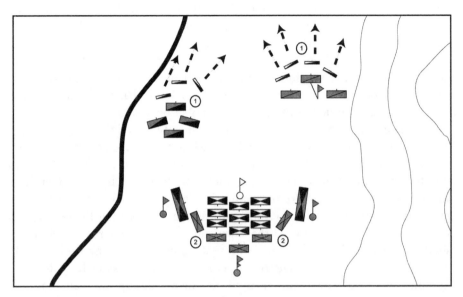

The Battle of Cannae, 216 BCE, Phase IV. The Carthaginian cavalry puts their Roman opponents to flight (1). The Carthaginian centre continues to withdraw, changing the formation from convex in shape to concave (2). The tightly-packed Roman infantry is slowly being drawn into a u-shaped 'killing sack,' from which escape may prove impossible.

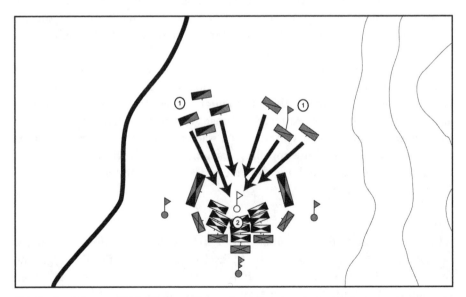

The Battle of Cannae, 216 BCE, Phase V. Breaking off their pursuit of the fleeing Roman horsemen, the Carthaginian cavalry turns its attention to the Roman infantry, charging into the rear of Varro's formation (1). As the Roman legionaries attempt to avoid the Punic horse, they begin to push against their comrades in the front. Men are knocked to the ground and trampled as the press gets tighter and tighter, beset on all sides by enemy troops (2). Varro's army is annihilated with perhaps as many as 60,000 killed and 10,000 captured.

Perhaps 60,000 Roman soldiers, including the consul Paullus, were killed and another 10,000 soldiers were taken prisoner as a result of this classic double envelopment.[176] Both of the consuls' *quaestors* were killed, as were twenty-nine of the forty-eight of Rome's military tribunes. Cannae also robbed Rome of no fewer than eighty senators or men of high office who would have likely become senators.[177] So thorough was the Roman defeat that never again did the Romans risk a large field army against Hannibal on Italian soil.

The defeat at Cannae underlined the vulnerability of the Roman heavy infantry-based tactical system. At Trebia, the legions managed to break through the Carthaginian centre, shattering the cohesion of the enemy army. At Cannae, the Romans massed their centre, determined to break through the Spaniards and Celts forming the centre of Hannibal's line. But this was the tactic of a pike phalanx and a misuse of Roman swordsmen. By massing the centre, the Romans were so tightly packed that they could not manoeuvre or wield their short swords effectively, especially with rank upon rank pushing from behind. The situation was further aggravated as the Romans, pushed from behind, 'tumbled' over their own and enemy dead, further disrupting their ranks.[178] Hannibal's men had no such problem as they gave way into a concave formation, setting up the killing field. Polybius puts Hannibal's losses at Cannae at about 4,000 Celts, 1,500 Spaniards and Africans, and 200 cavalry, while Livy states a total of about 8,000 men were killed.[179] The war treasure recovered from the battlefield of Cannae was also considerable. Besides prisoners and horses seized, arms and armour, horse trappings, and baggage was taken. Ancient sources report that the gold signet rings stripped from the fallen Roman knights alone amounted to three bushels in weight.[180]

The Battle of Cannae stands out as one of the most decisive and most written about engagements in history. Hannibal's execution of a perfect double envelopment has captured the imagination of generals, military theorists and historians ever since. Although Cannae was an important engagement in the annals of military history, it was not a watershed event in the history of the Second Punic War. Despite appalling casualties, Rome's will to fight was not broken and the battle did not provide a significant strategic advantage to Hannibal and his army.

After Cannae

The day after the victory at Cannae both Polybius and Livy inform us that one of Hannibal's favourite lieutenants, Maharbal, encouraged the Punic general to march on Rome, purportedly only five days away. When Maharbal sensed the apprehension in his master's voice, he reportedly replied, 'You know, Hannibal, how to win a fight; you do not know how to use your victory'.[181] Livy maintains that this failure to follow up on the spectacular success at Cannae saved the Eternal City.[182] Hannibal's refusal to besiege the Roman capital has generated a great deal of debate among modern historians. The march to Rome would have taken Hannibal's army twenty days, not five, plenty of time for the Romans to mount a spirited defence. Moreover, Hannibal's army was certainly fatigued from the Battle of Cannae itself, and not in the appropriate shape to not only make the forced march across the Apennines, but also take and hold the city.[183] The reduction of Saguntum in Spain two years earlier had taken Hannibal eight months, and the defences of Rome's capital city were of an entirely different order of magnitude.[184] Besieging a city in hostile territory was an even more difficult option. In ancient warfare, most successful sieges required prolonged periods of time and huge manpower reserves to move timber and earth, set up cordons, build and man siege engines, and maintain pressure against the enemy's fortifications, while simultaneously remaining vigilant against relieving enemy forces. This in turn required a reliable logistical line to friendly territory, something Hannibal did not have in the summer of 216. Moreover, Hannibal's sedentary Carthaginian army would have been at the mercy of Roman armies restricting his supply area and killing or capturing his foragers. Unwilling to die the death of ten thousand cuts, Hannibal not only refused to be bogged down in a dangerous siege, his logistical situation and lack of a sufficient siege train precluded him from even trying.[185]

In two years of campaigning, Hannibal had killed or captured between 80,000 and 100,000 legionaries and their commanders, robbing Rome of a third of its standing military force.[186] Seemingly, the loss of three Roman armies in as many years should have satisfied Hannibal's plans for the defeat of Rome, but once again the Roman Republic survived, refusing to capitulate to the Punic invaders. When Hannibal sent an envoy to Rome, he was rebuffed by the newly elected dictator's *lector*, relaying the message back to his general that Rome would not discuss terms of peace with a foreign enemy on Italian soil.[187] When he gave the Roman Senate the opportunity to exchange prisoners (a first step in peace negotiations), it declined, stating it had no use for the vanquished.[188] Rome was down, but not out. Rome would return to its Fabian strategy after Cannae, denying Hannibal another major victory on Italian soil.

Unable to coax his enemy into another set-piece battle, Hannibal was forced into a defensive posture in Italy and reduced to fighting smaller wars in Spain, Sicily, Sardinia and Illyria to damage Rome.[189] His army would be further reduced garrisoning defected cities. To further complicate Hannibal's strategic position in southern Italy, the bulk of the reinforcements he requested from Carthage were denied him, sent instead to buttress the failing Spanish frontier.[190]

That is not to say that Hannibal did not have some success in weakening the Roman confederation. By 212 most of the region of Campania and forty percent of Rome's other allies had defected to the Punic cause, with other regions like Etruria and Umbria wavering.[191] Even twelve of the thirty core Latin colonies refused to provide their annual levies to Rome in 209.[192] Yet despite these fissures in the Roman confederation, Hannibal was incapable of bringing the Second Punic War to a decisive conclusion, and time was now on the Romans' side.

The destruction of a large percentage of the Roman officer class at Cannae would give younger soldiers the chance to command. One of these men, a twenty-year old military tribune, survived the carnage at Cannae to emerge as one of these new commanders and the eventual hero of Rome. Like his distinguished father who shared his name, young Publius Cornelius Scipio understood the abilities of his Carthaginian enemy, and would spend the next fourteen years building a military reputation and a veteran army capable of finally defeating Hannibal once and for all.

Chapter 3

The Early Campaigns of Scipio

Scipio's Early Life and Building a New Army

The future saviour of Rome, Publius Cornelius Scipio, was born in Rome in 236 BCE. Little is known about his childhood, though we do know he was born into one of the most powerful of Rome's families, the Cornelii, a family which provided the Eternal City with consuls and magistrates for over a century. His family had become especially powerful during the decade leading up to the Second Punic War. In fact, of ten consuls elected in the years 222–219, three came directly from the Scipio family, while another four would have very close ties (most notably the consul killed at Cannae, Lucius Aemilius Paullus). Livy maintains that Scipio the Younger was a pious man, never engaging in any business, public or private, without first visiting the Temple of Jupiter on the Capitoline Hill. There is also some evidence that he was plagued by illnesses as a child, and that these maladies followed him throughout his life.

Scipio the Younger's military career began at seventeen years of age when he joined his father's consular army as it set out to intercept Hannibal in southern Gaul in September 218. Failing to stop Hannibal from crossing the Alps, Scipio the Elder sent his army on to Spain under the command of his older brother Gnaeus Cornelius Scipio. He then returned to Italy with his son, taking command of the Roman army in the Po Valley. It was here, at the small battle on the Ticinus, that young Scipio reportedly saved his father's life.

Emboldened by the Roman success against Carthaginian cavalry in the skirmish on the Rhone River, the elder Scipio offered battle with Hannibal, though he was outnumbered. Young Scipio was kept in the rear on a hill out of harm's way, protected by his own bodyguard. The momentum turned quickly against the Romans as the superior Numidian cavalry routed the Roman horse and light troops. Suddenly surrounded, the elder Scipio was wounded and knocked off his horse. Seeing his father in danger, the younger Scipio spurred his horse toward his father's position. Fearing the death of their charge, the bodyguard followed the teenager into the fray, scaring off the pressing Punic attackers.[193]

After the defeat at Ticinus, the Romans retreated and waited for the arrival of reinforcements from Tiberius Sempronius Longus, marching in from the Adriatic. Sempronius arrived in December and immediately decided to offer battle. He was soundly defeated at the Battle of the Trebia by Hannibal's forces, though a large portion of the Roman army actually succeeded in breaking through the Carthaginian centre and returning to Placentia. Recovered from his wounds, Scipio's father left for Spain to join his brother who had already scored several successes against the Carthaginians in Spain. We know nothing of Scipio the Younger's activities in 217, but in the course of this year, Hannibal destroyed the Roman consular army of Gaius Flaminius at Lake Trasimene, forcing the Roman Senate to proclaim a dictatorship under Quintus Fabius. But, as we have seen, the Romans soon soured on the delaying and harassment strategy advocated by Fabius and Rome prepared to meet and defeat Hannibal in a set-piece engagement.

In preparation for this upcoming battle, Scipio the Younger was elected as a military tribune, no doubt helped by his relationship with his father and the fame he had won at the Ticinus. Most probably he was already engaged to Aemilia by this time, the daughter of the current consul, Lucius Aemilius Paullus, and would serve under his prospective father-in-law at the Battle of Cannae, probably on the right side of the formation.

As the Battle of Cannae wore on and Hannibal's superior cavalry surrounded and annihilated the tens of thousands of Roman soldiers caught in the Carthaginian 'killing field', Paullus chose to stay and die. Scipio, on the other hand, was able to escape the carnage, fleeing with about 10,000 refugees to the large Roman camp. Most of these survivors waited in the camp to surrender, stunned by the magnitude of the defeat. But about 4,000 legionaries, among them Scipio, left the camp after nightfall, evaded Hannibal's cavalry patrols and made their way towards Canusium in Apulia. Along the road and still in great danger, the remnants of the army had an impromptu council and elected the twenty-year old Scipio and Appius Claudius as their new commanders.[194]

Livy tells us that while in council, news was brought to the new commanders of a mutinous plot by the son of an ex-consul, a man named Philus. Roman nobles, led by Lucius Caecilius Metellus, were contemplating fleeing Italy and taking service overseas with foreign kings. Scipio, seeing an opportunity to quell the rebellion before it took shape, moved quickly:

'Come with me', [Scipio] cried, 'instantly, sword in hand, if you wish to save our country. The enemy's camp is nowhere more truly than where such thoughts can arise!' With a few followers he went straight to where Metellus was staying. Assembled in the house were the men of whom Philus had spoken, still discussing their plans. Scipio burst in, and holding his sword over their heads, 'I swear', he cried, 'with all the passion of my heart that I shall never desert our country, or permit any other citizen of Rome to leave her in the lurch. If I willfully break my oath, may Jupiter, Greatest and Best, bring me to a shameful death, with my house, my family, and all I possess! Swear the same oath, Caecilius; and, all the rest of you, swear it too. If anyone refuses, know that against him this sword is drawn.' They could not have been more scared had they been looking into the face of their conqueror Hannibal. Every man took the oath and gave himself into the custody of Scipio.[195]

The rebellion disarmed, Livy tells us that Scipio and Appius moved their army to Venusia, reuniting with Varro and the remainder of the Roman army.

Rome's strategic position continued to deteriorate after the debacle at Cannae. The prosperous city of Capua, located about a hundred miles southeast of Rome, rebelled and joined the Punic cause. Capua was the most important city

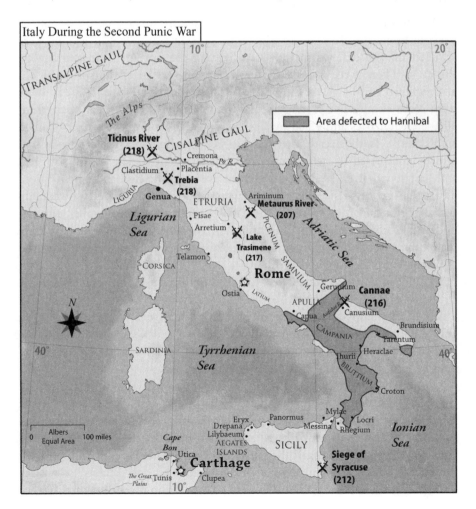

Italy During the Second Punic War

Area defected to Hannibal

to defect to Hannibal. Its population held Roman citizenship and many of its nobles had close relations with senatorial families.[196]

Hannibal then went on to capture the strategically important Roman city of Casilinum in Campania, controlling the land routes from the capital southward along the *via Appia* and *via Latina*.[197] Recapturing Casilinum became a Roman priority, and this city would be retaken by Rome in 215. In Sicily, the Greek city of Syracuse, formally an ally of Rome, joined Hannibal in 214, threatening Roman control over the island Rome had fought so hard to wrest from Carthaginian control in the First Punic War. Most ominously, the king of the Hellenistic kingdom of Macedon, Philip V (238–179 BCE), intrigued with Hannibal in 215 and declared war on Rome, initiating what would be the first of four conflicts between Rome and Macedon known to history as the Macedonian Wars (215–146 BCE). Philip began to mass men and material in Illyria with the intent of invading eastern Italy. Rome now faced a two-front war on their home soil.

Despite these setbacks, Rome did enjoy a significant manpower advantage over its Punic invaders. From 216 onward, record numbers of legions were enrolled for the defence of Italy and fighting the war in Spain and against Philip V. There were at least twelve legions in service in the spring of 215 and eighteen in 214.[198] At the peak of Roman mobilization in 212–211 there were some twenty-five legions in play representing a theoretical strength of 100,000 legionaries and 7,500 cavalry, supported by a similar number of allied auxiliaries.[199] In the decade after Cannae, between four and seven consular-size armies (comprised of two legions) and several single-legion armies patrolled and garrisoned Italy, keeping a watchful eye over the Roman confederation. There is some evidence that the Romans relaxed their property ownership requirements in order to make these goals, increasing the number of able-bodied men eligible to serve.[200] Hannibal, on the other hand, did not have large manpower reserves to draw on; and, like Rome, Carthage was fighting a war on multiple fronts in Italy and Spain.

In 214 Philip moved a small fleet to Illyria to threaten Roman interests there. In response, the Senate dispatched the *proconsul* Marcus Valerius Laevinus with a fleet of fifty ships to Apulia to watch Philip's activities in the Adriatic Sea. When Philip marched on Roman allies, Laevinus quickly crossed over to the eastern shore of the Adriatic near the city of Apollonia, forcing the Macedonian king to burn his own small fleet to prevent its capture.

Undeterred, Philip marched north up the coast of Illyria, capturing several cities and threatening to invade Italy itself. In response, the Roman Senate sought allies in Greece. In 211 the Romans approached the Athenian-led Aetolian League and formed an alliance against the Macedonians. Two years later, in 209, King Attalus of the Anatolian kingdom of Pergamum joined the Aetolians, though nothing came of this arrangement, and Attalus soon withdrew back to Asia Minor. Seeing an isolated foe, Philip invaded central Greece in 208 and after a few years of hard campaigning forced the Aetolians to sue for peace in 205. Still, the Romans got what they needed from the arrangement – Philip was neutralized and Italy was never invaded by Hannibal's Macedonian ally. The First Macedonian War was over.

Rome Resurgent and the Elder Scipios in Spain

The turning point in the Second Punic War came in 212 when Rome began to improve its strategic position and recover some of its losses in Italy. Roman armies had successfully kept Philip V at bay in Illyria, allowing the Roman Senate to concentrate on the Punic invaders in southern Italy. Hannibal had capitalized on his success at Cannae in the years since 216, capturing Thurii, Metapontum, Heracleia, and the very important port city of Tarentum. Only the strategic port city of Rhegium remained loyal to Rome. But in 212 the Romans captured Syracuse, taking a powerful Greek ally away from Hannibal's camp. With Syracuse in Roman hands, the Italians strengthened their control over the Strait of Messina and the sea approaches to Sicily and Italy, reducing Hannibal's ability to get sea-borne reinforcements from Spain and North Africa.

In 211 the Romans retook the mutinied city of Capua after a prolonged siege, beheading its leaders and enslaving its inhabitants as a warning to other potential defectors. Hannibal attempted to raise the siege by first attacking the Romans besieging Capua, and when this failed, marching on Rome itself. Beaten, Hannibal abandoned Capua and returned to friendly territory in southern Italy. But even the Punic general's successes there would be reversed when Rome recaptured Tarentum in 209, further reducing Hannibal's abilities to resupply by sea. The tide was slowly turning against Hannibal in Italy, and his brothers Hasdrubal and Mago were having similar problems in Spain facing two Scipios and their legions.

Gnaeus Cornelius Scipio had been operating in Spain since the war began in 218, having been sent there after the failed interception of Hannibal on the Rhone. Encouraged by Gnaeus' successes, the Roman Senate decided to send reinforcements to Spain under the command of his younger brother, Publius Cornelius Scipio (the Elder). Publius joined his brother in late 217, arriving with twenty or thirty ships and 8,000 men.[201] Together the two Scipios had advanced deep into the heart of Spain, marching their legions over the next few years south of the Ebro and deep into Carthaginian territory. Scipio the Elder was especially adept at persuading Spanish tribes to join (or sometimes rejoin) the Roman cause. In 214 they had even successfully recaptured the city of Saguntum, whose fall to Hannibal in 218 had started the war.

But, three years later in 211, Roman fortunes in Spain changed dramatically.[202] Hannibal's brother Hasdrubal Barca, recently back from North Africa where he had quashed a revolt, was attempting to join with his brother Mago and Hasdrubal Gisgo and confront the growing Roman presence. The Romans had added 20,000 Spanish allies or mercenaries and considered themselves

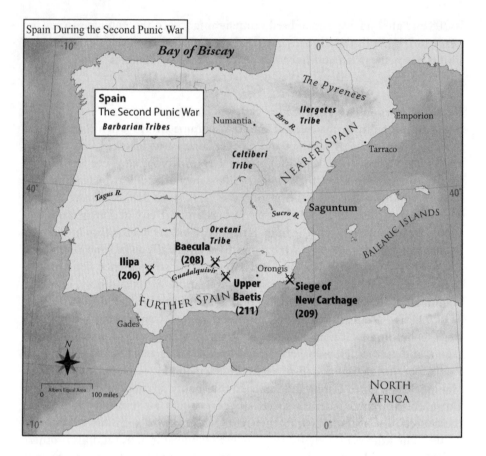

Spain During the Second Punic War

strong enough to confront the two Punic armies before they linked up, with Publius confronting Hasdrubal while his brother Gnaeus marched toward Mago and Gisgo's armies.[203] Hasdrubal Barca soon reasserted his influence over the Celtiberian tribes during secret negotiations and Gnaeus found his line of communication back to Roman Gaul in jeopardy and much of his newfound Spanish support evaporating. Greatly outnumbered, Gnaeus withdrew his troops.

Unknown to Gnaeus, his brother Publius had already suffered disaster. As the Roman troops drew near the camps of Mago and Gisgo near Castulo, their column was harassed mercilessly by Numidian light cavalry, commanded by a young prince named Masinissa, a warrior who would later figure prominently in the Second Punic War. After making and fortifying their camp, the Romans discovered that the Carthaginians were about to receive reinforcements from a powerful Spanish chieftain named Indibilis leading 7,500 of his Ilergetes tribesmen. Boldly, Publius decided to intercept this force before it arrived, leading the night march himself. The engagement, near the city of Castulo, was confusing, with neither side managing to form a proper line. To make matters worse for the Romans, Masinissa and his Numidian horsemen found them and attacked their exposed flank. Soon the main Punic army was surrounding the Roman position. With the Roman situation dire, Publius rode his horse in front of the troops to raise their spirits and organize their defence. Here, Publius was struck by an enemy javelin and killed. News of his death caused the Roman forces to rout, and the retreating legionaries and their allies were cut down by the pursuing Numidian cavalry and Punic light infantry.

Seeing an unprecedented opportunity to crush another Roman army, Mago and Gisgo rushed to join Hasdrubal before news of Publius' death reached his brother. Gnaeus' retreating column was eventually overtaken by the Numidian cavalry in the Punic army's vanguard, and knowing he could no longer march and fight, chose to make a stand around a rocky hill in an engagement known as the Battle of Ilorca. The ground here was too rocky for the legionnaires to dig their usual ditch and rampart, so the Romans made a makeshift barrier with their baggage and packsaddles. With the main Punic army joining the fray, the Romans' impromptu hill fort was eventually overwhelmed and Gnaeus was killed either defending the high ground or in the pursuit afterwards.

In less than a month's time, two of Rome's most celebrated generals and brothers were engaged in separate actions and killed, destroying two Roman armies and reversing seven years of progress in Iberia. Collectively, the two Roman defeats at Castulo and Ilorca are known as the Battle of the Upper Baetis. A few Romans did escape the slaughter, led by the equestrian Lucius Marcius. Marcius rallied the survivors of the two dead Scipios' armies and retreated north of the Ebro, holding some territory there as the last toehold for Rome south of the Pyrenees.

The psychological impact of losing the Roman armies in Spain is difficult to overestimate. For years the only good news the Roman people heard came from the exploits of the Scipio brothers, whose military accomplishments in Spain helped take the sting away from so many debacles in Italy. Moreover, years of Roman successes against Carthaginian forces for mastery of Iberia forced Carthage to send reinforcements to Hasdrubal and Mago instead of to Hannibal, thereby weakening the eldest Barca's position in Italy.

In 210, the Roman Senate sent Gaius Claudius Nero to Spain as a temporary commander. Nero did manage to stabilize the situation at the Ebro, but Rome's strategic situation in Spain was desperate, so desperate that on the day of the election in the capital no senior magistrates stepped forward to offer themselves up for the task of commanding Roman forces against the Carthaginians. Livy tells us the assembled citizens watched the faces of the likely candidates exchange apprehensive glances at one another:

> A murmur arose that things were desperate, that hope of saving the country had been so utterly lost that no one dared accept the Spanish command. Such was the general feeling when suddenly Publius Cornelius

Scipio, son of the Publius Scipio who had been killed in Spain and still a young man of about twenty-four, announced his candidature for the command.[204]

Scipio's election to the command was unanimous. And though Livy explains that many of those present later had second thoughts about entrusting *imperium* to such a young man and about sending another Scipio to Spain to fight where his father and uncle had been slain, Scipio won them over in an assembly.[205] Another Publius Cornelius Scipio would command in Spain.

Scipio the Younger and the Capture of New Carthage
Scipio the Younger arrived in Spain in late 210 at the head of an army of 10,000 infantry, 1,000 cavalry and thirty quinquiremes, securing a winter base at Tarraco (modern Tarragona) along the coast.[206] Throughout the winter he met with envoys from as many Spanish tribes as possible in an attempt to repair the damage caused in recent years. Like Hannibal, Scipio seemed to possess a certain confidence and charm which allowed him to get along with people from other cultures. Although a member of the class, Scipio did not exhibit the arrogance usually associated with Roman aristocrats, and his brilliant states-manship and ability to make personal connections with local chieftains laid the foundations of what would later become one of Rome's most prosperous provinces – Roman Spain.[207]

While in winter quarters, Scipio learned that his enemy had divided his forces into three armies to pacify the peninsula. Hasdrubal Barca camped near Saguntum, his brother Mago fought in the interior, while Hasdrubal Gisgo patrolled the southwest region around Gades at the southern tip of Spain. Noting the dispositions of his enemy, Scipio decided to target the capital of Carthaginian Spain, New Carthage (modern Cartagena), in one bold direct attack. This city was a natural stronghold located on a narrow peninsula pro-tected by an isthmus some 300 yards across. It was located on the direct sea route to Carthage and possessed deep and protected harbours perfect for large naval forces. The 1,000-man garrison also protected the Carthaginian treasury, and with strong Carthaginian armies within ten days' march of the city, the city guard did not fear attack.

Leaving 3,000 men with his official second in command, Marcus Junus Silanus, Scipio crossed the Ebro in the spring of 209 with 25,000 infantry and 2,500 cavalry, shadowed by his Roman fleet of thirty quinquiremes under the command of his senior legate, Gaius Laelius.[208] After arriving at New Carthage, Scipio ordered his ships to blockade the city from the sea while his legionaries constructed a line of contravallation facing outward to protect the besieging Roman army from Punic relief forces. According to Livy, Scipio clearly understood the importance of New Carthage to the Punic war effort on the Iberian Peninsula, and he explained to his men his reasoning for beginning the campaign with a siege:

> If anyone imagines that you have been brought here just to attack one town, he has made a better reckoning of your labour than your profit. It is indeed true that you are about the assault the walls of one town, but in that one town, you will have taken the whole of Spain.[209]

The following morning, Scipio ordered the first probe against one section of the defences. In preparation for this assault, the Carthaginian commander – another man named Mago – had buttressed his defences with an additional 2,000 citizen-soldiers, placing most of them on the landward walls in preparation of the attack.[210] The Romans pushed forward against the walls with scaling ladders, but the height of the wall and the weight of so many Romans on the ladders caused the attack to falter. At this moment Mago ordered the gates opened and the defenders sallied forth to attack the retreating Romans. Seeing this, the Roman general ordered a counterattack with his reserves that very nearly took the gate before the defenders rallied. Polybius explains that Scipio, watching the attacks from beneath the shields of three bodyguards, eventually called the attack off at mid-day.[211]

Now with a better idea of the city's defences, Scipio ordered a second, more comprehensive assault in the late afternoon against the entire length of the landward walls. He then ordered Gaius Laelius to command his marines in

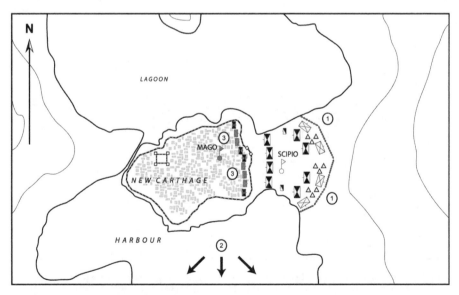

The Siege of New Carthage, 209 BCE, Phase I. Scipio's army, consisting of 25,000 infantry and 2,500 cavalry, arrives outside of New Carthage. While his troops construct lines of contravallation (1) to defend against any possible Punic relief force, his thirty quinqueremes under Gaius Laelius blockade the outer harbour (2). Inside the city, Mago presses 2,000 citizens into service to augment his 1,000-man garrison (3).

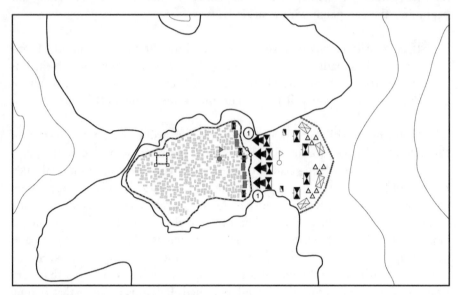

The Siege of New Carthage, 209 BCE, Phase II. Attempting to bring the siege to a quick end, Scipio orders an assault (1), but New Carthage's high wall and the weight of too many attackers on the scaling ladders render this first attempt fruitless.

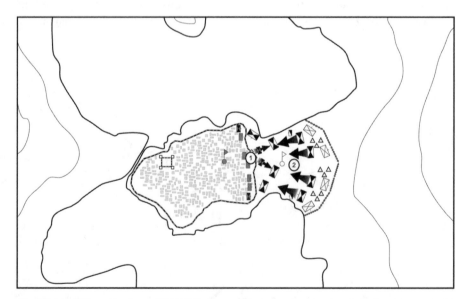

The Siege of New Carthage, 209 BCE, Phase III. Attempting to take advantage of the confusion outside the walls, Mago orders a force to sally from the main gate (1) to attack the Romans. Scipio recognizes the opportunity the open gates represent and quickly orders his reserves to counterattack (2), but the Carthaginians are able to rally and repulse the attack. Scipio calls off the attacks by midday.

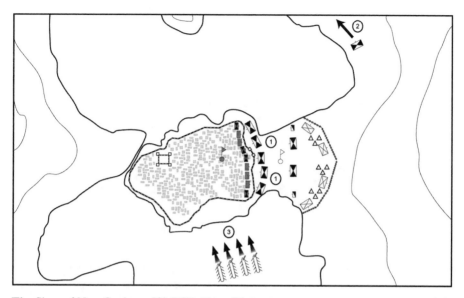

The Siege of New Carthage, 209 BCE, Phase IV. Scipio masses his troops for another assault (1), detaching a force to manoeuvre around the lagoon and approach from what he hopes will be an unwatched sector of the walls (2). To further stretch the defenders, Gaius Laelius is ordered to land a force of marines to assault the walls from the harbour-side (3).

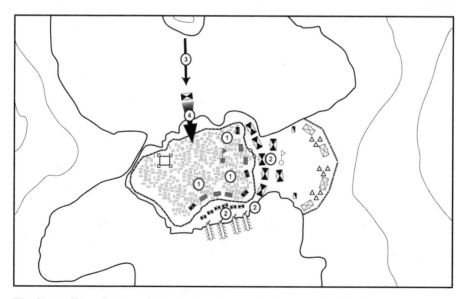

The Siege of New Carthage, 209 BCE, Phase V. The Punic defences thin (1) as Mago attempts to face the renewed assaults against the landward and harbour-side walls (2). Meanwhile, a 500-man Roman force wades through the shallow lagoon towards the city (3). The ebb tide allows the Romans to get close enough to the city's foundations to successfully scale the walls unopposed (4).

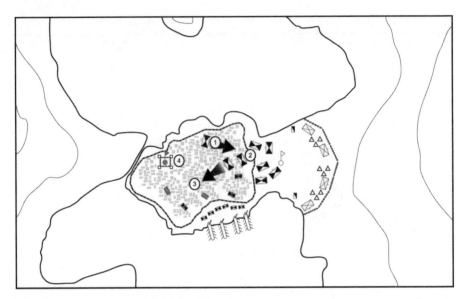

The Siege of New Carthage, 209 BCE, Phase VI. The Romans inside the city quickly clear the walls of defenders (1) and open the gates (2), allowing the rest of Scipio's army inside. The Romans kill every Carthaginian they encounter as they pour into the city (3). Mago and a portion of the garrison retreat to New Carthage's citadel (4), but surrender after a brief fight.

the harbour to assault the city from the sea, ensuring that every man of the garrison was engaged. Finally, Scipio stationed a contingent of 500 men with ladders at the edge of an unmanned side wall protected by a lagoon fed by tidal waters. At the climax of the assault, the tide began to ebb, exposing the foundations of the wall next to the lagoon. Here, the 500 soldiers waded through the shallow waters and set their ladders, scaling the undefended wall. These legionaries quickly cleared the walls and opened the gates, allowing their comrades access to the interior of the city. Polybius tells us that Scipio:

> let loose the majority of [the Romans] against the inhabitants, according to the Roman custom; their orders were to exterminate every form of life they encountered, sparing none, but not to start pillaging until the word was given to do so. This practice is adopted to inspire terror, and so when cities are taken by the Romans you may often see not only the corpses of human beings but dogs cut in half and the dismembered limbs of other animals, and on this occasion the carnage was especially frightful because of the large size of the population.[212]

Scipio himself led 1,000 men against the city's citadel where Mago was holding out with members of his garrison. After first putting up a fight, Mago eventually surrendered and handed over the citadel. Scipio then ordered an end to the slaughter and a beginning to the pillaging. As darkness fell, he ordered his soldiers to bring the city's spoils to the marketplace. There, next to the piles of plunder, the Romans slept their first night in New Carthage. The following morning, all of the wealth of the city was divided equally among the legions.

Polybius tells us that the Romans were very systematic about how plunder was taken and distributed. Sometimes a portion of the soldiers from a maniple or sometimes the maniple itself was picked to collect the spoils. The Romans never used more than half the army to collect the plunder, keeping the rest in their ranks for security reasons. All of those soldiers who were detailed to collect the plunder brought it back to their legions where tribunes evaluated its wealth and distributed it equally among the legionaries. Everyone in the legion was due a cut, including the protecting force, camp guards, those tending the sick, and those away on special duties.[213]

Scipio reached out to those Carthaginian citizens not killed in the storming of New Carthage. He offered to employ two thousand Punic artisans if they agreed to work for the Romans (New Carthage was famous for the quality of its armouries). Polybius says that the Romans adopted the Spanish short sword (*gladius hispaniensis*) and throwing *pilum* at this time, but it is more likely the Romans began using these weapons earlier in the century during their contacts with Spanish mercenaries in the First Punic War.[214] He also hired local sailors to row the captured ships in the harbour and freed the Spanish hostages kept in the prison there by the previous regime. After ordering Gaius Laelius back to Rome by sea with a report and spoils for the Senate, Scipio reconstructed the city's defences and, leaving a substantial garrison, returned north to Tarraco to drill his army and solidify his alliances for the remainder of 209.

The loss of New Carthage was a substantial strategic blow to Carthaginian interests in Spain. Without the support of a large navy, any Punic attempt to retake the city would have been fruitless. Well aware of their situation, the Barca brothers spent the winter of 209–208 shoring up their own Spanish alliances. Hasdrubal Barca also recruited and trained new troops which he intended to march to Italy by land to reinforce his older brother Hannibal, still reeling from the Roman capture of Capua and Tarentum.

The Roman Conquest of Spain (208–207 BCE)
When the campaigning season began in spring 208, Scipio moved quickly south from Tarraco at the head of an army of between 35,000–40,000 men and 10,000–15,000 Spanish auxiliaries to engage Hasdrubal, fearing that any delay would allow the three Punic armies the opportunity to converge. To further his chance of success, Scipio ordered Gaius Laelius' navy beached at Tarraco and he and his sailors added to his army's numbers, outfitted with captured or newly-made weapons and armour courtesy of the armourers at New Carthage.[215]

Scipio surprised Hasdrubal's 25,000–30,000 troops in the vicinity of Baecula, about twenty-five miles north of Jaen. Hasdrubal was also anxious to fight a decisive battle, having lost many key allies to the Romans over the winter. In fact, Polybius tells us that all of the tribes north of the Ebro had defected to Scipio's camp.[216] After learning of Scipio's approach, Hasdrubal ordered his light cavalry to delay the advancing Romans as he took a strong defensive position on a flat-topped hill, protected by a river in the rear and surrounded on the sides and front by steep banks. The front of the hill was also terraced and ringed with a parapet-like rim – an ideal location to make a stand against a numerically superior opponent.[217] Hasdrubal placed his African skirmishers and some Numidian cavalry on the terrace and the remainder of his army on the top of the plateau.[218]

Scipio probably camped somewhere east of Hasdrubal and waited two days before he approached the well-defended hill.[219] As he waited, the Roman general sent detachments to protect his position against the relief armies of Mago Barca and Hasdrubal Gisgo.[220] Scipio began the assault by sending some of his light infantry *velites* and a group of handpicked legionaries to engage the covering force stationed on the lower terrace.[221] The Roman army pressed hard against these forces, causing Hasdrubal to deploy his main army on the edge of the higher plateau to support his beleaguered troops. This may have been what Scipio had planned all along. Committing the rest of his light troops to the frontal attack, Scipio ordered his second in command Gaius Laelius around the left side of the hill with half the Roman heavy infantry legionaries while he went around the right with the other half. With the Roman pincers closing in on his position, Hasdrubal immediately ordered a hasty withdrawal, sacrificing

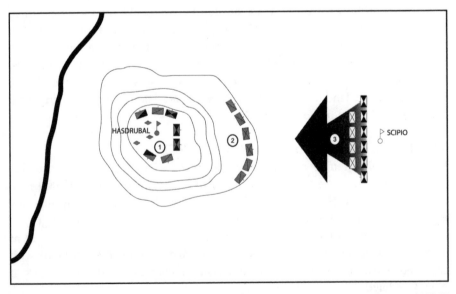

The Battle of Baecula, 208 BCE, Phase I. Hasdrubal arranges his main body on a flat-topped hill (1) with a skirmishing force of light infantry and Numidian cavalry deployed on a terrace below (2). Scipio's army approaches from their camp to the east where they have spent two days preparing for battle (3).

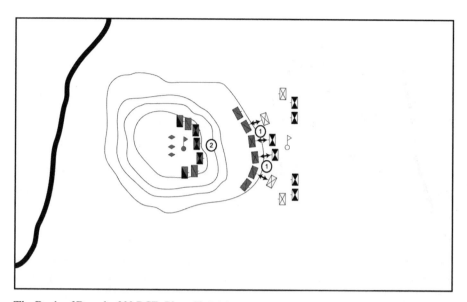

The Battle of Baecula, 208 BCE, Phase II. Scipio opens the action, throwing a force of *velites* reinforced by legionaries against the Punic forces arrayed on the lower terrace (1). Hasdrubal responds to the threat, deploying his main body to the edge of the higher plateau (2).

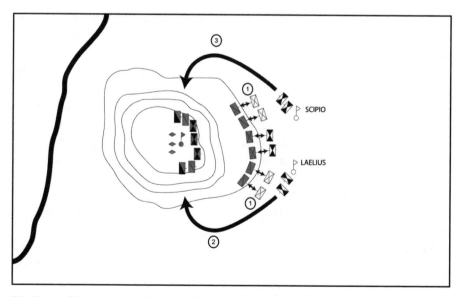

The Battle of Baecula, 208 BCE, Phase III. Scipio commits his remaining *velites* to the attack (1) against the Carthaginian skirmishers and Numidian light horse. He then orders half of his legionaries under Gaius Laelius to swing around the left flank (2) while he does the same on the right (3).

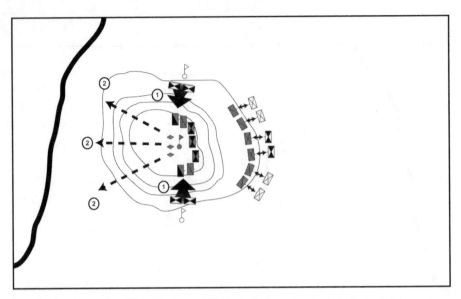

The Battle of Baecula, 208 BCE, Phase IV. Suddenly beset from both flanks by the Roman heavy infantry (1), Hasdrubal orders a quick withdrawal (2), abandoning his light troops. He loses perhaps as much as two-thirds of his army in this defeat.

his light troops to the melee and taking his elephants and treasury with him. Hadsrubal retreated up the Tagus valley, but left perhaps one half to two-thirds of his army to death or capture.[222]

Hasdrubal marched north and met up with his brother Mago and Hasdrubal Gisgo. There, he decided to march on to Italy with his army reinforced with Spanish recruits. He then ordered Mago to hand over his troops to Gisgo and go to the Balearic Islands to hire more troops, while Gisgo returned to friendlier territory around Gades. Interestingly, Hasdrubal Barca also ordered the brilliant young Numidian commander, Masinissa, to take his light cavalry and harass the Romans and their allies wherever he may find them.[223]

Having put things in order, Hasdrubal then slipped through one of the western passes of the Pyrenees into Gaul, evading Scipio's pickets along the eastern routes. Hasdrubal spent the remainder of 208 recruiting troops in Gaul in preparation for the invasion of Italy. Carthage sent a general named Hanno from North Africa to replace Hasdrubal and take command of Punic forces in Spain.

The Battle of Baecula was Scipio the Younger's first field command. His use of light infantry to hold the centre while his heavier troops manoeuvred and attacked the flanks would become a signature tactic, for he would use it again at the battles of Ilipa in 206 and the Great Plains in 203. Though his tactical judgment is lauded, for over two thousand years historians have wondered why Scipio did not pursue Hasdrubal after his victory at Baecula. Perhaps he recognized the danger of chasing Hasdrubal when there were two other Punic armies in the area, or perhaps he recognized the value of consolidating his political gains with other Spanish tribes after yet another battlefield victory over the Carthaginians. Whatever his reasoning, he probably did not have the military capability to stop Hasdrubal from crossing the Pyrenees if the Carthaginian general was bent on doing so, and with Hasdrubal now out of his theatre of operations, Scipio would have one less dangerous commander to deal with in his conquest of Spain.[224]

Scipio returned to his barracks at Tarraco after the battle and spent the remainder of 208 there. Polybius maintains that the year 207 witnessed a lull in operations in the Spanish theatre, though Livy records some very significant events.[225] According to Livy, the new Carthaginian general Hanno joined with Mago to recruit new Celtiberian tribes to the Punic cause, forcing Scipio to send a substantial Roman army of 10,000 infantry and 1,000 cavalry, under the command of Marcus Junius Silanus, to disrupt this activity. Silanus succeeded in destroying the Carthaginian army, even capturing Hanno, though Mago escaped with the cavalry and about 2,000 infantry. Scipio himself left Tarraco and pursued Hasdrubal Gisgo deep into the south of Spain near the city of Gades. Here, Gisgo dispersed his troops in the mountain towns, forcing Scipio to either take each town or withdraw. Scipio decided against such an arduous activity, and returned north, leaving his brother Lucius to secure a token victory by capturing the city of Orongis. Gisgo had successfully bought more time to recruit additional troops. But if the year 207 did not bring a decisive confrontation between Hasdrubal Gisgo and Scipio, it did see the death of Hasdrubal Barca and the destruction of the Carthaginian relief army by Roman forces at the Battle of the Metaurus River.

Hasdrubal Defeated: The Battle of the Metaurus River (207 BCE)

After wintering in Gaul in 208–207 Hasdrubal Barca crossed the Alps in the spring of 207 with an army some 20,000 strong using the same route that his older brother had used eleven years earlier, arriving in the Po Valley in May. Hannibal's strategic position in Italy had deteriorated in the years since his spectacular victory at Cannae in 216. For the most part, the Roman confederation had remained loyal to Rome, and what army Hannibal did possess was often tied up garrisoning those cities in southern Italy which had defected to the Punic cause. The Carthaginian general found himself with an army too small to both prosecute an offensive and guard his newly-acquired territory from Roman counterattack.[226] Hannibal sorely needed reinforcements to change this situation, and his brother Hasdrubal was determined to deliver them.

To stop the merging of the two Carthaginian armies, the Roman Senate ordered the two newly elected consuls to oppose the Barca brothers. Gaius Claudius Nero was sent to watch Hannibal in the south at Canusium in Apulia, while the other, Marcus Livius Salinator, was sent north to deal with Hasdrubal.

Hasdrubal moved to the east coast of Italy and then made his way south towards the Roman province of Umbria. In an attempt to contact his brother, Hasdrubal unwisely sent four Gallic and two Numidian horsemen with a letter stating his intention to link up with his brother in Umbria. After riding nearly the entire length of the peninsula, these couriers were captured by a Roman foraging party near Tarentum, revealing the plan. Nero sent a letter to the Senate in Rome asking for a change in strategy, arguing that this would be an ideal time for the two Roman armies to join forces and crush the new invading army. The Senate agreed, though if Hannibal learned that the Roman presence in southern Italy was weakened, he would be free to terrorize the region.

Leaving a covering force to watch the unsuspecting Hannibal at Canusium, Nero hand selected a lean contingent of 6,000 infantry and 1,000 cavalry and forced-marched this army north a distance of nearly 250 miles. He sent messengers ahead on the line of march to collect provisions from towns and farms in order to have them ready on the road for his troops' use, facilitating this amazing military feat.[227] Nero's strategy to defeat Hasdrubal Barca was very risky, and he expressed these dangers to his men. According to Livy, the Roman consul said:

> No commander has ever adopted a plan apparently more reckless, but actually more sure of success, than this of mine. I am leading you to certain victory. My colleague Livius did not leave for his field of action until forces sufficient to satisfy him had been granted him by the Senate, forces greater and better equipped than he would have needed against Hannibal himself. Our task now is to add a weight to the scale, never mind how small, to tip it in our favour. I shall see to it that the enemy gets no news of our approach; but once he knows, when the time of action has come, that another consul and another army have arrived, that knowledge will make our victory sure. Even a whispered word may settle a war – it doesn't take much to push a man towards hope or fear. It is we who shall reap the harvest of glory if this enterprise succeeds – for everyone forgets the water in the bucket and imagines it is the last drop that makes it overflow. You can see for yourselves how we are being acclaimed from the crowds of admiring faces along the road as we march by.[228]

Seven days later Nero linked up with Marcus Livius Salinator, already encamped near Hasdrubal, and joined his army under cover of darkness. Salinator even went so far as to quarter the newly-arriving troops with his own so as not to enlarge the size of the camp and tip off the Carthaginians, camped only five hundred yards away.[229] The following day a war council, or *consilium*, was held and it was agreed that the Romans would strike immediately. Livy tells us that orders were immediately given and the newly-combined armies formed a line.[230]

Hasdrubal's army was already deployed for battle. But as he reviewed his troops protected by a small cavalry detachment, he noticed some unfamiliar legionary shields among the enemy and some unusually stringy horses among what seemed to be a larger contingent of Roman cavalry. Concerned, he sounded the retreat and sent Punic scouts to reconnoitre the Roman camp. They brought back news that the trumpet had been sounded twice in Salinator's camp, indicating the presence of not one but two consuls. This confused Hasdrubal for he could not understand how another army could have entered the camp without his knowledge, and further inspection did not reveal extended ramparts or a larger Roman camp. This news worried him – either his brother's army had been destroyed or his letter had been intercepted. Either way, Hasdrubal was in a precarious position. He ordered his troops to extinguish their campfires and pack in silence at first watch. Hasdrubal's plan was to escape north under the cover of darkness, but in the confusion his guides lost their way and the retreating column floundered. Hasdrubal ordered the disorganized army to march along the bank of the Metaurus until first light, but the twists and turns of the river further compounded the confusion. Daylight revealed a river too wide to easily ford and the Roman cavalry overtaking their position.[231]

Nero and his cavalry were the first to appear, followed by one of Salinator's supporting commanders, the *praetor* Porcius Licinus and his light troops. Both Roman contingents proceeded to harass the jumbled Punic column, blocking Hasdrubal's attempt to organize his army and seize some high ground. When Salinator arrived with his legionaries already dressed for war, the Roman forces deployed for battle, with Salinator commanding the left, Nero the right and Licinus the centre.[232] Modern estimates put the Roman strength at between 37,000 and 47,000 troops, including Nero's 7,000 Roman reinforcements.[233]

Realizing he must fight, Hasdrubal placed his ten elephants forward to screen his own 20,000–30,000 troops as they formed.[234] He placed his Gauls on the left while he personally commanded the Spaniards on the right, his most trusted and veteran troops. Hasdrubal placed his Ligurian allies in the centre, fierce warriors from northwestern Italy who held no love for the Romans. The Punic array was deeper than it was wide, protected on the right by the river Metaurus and on the left by a deep ravine. Both Livy and Polybius make no mention of cavalry and their whereabouts are unknown.

The Battle of the Metaurus River opened on 22 June 207 with Hasdrubal attacking with the elephants, followed by his right wing and centre. The hardest fighting took place here between Salinator's Roman legionaries and Hasdrubal's Spaniards and Ligurians. At first the war elephants pressed the forward ranks of the Roman *hastati* back, but as the battle grew more ferocious six of the pachyderms began to stampede back through their own ranks, forcing their mahouts to put the wild beasts down by driving a spike into their necks. The other four elephants were later captured, their mahouts abandoning their mounts to the Romans.[235] Meanwhile, Nero found he could not get at the Gauls across the ravine. Undeterred, the consul took 2,000 legionaries and marched them across the Roman rear to fall on the Spanish flank. This motion decided the battle. Many of Hasdrubal's Spaniards and Ligurians were now encircled and slaughtered. Many of the Gauls, never the most reliable allies, deserted their position. Salinator restrained his men from killing the fleeing warriors so that they would return home with news of the Punic defeat. He did not show the same mercy to the drunk Gauls found sleeping in the Punic camp and 'slaughtered them like so many sacrificial victims'.[236]

Livy says 57,000 Carthaginians were killed, including Hasdrubal, making Metaurus the greatest single day of losses for the Carthaginians in the Second Punic War and a suitable revenge for Cannae.[237] Polybius is much more conservative in his casualties, putting Punic losses at 10,000 killed and 2,000 captured.[238] Hasdrubal died in the last moments of the battle, ending any hope of a relief army reaching Hannibal Barca.

Wanting to maintain the initiative, Nero gathered his men and returned south in another forced march to rejoin the remainder of his army at Casunium. He hoped to slip back into his camp without Hannibal ever knowing he was gone or that his brother's army had been located and defeated. He succeeded. Livy relates to us that Hannibal only learned of his brother's death when Hasdrubal's head was catapulted into one of his outposts. Later, two Carthaginian prisoners were released to recount the disaster.[239] When

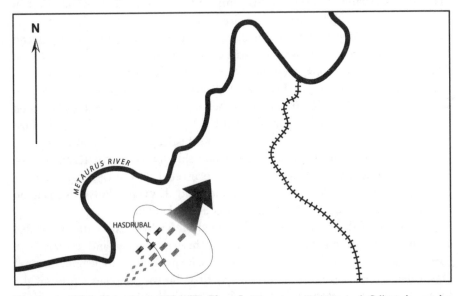

The Battle of Metaurus River, 207 BCE, Phase I. After reconnaissance reveals Salinator's army has been reinforced by a 7,000-man force under Nero, Hasdrubal elects to withdraw north along the Metaurus River under cover of night. The retreat is disorderly as darkness and the winding course of the river work against the Carthaginians. Dawn reveals an unfordable river and a fast-approaching Roman cavalry force on their heels.

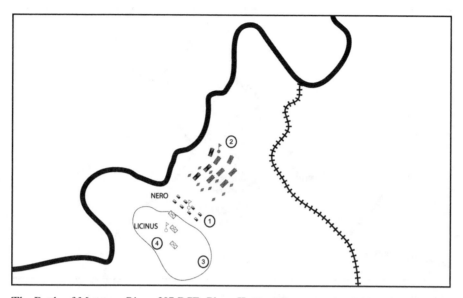

The Battle of Metaurus River, 207 BCE, Phase II. Nero's Roman cavalry (1) keeps pressure on the jumbled Carthaginian columns (2), preventing Hasdrubal from occupying a hilltop from which to make a stand (3). Nero's force is closely followed by light troops under Porcius Licinus (4), creating even more pressure on the Punic army.

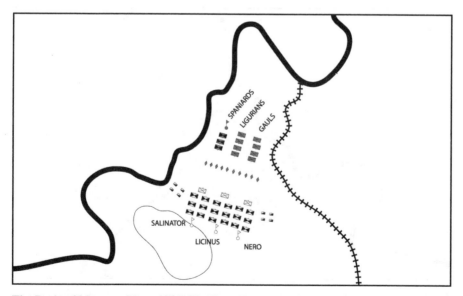

The Battle of Metaurus River, 207 BCE, Phase III. Hasdrubal's army deploys in a deep formation, protected by a deep ditch on their left, and the river on their right. He takes personal command of his most reliable Spanish troops on the right, a Ligurian contingent in the centre, and the unreliable Gaul's on his left, screening his army with ten elephants. Facing them, the Roman left is commanded by Salinator, the centre by Licinus, and the right by Nero.

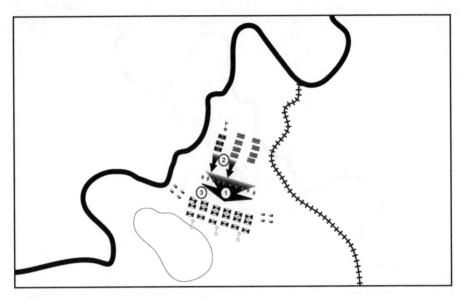

The Battle of Metaurus River, 207 BCE, Phase IV. Hasdrubal opens the battle with an assault by his elephants (1) that press the Roman *hastati* backwards. As the elephants move out, he orders his Spanish and Ligurian troops to advance as well (2). The fighting is ferocious as the Spaniards and Liguarians make contact with Salinator's legionaries on the Roman left (3).

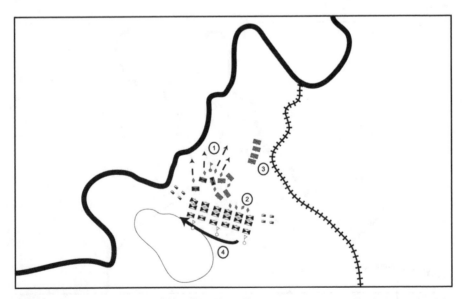

The Battle of Metaurus River, 207 BCE, Phase V. As the action grows more ferocious, six of the elephants stampede back through the Ligurian and Spanish infantry (1). The beasts are killed by their mahouts, but Hasdrubal's attack is dealt a heavy blow. The four surviving pachyderms are captured by the Romans (2). On the Roman right, Nero looks for an opportunity to attack but finds the ditch prevents him from striking the Gauls on their flank (3). He elects to march his legionaries across the Roman rear to the left (4).

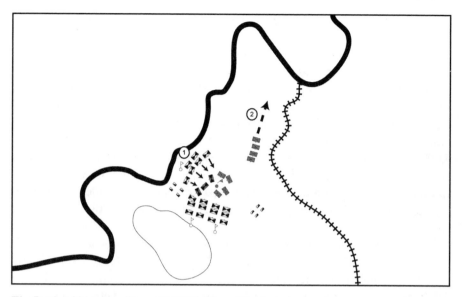

The Battle of Metaurus River, 207 BCE, Phase VI. Nero's turning movement proves decisive as he attacks the Spanish and Liguarian flank (1). Hasdrubal and many of his most reliable troops are slaughtered as they find themselves encircled by the Roman legionaries. The Gauls witness the disaster and desert their positions (2) bringing the action to an end.

news of the victory reached Rome, the Senate declared three days of public thanksgiving honouring the achievement of the consuls Nero and Salinator and gave them a joint triumph at the end of the year.[240]

The entire Roman campaign surrounding the victory at the Metaurus River demonstrated a higher efficiency and greater flexibility of the Roman military machine compared to earlier in the Second Punic War. Nero had responded quickly to news of Hasdrubal's presence in Umbria, marching 250 miles in seven days to buttress Salinator's army and provide the Romans with an element of surprise and added mass to win the day, while his tactical acumen to march from one wing to the other in the battle to outflank his enemy illustrated a degree of tactical flexibility unimaginable in the legions at the start of the war.[241]

Scipio's Masterpiece: Ilipa (206 BCE)

The Romans recorded some significant victories outside of Italy and Spain in 208 and 207. In 208 the Roman Senate sent proconsul Marcus Valerius Laevinus, now in charge of the Roman navy in Sicily, and a flotilla of one hundred quinquiremes to raid the coast of North Africa around the cities of Utica and Carthage. Laevinus encountered a Carthaginian fleet off Clupea, capturing eighteen of its ships.[242] A year later he returned and defeated another Punic fleet, sinking four ships and capturing another seventeen.[243] And although the Roman fleet was reduced in Sicily in 206, it is likely the Carthaginian government saw this naval activity off their coast as a prelude to invasion, giving Hasdrubal Gisgo and Mago Barca more reason to bring Scipio to battle. Except for the destruction of the Carthaginian army commanded by the newcomer Hanno, Roman activities in Spain witnessed a respite in 207, allowing Scipio to consolidate his gains.[244]

In Spain, news of the victory at the Metaurus elevated Roman spirits, while dashing those of the Carthaginians. Gisgo and Mago spent the winter of 207–206 recruiting new troops and strengthening their army for one last offensive. Amassing an enormous host consisting of perhaps 70,000 infantry, 4,000 cavalry and thirty-two elephants at Gades, Gisgo and Mago marched this army east in the spring of 207 to challenge Scipio for mastery of Spain.[245] The Carthaginians stopped near the city of Ilipa near modern Seville, camping on high ground and sending a powerful message to Scipio that they were ready and willing to fight.[246]

Scipio concentrated his forces near Baecula, well aware of his enemy's intentions. His army had been weakened by the need to garrison newly-acquired Spanish territories. He was able to muster 45,000 infantry and some 3,000 cavalry, although just over half of these were a core veteran contingent of two Roman legions and other Italian auxiliaries. The remainder were allied troops, many of which were recently-raised Spanish tribesmen whose allegiance was always suspect. No doubt Scipio realized he was fighting near where his father and uncle were killed only five years earlier and knew the tendencies of his new allies. Despite these reservations and a numerically-inferior army, Scipio marched to confront Gisgo and Mago in a decisive engagement for the future of Spain.

When the Carthaginian army was located, Scipio commanded his army to make camp on a line of low hills facing the enemy. Knowing the predilections of his enemy, Scipio concealed a unit of Roman cavalry behind a nearby hill and waited for a possible Punic cavalry raid on his main column marching to the camp. He was not disappointed. As the Punic horseman, led by Mago and the Numidian prince Masinissa, swept down on the marching Roman legionaries and their allies, the Roman cavalry charged unexpectedly across their flank, destroying the momentum of the attack. With the arrival of Roman reinforcements, the Carthaginian raid was pushed back until the retreat turned into a panicked flight.[247] Elated by their victory, the Romans fortified their camp and rested for the upcoming battle.

Over the next few days, the two armies deployed for battle though neither host advanced far enough to precipitate a fight. Each day Hasdrubal Gisgo probed the Roman lines with his cavalry and light forces, then deployed for battle around midday, playing his best infantry, the Libyans in the centre, the Spanish on their flanks and the cavalry and elephants on the wings. Scipio would then order his own army from their camp to form up for battle, placing the legionaries in the centre, allied Spanish troops on the flanks, and cavalry on the wings. Livy tells us that neither side 'made any forward movement, no missile was thrown, no sound was uttered'.[248] As the daylight faded, Hasdrubal would order his own troops back into the camp first, with Scipio following suit.

Having witnessed this martial dance over a few days, Scipio decided to use his enemy's routine to his advantage. The next night he ordered his infantry to have their meal and be dressed for battle before dawn. As first light broke, Scipio ordered his cavalry and *velites* against the Punic outposts, then marched his main army out of the camp, altering their deployment in order to wrong-foot his opponent. He placed his Spanish troops in the centre and one legion and auxiliaries on each of their flanks, in effect reversing the deployment of the last few days. With his outposts caving in, Gisgo ordered his troops to march out and deploy, but in the confusion he did not realize his enemy had altered his battle order until it was too late. For hours the two lines stared at one another, their light troops making probing attacks. Finally, Scipio recalled his *velites* to the wings and ordered an attack around midday.

Scipio commanded the right and the left was led by his second in command Marcus Junius Silanus and Lucius Marcius, the man who had rallied the Roman forces in Spain when his father and uncle had been killed in 211. We are not sure who commanded the Spanish allies in the centre, though these troops were ordered to advance slowly, creating a concave formation as the line marched forward. Contrary to standard Roman doctrine, Scipio next ordered the legionaries and their auxiliaries on the wings to switch from line of march to column, with both legions marching away from the centre and then turning ninety degrees toward the enemy. Now marching in column, the two legions and their auxiliaries advanced quickly against the less-reliable Spanish infantry on the Punic flanks, wheeling again from column to line as they engaged the enemy. The Roman legionaries and their Italian allies struck hard against these raw recruits who were already worn down due to lack of food and water in the midday heat. Livy recounts

> Tired and discouraged as a result of all this, the Carthaginians began their retreat; but it was still an orderly retreat with the appearance, at any rate, of a planned withdrawal by an unbroken line. But this was not to last, for when the victorious Romans saw their advantage they redoubled their weight of their attacks from every side. The Carthaginians could no longer hold them; Hasdrubal [Gisgo] did all he could to keep them in hand and stop the rot, crying out again and again that if only they withdrew slowly and in order they could find safety amongst the hills in their rear. But panic proved stronger than discipline and, as their comrades in the van began to fall, the whole line suddenly faced about and took to flight.[249]

The Carthaginians fled to the base of the hill beneath their own camp and began to rally, only to be put to rout once more when the Romans arrived again in force. The fighting only ended when a timely deluge of rain allowed the

Punic forces to escape into the night.[250] By morning Gisgo's Spanish allies had evaporated, forcing the remainder of the Punic army to fight from its hilltop camp. Seeing that all was lost, Gisgo managed to make it to the coast and take ship to North Africa, while Mago Barca fled to Gades. Later he would be called home to Carthage. His departure marked the end of several hundred years of Carthaginian rule in Spain.

Scipio's victory at Ilipa was a masterpiece of strategic planning and tactical execution. Scipio successfully manipulated to his own advantage the rituals of a formal battle, with its characteristic days of delay, skirmishes and displays of confidence, and then dictated how and when the battle would be fought. He surprised his opponent and pressed his advantage by wrong-footing his opponent, gaining a substantial tactical advantage.[251] His audacious plan to march perhaps 25,000 Roman legionaries and auxiliaries from line to column, and then again to line, illustrated the superior drill and discipline these Roman soldiers possessed compared to their comrades who fought a decade earlier at Cannae.[252]

After the Punic army disintegrated, Scipio divided his own forces and mounted punitive expeditions against those Spanish chieftains who refused to submit. Complicating his attempt to consolidate his gains, Scipio fell seriously ill and a rumour of his death spread quickly throughout the tribes. Indibilis, a chieftain of the Ilergetes tribe in northeastern Spain, seized this opportunity to

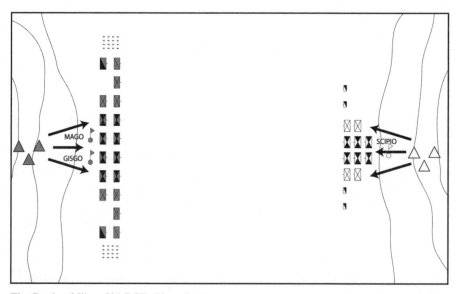

The Battle of Ilipa, 206 BCE, Phase I. The Roman and Carthaginian armies face each other over a period of several days, deploying for battle each day, but never advancing far enough to precipitate an engagement (1). Gisgo positions his high-quality Libyan infantry in the centre, his Spaniards on each flank, and his cavalry and elephants on each wing. Scipio matches his foe's deployment with his legionaries in the centre, Spanish infantry on the flanks, and his cavalry on each wing.

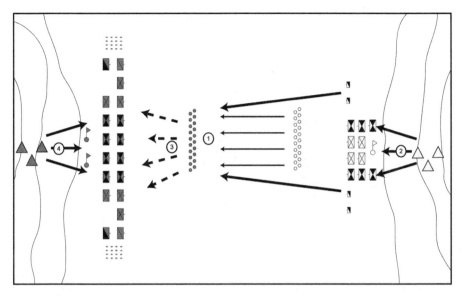

The Battle of Ilipa, 206 BCE, Phase II. Scipio decides to alter the daily routine of deployment, probing, and returning to camp. He readies his army before dawn and orders his cavalry and *velites* to attack Gisgo's outposts (1) while his main force deploys from camp (2). This time, Scipio places his legionaries on the flanks, with his Spanish troops in the centre, hoping to deceive his opponent. As his outposts break under Roman pressure (3), Gisgo orders his army to deploy from their camp (4).

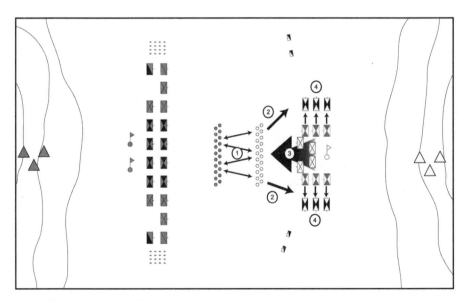

The Battle of Ilipa, 206 BCE, Phase III. Both sides' skirmishers probe back and forth (1), searching for an opening, as the main forces stand fast. Gisgo doesn't recognize the change in the Roman disposition. At midday, Scipio recalls his *velites* (2), orders his Spaniards forward slowly in a concave formation (3), and deploys his legionaries in an unorthodox manner, marching to the flanks in column (4).

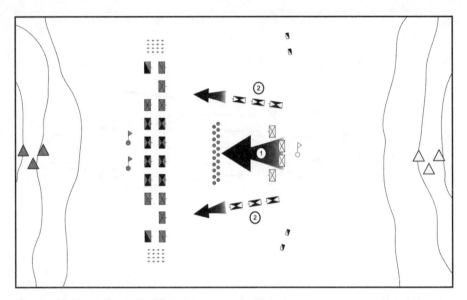

The Battle of Ilipa, 206 BCE, Phase IV. As the Roman's Spanish infantry continues their advance (1), Scipio's legionaries turn towards the Punic line, maintaining their column formations and speeding towards the unreliable Spaniards on Gisgo's flanks (2).

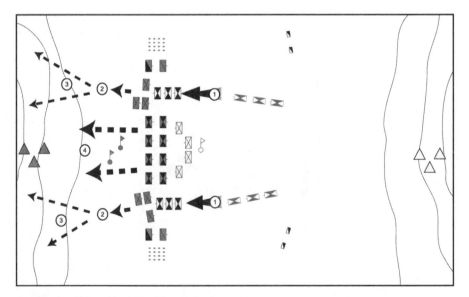

The Battle of Ilipa, 206 BCE, Phase V. As the legionaries close with the Spanish recruits, they change formation from column into line (1). Already suffering from the midday heat, lack of water, and short rations, the raw Carthaginian troops begin to give way (2). Orderly withdrawal gives way to headlong flight (3) as the Roman infantry increases the pressure on the flanks. Many of the Carthaginians retreat to the base of the hill below their camp (4) where they begin to rally.

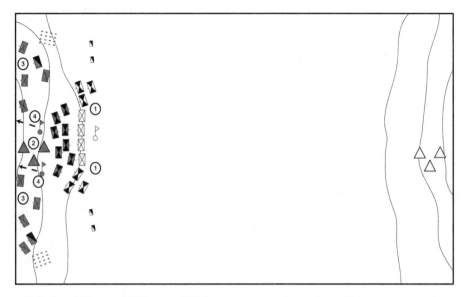

The Battle of Ilipa, 206 BCE, Phase VI. This stand proves short-lived as the Roman army presses its advantage (1). An intense downpour and the onset of darkness allow the remaining Carthaginians to retreat to their camp (2). The unreliable Spanish troops disappear by morning (3) and all is lost. Gisgo and Mago flee the field (4), abandoning the remnants of the Punic force to the Romans.

organize some tribes and rebel against the Romans. Scipio recovered and the rebellion was crushed, but the Roman general also faced a mutiny from 8,000 of his Roman soldiers in the city of Sucro. Many of these legionaries had not been paid in ten years and their demands to be released from service and return home fell on deaf ears. The mutiny was suppressed, ringleaders killed, and wayward soldiers forced to retake their oaths.[253]

Before Scipio left Spain he began to anticipate a campaign to strike Carthage directly, and to further this aim, reopened negotiations with the Numidian king Syphax, even sailing across the Straits of Gibraltar to visit him in his kingdom. This event resulted in a strange incident where Scipio and Hasdrubal Gisgo and their retinues sat down together as guests of Syphax only a few months after Ilipa. And though negotiations with King Syphax ultimately failed, the talented Prince Masinissa did agree to fight for Rome. His defection would be a key reason for Scipio's success in his North African campaign and later victory over Hannibal at the Battle of Zama.[254]

Scipio Returns Home and Builds an Army (205–204 BCE)

Scipio returned to Rome to give his report to the Senate. Although his achievements in Spain were spectacular, he was denied a triumph because he had never held the appropriate rank of magistrate. He did, however, stand for the consulship of 205, even though at around thirty-one years old he was well below the minimum age of forty. Scipio made it clear to the Senate that he wanted to bring the war directly to the heart of Punic territory and invade North Africa, and his enthusiasm and perceived arrogance evoked powerful opposition among some Senators, chief among them the aged Fabius Maximus.

Too old to fight in the field anymore, Fabius argued that Hannibal Barca was still undefeated on Italian soil in Bruttium, despite numerous Roman campaigns to dislodge or defeat him. And even if an invasion of Africa were attempted, fighting a war on the other side of the Mediterranean was a difficult task, something Fabius would have remembered from Regulus' defeat at Tunis fifty years earlier in 255, during the First Punic War.[255] Perhaps Fabius understood that such a defeat on foreign soil could give the Carthaginians hope and change the direction of the war.

To make matters worse for Scipio, rumours began to circulate that the young general would use drastic means to secure his plan to attack Africa, going so far as persuading a tribune to pass a law in the Plebeian Assembly giving him Africa as his province if the Senate denied him. Even though this action was technically legal, Scipio's perceived willingness to use the plebeians against the Senatorial class put off many of Scipio's supporters.[256] When asked point blank by the respected four-time consul Quintus Fulvius Flaccus if he would challenge the Senate, Scipio stated that he would abide by whatever decision the Senate made.[257]

Despite reservations, the Senate granted Scipio a consulship in mid-March of 205, giving him Sicily as his province and endorsing his plan to invade North Africa if he believed it to be in Rome's best interest.[258] The other consul for the year, Publius Licinius Crassus, also held the religious office of *pontifex maximus* or Rome's high priest, an elected position that required him to stay in Italy, freeing Scipio to fulfill his African ambitions without consular meddling.

At the head of thirty newly-commissioned warships, Scipio probably arrived in Sicily in late May or early June and began selecting and training his forces.[259] He had no shortage of troops to choose from. The young consul could draw from a substantial garrison already on Sicily, and other communities throughout Italy sent their young men to join the African expedition. In all 7,000 men came forward, swelling Roman forces.[260] Unfortunately, we do not know how many men Scipio took with him to North Africa. Livy mentions three different totals, ranging from 10,000 infantry and 2,200 cavalry, through 16,000 infantry and 1,600 cavalry, to the maximum troop strength of 70,000 men split evenly between horse and foot.[261] A modern estimate of 25,000–30,000 men (including allies) is most realistic, with perhaps one-in-ten being cavalry.[262]

Whatever the final troop figure, Scipio decided to winter in Sicily and invade North Africa in the late spring of 204, though he did order a squadron of thirty Roman quinqueremes to raid Carthaginian territory. Led by his trusted senior legate Gaius Laelius, the Romans raided the city of Hippo Regius on the coast, an area not yet affected by the war.[263] Laelius spread destruction far and wide, precipitating an invasion scare in Carthage. The Carthaginians immediately levied troops and attempted to secure their alliances with their subject peoples, most importantly the Numidians, who were now embroiled in a civil war.

Masinissa's father, Gala, had died, forcing a succession struggle among the Maesulian branch of the Numidian nation. The young prince defeated his rivals, but his strategic position was further complicated when the Carthaginians managed to convince King Syphax that Masinissa posed a threat to both him and Carthage. Syphax invaded Maesulian territory and routed Masinissa's army, putting the prince on the run and nearly killing him on a few occasions. Masinissa managed to escape to the coast, where he made contact with the Romans. Laelius reassured him that the Roman invasion was imminent, then returned to Sicily and assisted with the invasion preparations.

The core of Scipio's African army consisted of the two Cannae legions which had served as the garrison for the island since the debacle in 216. But even these legionaries were more accustomed to raids and sieges than set-piece battle, with as many as fifty percent of them recent replacements from Scipio's volunteers.[264] From his experiences in Spain, Scipio understood the necessity of having a well-disciplined and well-trained army to meet and defeat the enemy in the open field, and he would spend a year drilling his new recruits and veterans alike to these same standards. Scipio also needed to stockpile supplies in Sicily to maintain his logistical lines while operating in North Africa. In fact, the majority of the food consumed by Roman forces during the two-year African expedition was brought across the sea from Sicily or Italy, illustrating the importance of logistics to the success of the campaign.[265]

Scipio's invasion preparations in Sicily were complicated by a scandal that threatened his command of the expedition. Late in the campaigning season of 205 a group of prisoners from the Punic held city of Locri on the toe of Italy offered to betray the city to Rome. Scipio jumped at the chance to deny Hannibal one of his strongholds in southern Italy, and ordered one of his *legati*, Quintus Pleminius, and 3,000 of his men to march from Rhegium to Locri to retake the city. When the Romans arrived, the Punic garrison withdrew back to Hannibal's position. The scandal erupted when the Romans sacked Locri, plundering the houses and temples and assaulting and raping the citizens. The situation further disintegrated when the Roman garrison split into two rival bands, one under the legate Pleminius and the other commanded by the tribunes Marcus Sergius and Publius Matienus. Squabbling over booty, Pleminius ordered the tribunes arrested and flogged, precipitating a retaliatory attack by the tribunes' men, who wounded Pleminius, leaving him for dead. Scipio, hearing of this disturbance, crossed the Straits of Messina to Italy and arrested the tribunes, leaving the senior officer Pleminius in charge. Incensed at Scipio's lenient treatment of the tribunes, Pleminius executed the two men.[266] When news of this event made its way to Rome, Scipio's enemies attempted to remove him from his command. A fact-finding commission was eventually sent to Sicily to ascertain what Scipio's role was in the Locrian fiasco and to checkup on the invasion preparations. After a few days of witnessing the fruits of months of Roman drill and training, the commission confirmed Scipio's command and returned home.[267] His consulship now expired, Scipio was granted the rank of *proconsul* and prepared for the launch of his invasion fleet.

Chapter 4

The African Landings and the Battle of Zama

The African Landings (204 BCE)

After performing the traditional sacrifice of flinging animal entrails into the sea, Scipio ordered the Roman invasion fleet to set sail from Sicily for North Africa early in the campaigning season of 204, probably in the month of June or July. The Roman flotilla consisted of four hundred transports, escorted by only forty warships.[268] There is some controversy concerning why Scipio's fleet was escorted by only forty warships. Perhaps he was only able to man these few ships with qualified crews, or perhaps Gaius Laelius' raid the year before had exposed a weakness in the Carthaginian defence, convincing the proconsul that a small escort would suffice.[269] Scipio and his brother Lucius commanded the twenty warships on the right, while Laelius and Scipio's quaestor, Marcus Porcius Cato (later Cato 'the Elder'), commanded the twenty warships on the left. The fleet sailed close together through fog and sighted the African coast on the second day, a promontory west of Cape Bon known today as Cape Farina. Scipio ordered his pilots to steer for this landform, disembarking unopposed about twelve miles north of Utica. Fourteen years into the Second Punic War, the long-anticipated Roman invasion of North Africa had now begun.

Livy tells us that Scipio ordered forty-five days worth of rations and fresh water prepared for the troops, with fifteen days pre-cooked and ready for issue (this probably was grain baked into bread or hard tack).[270] Scipio understood the necessity of keeping his soldiers well fed and well watered in the crucial first stages of the operation, when the beachhead needed to be secured and communication lines set up between North Africa and Sicily. Scipio sent his warships to reconnoitre the coast near Utica and moved inland to secure some coastal hills. It was here that the first engagement of the African campaign took place when a Carthaginian officer named Hanno and 500 Punic cavalry crossed the Roman outposts. Sent by Carthage to spy on the Roman expedition, Hanno was killed and his men dispersed.[271] Scipio followed up this encounter by plundering the countryside and capturing a local town, sending both its treasure and 8,000 captives back to Sicily on transports.

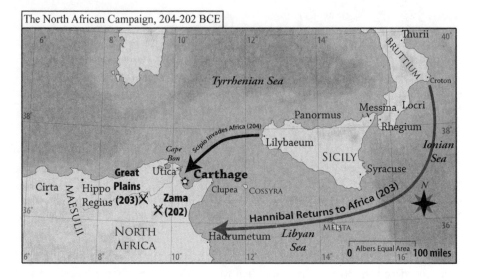

The North African Campaign, 204-202 BCE

The Roman expedition received a boost shortly afterwards with the arrival of Prince Masinissa and 2,000 Numidian cavalry.[272] Masinissa had successfully evaded the armies of Syphax and his presence in the Roman camp meant the invaders now had an ally well versed in the local terrain and the combat capabilities and martial predilections of their North African adversaries. Scipio put these new resources to work when a second Punic cavalry force, again commanded by an officer named Hanno, seized a town called Salaeca only twelve miles away from the Roman camp. Scipio ordered Masinissa and his men to ride up to Salaeca and try to lure the Punic horse out of the city. The provocation worked perfectly. Hanno and his men pursued the Numidians past the high ground where Scipio was waiting in ambush just as he had at Ilipa two years earlier. The Romans fell on the flanks of the Punic horse, while Masinissa wheeled and struck the front of the formation. Livy says that Hanno fell with a thousand of his men, while another thousand were killed or captured in the pursuit.[273] Scipio now secured the area and struck out towards Utica.

Capturing the port city of Utica was high on Scipio's list of priorities, and he brought with him a siege train specifically for this purpose. But after a forty-day siege, Scipio was forced to abandon the action. Hasdrubal Gisgo and Syphax were now massing a substantial army in the area, and the proconsul needed to secure winter quarters. He picked a peninsula just east of the city and prepared camp for the coming winter. The preparations were impressive enough for Julius Caesar to remark on them a century and a half later, calling the site Castra Cornelia, or the 'camp of Cornelius'.[274] Scipio also blockaded Utica by sea to keep its garrison from sallying out and attacking the Roman position.

This was a precarious time for the Roman expedition. Unable to secure Utica, Scipio and his men now faced a long winter cut off from their maritime supply lines and facing a numerically superior enemy on his own soil. Both

Livy and Polybius claim that Hasdrubal and Syphax had armies watching the Roman position from separate camps just eight miles away over the winter, with Gisgo commanding 30,000 infantry and 3,000 cavalry and the Numidian king mustering 50,000 foot and 10,000 horse.[275] Spring brought Scipio good news from Rome. On the Ides of March 203, the two newly elected consuls took office and renewed Scipio's *imperium* for the duration of the African campaign.[276] Spring also brought a renewed effort to take Utica. To this end, Scipio used both negotiations and preparation to meet his objective.

Throughout the winter Scipio attempted to win Syphax over to the Roman cause, but the Numidian king was a hard sell. Hasdrubal Gisgo had married his daughter Sophonisba off to the barbarian king, and her influence went a long way in securing the Numidian alliance for Carthage. For his part, Syphax enjoyed his role as wedge between the Carthaginians and Romans, and attempted to use this leverage to secure a Roman evacuation of Africa and the return of Hannibal from Italy.[277] Scipio maintained that he favoured the Numidian king's plan, but that his own *consilium,* or council of officers, vetoed the idea.[278] Scipio's negotiations seemed to have been a ruse to stall his enemy until he was ready to strike. This dialogue allowed the Roman delegations (and legionary spies dressed as slaves) to map out the defences and interior of the camps, providing Scipio with valuable intelligence.

Believing the time was ripe for an attack, Scipio prepared his war council, summoning the tribunes to him at noon. He informed them that he proposed to use the normal nightly trumpet blasts which signaled the changing of the watch as the signal for the attack. Quietly, the Roman camp prepared for battle. Scipio's plan was simple: he would split his attacking force into two parts, with half the main force commanded by Laelius, supported by Masinissa's Numidian troops. Their objective would be Syphax's camp. Scipio would lead the other half of the force against Gisgo and his Carthaginian troops. When the trumpets sounded, Laelius attacked first, assisted by allied Numidian troops that were strategically stationed at all routes in and out of the enemy Numidian encampment. The Romans set the poorly-constructed Numidian huts on fire, creating a chaotic scene. According to Polybius

> Many were trampled by their own comrades in the exits from the camps, many were surrounded by the flames and burned to death, while all those who escaped from the blaze ran straight into the enemy and were slaughtered before they knew what they were doing or what fate had overtaken them.[279]

Panic spread to the nearby Punic camp, whose soldiers rushed out to help their allies fight the flames. At this moment Scipio sent his own troops to attack the Carthaginian camp, setting the timber barracks alight. Again, Punic soldiers either perished in their burning quarters, or were cut down by the Romans as they fled. The surprise attack worked perfectly, though both Gisgo and Syphax escaped. Scipio kept the initiative by ordering his tribunes to pursue the broken armies and by the end of the next day's pursuit both armies had been dispersed. Although casualty figures given by Livy and Appian are unreliable, Polybius believed that Gisgo retreated from the scene with less than 500 cavalry and 2,000 infantry.[280] Polybius maintains that the surprise attack on the enemy camps ranks as Scipio's greatest military achievement, and there is no doubt that coordinated night attacks, in any age, are difficult strategies to successfully implement.[281] Scipio used diplomacy to soften his enemy, and then boldly struck a numerically-superior enemy, wielding fire and sword.

The local city near the battle surrendered immediately, and though Scipio agreed to spare its citizens from the customary sack, he did allow his soldiers to plunder two nearby towns.[282] With his logistical lines again flowing from Sicily, Scipio beefed up the siege of Utica, going so far as to equip blockade ships with siege weapons to attack the seaward walls.[283] Meanwhile, Roman scouts had located a Carthaginian and Numidian army reforming on the 'Great Plains' (probably the plain of Souk el Kemis, near Bou Salem), some seventy miles southwest of Utica.

During the previous thirty days, Syphax had retreated to the city of Abba where he reformed his army. While licking his wounds at Abba, the Numidian king was met by Punic ambassadors urging him to stay faithful to the Carthaginian cause and rejoin Hasdrubal Gisgo again. Syphax, perhaps encouraged by his wife, stayed the course and joined the Punic commander on the Great Plains. Their combined reconstituted force included Carthaginians, Numidians, and a contingent of 4,000 Celtiberian mercenaries from Spain. In all, Gisgo and Syphax had some 30,000 troops at their disposal, an impressive force gathered in a short amount of time.[284] Seizing the opportunity to destroy this Punic army in a set-piece battle, Scipio left his navy and a covering force on the coast and marched with light kits into the interior of Africa.

The Battle of the Great Plains (203 BCE)

Although none of the ancient sources give a definitive account of the size of Scipio's army, it was most probably around 20,000 men and contained most of the Roman and Numidian allied cavalry.[285] The Roman army reached the Great Plains in five days and seized a nearby hill about three miles away from the enemy host. The following day, they moved off the hill, forming a cavalry screen and marched within 1,200 yards of the enemy before erecting a second camp. Over the next two days, both sides sent their cavalry and light infantry to skirmish, but no major engagement took place. On the fourth day both armies marched out from their camps and deployed for battle.[286]

Scipio drew up his army in traditional Roman fashion in three lines, with the *hastati* in front, the *principes* in the centre, and the veteran *triarii* in the rear. He then formed his Roman and allied Italian cavalry under the command of

Gaius Laelius on the right wing and Masinissa's Numidian cavalry on the left wing. We are unsure how many of the estimated 20,000 Roman and allied troops were cavalry, though the number was probably less than 4,000.[287] Hasdrubal Gisgo and Syphax formed up their 30,000 troops with the Carthaginian foot and horse on the right, Numidian foot and horse on the left and mercenary Celtiberians in the centre.

The Battle of the Great Plains began when Scipio ordered his cavalry under the command of Laelius and Masinissa to charge their counterparts, sweeping the enemy cavalry from the battlefield. The disappearance of their horseman must have had a debilitating effect on the Punic infantry, because a general rout of Carthaginian and Numidian foot soldiers ensued shortly afterwards, leaving the Celtiberians to fend for themselves. These mercenaries fought bravely, but were eventually engaged by the Roman infantry. Polybius remarks that when the cavalry 'wings gave way, the whole of their contingent was quickly encircled by the *principes* and *triarii* and cut down where they stood, except for a few survivors'.[288] Although neither Polybius nor Livy mention it explicitly, it is most likely the *hastati* engaged the Celtiberians first, then were assisted by the *principes* in the second line and the *triarii* in the third line, who deployed from line to column and struck the barbarian force in both flanks.[289] We do not know whether one entire line went to left and the other to the right, or whether both lines split and half the *principes* and *triarii* attacked each flank.[290]

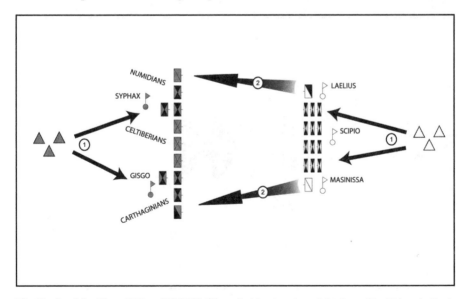

The Battle of the Great Plains, 203 BCE, Phase I. After four days of desultory skirmishing, the Punic and Roman armies deploy from their camps (1). Gisgo commands the Carthaginians on the right of the Punic line, Syphax the Numidians on the left, and a Celtiberian mercenary force holds the centre. Scipio commands the Roman legionaries in a conventional three-rank deployment, while Masinissa commands the allied Numidian light horse on the left and Gaius Laelius the Italo-Roman horse on the right. The action opens as Scipio orders a cavalry charge against the opposing horse (2).

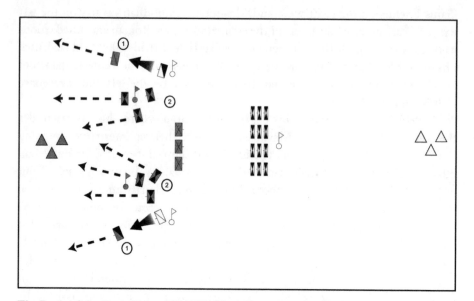

The Battle of the Great Plains, 203 BCE, Phase II. The Punic cavalry is quickly routed by Laelius and Masinissa (1). Watching their mounted companions bolt for the rear proves more than the Numidian and Carthaginian foot can handle and they begin to rout as well (2), leaving the Celtiberian infantry to face the oncoming legionaries alone.

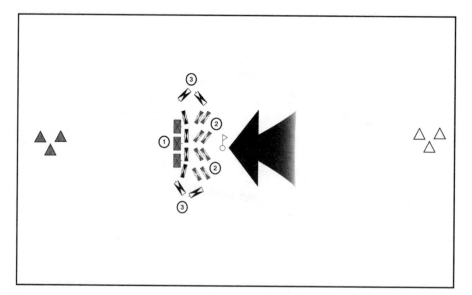

The Battle of the Great Plains, 203 BCE, Phase III. As the Roman infantry closes with the Celtiberians, the mercenaries bravely hold their ground (1), allowing their comrades to make good their escape. The Roman *hastati* very likely pinned the Punic infantry, while the *principes* and *triarii* deployed from line (2) to column (3) to fall on the enemy flanks, though whether it was a single or double envelopment is not known. Regardless, the outcome is the same, as the Celtiberians are quickly destroyed.

We do know that the spirited defence offered up by the Celtiberians assisted the fleeing Punic and Numidian contingents, delaying a Roman pursuit. Syphax withdrew to the safety of his own territory, while Gisgo limped back to Carthage. Scipio called his *consilium* together to discuss the next course of action, deciding to send Laelius and a contingent of Roman infantry and Masinissa and his Numidians to harass Syphax's retreat, while the remainder of the Roman army stayed in the vicinity of the Great Plains to gather supplies, make alliances and plunder. Polybius makes the point that much of Punic-held Africa was ready for a change of government, having suffered hardship and high taxation for a long time due to the war.[291] Many townships offered their allegiance to Rome, while others were assaulted and taken.

Laden with booty, Scipio decided to threaten Carthage itself, marching his army to the ancient city of Tunis, which was easy to invest since its garrison abandoned the city. Located only fifteen miles away from the capital, Scipio was able to see Carthage's walls and its magnificent harbours from his headquarters in Tunis. This action was no doubt designed to intimidate the Punic population and put pressure on the suffetes and Council of Elders to sue for peace. Some of the Carthaginian elite wanted to capitulate, while others wanted to recall Hannibal from Italy to assist with the defence of the homeland. The latter proposal was agreed on and a party of Punic politicians was sent to southern Italy to deliver this order to Hannibal.[292] For the short term, the Carthaginian legislature remained resolute, ordering the city to prepare for a siege and out-fitting and manning a fleet to threaten the Roman supply line from Sicily and Italy. In fact, this maritime strategy was adopted immediately when Carthage ordered its fleet against the Roman siege at Utica.

Scipio witnessed the Punic fleet as it left the harbour at Carthage, recognizing immediately the vulnerability of his own fleet supporting the siege at Utica. Abandoning his new position at Tunis, Scipio marched in haste back to Utica, arriving at Castra Cornelia one day before the Carthaginian fleet. Scipio found his warships carrying siege equipment or supplies and his trans-ports bow-up on the shore and not prepared for naval action. He immediately ordered his ships lashed together, surrounding his line of warships with transports three or four deep. He then stationed 1,000 hand-picked men to act as marines armed with copious amounts of missiles to protect the floating battlefield from attack.[293] When the Punic fleet arrived, they waited a while to see if the Romans would come out and fight. After a while, the Roman strategy became apparent and the Punic ships rowed in to engage the tethered fleet. Livy writes:

> What followed had no resemblance to a sea fight; it looked, if anything, more like ships attacking walls. The Roman transports were higher out of the water than their opponents, and the Carthaginians on their warships, forced as they were to lean back in order to discharge their missiles at the

mark above their heads, failed more often than not to score a hit, whereas the striking power of their enemies' [the Romans'] missiles was, from the fact of their positions, much greater and effective.[294]

The Carthaginians made little headway against the lashed ships, probably because the Roman transports' superstructures were much higher than the Punic warships, providing the Roman defenders with an advantage. Nevertheless, the Carthaginians did manage to cut away some sixty transports and tow them back to Carthage in triumph.[295] There, the population's celebration was cut short with news of the defeat and capture of King Syphax.

After a fifteen-day ride, Gaius Laelius and Masinissa reached Numidia. In an interesting turn of events Masinissa was proclaimed king by his father's tribe, the Maesulii, who then proceeded to eject Syphax's officers and garrisons. Syphax soon surrounded himself with his own loyal subjects, the Masaesulii, returning to his kingdom to raise a new army of raw recruits. Recognizing the importance of striking Syphax before he had time to train his army, Laelius and King Masinissa marched into Masaesulii territory and confronted Syphax. Livy mentions that the Masaesulii's superior numbers in cavalry first had a good showing against the Roman and allied cavalry, but after Roman light infantry entered the fray, the balance began to shift in favour of the Romans. Laelius then ordered his legionaries forward, but the sight of the approaching Roman heavy infantry caused panic within the ranks of the Masaesulii. In a last ditch effort to rally his faltering men, Syphax rode his horse up to the Roman lines, where it was shot out from under him.[296]

Masinissa followed up the victory by taking Syphax back to the captured king's own capital of Cirta, followed by Laelius and the Roman army. At the sight of their king in chains the city elders surrendered the city without bloodshed. When Masinissa reached the royal palace, Livy tells us that he was so mesmerized by the youth and beauty of Syphax's Punic wife, Sophonisba, that he vowed to marry her. Laelius, displeased with the idea of having to give up such a high profile political prisoner, convinced Masinissa to allow Scipio to make the decision. When the Roman expedition returned to Utica just after the successful defence of the tethered fleet, Scipio denied the new king's request, and Masinissa is said to have sent a slave to Sophonisba with poison, which she took.[297] Although Scipio denied the marriage, he did parade Masinissa in front of his Roman troops and address him as King, bestowing both titles and gifts on his young royal ally.[298] Both of these stories have been doubted by some historians, though neither is beyond the realm of possibility.

Armistice and Hannibal Recalled
After defending his fleet at Utica, Scipio returned to Tunis, where he was greeted by a peace delegation from Carthage.[299] The capture of Syphax changed the complexion of the war for many of the Carthaginian elite, who now believed

that, without Numidian support, continuing the war with Rome was futile. Thirty senior legislators met with the Roman proconsul, blaming Hannibal Barca and his supporters for the origins of the war.[300] Scipio listened to the delegation and offered his terms. According to Livy, Carthage was to pay a large indemnity (either 5,000 talents or 5,000 pounds of silver), and:

- Return all prisoners, deserters and runaway slaves
- Withdraw all armies from Italy and Cisalpine Gaul
- Stop interference in Spain
- Evacuate all islands in the western Mediterranean
- Surrender all but twenty warships
- Supply the Roman army with 500,000 measures of wheat to feed troops and 300,000 measures of barley to feed the animals [301]

To Livy's account, the historian Appian of Alexandria added clauses forbidding the Punic state from recruiting mercenaries, a primary source of military man-power, and demanding the recognition of Masinissa as king of all Numidia.[302]

Scipio gave the Punic delegation three days to consider his demands. The Carthaginians eventually agreed to the proconsul's terms, an armistice was concluded and Punic envoys sent to Rome where the treaty was ratified by the Roman Senate.[303] Livy maintains that the Carthaginians were simply biding their time until Hannibal could return and redress the military situation.[304] Since 205, Hannibal had been operating in Bruttium, though not unmolested. In 204 he defeated the consul Publius Sempronius Tuditanus near the city of Croton, though he experienced a setback when Sempronius was joined by the proconsul Publius Licinius Crassus.[305] Hannibal continued to lose ground in southern Italy to the Romans in 203, so when he was summoned to return to Africa, the order may, from a purely military point of view, have been welcome.[306] Hannibal's brother Mago landed in Italy near Genua (modern Genoa) in 205 and began immediately recruiting troops in Etruria. Two years later, in 203, he advanced out of the region, but like his older brother, Mago's activities were challenged by the Romans. The proconsul Marcus Cornelius Cethegus and the *praetor* Publius Quinctilius Varus defeated Mago in territory controlled by the Insubres, wounding the Punic general in the fray.[307] When the Punic soldiers saw their commander carried off the battlefield, discipline disintegrated and retreat turned into rout. Mago was able to return to the west coast of Italy, where he met with Carthaginian envoys summoning him home. Livy believes Mago died of his wounds on the return voyage to Africa, and most of his ships and troops safely returned home.[308]

Hannibal probably left Italy in the autumn of 203, landing at Leptis Minor, between Hadrumentum and Thapsus.[309] He would later make his winter camp outside of Hadrumentum. The sources do not mention how many troops he arrived with, though we do know he abandoned some of his soldiers in Italy, a rabble he described as a 'useless crowd', which he distributed among the garrisons of his allied cities.[310] Appian tells of the slaughter of 4,000 horses and a substantial number of pack animals on his departure, no doubt because of limited space on the return voyage.[311]

The armistice continued throughout the winter months, but events in the early spring of 202 would destroy the peace. Scipio's African army was still dependent on supplies sent from Roman territory, especially Sicily and Sardinia. When a large convoy of some 200 transports escorted by thirty warships was struck by extremely high winds, the oared vessels were able to make landfall, but the sailed merchantmen were blown way off course and scattered along the North African coast. Many of these vessels blew into the wide bay overlooking Carthage itself. Bending to the will of public demonstrations, the Carthaginian legislature dispatched Hasdrubal Barca and fifty warships to round up the now-abandoned merchant ships, whose grain cargos were added to Carthage's own dwindling supply.[312]

Provoked by the action, Scipio dispatched three ambassadors from Castra Cornelia on board a quinquereme to Carthage to demand the return of the vessels and the cargo, complaining to both the Council of Elders and the Popular Assembly that the seizure of the ships had violated the terms of the armistice. But the mood had changed in Carthage with the return of Hannibal Barca and his veteran soldiers. The Carthaginians now believed they had the upper hand and wanted to resume hostilities. The Roman delegation was attacked by the exuberant mobs of Carthage, only saved from death by the city's magistrates. In fact, the Roman quinquereme was given a Punic escort back to the Roman fleet, though even this gesture did not keep the Roman warship safe. Passing Utica, three Carthaginian triremes put out to intercept it. Only by skillful piloting and superior height was the Roman warship able to defend itself from both ramming and boarding, although Livy and Polybius reported many casualties.[313]

The armistice was now over and Scipio resumed hostilities immediately. He revisited cities which he had offered terms to and enslaved their populations in an attempt to provoke Carthage into a set-piece battle. Although the Roman general's *imperium* had been extended by the Senate until he finished the war, he no doubt understood that the strategic position was rapidly changing with the return of Hannibal to African soil. To complicate matters for Scipio, the political situation in Rome was also in flux. One of the consuls for 203, Gnaeus Servilius Caepio, had traveled to Sicily late in the year in the hopes of taking a rival army to Africa. Though the dictator appointed to hold elections for 202 called Servilius Caepio back, both of the consuls elected in March of 202 hoped to be given Africa as their province. Fortunately for Scipio, his popularity in Rome with both the Senate and the Assembly continued, and his *imperium* was extended again. However, the Senate did send a fleet of fifty quinqueremes under the command of one of the newly-elected consuls,

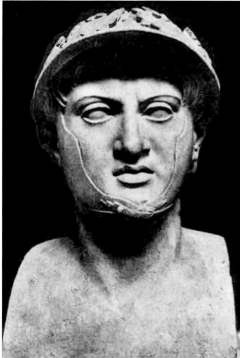

Pyrrhus of Epirus whose intervention failed to halt Roman expansion in Italy and Sicily prior to the First Punic War. *(National Museum of Roman Civilization, Rome)*

A marble bust found at Capua thought to be that of Hannibal Barca, considered a strategic and tactical genius. *(National Museum, Naples.)*

Obverse of a Numidian coin bearing the likeness of King Syphax, who sided with Carthage late in the conflict. *(British Museum)*

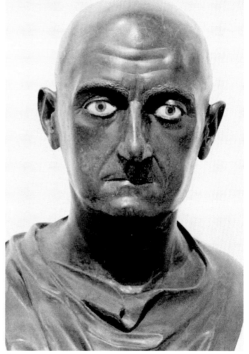

Black marble bust of Scipio Africanus, the victor of Zama. *(National Museum, Naples)*

Hannibal Crossing the Rhône, by Henri Paul Lamotte (1846-1922). When Hannibal marched on Italy in 218 BCE, transporting thirty-seven war elephants across large rivers and high mountains proved to be difficult, but Punic engineers successfully negotiated these barriers.
Inset: Reverse of a Carthaginian silver double shekel depicting a war elephant. Larger Indian elephants were used in Hellenistic warfare, but Carthage preferred the smaller African forest elephants (shown here) because they were easier to acquire and train.

(*British Museum*)

A fourth century BCE example of an Iberian *falcata*. *(National Archaeological Museum of Spain, Madrid)*

Below, a Roman *gladius*. Spanish warriors fought with either a cut-and-slash falcata, or a short double-edged thrusting sword, from which the Roman *gladius hispaniensis* was patterned.

Roman 'Montefortino' type helmet. Celtic in origin, the Romans added cheek guards for greater protection. *(Archaeological Museum of Bologna)*

Sculpture of a Numidian horseman. *(The Louvre, Paris)* The Numidians, a fierce semi-nomadic people from the remoter parts of what is now Tunisia, supplied Carthaginian armies with their finest light cavalry.

Found in a tomb at Ksour-es-Sad in Tunisia, this ornate bronze triple-disc cuirass is of southern Italian origin and may have been taken back to Africa by one of Hannibal's soldiers. *(The Bardo Museum, Tunis)*

Carthaginian armour and shield as depicted on a Roman triumphal frieze in Tunisia. Triumphal arches were built to celebrate Roman victories, depicting the captured arms and armour of vanquished foes.

Obverse of a gold stater with an image of Titus Quinctius Flaminius, who defeated Philip V of Macedon at Cynoscephelae in 197 BC. *(British Museum)*

Coin of Philip V of Macedon. Philip entered into an alliance with Carthage against Rome in 215 BCE, initiating the First Macedonian War. Unable to make headway against Italy, he turned his attention towards Greece. He was finally defeated in the Second Macedonian War in 192 BCE.

King Antiochus III of Syria, attempted to fill the vacuum created by the defeat of Philip V, but his actions drew him into conflict with Rome and he was defeated at Magnesia in 190 BCE. *(British Museum)*

A modern view of the harbour of Carthage. The ancient city of Carthage's most impressive and imposing features were its city walls and its complex of harbour and docks, whose outline can still be seen here. The city was built on a naturally defensible position and then heavily fortified, protected by two restricted land approaches. A twenty-two mile city wall enclosed the great harbour as well as the citadel that was constructed on the Byrsa hill overlooking the harbour.

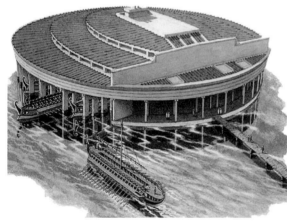

Artist's conception of the ship storage shed and admiral's headquarters that lay in the centre of the military harbour at Carthage, reported to have a capacity for 220 vessels.
(University of Texas at Austin)

The Carthaginian ship found off the coast of Sicily in the area of Lilybaeum.
(The Regional Archaeological Museum Baglio Anselmi, Marsala, Sicily)

Carthaginian ruins at Kerkouane on the Cap Bon peninsula, Tunisia. One of the few sites not razed and built over by the Romans.

Roman ruins at Carthage. Although the complete destruction of Carthage after the Third Punic War is a myth (archaeologists have found several walls dating back to Carthaginian occupation), the largest walls and fortifications were torn down and those cities that sided with Carthage were destroyed. Rome annexed 5,000 square miles of Carthaginian territory to form the new province of 'Africa' and then reinhabited the site where Carthage had stood. Today, most of the ruins found in this area date back to the Roman period.

'The Capture of Carthage' by Giovanni Battista Tiepolo (1696-1770).
(The Metropolitan Museum of Art, New York).

Publius Cornelius Scipio Aemilianus oversees the sack of Carthage. The natural son of Aemilius Paullus and grandson by adoption of Scipio Africanus, he was destined for political pre-eminence in Rome. In 151 BCE, he volunteered to fight in Spain when Roman reverses had severely impacted on recruiting. He distinguished himself there and also in North Africa, where his political skills won him respect with Numidian and Carthaginian commanders. When the Third Punic War was bogged down, he was elected as consul and returned to North Africa to end the siege and oversee the destruction of Carthage in 146 BCE, ending nearly seven hundred years of Punic civilization in Africa.

Tiberius Claudius Nero, to support Scipio's land campaign. Livy makes it clear that Nero held the rank of *imperator* on par with Scipio.[314] When the campaigning season began in 202, Scipio understood that a decisive battlefield victory over Hannibal Barca was required to end the war quickly and cement his political and military reputation.

Parley on the Plain and Locating the Battlefield
Scipio's brutal campaign against the African towns pressed the Punic government to act in their defence. Hannibal was ordered to stop the depredations, but he refused to leave his camp near Hadrumentum before he had raised an army capable of defeating Scipio. Weak in cavalry, Hannibal sought to buttress this arm through an alliance with a relative of Syphax named Tychaeus, a man who reportedly commanded the best cavalry in Africa.[315] Hannibal was successful and 2,000 Numidian light horse joined his army. Satisfied with his forces, Hannibal decided to break the stalemate and marched his army five days west of Carthage to an area Polybius identifies as Zama.[316] Pausing there, he sent scouts and spies out to locate the Romans and evaluate their strength.

After the breakdown of peace negotiations, Scipio left his stronghold at Castra Cornelia and advanced up the Bagradas River past the site of his victory at the Great Plains, partly to provoke Hannibal and partly to secure his lines of communication with King Masinissa and his Numidian troops.[317] Hannibal knew Scipio was in the area, but was not sure whether his Roman enemy had already been joined by Masinissa. It is possible that Hannibal marched west of Carthage to Zama in order to put himself between Scipio and his Numidian ally. Perhaps Hannibal believed Scipio would not engage him without Masinissa's reinforcements, or perhaps he felt he could intercept the Numidian king before he rendezvoused with the Roman general and deal with him separately.[318] Divided, the Roman and Numidian armies might be manageable. Combined, they presented the Carthaginian general with a substantial threat. No doubt Scipio was aware of this as well, and this might explain why he treated three captured Carthaginian spies the way he did.

These three spies were taken prisoner by the Romans about the same time that Masinissa arrived at the camp with Numidian reinforcements. This force consisted of 4,000 light cavalry and 6,000 infantry.[319] Polybius and Livy differ on the timing of these events. Livy maintains that the spies arrived after Masinissa, and reported back their numbers, while Polybius states that the Numidian king arrived the next day unobserved by the spies.[320] Both authors agree that Scipio ordered the spies to be treated well and given guided tours of the camp and to report back to Hannibal what they observed. Polybius' account would make sense if it were Scipio's intention to mislead Hannibal into believing the Roman's were weak in cavalry. This may be why Hannibal continued to march west towards Scipio. Livy's account would ring true if the spies returned to Hannibal's camp with intelligence on Roman troop strengths that worried the Punic general.

Hannibal Barca sent word to Scipio that he wanted a conference with the Roman general. Livy maintains that Hannibal was 'alarmed' by the confidence of his Roman foe and thought 'that he would get better terms from Scipio if he approached him while his army was still intact than after a defeat'.[321] Whether this was Hannibal's idea or that of the Carthaginian government, Livy does not say. Polybius has a slightly different take on the reason for the meeting, proposing that Hannibal was so 'impressed by the courage and lofty spirit which Scipio had shown [the captured spies] ... that he conceived the surprising idea that the two should meet and talk with one another'. Either way, the Roman camp was located and Hannibal ordered his army to take up position on a hill just under four miles away from the Roman camp, virtually ensuring a set-piece battle would take place. The Roman position was defensible and 'within javelin range' of a reliable water supply, while the Punic camp was also defensible, but without easy access to water.[322]

The next day Hannibal and Scipio, accompanied by small detachments of horsemen, rode out to meet one another in full view of both armies. Dismounting, the two men walked towards each other. Livy records:

> Exactly halfway between the opposing ranks of armed men, each attended by an interpreter, the generals met. They were not only the two greatest soldiers of their time, but the equals of any king or commander in the whole history of the world. For a minute mutual admiration struck them dumb, and they looked at each other in silence. ...[323]

The two men then conversed, though what we know about this conversation comes from Polybius' later reconstruction based on testimony of the interpreters. Hannibal spoke first, declaring that 'he only wished that the Romans had never coveted any possessions outside of Italy, and Carthage outside of Africa'.[324] He then asked Scipio if there was any way they could resolve their differences without fighting. Scipio retorted that it was Carthage, not Rome, which had started the war, invading Italy and slaughtering thousands of Romans. Scipio then recounted Rome's grievances, which both Livy and Polybius discuss in some detail. Scipio reportedly ended the conversation with an ultimatum: 'The fact is that you must either put yourself and your country unconditionally into our hands, or else fight and conquer us'.[325] After this exchange, Hannibal and Scipio parted, returning to their camp for the evening, and prepared for the coming battle.

Precisely where the Battle of Zama occurred is still a matter of some debate.[326] History records no less than three different places in ancient Tunisia called Zama, and Polybius' account has Hannibal moving away from there to take up position near Scipio's camp. So although history will forever record the name of this engagement as the Battle of Zama, it is the location of Scipio's camp where the actual battle took place. Polybius identifies Scipio's camp at a place called Margaron, which has never been accurately identified, while Livy calls the site Naraggara, which is known and is usually located at the modern Sidi Youssef. Unfortunately, this area is too hilly and does not fit the physical description of the battlefield. One modern historian posits that the Battle of Zama was fought in the plain of Draa el Metnan, a little south of the road from Sidi Youssef to El Kef.[327] Here, the topography fits the description of the battle site. Unfortunately, we will probably never know for certain the precise location of this epic confrontation.

The Battle of Zama (202 BCE)

At daybreak the following morning the opposing generals drew up their armies in large formations facing each other on the plain. The ancient authorities do not agree on the precise size of the armies involved. Hannibal's troop strengths are taken from a calculation from Polybius who states that the first line of infantry consisted of 12,000 men. Historians assume that each of the three lines held similar numbers for a total of 36,000 infantry.[328] Polybius also states that the Numidian prince Tychaeus brought with him 2,000 horse when he joined Hannibal's army.[329] Appian increases the total Punic forces to 50,000 men.[330] There is even less information from the sources on Roman troop strengths. Both Polybius and Livy give no figures other than remarking on the 6,000 infantry and 4,000 cavalry Masinissa brought with him. Appian gives Scipio an army of 23,000 Roman infantry and 1,500 cavalry, to which we add the above numbers, plus a further 600 Numidian horsemen brought by another chieftain named Dacamas.[331] It is likely that Scipio's army had swelled to 29,000 infantry and over 6,100 cavalry with the addition of the Numidian reinforcements, though it was still smaller than Hannibal's 36,000 infantry, 4,000 horse and eighty war elephants.[332]

We do possess more information on how the two armies were arrayed for battle. Scipio drew up his veteran Roman and allied heavy infantry troops in the typical three-line formation. But instead of staggering the *hastati, principes* and *triarii* maniples in the customary checkerboard formation or *quincunx,* Scipio aligned his three lines directly behind one another to create corridors through his ranks. He then filled the corridors between the *hastati* in the first line with light infantry *velites.* According to Polybius, these corridors were designed as an anti-elephant defence, allowing the attacking pachyderms to be ushered through the ranks of Roman infantry by the *velites,* who, if pressed, could either retire backwards along the corridor or withdraw sideways between the lines of their more-heavily armoured comrades.[333] Scipio then placed his cavalry on the wings of this novel infantry formation, with Masinissa and all of his 4,000 Numidian horse on the right and Laelius and the 1,500 Italian cavalry on the left. We do not know where Dacamas and his contingent were placed, but it is likely they formed up with the Roman horse on the left to balance the wings.[334]

Hannibal also arrayed his army in three lines, and the composition of his forces reflected the multinational character of the Carthaginian army. The first line consisted of a mix of heavy and light infantry 12,000 strong, comprised of Ligurian and Celtic infantry of the line and Balearic slingers and Moorish archers.[335] Many of these men were remnants of Mago Barca's ill-fated expedition that had been called home from northern Italy in 203.[336] Behind this mixed first line stood 12,000 heavy infantry from the Carthaginian levies, taken from the city and the region around the capital. Livy also places a large contingent of 4,000 Macedonian infantry among these troops, sent by Philip V to help his ally Hannibal.[337] Polybius, our most detailed chronicler, makes no mention of these Greek troops, and most modern historians fancy this addition as later Roman propaganda. Hannibal's third line was made up of his veteran troops from his Italian campaigns, drawn up less than two hundred yards behind the second line.[338] Perhaps 12,000 in number, these veteran troops consisted mainly of allied Bruttians from southern Italy, though there were no doubt African, Numidian and Spanish soldiers present who had marched with him from Spain seventeen years earlier in this formation, as well as Celts recruited in northern Italy in the first years of his campaigning on the peninsula. Hannibal's placement of his veterans in the back suggests he regarded his front two lines as expendable, fodder for Roman swordplay before his best infantry were committed. Hannibal positioned his best Numidian cavalry on his left to face Masinissa, and his Carthaginian cavalry on the right to face Laelius. Finally, in the tradition of Hellenistic warfare, Hannibal placed eighty war elephants in front of the entire formation to screen his forming troops and act as a ward against enemy cavalry attacks.

Interestingly, both deployments were very similar and illustrated just how much the Roman and Carthaginian art of war had learned from one another during the long war.[339] In his numerous battles against the Romans, Hannibal had been well served by a strong cavalry arm. Punic cavalry, with a strong Numidian contingent, had enveloped the enemy at both Trebia in 217 and Cannae in 216. But Hannibal did not enjoy an advantage in cavalry at Zama, so his strategy reflected the realities of his force structure, raising the role of infantry in the coming battle plan. Hannibal would attempt a direct assault into the Roman infantry, sending first his elephants, and then his less reliable allied infantry, holding his veteran troops in reserve until precisely the right moment. Perhaps Hannibal was taking a page from the history books, for this battle plan served the Greek mercenary Xanthippus well against Regulus at the battle of Tunis in 255, a battle fought not too far from where these two great hosts were deployed.[340] Scipio's battle plan, on the other hand, relied on his superiority in cavalry, an arm not usually associated with the Roman art of war. But Scipio's army was forged in Spain and honed on the battlefields of North Africa 'and represented one of the best trained forces ever produced by the Roman military system'.[341]

With their armies arrayed for battle, both generals addressed their troops. According to Polybius, Scipio rode up and down their front ranks and reminded his men to:

> Remember the battles you have fought in the past and bear yourselves like brave men who are worthy of your reputation and of your country. Keep this fact before your eyes: that if you overcome the enemy not only will you be the complete masters of Africa, but you will win for yourselves and for Rome the unchallenged leadership and sovereignty of the rest of the world. If the battle should turn out otherwise, those of you who fall will meet a death that is made forever glorious by this sacrifice for your country, but those who save yourself by flight will be left with a life that brings them nothing but misery and disgrace. . . . So when you go to meet the enemy, there are only two objects to keep before you, to conquer or to die[342]

For his part, Hannibal also reminded his troops of the glories of the past. Again according to Polybius, he ordered his mercenary officers to address their men in their own languages, telling them to convey to the men what would happen to their wives and children should the Romans be victorious. He then addressed his Punic officers directly, calling on them to remember their seventeen years campaigning together, stating:

> In all those actions you proved yourself invincible and you never gave the Romans the smallest hope they could defeat you. Let us forget for a moment the scores of minor engagements; I ask you to remember above all the Battle of the Trebia which you fought against the father of this Scipio who commands the Romans today, the Battle of Lake Trasimene, when your opponent was Flaminius, and of Cannae when we defeated Paullus. The struggle which awaits us today bears no comparison with any of those battles, whether you consider the numbers of our adversaries or their courage.[343]

Hannibal went on to emphasize the inferiority of the Roman troops, both in numbers and experience, ending his speech with a reminder that many of the men facing them in Scipio's army were the sons of legionaries they had murdered in past battles or remnants of legions which they had time and again defeated on Italian soil.[344]

The Battle of Zama opened in standard fashion with skirmishing between the opposing Numidian covering forces. It was Hannibal who made the first decisive move, sending his eighty war elephants forward in a massive charge, probably followed closely by his first and second lines.[345] The Punic commander had never had so many pachyderms at his disposal, and the charge of so many of these beasts was something Scipio's men had never faced before.[346] No doubt he hoped the elephants would disrupt the Roman first line, providing an advantage to his own infantry advancing on the pachyderms' heels. But the use of elephants in war was often a double-edged tactic, for as the elephants closed with the enemy, the blast of Roman trumpets and horns terrified some of the animals, who wheeled back and stampeded through the Numidian cavalry on the Carthaginian left. Masinissa, seeing this opening, counter-charged, driving these Numidian horsemen from the field and exposing the Carthaginian left flank. Still, some of the war elephants in the centre did reach the Roman ranks, causing great losses to the Roman *velites* before they were either murdered on the spot or ushered down the corridors Scipio had put in place. Still other pachyderms broke to the right and were driven from the field by showers of javelins. Like Masinissa, Laelius took advantage of the confusion caused by the wounded elephants and charged his opposing Punic cavalry, sweeping them from the field and exposing the Punic right flank. In Livy's words, 'the Carthaginian army had now been stripped of cavalry support on both sides when the infantry closed, and was no longer equal to the Roman forces either in hope or in strength'.[347] With the Roman cavalry in pursuit of the Punic horse and the war elephants no longer a threat, the Battle of Zama quickly became an infantry engagement.

We know that Hannibal sent his first two lines forward but held his veteran third line in reserve. Again according to Livy, the Romans shouted their war cries in unison and clashed their spears against their shields, while the Punic forces shouted a babble of different languages.[348] As the two infantries closed, the inherent advantages of the Roman maniple over the hodgepodge of Punic fighting styles became gradually apparent. Whereas the Roman *hastati* and *principes* were all armed with *pila* and short swords and fought in an identical fashion, the Punic forces they faced in these first two lines fought according to their national preference. Some of these troops used missile weapons, others used swords or short thrusting spears, while still others fought in Hellenistic-style phalanxes. These Punic troops, with their thrusting swords, slashing *falcatas* and forward-facing pikes and thrusting spears, at first worked murderously well in forward engagements against the Roman legionaries. Polybius remarks, 'In this contest the courage and skill of the mercenaries at first gave them the advantage and they succeeded in wounding a great number of the Romans'.[349] But as the Roman and Carthaginian soldiers pressed closer, a type of hand-to-hand combat that favoured the Roman legionary and his short sword in close-quarter battle ensued. Again, Polybius praised 'the steadiness of their ranks and the superiority of their weapons' which 'enabled Scipio's men to make their adversaries give ground'.[350] Polybius also makes note of the support the Roman rear lines gave their comrades-in-arms already engaged with the enemy.

Eventually, the first-line mercenaries gave way and actually started to attack the Carthaginians in the second line, compounding the confusion of their retreat. Although Polybius suggests that it was Hannibal's strategy all along to place his least reliable troops (mostly Gauls and Ligurians and the remnants of Mago's troops) in the first line, and that the retreat of the first line 'actually forced the Carthaginians to die bravely in spite of themselves, for when they found they were being slaughtered by the mercenaries, they were obliged to fight both the barbarians and the Romans at the same time'.[351] Polybius' low opinion of the Punic forces might cloud his appraisal, for it is certainly possible that the mercenaries were not allowed to retreat through the Carthaginian second line, forcing an armed response.[352] Pressed between a Punic phalanx and the advancing Roman first line of *hastati*, the mercenaries were cut down.

The Carthaginian second-line's counter-attack did throw some of the *hastati* maniples backward in confusion, but the Roman officers commanding the *principes* held their ranks firm, and the attack was blunted either by the *principes* or the recovering *hastati*. Soon, the Carthaginian soldiers of the second line broke and ran, but Hannibal refused to let these men retreat through the ranks of his veteran third line, forcing these men to take refuge on the wings or in the open country.[353] Polybius describes the battlefield that lay between Scipio and Hannibal at this moment:

> The space between the two corps which still remained on the field was by now covered with blood, corpses and wounded men, and the physical obstacle created by the enemy's rout presented a difficult problem for the Roman general. Everything combined to make it hard for him to advance without losing formation: the ground slippery with gore, the corpses lying in blood-drenched heaps, and the spaces between encumbered with [weapons] that had been thrown away at random.[354]

Taking this moment to tend to his wounded and redress his lines, Scipio ordered the wounded to be carried to the rear and recalled the *hastati* that were pursuing the enemy with bugle blasts. He then commanded the *principes* and *triarii* to deploy on the wings of the reformed *hastati* until one long line was created. Some of these older legionaries had actually fought at Cannae and were no doubt eager for their revenge. Confident in this new formation, Scipio ordered his legionaries forward toward Hannibal's remaining veterans.[355]

When the Roman and Carthaginian infantry clashed, Polybius points out that the antagonists 'were equally matched not only in numbers but also in courage, in warlike spirit and in weapons', and that the battle 'hung for a long while in the balance'.[356] The tipping point came with the return of Masinissa

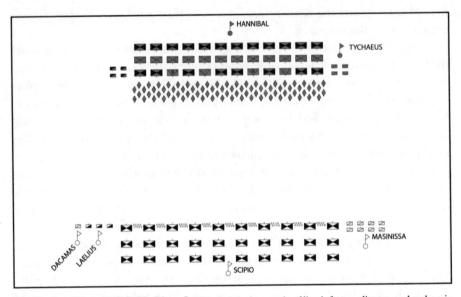

The Battle of Zama, 202 BCE, Phase I. Hannibal deploys a mix of line infantry, slingers, and archers in his first line, his Carthaginian levies in the second, and his veteran infantry in the rear. Tychaeus leads the Numidian cavalry on the left flank. The Carthaginian cavalry is placed on the right and the army is screened by 80 elephants. Scipio deploys in an unusual manner, aligning rather than staggering his three ranks of legionaries, thus creating lanes in his formation. These lanes are rendered invisible to Hannibal by deploying *velites* in the intervals. Masinissa commands the Numidian horse on the right, Laelius and Dacamas a mixed cavalry force on the left.

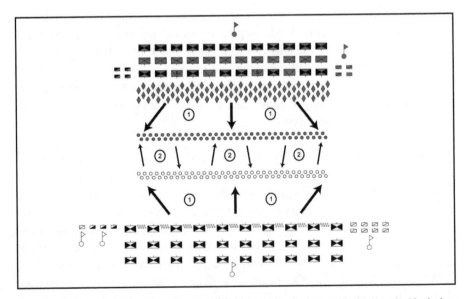

The Battle of Zama, 202 BCE, Phase II. The action opens in typical fashion as each side deploys skirmishers (1) and engages their opposite number on the plain between the two armies (2). Neither side gains an advantage.

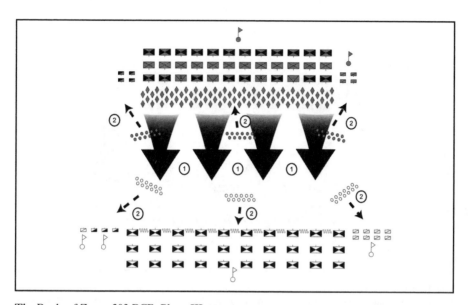

The Battle of Zama, 202 BCE, Phase III. Hannibal orders his elephants to charge (1), hoping that the large number of massive beasts will be able to strike a decisive blow against the Roman infantry. The skirmishers of both sides disperse (2) as the pachyderms surge forward, goaded on by their *mahouts*.

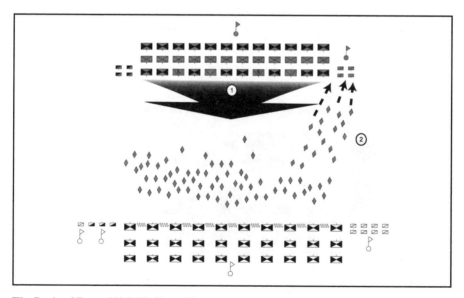

The Battle of Zama, 202 BCE, Phase IV. Hannibal orders his army forward in the wake of the elephant charge (1). As the animals draw closer, trumpets and horns blast out from the Roman ranks, causing some of the beasts to turn and stampede back through the Numidian cavalry on the Punic left (2).

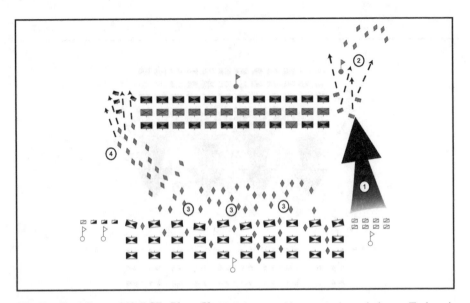

The Battle of Zama, 202 BCE, Phase V. Masinissa sees his opportunity and charges Tychaeus's disrupted formations (1), sweeping them from the field (2). Meanwhile, many of the elephants in the centre close with the Roman line (3), some being killed, others driven back, while still others are funnelled into the lanes through the Roman formations where they are more easily dealt with. Roman losses are heavy but the ranks hold fast. Some of the wounded elephants stampede towards the Carthaginian horse on Hannibal's right, disrupting those formations (4).

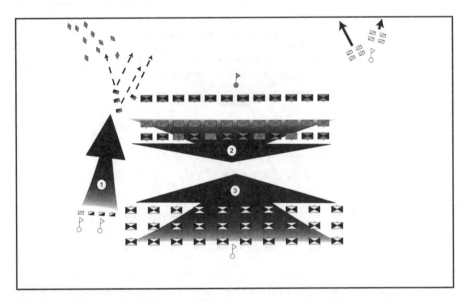

The Battle of Zama, 202 BCE, Phase VI. Laelius and Dacamas charge (1), putting the Carthaginian cavalry to rout. The fight is now between the infantry of each side and Hannibal orders his first two ranks forward (2) against the Romans, who dress ranks and advance to meet their foes (3).

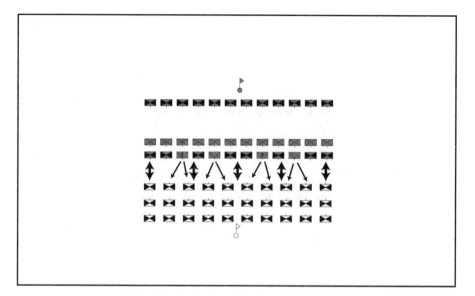

The Battle of Zama, 202 BCE, Phase VII. As the opposing foot soldiers close with each other (1) the Punic forces initially exercise an advantage, as they employ a variety of weapons types and fighting techniques the Roman short swords and *pila* cannot counter.

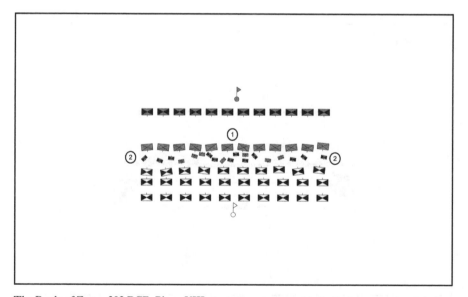

The Battle of Zama, 202 BCE, Phase VIII. As the Romans close with the Punic mercenaries, their short swords and discipline quickly gain the upper hand. Many of the mercenaries in the front rank attempt to flee, but their path is blocked by the levies in the second rank (1). Fighting ensues as the panicking troops try and cut their way through their erstwhile comrades. Trapped between the legionaries and the Punic second rank, the mercenaries are destroyed (2).

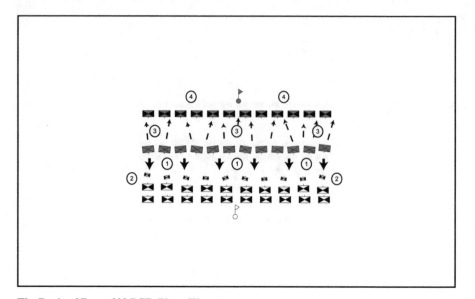

The Battle of Zama, 202 BCE, Phase IX. The Punic second line counterattacks (1), pressing the *hastati* back in some confusion (2). The Roman *principes* stand firm, however, and the *hastati* rally, driving the Carthaginian levies back until they break (3). Hannibal's line of veterans (4) rebuffs their attempt to force through the line, and those survivors that can flee towards the open plains on the flanks.

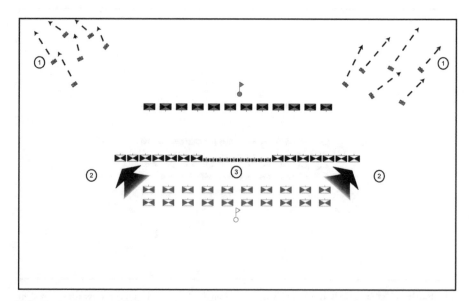

The Battle of Zama, 202 BCE, Phase X. The routing of the Carthaginian second line (1) still leaves the third line to deal with. Scipio redresses his formations, ordering his *principes* and *triarii* (2) to deploy to the flanks of the surviving *hastati* (3), forming one continuous line facing Hannibal's veteran infantry across the corpse-strewn plain.

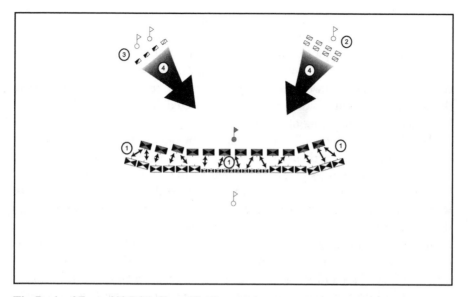

The Battle of Zama, 202 BCE, Phase XI. The action hangs in the balance as both sides trade blows in fierce hand-to-hand fighting (1). The sudden reappearance of Masinissa's Numidian horse (2) and Laelius and Dacamas with their cavalry (3) tips the scales in Scipio's favour. The horsemen swiftly deploy and charge into the rear of the struggling Carthaginian formations, killing most of Hannibal's veterans where they stand. The survivors are quickly ridden down, though Hannibal manages to flee the field.

and Laelius to the battlefield, whose cavalry fell on the rear of Hannibal's third line, killing most of the Punic soldiers where they stood. Those few who escaped this slaughter were easily run down in the open country by the Numidian and Roman horse. Scipio pursued the enemy as far as their camp, which he sacked, before returning to his own. Hannibal managed to escape with a few of his horsemen, riding hard until he reached the safety of his base at Hadrumetum.

Polybius states Roman casualties at 1,500 killed, while the Carthaginians lost more than 20,000, with nearly as many taken prisoner.[357] Appian reports Roman casualties at 2,500 and Punic killed at 25,000, though he estimates the amount of prisoners taken at only 8,500.[358] Livy adds that the Romans captured 132 Punic military standards and eleven war elephants.[359] Whatever the final numbers, it is somewhat ironic that Hannibal's army was finally destroyed by being held in place by infantry and attacked and struck down by cavalry, the same tactic the Carthaginian general used to spectacular effect against the pride of Rome at Cannae fourteen years before.

Scipio Africanus: 'Greater than Hannibal'?
Scipio's victory at the Battle of Zama was decisive and it broke the Carthaginian government's will to continue the Second Punic War. But the outcome of the battle was not inevitable, even taking into consideration the Roman general's

clear advantage in cavalry. In fact, in many ways this engagement was a near-run thing. Hannibal's basic strategy was brilliant in its simplicity – strike the Roman centre and hope to win the day. He understood well his quantitative advantage in numbers did not necessarily translate to a qualitative advantage in combat power. He was weak in cavalry, a tactical system he used to great effect throughout his military career, and he respected his enemy's advantage in horsemen on the morning of Zama.

Hannibal also understood that although he possessed more infantry than his Roman counterpart, perhaps two-thirds of his footmen (the first two lines) were not as well-trained or as disciplined as the veterans in Scipio's ranks. Hannibal's only real chance of victory was to break the Roman centre with wave after wave of attack, beginning with a war elephant charge to break up the Roman first line, followed by three waves of infantry to punch through the Roman ranks. In reality, this strategy worked exceptionally well, for the commentators make note of how exhausted the *hastati* were after fighting the first line of mercenaries and the second line Carthaginian levies, whose advances also pushed into the second line Roman *principes*. It is here that we see the fruits of the Roman military system's superior training and tactical articulation, for after the rout of the Punic second line, Scipio was able to redress his lines, pulling back his battle-tested *hastati* and pushing forward his *principes* and *triarii* to form a single line, before advancing against Hannibal's veteran third line. Still, according to Polybius, Hannibal's strategy nearly worked, for the battle 'hung in the balance' until the return of the Numidian and Roman cavalry.[360]

History will never know for certain if the Carthaginian phalanx would have prevailed had Masinissa and Laelius not returned when they did, but we can surmise that if the Roman lines had broken, it probably would have meant an end to Rome's African expedition and a very different conclusion to the war. Scipio needed a decisive victory at Zama to secure his precarious political position in Rome and his proconsulship in Africa, whereas Hannibal needed to break the enemy and escape with enough of his army to fight again if necessary. Scipio and his veterans did not give Hannibal that opportunity.

So, how do Hannibal and Scipio compare as tacticians and strategists? Polybius concludes that Hannibal did all that a good general could do, but that he was simply bested by a better man.[361] There is something to this appraisal. Hannibal was a master tactician, who understood both the combat capabilities and motivations of his multinational troops. Like Alexander before him, who he no doubt imitated, Hannibal used cavalry as his decisive arm, the hammer to his infantry's anvil. Infantry, in Hannibal's art of war, was used defensively and in support of his more mobile and more highly-skilled cavalry arm. This can be seen in his defeat of the Romans at Trebia in 218 and Cannae in 216. Hannibal understood the limitations of his forces and created a winning strategy to fit these limitations. Weak in cavalry at Zama, the Punic general was forced to reconsider his usual tactics, opting to use his war elephants and infantry as his offensive striking force. And even with inferior foot soldiers, Hannibal nearly carried the day. Additionally, the heterogeneous character of his fighting force always hampered Hannibal. His army was made up of people from many nations, a fact which presented numerous problems in battlefield command, control and communication.

Scipio also possessed superior skills as a tactician, and unlike his adversary who was always cobbling forces together in a hostile environment, the Roman general always had as the core of his fighting force the well-trained and disciplined legionary, a soldier produced from the seemingly inexhaustible manpower resources of the Roman confederation. Unlike Hannibal, Scipio used his infantry often as an offensive striking force, as his victories at Baecula in 208, Ilipa in 206 and Great Plains in 203 illustrate. True to the Roman art of war, infantry held a central place in Scipio's tactics, and the centrepiece of the Roman heavy infantry organization was the maniple.

But Scipio had the luxury of adding an impressive cavalry force to his army with the recruitment of Masinissa to his cause, creating a very impressive combined-arms army featuring cavalry, unusual in the annals of Roman warfare. With a large Numidian contingent attached to his army, Scipio could afford to alter his own tactics at Zama. There, he used his numerically superior cavalry to best the enemy, and then used his better-trained and equipped infantry in a defensive capacity, standing firm against the repeated Punic onslaughts until the Roman horse returned.

When we compare the two men as strategists, both Hannibal and Scipio rate as bold and prudent, though it should be noted that the Punic commander faced a very different strategic reality than his Roman adversary. Hannibal inherited his father Hamilcar Barca's plan to bring the war to Italy and assembled a massive army of 90,000 men to carry out the plan. After reducing the Roman allied city of Saguntum in the summer of 218, Hannibal's task was to evade an enemy army sent to intercept him in southern Gaul, cross the Alps in bad weather, and then, with his army depleted, quickly defeat two Roman armies at Ticinus and Trebia in late 218 to bolster his men's morale and help recruit a new army from foreigners in a hostile environment. With his numbers replenished with Celtic allies, Hannibal pushed south into Italy, evading one Roman army and ambushing and annihilating another at Lake Trasimene in 217. Maintaining the initiative, he skirted the Eternal City, realizing its walls were too strong and fearing a prolonged siege would trap his army in place. Here, Hannibal showed great restraint and situational awareness, crossing the Apennines again into the fertile plains of Campania, looting and burning the countryside before returning to Apulia to winter.

With three victories over the Romans in just two years, Hannibal recognized that the Romans were preparing for a massive set-piece battle, so in the spring of 216 he moved to the old Roman citadel at Cannae and handpicked the next killing field, seized the high ground and waited. Outnumbered nearly two-to-one, Hannibal met the largest Roman army ever assembled, over 80,000 men, and annihilated three-quarters of the enemy host in a brilliant double-envelopment. Historically, Cannae became the military debacle against which all other Roman losses would be judged. After Cannae, the Romans would not risk another large set-piece battle against the eldest Barca son, preferring instead to pursue a 'Fabian' strategy of delaying and harassment.

For the next thirteen years Hannibal fought the Romans in southern Italy while simultaneously cultivating alliances with the Greeks and other captive peoples of the region. Hannibal's formidable diplomatic skills kept him in good standing with some of the indigenous peoples, but the Roman confederation did not unravel as his father Hamilcar had predicted, and despite overwhelming battlefield victories in the first three years of the war, the Punic general was never able to sow the seeds of rebellion necessary for the destruction of Rome as a regional power. Nor was Hannibal able to muster a large enough fighting force after Cannae to compel his enemy to fight on his terms. Attempts to reinforce his army by his younger brothers were crushed, first when Hasdrubal Barca was killed at Metaurus River in 207 and again when Mago Barca was held in place in northern Italy from 205 until his recall to Africa in 203. In the end, Hannibal's strategic miscalculation doomed the Punic expedition, while Rome's 'Fabian' strategy kept him effectively confined to southern Italy and away from the new theatre of operations, Iberia.

After Cannae, the Roman Senate understood the necessity of a mirror strategy in defeating the Carthaginians, though the question remained where to push back against Punic aggression. Despite Polybius' claim that the original strategy was to invade North Africa as early as 218, the Senate adopted a more prudent strategy of taking the war to the Iberian Peninsula and sent the elder Scipio brothers and then the younger Scipio to Spain to attack the house that Hamilcar Barca built.[362] Like his father and uncle before him, Scipio made his military reputation in Spain, honing his skills as a strategist there when he took over the command of Roman forces after the loss of both elder Scipios and their armies in 211.

When the younger Scipio arrived in Spain in late 210 he inherited a theatre of operations in complete disarray. The destruction of two armies set the Romans back on their heels and Roman influence waned quickly in Iberia. With his army of 11,000 Scipio secured a winter quarters at Tarraco and immediately began to court the assistance of local Spanish tribes and reconnoitre his enemy's location. When he learned that the Carthaginians had split their forces into three armies to pacify the peninsula in 209, the young Roman general decided to strike the political, military and psychological heart of Punic Spain – the city of New Carthage. Undaunted by the city's strong defensive position, Scipio took New Carthage by storm quickly, which was essential with three enemy armies in the region. This bold plan paid huge dividends, for, once New

Carthage was in Roman hands, the Punic forces lost their major port in Spain and would never regain their strategic balance.

In the spring of 208 Scipio struck out with a substantial Roman army aided by Spanish mercenaries with the goal of destroying the Punic forces on the field of battle. But with Hasdrubal Barca, Hasdrubal Gisgo and Mago Barca and their three armies in the vicinity, this was a dangerous strategy. If engaged individually, Scipio had the advantage over the three Punic armies, but if the enemy converged on him, the Roman army would be in a dangerous position. Scipio surprised Hasdrubal Barca's troops in the vicinity of Baecula, killing or capturing perhaps as many as two-thirds of the Punic army. After Baecula, Scipio resisted the temptation to pursue his enemy into the coastal southern mountains in what would have certainly been a guerrilla war against the Romans, instead deciding to regroup and wait for a better opportunity to bring his enemy to battle. Two years later in 206, Scipio would have this opportunity, following up on his win at Baecula with a stunning victory over Gisgo and Mago at Ilipa, scattering the remaining Punic forces to the wind. Scipio was now master of Spain, and used the political capital these successful campaigns won him to secure a consulship in Rome and a new army for the invasion of North Africa.

Even as Scipio was preparing to leave Spain for Italy, he was in negotiations with the royalty of Numidia to join Rome in their fight against Carthage. These negotiations divided this key Punic ally and brought to the Roman cause Prince Masinissa, whose cavalry would prove the decisive arm at Zama. Scipio's ability to secure this key alliance, ironically, did to the Carthaginians in North Africa what Hannibal had tried for fifteen years to do to the Romans in Italy – deprive his enemy of key manpower resources. In fact, when we compare both Hannibal and Scipio as strategists we should keep in mind the vast discrepancy between available manpower for their campaigns. Here Scipio clearly had the advantage, for not only was Rome able to raise large, consular-size armies and several single-legion armies to patrol and garrison northern and central Italy and keep an eye on Hannibal in the south, but the Senate could also muster enough troops to fight against Carthaginian interests in Spain. Hannibal, on the other hand, did not have large manpower reserves to draw on; in fact, the Punic campaigns in Spain often took precedence over his in Italy, forcing Hannibal increasingly to do more with less as the war wore on. All of this makes Hannibal's achievements even more remarkable.

But how would Hannibal rate himself as a general? Livy tells us that these two generals met a second time at Ephesus in 193 BCE. Scipio was sent to the Levant by the Roman Senate to ascertain the motives of the Syrian king Antiochus III, a Hellenistic monarch from the Seleucid dynasty who was expanding his influence in the eastern Mediterranean. Hannibal was in exile there, serving as the Syrian king's military advisor. When Scipio arrived, he asked to see his Punic rival, and it seems these men met and talked on a few occasions. During one of these encounters, Scipio asked

> ... who, in Hannibal's opinion, was the greatest general of all time. Hannibal replied, 'Alexander ... because with a small force he routed armies of countless numbers, and because he traversed the remotest lands....' Asked whom he placed second, Hannibal said: 'Pyrrhus. He was the first to teach the art of laying out a camp. Besides that, no one has ever shown nicer judgment in choosing his ground, or in disposing his forces. He also had the art of winning men to his side. ...' When Scipio followed up by asking whom he ranked third, Hannibal unhesitatingly chose himself. Scipio burst out laughing at this, and said: 'What would you be saying if you had defeated me?'
>
> 'In that case,' replied Hannibal, 'I should certainly put myself before Alexander and before Pyrrhus – in fact before all other generals!' This reply, with its elaborate Punic subtlety ... affected Scipio deeply, because Hannibal had set him apart from the general run of commanders, as one whose worth was beyond calculation.'[363]

The story may well be apocryphal, but both Livy and Plutarch report it, so it might have happened.

The End of the Second Punic War

The defeat of Hannibal's army left Carthage with no choice but to sue for peace. Livy states that Hannibal was summoned from his main base at Hadrumentum to the Punic capital. It was the first time Hannibal had set foot in his native city in some thirty-six years. Hannibal personally addressed the Carthaginian assembly and admitted that the defeat of his army at Zama was also the defeat of Carthage in the war. The last surviving son of Hamilcar Barca and long-time champion of Carthage advocated making peace with the Romans.[364]

After the Battle of Zama, Scipio rounded up his Punic prisoners and sacked their camp, securing great amounts of treasure. When he returned to the coast he received good news that a Roman convoy commanded by one of the consuls for 201, Publius Cornelius Lentulus, had arrived at Utica with fifty warships and one hundred transports with much-needed supplies. Deciding the moment was right to follow up on his battlefield victory, Scipio sent Laelius again to Rome to deliver news of the victory over Hannibal, then ordered his legions to march to Carthage by land, while he set sail from Utica towards the harbour at Carthage, augmented by the newly-arrived warships.[365]

Not far from the harbour, Scipio was met by a single Punic ship wreathed in olive branches and carrying ten of the leading men of Carthage. According to Livy, as they drew along side the stern of the Roman flagship, this delegation 'held out the symbols of supplication, begging and praying for mercy and protection'.[366] Scipio ignored these prostrations, save for asking the delegation to meet him later at Tunis, where he would be setting up his new headquarters. Scipio then sailed on to Carthage with his massive fleet in a demonstration of Roman power. In actuality, the Romans posed no immediate military threat to the citizens of Carthage, safe behind their massive walls. Satisfied, Scipio ordered his fleet back to Utica and prepared his army for its march to Tunis.

While marching from Utica to Tunis, Scipio learned of a new military threat in the form of a Numidian army racing to the aid of Carthage. Raised by Syphax's son, Vermina, this North African column was quickly located, surrounded and attacked by Roman cavalry supported by some infantry in mid-December 202. Although Vermina escaped, he lost 15,000 of his fellow tribesmen, with another 1,200 captured by the Romans.[367] This was the final engagement of the Second Punic War.

When Scipio reached Tunis he found a Punic delegation of thirty men waiting for him there, probably made up of the city's Council of Elders. Livy maintains that Scipio's *consilium* was at first eager to destroy Carthage, but that further deliberation brought them around to the idea of negotiation. Despite his earlier posturing, Scipio recognized the need to come to terms with the Carthaginians quickly. The Roman general and his war council knew a prolonged siege of Carthage was out of the question and there was mounting pressure from Rome for a change of command in Africa, an act that would have taken the glory from Scipio and his men.[368]

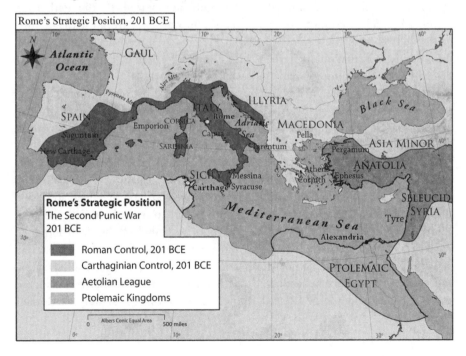

Rome's Strategic Position, 201 BCE

The terms Scipio set to end the Second Punic War were very harsh, no doubt set as a reminder to the Carthaginians of the truce which they broke when the convoy was attacked off the coast of Carthage in early spring 202. According to the treaty Carthage would:

- Lose all territory outside of Africa and recognize Masinissa as the king of a greatly expanded Numidia.
- Reduce her fleet to only ten triremes.
- Have all her war elephants confiscated.
- Pay an annual indemnity of 10,000 silver talents for fifty years.
- Refrain from making war outside of Africa unless Roman permission was obtained.
- Return all Roman prisoners and deserters without ransom.
- Supply Rome with three month's worth of food and supplies and pay the occupying Roman army's wages until the treaty was ratified by the Roman Senate.
- Pay reparations for the loss of the convoy and its supplies.[369]

Finally, Scipio demanded hostages from the leading Carthaginian families to ensure their cooperation.

Not all of the Carthaginian statesmen were willing to bow to the Roman demands. Livy recounts that a Carthaginian politician came forward to oppose the peace and, while giving his speech, was pulled down from the platform by Hannibal himself. Hannibal immediately apologized to the gathering, blaming his lack of etiquette on his thirty-six year absence from Carthage, then proceeded to urge the capital's leading citizens to accept Scipio's terms. In the end the Carthaginians agreed with the Punic general and dispatched a delegation to Rome to confirm the terms of the treaty.[370]

After heated debate in the Roman government, the Senate finally agreed to accept the peace terms Scipio had proposed. Consistent with Roman custom, the Senate ordered the fetial priests to go to Carthage and sanctify the peace treaty. The Carthaginian envoys were released and in early spring 201 returned from Rome and met with Scipio in North Africa. True to their word, they surrendered their warships, deserters, runaway slaves and 4,000 Roman prisoners of war. Scipio then had nearly the entire Carthaginian fleet, some 500 ships in all according to Livy's sources, towed out to sea, where they were set ablaze in full view of the city of Carthage as a symbol of the destruction of the Carthaginian thalassocracy.[371] Scipio then brought forward the deserters (precisely how many we do not know) and had the Roman legionaries crucified and the Latin soldiers beheaded.[372] With Carthage now officially considered another subject people of Eternal Rome, Scipio returned to Italy as Rome's greatest hero.[373]

Chapter 5

In Zama's Wake – The Growth of Roman Imperialism and the Third Punic War

Hannibal After Zama (201–183 BCE)

It is curious that Hannibal Barca's surrender to Rome was not one of Scipio's conditions. Perhaps Scipio held his rival in too high esteem to bring him back to Italy in chains, or perhaps the Roman general understood that Carthage needed a charismatic and able statesman to implement the conditions of the treaty. Whatever the case, Hannibal was appointed one of the two suffetes of Carthage in 201 and spent the next seven years attempting to reconstruct the Carthaginian economy and pay the high reparations demanded by Rome. Despite nearly two decades of war and the loss of Spain and its navy, Carthage continued to prosper, mostly due to very close commercial contacts with the Levant and its colonies on the southern littoral of the Mediterranean, areas where Rome had yet to interfere.

As one of the chief magistrates of Carthage, Hannibal found himself butting up against traditional enemies of the Barca clan, those who believed that trade, not war, was the main occupation of the Punic state. This political faction had plagued his father Hamilcar Barca and other influential military families throughout the third century BCE who were hawkish in their pursuit of Carthaginian foreign policy. Hannibal understood that Rome's influence in the western and central Mediterranean had now grown to the point that it would no longer tolerate a balance of power with Carthage. Hannibal watched as this peace faction laid the blame for the loss of the Second Punic War entirely at his feet, and retaliated by denouncing a number of prominent Carthaginian officials whose peculations he had uncovered.

To make matters worse for Hannibal, he continued to have powerful enemies in Rome. There were many senators who felt Scipio's peace terms were too lenient and this, combined with Hannibal's ability to raise the large annual war indemnity, enraged those Romans who wanted to use this failure as an excuse to invade North Africa. Although Scipio intervened on behalf of his former enemy, admonishing his fellow Romans for their interference in Carthaginian affairs, it did not take long for the Punic peace faction and these bellicose Romans to form an alliance with the primary goal of ousting Hannibal from power. Ultimately, this strange alliance proved too strong, and when combined with the charge in 195 that he was conspiring with another enemy of Rome, the Seleucid king Antiochus III ('the Great') of Syria, Hannibal calculated that his days were numbered and prepared his escape from Carthage.

In 195 BCE the Romans sent a commission to Carthage to investigate the alliance between Hannibal and Antiochus. Ordered to North Africa by one the new Roman consuls, Marcus Porcius Cato (Scipio's former *quaestor*, known to history as Cato 'the Elder'), this commission was determined to bring Hannibal back to Rome as a prisoner. Hannibal knew well that his enemies in Carthage were about to betray him to his long-time enemy, so he put into effect his escape plan. After receiving the Roman envoys, he had them escorted to their quarters in the citadel on the Byrsa Hill above Carthage, then continued his normal activities in the city during the day. On the pretext of taking his evening ride, he set out for a villa near Hadrumetum, using horse relays set up beforehand to make good time. Once there, he slipped on to a waiting ship, his personal belongings and private fortune already sent ahead. Weeks later he made his way to the ancient Phoenician city of Tyre and to the court of King Antiochus, where he would serve as the Hellenistic king's military advisor. Hannibal was about fifty-two when he went into exile in the Levant. He would spend his last thirteen years in the eastern Mediterranean and Anatolia, serving kings and evading the Romans.

Although celebrated as a hero by the enemies of Rome in the eastern Mediterranean, Hannibal was not always warmly received by the generals and advisors who surrounded Antiochus. Hannibal wished to use the Syrian king's resources to make war with Rome again. As usual, the Punic general's plan was bold. He would take a Syrian force of 100 ships, 10,000 infantry and 1,000 cavalry with him to North Africa and induce the Carthaginians to revolt, while Antiochus threatened to invade Italy across the Adriatic. Once Carthage was secured, he would invade Italy directly from North Africa.[374] In the end, Antiochus refused Hannibal's wishes because the advancing shadow of Rome was now directly threatening the Balkans and Antiochus' territory in Asia Minor.

King Philip V of Macedonia had been busy since the end of the First Macedonian War in 205. Over the next two years he pressed westward into the Roman protectorate of Illyria, but protests from Rome forced him to seek lands elsewhere. In 202 the Macedonian king entered into a secret pact with Antiochus with the ultimate goal of attacking and dividing up the Ptolemaic kingdom of Egypt, a monarchy hamstrung by civil war. Under this agreement, Philip would expand eastward into Thrace in order to seize control of the important Black Sea shipping lanes, while Antiochus would expand south into

Palestine and threaten Egyptian territory from the northeast. By 201 Philip was fully engaged against King Attalus of Pergamum and the powerful naval power of Rhodes. When Philip threatened Athenian territory in Attica in 200, pleas for aid from Athens, Pergamum and Rhodes finally piqued the Roman Senate's interest in the region, initiating a Second Macedonian War (200–196 BCE).

In 200 BCE, the Romans sent the consul Publius Sulpicius Galba to Greece to support their Athenian allies against the Macedonians. Over the next three years, the Romans and Macedonians sparred, with neither side gaining a significant advantage. But in 197 the Roman Senate sent the young consul Titus Quinctius Flamininus (he was only thirty years old at the time) to Greece with hopes of bringing the war to a successful conclusion. In the hilly region of Thessaly, Flamininus' and Philip V's columns unexpectedly bumped into one another as they approached a pass from opposite directions. The opposing armies were almost equal in number.[375] The resulting Battle of Cynoscephalae was a stern trial between the Roman legion and the classical Macedonian phalanx, the legion's flexibility eventually proving superior. Faced with a crushing defeat, Philip was forced to settle with Rome.

The Second Macedonian War ended in 196 with Philip giving up all claims on Greek territory and paying an indemnity of 1,000 talents of gold. The Greek *poleis* in the Balkans were placed under Rome as a protectorate, as were any Greek city-states in Anatolia, further blunting Philip's aspirations to expand eastward into Asia Minor. But the increased Roman presence in Asia Minor would also place Rome in direct conflict with Antiochus, who considered this

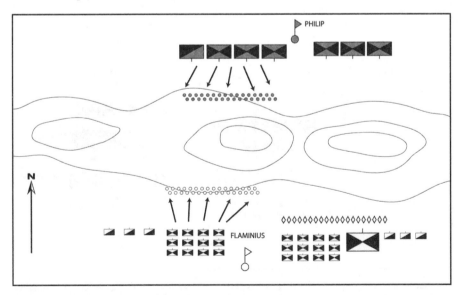

The Battle of Cynoscephalae, 197 BCE, Phase I. Titus Quinctius Flamininus leads an army consisting of 18,000 legionaries, 8,000 Athenian-led phalangeal infantry from the Aetolian League, 2,000 cavalrymen, and 20 elephants. They face a Macedonian army of 25,500 infantry and 2,000 cavalry under Philip V. Both sides deploy skirmishers to search for the enemy.

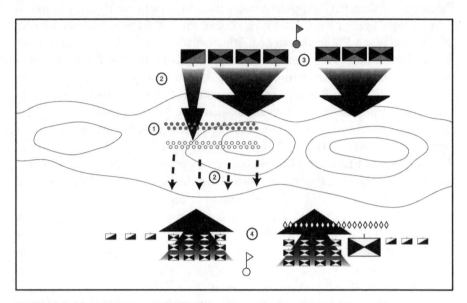

The Battle of Cynoscephalae, 197 BCE, Phase II. The battle opens as the skirmishers clash in the fog-enshrouded Cynoscephalae hills (1). After initially holding the upper hand, the Roman light infantry retreats in good order as the Macedonian cavalry advances against them (2). Philip orders his infantry forward, occupying the ridge line (3). The Romans begin to advance as well (4).

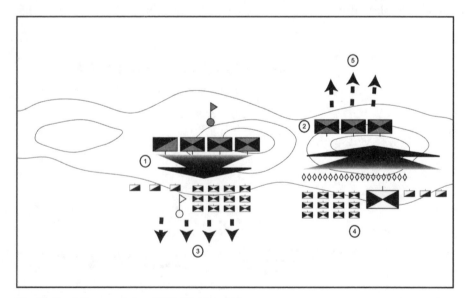

The Battle of Cynoscephalae, 197 BCE, Phase III. The Macedonians launch a downhill charge against the Roman left (1), but the move occurs before their own left has fully deployed (2). The Roman's left is pressed back by Philip's charge (3), but Flamininus's right attacks the lagging Macedonian left (4) and pushes them back as well (5).

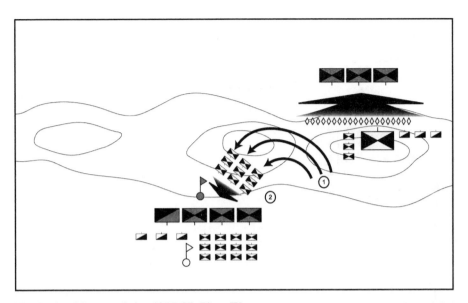

The Battle of Cynoscephalae, 197 BCE, Phase IV. As the Roman right pursues the Macedonian left, a Roman tribune orders his maniples to wheel to the left (1) and engage Philip's victorious right in the rear (2). The Macedonians, unable to protect themselves against this unanticipated onslaught, raise their sarissas in surrender. The Romans fail to understand the gesture and slaughter Philip's infantry.

peninsula to be in his sphere of influence. Soon the realities of garrisoning the Greek world sunk in, and Flamininus announced at the Isthmian games in Corinth a 'Treaty of Freedom' giving the Greeks the autonomy to live their lives under their own laws and customs free from Roman or Macedonian control. This brilliant political move not only freed up valuable Roman manpower to deal with future threats, most notably Antiochus of Syria, but also expanded Roman influence in the East while securing Greek friendship and loyalty. By the end of 196 the Romans had removed all of their forces from Greece.

Interestingly, Rome's containment of Philip V allowed Antiochus to expand westward in 195, across the Bosporus and into Thrace. Now the Syrian king was threatening to control the Black Sea sea-lanes and intervene in Greek affairs. It was during this tense time that Scipio Africanus and Hannibal Barca had their famous second meeting, when Scipio was dispatched by the Senate to Ephesus to ascertain Antiochus' intentions. After five years of tension the Roman Senate ordered Lucius Cornelius Scipio, younger brother of Scipio Africanus, to march through Greece and into Asia Minor, where he defeated Antiochus at the Battle of Magnesia in 190, after nearly two weeks of manoeuvring to gain a tactical advantage. Scipio Africanus was present at this battle.

After his defeat at Magnesia, Antiochus made peace with the Romans and withdrew from most of Anatolia, leaving it to the Romans and their allies.

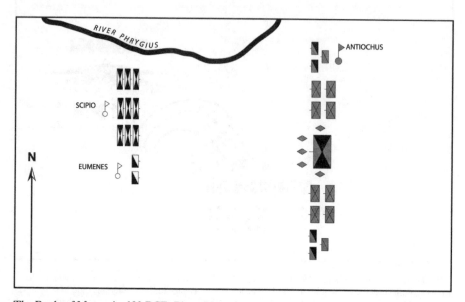

The Battle of Magnesia, 190 BCE, Phase I. After two weeks of manoeuvring, Lucius Cornelius Scipio brings the army of Antiochus to battle near Magnesia in Anatolia. The 35,000-man Roman army is outnumbered two-to-one by the Seleucid force. Scipio commands the Roman centre, while Eumenes II, King of Pergamum, commands the cavalry on the right wing.

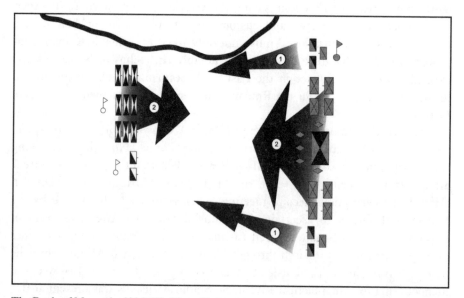

The Battle of Magnesia, 190 BCE, Phase II. The Seleucid cavalry, the right commanded by Antiochus himself, charge the Roman flanks (1) as the armies advance towards each other (2).

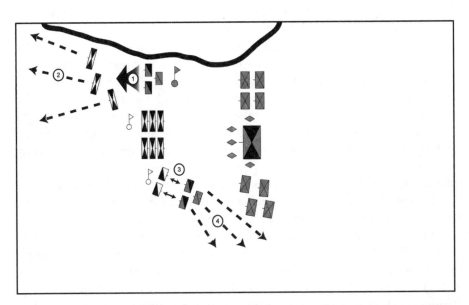

The Battle of Magnesia, 190 BCE, Phase III. Antiochus's cavalry slams into the Roman's left flank (1), scattering the infantry (2). The Seleucid horse mounts a pursuit. Events take a very different course on the Roman right, as Eumenes succeeds in breaking the enemy cavalry (3) and driving them from the field (4).

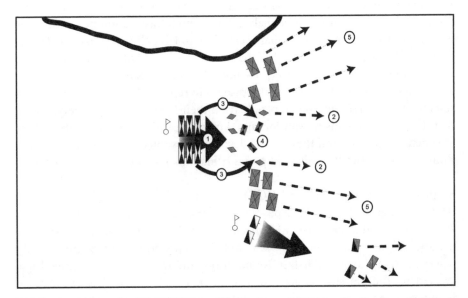

The Battle of Magnesia, 190 BCE, Phase IV. The Roman legionaries advance against the Seleucid phalanx (1), which is reinforced by elephants deployed between the infantry sections. The pikemen put up a good fight, but the Romans succeed in killing or driving off the elephants (2). They then outflank the less-manoeuvrable formation (3) and annihilate the foot soldiers (4). Having lost their advantage in cavalry and with their elite phalangeal infantry destroyed, the Seleucid army is driven from the field (5).

Hannibal, realizing that his presence in the Syrian court was no longer desired, quickly and quietly fled the Levant for the island of Crete, famous as a haven for pirates and refugees. Hannibal settled near the city of Gortyna, a few miles inland from the southern coast. One story, possibly apocryphal, has him openly depositing his sizable treasure in large clay vases at the temple of Artemis. Such actions were common in the ancient world, with temples acting as banks. In reality, Hannibal had weighed these pots down with lead, disguised with a scattering of gold. His treasure was instead well hidden in hollow bronze statues on his property. By the time the Romans finally heard about a wealthy Carthaginian living on the island, Hannibal had already slipped away by sea, abandoning his clay pots to the priests of Artemis and curious Roman soldiers.

Hannibal fled to the remote kingdom of Bithynia in northwestern Anatolia on the eastern edge of the Propontus (the modern Sea of Marmora). But even on the edge of the civilized world, Hannibal could not evade the long reach of Rome. When Bithynia became entangled in a war with its neighbour Pergamum, a client state of Rome, Hannibal was asked to serve the Bithynian king, Prusias. The Punic general agreed and secured a naval victory against Rome's ally. Curious, the Roman Senate asked Prusias to send envoys to Rome to explain why they were at war with Pergamum in the first place. Although Prusias was willing to keep Hannibal's presence secret, one of his envoys betrayed him to the Romans. It was 183 BCE, nearly twenty years after his defeat at Zama, and Hannibal's name still evoked passion in the senatorial chambers. The Senate dispatched the hero of Cynoscephalae, Titus Quinctius Flamininus, eastwards to Bithynia to apprehend Hannibal. According to Livy, Prusias, to court favour from the Romans, dispatched his men to Hannibal's villa, surrounding the estate with guard posts before approaching the house. Hannibal was sixty-four years old when he took his life with poison. He reportedly said right before his suicide, 'Let us free the Roman people from their long-standing anxiety, seeing that they find it tedious to wait for an old man's death'.[376] His death denied his old enemies the triumph they had so desperately wanted. No longer would the Roman people fear *'Hannibal ad portas'* ('Hannibal at the Gates').

Scipio After Zama (201–184 BCE)

After securing the terms of the peace from Carthage, Scipio set sail for home in 201, stopping off at his base in Lilybaeum in Sicily. Once in Sicily, he sent the majority of his troops ahead by sea, and then crossed over to southern Italy where he made his way north to Rome. Along the way the Roman general was greeted by the grateful subjects of Rome. In Livy's words, 'Everywhere he found rejoicing as much on account of the peace as for victory, when the towns poured out to do him honour and crowds of peasants held up his progress along the roads'.[377]

Scipio entered the capital and was accorded a triumph unlike any which had ever been seen before. On this special day, Scipio traveled at the head of his conquering legions through the garlanded streets of Rome, preceded by captured Carthaginian war elephants shipped to the city to amaze the Romans especially for this occasion. He brought 123,000 pounds of silver to the treasury, and was granted the cognomen 'Africanus' – the first Roman general to be addressed by a name derived from the location of his greatest campaign.[378] This celebrity resulted in Scipio being named the chief of the Senate (*princeps senatus*), a position he held for twelve controversial years.

Although a national hero, Scipio Africanus' fame did not long insulate him from the jealousy of his political rivals. The expansion of Rome's imperium into Spain, southern coastal Gaul and Illyrium created new wealthy classes within Roman society as the spoils of these newly-conquered regions and protectorates flowed back to Italy, while exposure to foreign ideas, especially Greek ideas, was slowly transforming Roman culture. This gradual Hellenization of Roman society began after the conquest of *Magna Graecia* during the Tarentine Wars of the early third century BCE, but intensified with sustained contacts with Hellenized Sicily and Greece itself in the late third and early second centuries. But not everyone in Rome was happy with this increased Greek influence, and Roman political structures began to divide between those who despised Hellenism, and those who would embrace it. Scipio Africanus and his clan were seen as lovers of Greek art and culture, and the Roman general's extravagant lifestyle in Spain and especially in Sicily only reinforced these perceptions that Scipio was not respecting the *mos maiorum* (custom of the ancestors).

Levelling these charges against the hero of Rome was the leader of this new group of Roman conservatives, Marcus Porcius Cato (Cato the Elder). Cato was a wealthy farmer from Tuscany who attracted broad support in the Senate due to his unwavering integrity and traditional attitudes. Cato's antagonistic relationship with Scipio began during the Second Punic War just before the African expedition was launched in 205. Cato had followed Scipio to Sicily as a *quaestor*, where his protest against the Roman general's spending provoked an official commission from Rome. Later Cato served as commander of Scipio's supply fleet, and witnessed first hand the defeat of Carthage. Perhaps it was during his time in North Africa that Cato perfected his life-long hatred of Punic culture, and his negative attitudes exerted a powerful influence on the course of republican Rome's history.

Cato used his position in the Senate and his powerful political alliances to deny Scipio important military commands and accuse him of misappropriating funds in the Syrian War (192–189) against Antiochus. His brother, Lucius, the victor at Magnesia, was formally charged with the latter count, a charge which sent Africanus into a rage, culminating in the destruction of the campaign receipts on the floor of the Senate. He pointed out that thousands of talents of silver had come into the public treasury through his efforts, and that his victories had given Rome not only Spain, but also Africa and increased Roman influence in Asia Minor. Harassed by insults from his political rivals,

Scipio Africanus retired from public life, physically sickened and emotionally embittered that the republic he had saved from the Punic menace would treat him as an enemy. In 184 BCE, just one year before Hannibal took his life in Bithynia, Scipio Africanus, the hero of the Second Punic War, also died in exile at the villa of Liternum in northern Campania.

Rome Expands in the Mediterranean (201–149 BCE)

The period between the Second and Third Punic Wars (201–149 BCE) witnessed the expansion of Rome across the northern littoral of the Mediterranean basin, with Roman legionaries eventually garrisoning cities from Spain to Macedonia. After the Syrian War against Antiochus III, the Romans continued to look to the east, but matters in Cisalpine Gaul and Spain took precedence. On the Gallic frontier, a Celtic rebellion forced the Romans to intervene militarily. Once the insurgency was put down, the Romans invested heavily in building up the infrastructure (roads and colonies) to finally bring this region under Roman hegemony. Further west in the newly created province of Hispania (modern Spain), attacks by the Turdenati and Celtiberians continued to bother the Romans, bleeding both men and resources westward.

Troubles continued in the east as well. In Macedonia, Rome defeated Philip V in the Second Macedonian War in 196; but, following Philip's death, his son and successor Perseus took steps to strengthen his kingdom. He arranged a marriage alliance with Antiochus III and instituted debt relief in his kingdom.

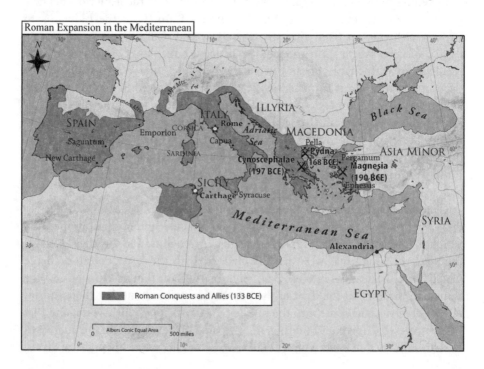

Roman Expansion in the Mediterranean

Roman Conquests and Allies (133 BCE)

This second action undercut Roman profits, which raised the ire of wealthy Romans operating in the region. He also moved militarily, north into Illyrium and south into Greece, in clear violation of the treaty his father had penned with the Romans. All of this proved too much for the Romans, and the Third Macedonian War (171–168) was launched in 171.

Over the next two years, Roman legions plundered Greece, but were unwilling to bring Perseus to battle. Perseus, for his part, was able to regain many of his losses in 169 and took a strong position on the Elpeus River in northeastern Greece, north of the sacred Mount Olympus and near the strategically important port of Pydna. There, he wintered and consolidated his gains. The election of Lucius Aemilius Paullus (later known as 'Macedonicus') to consul in 168 changed the complexion of the war when he arrived in theatre and raised an army with the explicit purpose of defeating Perseus. In fact, the army raised by Rome would be 'the last gasp of the generation of Romans which had fought and defeated Hannibal.'[379] The Romans won the Battle of Pydna because of the virtues of Roman small unit tactics and the initiative of individual centurions leading their men through the gaps in the phalanx's rank and file, attacking the helpless Macedonians in their flanks.

After his defeat at Pydna, Perseus was brought back to Rome and put on display in Paullus' triumph. Afterwards, he was exiled to the small Italian villa of Alba Fucens, where he lived out his life in relative obscurity. Unlike after the First Macedonian War, when Rome left the Greeks to govern their selves,

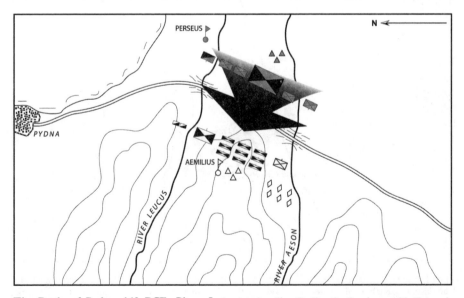

The Battle of Pydna, 168 BCE, Phase I. Lucius Aemilius Paullus finally closes with Perseus's Macedonian army near Pydna. Aemilius encamps on higher ground in rough terrain to offset the power of the Macedonian phalanx. The Roman commander holds his position, wanting the afternoon sun to be in his opponents' eyes. Weary of waiting for the Romans to attack, Perseus orders his army forward. The Macdeonians advance with a shout, moving swiftly against the Romans on the ridge (1).

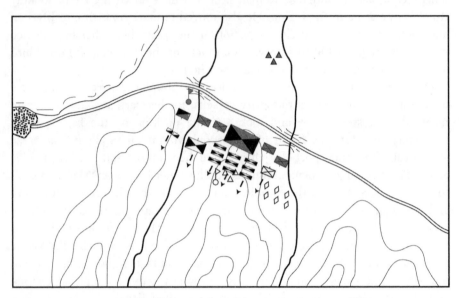

The Battle of Pydna, 168 BCE, Phase II. Faced with a wall of bristling pikes, the legionaries are pressed back, though they stay in good order.

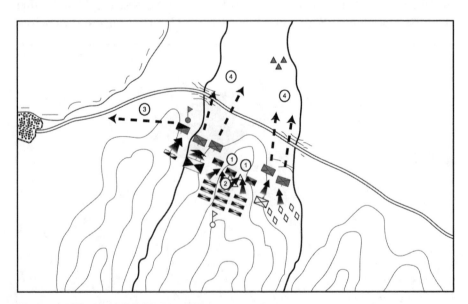

The Battle of Pydna, 168 BCE, Phase III. As the Macedonian phalanx leaves the plain and advances up the ridge, the rough terrain causes gaps to open in their formation (1). The Roman maniples take advantage of their tactical agility and charge into the gaps (2). Most of the Macedonian infantry in the phalanx are killed. Perseus, witnessing the destruction of his best foot soldiers, flees the field (3). The now-leaderless Macedonians melt away as the Romans counterattack (4).

the Senate ordered the kingdom of Macedonia split up into four republics, then denied each new state the ability to trade with one another. It seems Rome was very disappointed with how much local support Perseus received from the Balkan states, and wanted to punish their disobedience. Local magistrates were removed from power and shipped off to Rome in chains. Even the kingdoms of Illyrium and Epirus, once loyal subjects of Rome, were not spared and these lands were similarly ravaged and split up. Much of this rage was focused on Epirus. Paullus was authorized by the Senate to sack seventy coastal towns. An untold number of lives were lost and perhaps 150,000 Epirotes were sold into slavery.[380]

Despite the overwhelming victory in the Third Macedonian War and the reorganization of the Macedonian kingdom into four republics, Roman troubles in the east continued. Once again the Senate refused to garrison the Balkans and with the appointment of greedy *praetors* anti-Roman sentiment flared. The situation continued to disintegrate as Cilician piracy plagued the region's coasts and sea-lanes. By 149, the Romans were forced to intervene again in the Fourth Macedonian War (149–148) when a pretender to the abolished throne of Macedon, Andriscus, reunited the four republics and defeated a small Roman force dispatched to put the rebellion down. Undaunted, the Senate then sent the *praetor* Quintus Caecilius Metellus to Macedonia, where he quickly crushed the revolt and chased Andriscus from the country. A year later, the Romans officially annexed Macedonia and its recalcitrant neighbour, Epirus, then moved south into Greece to crush another rebellion, this time led by Corinth. Metellus razed Corinth, selling its inhabitants into slavery, and then disbanded the Achaean League. By 146 Greece followed in Macedonia and Epirus' footsteps, becoming a direct subject of the growing Roman imperium.

The Third Punic War (149–146 BCE)
The same year the Roman Senate sent legions to Macedon to deal with the pretender Andriscus it also initiated the Third Punic War (149–146) against Carthage. For half a century tensions had grown between Rome and Carthage, culminating in a war rare in history in that it ended with the eradication of an entire civilization.

In the years after Carthage's defeat at Zama in 202 and the close of the Second Punic War, Hannibal was successful in meeting the punitive conditions of the Roman peace, while simultaneously cleaning up corruption in the Carthaginian government and strengthening the economy. When Hannibal finally fled Carthage in 195 for Syria, he left his homeland stronger financially than he found it. Four years later in 191, the Carthaginians offered to pay off their annual reparations in one large payment, but Rome refused, not wanting Carthage to be released from its obligation. That same year, Carthage even sent half of their tiny reconstituted fleet to Rome's aid in its battle against Antiochus III. Carthage had demonstrated that it was a faithful ally of Rome.

Rome, on the other hand, kept a wary eye on their North African subject. To keep Carthage off balance, Rome continued to support their Numidian ally, King Masinissa, even encouraging him to seize Punic lands in North Africa. Masinissa launched major campaigns into Punic territory in 193, 182, 172 and 162 BCE, and when Carthage sent ambassadors to Rome protesting the Numidian incursions, the Senate ignored their pleas. These invasions increased in the 150s, as did the Punic pleas for Roman assistance. Rome was content to use Numidia as a counterbalance to Carthaginian expansion, especially at a time when it had its hands full fighting in Spain, Macedon and Anatolia. But a pro-war faction in the Roman Senate, led by Cato the Elder, continued to press for renewed hostilities against Carthage. In 153, Cato led a Roman delegation to Carthage to investigate the impact of Masinissa's depredations. While touring Carthage and its territories, Cato was awestruck by the wealth of the resurgent Punic civilization.

When he returned to Rome, Cato's sophistry was key in the Senate's decision to resume hostility against Carthage. Plutarch relates how he, while making a speech before the Senate, shook the folds of his toga and dropped some large African figs as if by accident. As his fellow Senators admired the size and plumpness of the figs, Cato reminded his colleagues that this produce could be found just three days away by sail in Carthage.[381] This political theatre was designed to illustrate the prosperity of Carthage, a prosperity Cato believed would eventually allow the Punic state to rise again and challenge Rome for mastery of the Mediterranean. Cato's fear of Carthage can best be illustrated in the strange way he ended all his speeches or rebuttals in the Forum with: 'It seems to me that Carthage should be destroyed'.[382] Cato continued to spearhead this campaign in Rome until war was declared in 149.

The situation in Carthage changed dramatically in 151 when the city-state paid off its fifty-year debt with Rome and a Punic government came to power that was antagonistic to Roman apathy towards Numidian transgressions. No longer bound by the treaty that ended the Second Punic War and unwilling to sit back idly and watch Masinissa raid their territory, the Carthaginians raised an army of 25,000 raw recruits in response to the Numidian king's investment of an important Punic city called Oroscopa, the location of which remains unknown.[383] The Numidians easily crushed the inexperienced army, but a witness to this defeat, the Roman tribune Publius Cornelius Scipio Aemilianus (grandson of Scipio Africanus through adoption), reported back to the Roman Senate and his description was construed as a Carthaginian violation of its treaty with Rome. Tensions rose over the next two years as Punic attempts to placate the Romans were refused. In 149 Rome declared war on Carthage.

Even before war was declared, the important North African harbour town of Utica defected to the Romans, providing Rome with an ideal base for the attack on Carthage. As in the campaign of 205–204, the Romans concentrated their forces at Lilybaeum on Sicily, landing in Utica in 149. The Senate had dispatched both consuls on this campaign. Manius Manilius was placed in command of the army, while Lucius Marcius Censorinus commanded the fleet. The Carthaginians sent a final embassy to the consuls' headquarters at Utica. Censorinus met the delegation, demanding that Carthage hand over massive amounts of military equipment, including 200,000 panoplies and 2,000 torsion engines (including javelin-throwing 'scorpions' and stone-throwing 'onagers'), as well as large numbers of javelins, arrows and siege ammunition.[384] After Carthage reluctantly complied, Censorinus upped the ante, demanding that the citizens of Carthage abandon their capital and move to a new settlement of their choice, providing it was ten miles inland from the coast. The Roman consul told the Carthaginian envoys that their city would then be razed. After being roughly ejected from the Roman camp, the Carthaginian delegation returned to their city and relayed the Roman demands. The Carthaginian government rejected these harsh demands, going so far as to kill any Carthaginian sympathetic to the Roman position in their ranks, as well as any Italian merchants unlucky enough to be in the city that night. Recognizing the intractable position of their enemy, the Carthaginians finally declared war on Rome. The third and last Punic war was now on.

Appian claims the Roman army which assembled at Scipio Africanus' old fortress, Castra Cornelia, was the largest Roman army fielded since the battle of Cannae in 216, consisting of 80,000 infantry and 4,000 cavalry and supported by fifty quinqueremes and one hundred smaller galleys.[385] Our source tells us that there was no shortage of recruits for the African campaign, with volunteers streaming in from all over the republic to fill the troop rosters. The possibility of an easy victory over Rome's greatest adversary no doubt attracted these men, as did the prospect of sacking the only city in the western Mediterranean which rivalled Rome's opulence.

A large army would be needed to breach the impressive walls of Carthage.[386] The city was protected by twenty-two miles of circuit walls and difficult to besiege and blockade because of its unique defensive position and large, well-defended harbours. A triple line of defence protected the northern approach to the city on its landward side, beginning with a sixty-foot-wide ditch and timber palisade, backed by a wall over fifty feet in height and thirty feet wide, with towers placed at two hundred feet intervals. This wall was built across the 3,000-yard wide isthmus and was divided into two stories. Appian tells us that in the lower space there were stables for 300 elephants, while above there were stables for 4,000 horses. This wall also contained barracks for 20,000 infantry and 4,000 cavalrymen.[387] Despite fifty-years of manpower restrictions, the Carthaginians were able to muster enough defenders to man the walls, although the relinquishing of critical armour and siege equipment must have weakened the defenders' position.

The Romans attacked Carthage from two directions. The consul Manius Manilius led his legionaries against the northern wall protecting the isthmus, while the other consul, Lucius Marcius Censorinus, used the Roman fleet to attack a weak stretch of wall near a narrow spit of land edging Lake Tunis to the south of the city. Here, legionaries using scaling ladders mounted on the prows of warships tried to climb the wall. Both attacks were met with a hail of missile fire from Carthage's walls, forcing the attacking Romans to retreat. Manilius and Censorinus attempted a second assault with the same results. Unable to quickly storm their objective, the Romans settled in for a longer siege and constructed camps near the city's long walls.[388]

The Roman siege was complicated by the existence of a strong Carthaginian presence outside of the walls, an army of 30,000 led by a man named Hasdrubal. This Punic force harassed the Roman lines, while another under the command of one Himilco Phameas massacred a Roman foraging party gathering wood, killing five hundred soldiers. Manilius was able to secure enough wood to construct ladders and a third assault against Carthage's northern walls was attempted, but failed to breach the span.[389]

Meanwhile, Censorinus continued his assault against the southern wall, filling in a portion of the lake in order to utilize two large battering rams. Appian tell us that these massive machines were supposedly manned by 6,000 men apiece, the first with a crew made up of legionaries and commanded by tribunes, and the second made up of sailors and officers from the fleet. Appian believed the consul used the service rivalry to spur a competition to breach the walls.[390] It worked, as two breaches were made, but the Carthaginians managed to drive the Romans back late in the day, executing repairs on the wall that evening. The Punic defenders even managed to sortie out under cover of darkness and burn both battering rams, making both engines inoperable. Unfortunately, the Carthaginians were unable to complete their repairs, providing the Romans with another opportunity to enter the city. To defend this gap, the Punic defenders formed a makeshift and poorly-armed mob behind the breach and stationed throngs of missile throwers on the walls and on the roofs of nearby homes. Taunted by the Punic defenders, the Romans hastily mounted an assault, but the attack was poorly organized and bogged down after the initial push through the walls. It was at this moment that one of the military tribunes, Publius Cornelius Scipio Aemilianus (the adopted grandson of Scipio Africanus and the same man whose report back to the Senate in 151 helped escalate tensions between Rome and Carthage) enhanced his military reputation, holding back his men from the initial assault and covering the Roman retreat when the attack began to disintegrate and the legionaries were expelled from the city.[391]

Scipio Aemilianus' actions are significant in that he was the only senior military officer to win distinction during the early phases of the Third Punic War, raising his stock in the eyes of the Roman Senate back home. No doubt, Scipio's impressive lineage helped keep the Senate's focus on his career. The youngest of four sons of the victor at Pydna, Aemilius Paullus, Scipio

Aemilianus was adopted by Publius Scipio, the son of Africanus. Roman custom allowed for the adoption of young men between prominent families, and Scipio Aemilianus' connection to two of the most prominent families in Rome placed enormous pressure on the young tribune to succeed. Groomed since birth to be a military leader, Scipio saw his first combat as a teenager at Pydna, where his enthusiastic pursuit of the enemy nearly had him declared missing in action. Later, in 151, he would take the position of tribune in the Spanish campaign, even personally killing an enemy champion in single combat.[392] One distinguished historian of the Punic Wars explains that 'it was perhaps his service in Spain that taught Scipio the importance of maintaining a reserve and cautious pursuit, for the tribes of the [Iberian] Peninsula were quick to punish careless attackers'.[393]

The Roman strategic position eroded further when disease began to spread throughout Censorinus' camp near the shore of Lake Tunis, forcing the tribune to relocate his camp closer to the sea. The Carthaginians also sent fire ships against the Roman fleet, coming, according to Appian, 'a little short of destroying the whole fleet'.[394] Emboldened, the defenders launched a nocturnal attack against Manilius' camp on the isthmus, crossing the Roman defensive ditches with planks and tearing down the wooden palisades. As the Romans within the camp panicked at the suddenness of the attack, Scipio Aemilianus led a cavalry detachment out of the rear gate and swung around the camp, striking the attacking Carthaginians in the flank, scattering the Punic troops.[395] After this near disaster, Manilius strengthened the defences of the camp and constructed another fort near the shore to cover Roman supply ships as they unloaded their cargo. Unable to quickly take Carthage over the campaigning season, the Roman expedition was settling in for the winter.

Censorinus returned to Rome to oversee the election of new consuls, leaving his colleague to carry on the siege. Manilius organized a strong contingent of 10,000 Roman infantry and 2,000 cavalry to punish the loyal regions around Carthage and to forage for food and wood for the winter. The Roman's inexperience precipitated disaster as groups of foragers were attacked by Himilco Phameas and his Numidian and Moorish allies, leading to terrible loss of life. Once again, Scipio showed his military acumen by keeping his foragers close to his troops and supporting the infantry guards with cavalry. When Manilius brought his column back to the main Roman camp, the Carthaginians mounted another night attack, this time against the small fortress protecting the Roman fleet. As the Punic forces threatened the smaller fort, Scipio took 300 Roman cavalry armed with torches into the night to create an impression of a larger force. The ruse worked and the Punic forces withdrew.[396]

Unable to bring a decisive conclusion to the siege, Manilius decided to seek out Hasdrubal's main army and destroy it. Hasdrubal was camped around the city of Nepheris, about twenty miles southeast of Tunis. The Carthaginian general made his camp on higher ground beyond a small river at the end of a valley, a very defensible position and one that forced the Romans to attack in column and not in line. Although Scipio Africanus was able to use this very difficult manoeuvre at Ilipa during the Second Punic War, the tactical articulation of the Roman army during the Third Punic War was not nearly as refined as a half century before. Ignoring this fact, and against the protests of Scipio Aemilianus, Manilius ordered a direct assault against the Punic position straight out of the march, not bothering to fortify his own camp and rest. Perhaps the Roman consul believed surprise would serve him well and his men did initially make some headway, fording the river and pushing the Carthaginians back up the slope. Hasdrubal waited patiently as the Roman troops tired and began to pull back, then ordered a ferocious counterattack. Bottle-necked at the ford, the legionaries were cut down by the Punic troops. Once again, Scipio saved the day, taking his contingent of 300 cavalry, and any other Roman horsemen he could gather along the way, and galloping towards the ford. Once there, Scipio divided his horsemen into two groups and led a series of controlled charges against the pursuing enemy, keeping his lines close and rotating his cavalry attacks in order to keep constant pressure on the enemy lines. His decisive intervention allowed the majority of the legionaries to cross the river to safety, with his own horsemen barely making it across the ford.[397] Scipio went on to lead another daring rescue mission, freeing four Roman units (probably maniples) who had taken refuge on a hill at the beginning of the melee. Scipio even managed to secure the bodies of several fallen tribunes from Hasdrubal, illustrating his penchant for negotiating with the enemy.[398]

The fact that it was Scipio, and not the consul and commander Manilius, who negotiated for the return of these fallen officers illustrates the young tribune's understanding of North African culture and the personal relationships forged with Punic and Numidian leaders in the years before the start of the war. At times, these relationships spurred rumours of collaboration (often spread by the tribune's jealous rivals in the Roman army), but Scipio's knowledge of his enemy made him a better commander in the field, while also placing him in a stronger position to take on greater responsibility as the war continued. Perhaps more interestingly, Scipio's lineage as the adopted grandson of Africanus presented an unusual opportunity for the Roman cause in North Africa. When ninety-year-old King Masinissa died in the early months of 148, his will called for Scipio to oversee the division of his assets among the old king's three legitimate sons. Scipio completed this task and persuaded one of these sons, the Numidian prince Gulussa, to join the Roman effort against Carthage.

Overall, the Roman expedition against Hasdrubal's camp near Nepheris was a disaster, and the Roman column was even attacked again by Himilco while trying to return to the main Roman camps near Carthage. The consul would mount a second, better organized, attack against Nepheris in the early spring of 148, but this campaign also failed to destroy Hasdrubal's army. The only bright spot in this second campaign was the defection of Himilco Phameas and 2,200 of his cavalry to the Roman cause, an act secretly negotiated by Scipio.[399] When Scipio was called back to Rome in 148, Himilco accompanied him to the Senate, where he received, according to Appian, 'a purple robe with gold clasps, a horse with gold trappings', as well as a fully-furnished tent and great sums of silver.[400] Scipio Aemilianus had in Himilco what his grandfather secured in his alliance with Masinissa – a faithful North African ally in his war with Carthage.

The Siege Perfected and the Fall of Carthage, 147–146 BCE

While in the Eternal City, Scipio planned to stand for the office of *curule aedile*, a logical next step for a young, well-connected aristocrat. But his name was submitted by the *comitia centuriata* as a candidate for the consulship of Rome for 147–146. As a man of thirty-six or thirty-seven, he was still a few years short of the minimum age of forty required to stand for consul. This technicality was overcome with a Senatorial annulment of the old law, allowing Scipio to stand for election, just as his underage grandfather had done in 205. Granted Africa as his command region, Scipio raised a new army from volunteers and returned to the war, sailing first to Sicily, then on to Utica.[401]

Roman actions during the previous campaigning year (148) made little headway in North Africa. The consul in charge, Lucius Calpurnius Piso Caesoninus, maintained a loose blockade around Carthage, but placed more emphasis on subduing cities in the region. Unfortunately, no strategically-important cities were taken and the campaigning season ended without any significant gains. Hasdrubal, the leader at Nepheris, assumed command in Carthage and, after disposing of his rivals, continued the defence of the city.

As the Roman blockade of Carthage continued into early 147, the Roman commander of the fleet, Lucius Mancinus, decided to exploit an apparent weak spot in the city's defence, a section where the natural defences were so strong that a strong wall seemed unnecessary. Mancinus sent men with ladders to scale the cliffs, but their assault was noticed by the Punic defenders, who sallied out of a nearby gate to attack the Romans. The Romans soon put the Carthaginians to flight, and then pursued the enemy through the portal and into the city. Mancinus poured all of his available resources into the city. Unfortunately, of these 3,500 men, only about 500 were fully-equipped legionaries, while the rest were poorly-armed and -armoured sailors. After nearly two years, a small corner of Carthage was now in Roman hands. Well aware that his men did not have adequate supplies to hold the city, Mancinus sent messengers to the consul Piso (who commanded the field army) and the Roman base at Utica asking for reinforcements. As luck would have it, Scipio had arrived in Utica that evening and immediately prepared an expedition to relieve Mancinus. After releasing some Punic prisoners with the hope that his arrival would strike fear into the Carthaginians, Scipio set sail in the early morning for

Carthage. First light brought a renewed attack against Mancinus and his men, an attack which only stalled when Scipio's fleet came into view, with legionaries crowding the decks to suggest the arrival of a new army from Italy. There was enough of a pause in the fighting to allow Mancinus and his men to escape the city on the decks of Roman ships.[402]

Assuming command of the African campaign, Scipio concentrated his army outside of Carthage, reinvigorating a strategy with the capture of the Punic capital as its centrepiece. The new consul inspected his troops, dismissing those men who he felt were there to loot and not to fight.[403] A year of battlefield reverses weighed heavily on the remaining Roman veterans, and the task of integrating raw recruits brought from Italy compounded the problem. Scipio understood that he did not have sufficient time to fully train his new army, but he also understood the importance of military success in healing the psychological wounds inflicted by the long siege. Mancinus' successful capture of a corner of Carthage inspired the young consul, and he ordered two simultaneous Roman assaults against the Megara, one of the largest suburbs surrounding the Byrsa or old citadel. These attacks were launched at night and against two widely-separated sections of the wall. Punic defenders hurling missiles repulsed these two assaults, but the Romans were able to seize an abandoned tower adjacent to the wall. Using planks as a gangway, the Romans bridged the gap and fought their way onto the rampart, finally seizing a nearby gate and admitting Scipio and 4,000 of his legionaries.[404] The Punic defenders panicked, fleeing back to the protection of the Byrsa. Scipio and his men slowly moved through the dark streets and city orchards and gardens, but were wary of the numerous areas suitable for ambush and disturbed by the lack of defensible positions in this area of the city. Wisely, Scipio ordered a withdrawal from the city back to his main camp.[405]

The success of the Roman assault greatly upset Hasdrubal, who reacted to the incursion by ordering Roman prisoners taken to the walls and tortured to death in full view of their comrades, an act incensing the Italian besiegers. This was the action of a desperate commander. Hasdrubal understood his city was now very vulnerable to storm and he wanted to send a message to his own population that the Romans, should they enter the city again, would not show any quarter. This act angered some members of the Carthaginian Council of Elders, but when they protested, Hasdrubal had them arrested and executed.[406]

Scipio recognized that he now possessed the initiative in the siege, and he pressed his advantage by instituting a tighter blockade of the city. The consul ordered the abandoned camp by Lake Tunis to be burned, then moved his own main camp closer to Carthage's walls on the isthmus. Scipio fortified this new position in the traditional rectangular manner, taking twenty days and nights to dig ditches (filled with sharp stakes) and erect a rampart twelve-feet high with towers at regular intervals and a tall tower in the middle of the wall facing Carthage to act as an observation post. Appian states that this tower was tall enough for Scipio to observe what was going on in the streets of Carthage.[407] Roman commanders had long used engineering projects to impose drill and discipline among their soldiers, and the construction of such a large camp no doubt helped build an esprit de corps among the troops, helping to integrate the new recruits with the veterans. This new Roman fort dominated access to the city on the landward side.

With the isthmus under Roman control, Scipio next tackled the porous nature of the naval blockade. Throughout the Roman siege of Carthage, Punic ships regularly ran the blockade and brought much-needed supplies into the city via the seventy-foot-wide harbour entrance. These supplies were essential in maintaining the fighting spirit of Hasdrubal's 30,000 active defenders, though this was done at the expense of the rest of the population, creating a famine in the city.[408] Scipio decided to cut off the harbour with the construction of a mole, hoping to seal the fate of the city. The mole was designed to cut across the harbour entrance from the isthmus to an earthen tongue or natural quay which projected outward on the seaward side of the harbour entrance.

As the Romans went about the business of filling the causeway, the Punic defenders began to secretly cut a new channel to the sea, with work being done at night using all available labour, including women and children. In addition to cutting a new passage, the Carthaginians used the wood within the city to construct a fleet of fifty triremes and lighter support ships from scratch. Appian tells us that the Romans knew nothing of either activity until dawn one morning when the fleet sailed from the mouth of the harbour utilizing the new passage.[409] The sudden appearance of this sizeable fleet unnerved the Romans, but inexplicably, the Carthaginians did not seize the element of surprise and immediately attack the Roman fleet, instead taking the ships out for sea trials before returning to the safety of the harbour. It was only three days later that the Punic fleet sailed out again, this time with the intent of engaging the Roman flotilla. The sea battle that took place near the coastline of Carthage was the last naval engagement of the Punic empire. Appian tells us that

> Loud were the cheers on both sides as they came together, and rowers, steersmen, and marines exerted themselves to the utmost, this being the last hope of safety for the Carthaginians and of complete victory for the Romans. The fight raged until midday, many blows and wounds being given and received on both sides. During the battle the Carthaginian small boats, running against the oarage of the Roman ships, which were taller, stove holes in their sterns and broke off their oars and rudders, and damaged them considerably in other ways, advancing and retreating nimbly.[410]

Despite the greater manoeuvrability of the triremes versus the larger Roman quinqueremes, this battle ended in stalemate. The Punic ships were ordered to withdraw back into the Great Harbour, probably to repair and refit and fight again the next day. During this retreat, the Carthaginians' situation began to disintegrate when the smallest vessels attempted to enter the newly-cut passage. Here, some of the smaller ships collided, blocking the entrance. Unable to return to the harbour, the remaining Punic ships pulled back and moored against the stretch of the earthen quay previously used to unload merchant ships too large to enter the harbour. This quay had been fortified over the duration of the siege with a rampart designed to deny the Romans with this landing from which to mount an assault. The Punic captains adroitly backed their ships up to this landing, bow rams facing outward. The Roman ships attacked this position, but suffered heavy casualties from the defending ships and defenders attacking the vessels from the rampart before finally gaining an advantage. Appian tells us that 'many' of the Carthaginian warships were able to escape back into the harbour, presumably after the removal of the damaged ships.[411]

Scipio now recognized that capturing the earthen quay provided the Romans with their best opportunity to enter the city. He ordered his legionaries to attack the quay's rampart across the newly-constructed mole. Huge siege engines and battering rams were pulled into position, and the wall was successfully breached in several places. But brave Carthaginians swam naked across the harbour with dry torches and set many of these artillery pieces and rams on fire, causing the Roman forces manning the engines to rout. Fearing the loss of this strategically-important position, Scipio led a cavalry charge across the mole in an attempt to restore order. When the fleeing soldiers refused to stop, Scipio and his horsemen cut them down.[412]

In the morning, the Carthaginians began to repair the rampart, free from the molestation of Roman arms. Although new towers were constructed, the Punic fighters were not able to stop the Romans from renewing their efforts. Scipio ordered the construction of new siege engines and assault ramps, and the Romans were eventually able to force the Carthaginians to abandon the ramparts. Scipio next commanded the construction of a brick wall on the quay, one facing the main city wall and equal to its height. It was a large wall, for Appian says it was capable of holding 4,000 Roman attackers.[413] This massive project took until the autumn of 147 to complete. Scipio would mount the final assault on the city from this position when the campaigning season began again in the spring of 146.

Before Scipio could launch the final attack on Carthage, he needed to destroy the Punic army wintering in the well-defended position outside of Nepheris. Taking note of Manilius' botched campaign two years before, Scipio approached the enemy carefully, breaching the encampment's walls and then feeding his own reserves inside as another party attacked the far side of the camp. Those Punic defenders which did manage to escape were hunted down by the Numidian prince Gulussa and his cavalry and elephants. Appian recounts a 'great slaughter, with as many as 70,000, including non-combatants, being killed'.[414] Scipio went on to take the city of Nepheris itself. Soon, all of the nearby communities yielded to the Romans. Scipio was now free to complete the reduction of Carthage without fearing an enemy army at his rear.

When the new Roman year began in March 146, the Senate rewarded Scipio with a continuation of his *imperium* in North Africa, allowing the former consul to complete his task of taking the Carthaginian capital. The main assault on the city was renewed that spring, using the newly-fortified quay as the base of operations. Fearing this, Hasdrubal set the warehouses on fire in the rectangular civilian harbour adjacent to the newly-erected Roman wall. Despite this action, it was near this area that one of Scipio's lieutenants, a man named Gaius Laelius (the son of Scipio Africanus' loyal friend by the same name) led a raiding party at night over the walls and into the round, innermost military harbour. Punic resistance was light, allowing Laelius to press into the city itself, seizing the *agora* (marketplace) next to the square civilian harbour. In the morning, Scipio personally led a force of 4,000 legionaries into the city to support his lieutenant.[415] As the Roman soldiers moved through the city streets, the gilded temple of Apollo caught their eye and the troops broke rank and stripped the temple of all of its gold, reportedly equivalent to the amount of 10,000 talents. Scipio and his officers were unable to persuade their men to return to duty until the religious building was thoroughly picked over.[416] This pillaging stands in stark contrast to the discipline showed by Scipio Africanus' legionaries when they stormed New Carthage in 209 during the Second Punic War. Long gone were the days of Roman military restraint and the even distribution of all booty seized by soldiers during the storm of a city. Only after a thorough sacking of the temple did Scipio's men rejoin their general and proceed deeper into the city towards their target, the Byrsa citadel.

As the Romans began to slowly ascend the hill towards the Byrsa, the Carthaginian defenders made their presence known.[417] According to Appian

The streets leading from the market square to the Byrsa were flanked by houses of six storeys from which the defenders poured a shower of missiles onto the Romans: when the attackers got inside the buildings the struggle continued on the roofs and on the planks covering the empty spaces; many were hurled to the ground or onto the weapons of those fighting in the streets. Scipio ordered all the sector to be fired and the ruins cleared away to give a better passage to his troops, and as this was done there fell with the walls many bodies of those who had hidden in the upper storey and been burned to death, and others who were still alive, wounded and badly burnt. Scipio had squadrons of soldiers ready to keep the streets clear for the rapid movement of his men, and dead or living were thrown together into pits, and it often happened that those who were not dead yet were crushed by the cavalry horses as they passed, not deliberately, but in the heat of battle.[418]

Urban fighting in any era is a grisly business, with soldiers clearing buildings floor by floor and subject to sudden ambush from unfamiliar doors, halls and stairwells. After the first buildings were taken, legionaries laid planks from rooftop to rooftop across the alleyways and then cleared adjacent buildings, allowing the soldiers in the street to slowly proceed up the hill toward the Byrsa. Once the citadel was reached, Scipio ordered the buildings running along the streets to be burned behind him. This was done to create a larger path suitable for the siege engines and reinforcements required for the reduction of the citadel. As the buildings fell, Roman working parties filled the holes and leveled the wreckage, creating solid wider paths. This project took six days to complete. Scipio was now ready to attack the walls of the Byrsa itself.[419]

The following day, a Carthaginian delegation carrying olive branches walked out of the Byrsa offering to surrender. Scipio granted the request, and a throng of 50,000 men, women and children emerged from the gates, only to be sold into slavery by their Roman captors. Only the Roman and Italian deserters, some 900 in number, refused to surrender. These men barricaded themselves into the temple of Aesculapius, where they eventually burned themselves alive rather than be taken by the Romans. Hasdrubal, abandoning his wife and children, surrendered to the Romans, while his wife killed their children and then herself.

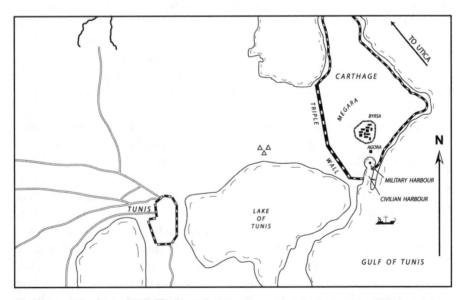

The Siege of Carthage, 147 BCE, Phase I. Roman forces blockade Carthage from both land and sea. The Roman fleet commander, Lucius Mancinus, attempts an assault against an area with strong natural defences that has a lower wall and fewer defenders than other areas. Though he succeeds in gaining a foothold, the attempt is unplanned and poorly executed. Mancinus's sailors and legionaries manage to escape by sea as reinforcements under Scipio Aemilianus arrive from Utica.

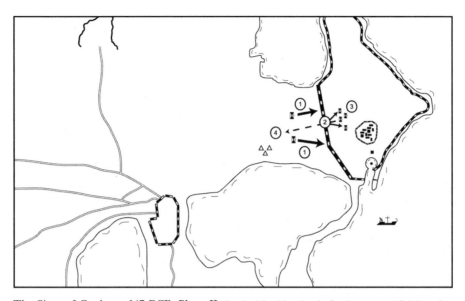

The Siege of Carthage, 147 BCE, Phase II. Inspired by Mancinus's fleeting success, Scipio orders assaults against two widely separated points of the city wall (1). The Romans manage to seize an adjacent tower, gain the rampart, and open a gate, admitting Scipio and 4,000 legionaries (2) who move into the urban landscape of the Megara (3). Scipio realizes his small force is vulnerable to ambush, that the Megara lacks defensible positions, and orders a withdrawal (4). Hasdrubal responds to the incursion by hauling Roman prisoners atop the walls and torturing them in view of their comrades.

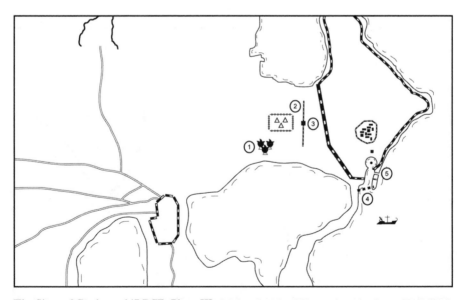

The Siege of Carthage, 147 BCE, Phase III. Scipio orders the old camp along the shore of Lake Tunis burnt (1) and constructs a new, fortified camp closer to the city walls (2). The Romans also build a twelve-foot-high rampart with a tall central tower to better observe Carthaginian activity inside the city (3). To tighten the noose to seaward, Scipio orders a mole to be constructed across the mouth of the harbour (4). Hasdrubal counters by ordering a channel cut at night (5). Fifty additional triremes and support ships are built to bolster the Carthaginian fleet.

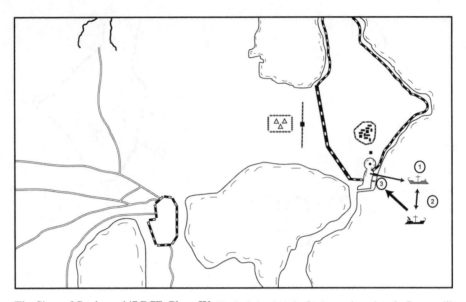

The Siege of Carthage, 147 BCE, Phase IV. Hasdrubal orders the fleet to sortie against the Romans (1) and a sharp naval battle ensues (2). The manoeuvrable triremes fail to defeat the larger Roman quinqueremes and the Carthaginians attempt to re-enter the harbour via the cut in the quay. Several ships collide, blocking entrance, and the remaining vessels back against the quay next to a rampart (3), where they are able to stave off several Roman attacks. The channel is finally cleared and the surviving Carthaginian vessels return to the harbour.

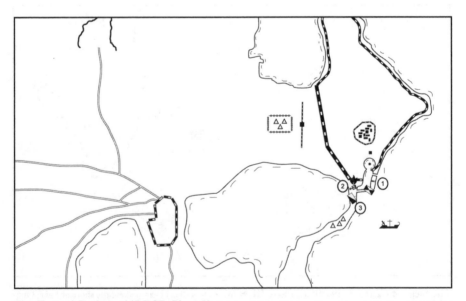

The Siege of Carthage, 147 BCE, Phase V. Scipio realizes the quay may prove to be the chink in the Carthaginian armour and orders an assault against the rampart (1). Siege engines and rams breach the wall in several places, but the Roman artillerymen are put to flight and their pieces burned (2) by Carthaginians who have swum across the bay. The Roman attack wavers and Scipio leads a cavalry force across the mole (3). The infantry fails to rally and the cavalrymen ride them down.

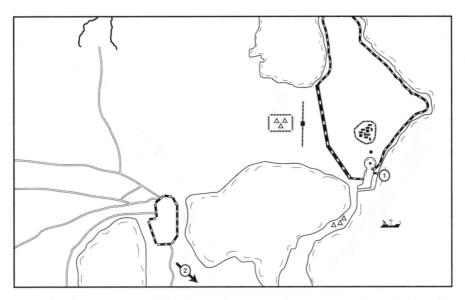

The Siege of Carthage, 147–146 BCE, Phase VI. Scipio orders new siege engines built and constructs assault ramps, finally forcing a Carthaginian withdrawal. He then refills the cut in the quay and builds a wall equal in height to the city wall from which to launch an assault in the spring of 146 (1). During the winter, Scipio attacks and destroys a Carthaginian army near Nepheris, to the southeast of Carthage (2), allowing him to fully concentrate on his siege of the city.

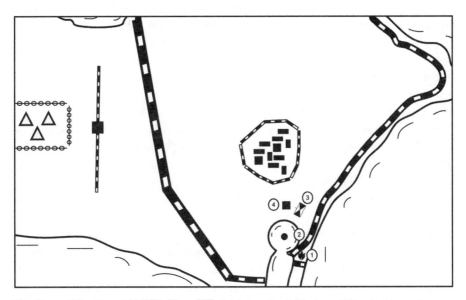

The Siege of Carthage, 146 BCE, Phase VII. Scipio launches the final assault from his base on the quay. Hasdrubal orders the warehouses next to the Roman's wall set afire (1), but this fails to check the assault. A raiding party under Gaius Laelius (3) overcomes light Carthaginian resistance, enters the military harbour area and seizes the adjacent Agora (4). Scipio reinforces the raiders with 4,000 legionaries, but the Roman infantrymen stop to loot the gold-covered Temple of Apollo near the Agora.

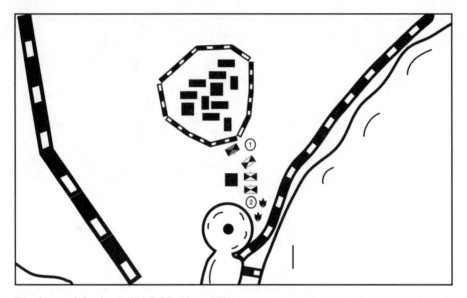

The Siege of Carthage, 146 BCE, Phase VIII. The Romans push through the streets against stiff Carthaginian resistance (1). Scipio finally gains the walls of the Byrsa and orders the buildings leading back to the breach burned to make way for the siege engines. After six days of pounding, the Carthaginians offer to surrender. Scipio accepts and then sells the populace into slavery. Nine hundred Roman and Italian deserters retreat to the Temple of Aesculapius and burn themselves alive rather than fall into Roman hands. Hasdrubal surrenders to Scipio, while his wife kills their children before committing suicide.

With the Byrsa now in Roman hands, the siege of Carthage was complete. In accordance with Roman custom, Scipio allowed his soldiers several days of pillage. Interestingly, he did place the cities' temples off limits and denied those men who sacked the Temple of Apollo from sharing in the spoils. Some of the plunder was placed on a messenger ship and sent to Rome, precipitating rejoicing throughout the city. Rome sent a commission consisting of ten Senators to Carthage to supervise Scipio's razing of the city. Although the complete destruction of Carthage is a myth (archaeologists have found several walls dating back to this period), the days of the Punic Empire were no more. Those cities which had sided with Carthage were also destroyed, while those which had aided Rome were rewarded with freedom and grants of former Carthaginian lands. Finally, some 5,000 square miles were annexed to form the new Roman province of 'Africa'.

Scipio Aemilianus returned to Rome and celebrated a triumph fit for a general who had destroyed Carthage. Like his grandfather, he took the cognomen 'Africanus', but unlike his namesake, he enjoyed a long and fruitful political career. He even served as consul again in 134, returning to Spain where he finally subdued the peninsula, ending the Celtiberian War. Scipio Aemilianus 'Africanus' died in 129, a celebrated man who represented the ideal second-century aristocrat – an honourable Roman soldier and statesman who appreciated Greek culture.

Rome Transformed: The Legacy of the Punic Wars

After Scipio Aemilianus Africanus' passing, Rome entered the last century of the Republic, a tumultuous time when the fruits of empire building would be challenged by the realities of governing an empire. Rome's victory in the three Punic wars (264–146 BCE) had catapulted the Italian power from a regional hegemon to master of the western Mediterranean, while simultaneous wars in Macedon, Greece and Anatolia had placed the Romans in an ideal position to continue their conquest of the remainder of the Mediterranean coastline. By 146, six permanent overseas provinces had been established (Sicily; Sardinia and Corsica ruled as one; Nearer Spain; Further Spain; Africa and Macedonia), with two more established by the end of the century (Asia and Transalpine Gaul).[420] In little more than a century, Rome's conflict with Carthage had produced a political, military and economic juggernaut and laid the foundations of a lasting Mediterranean empire.

But was Rome seeking an overseas empire when it initiated hostilities against Carthage in 264 BCE? Polybius offers the theory that Rome went to war with Carthage for purely defensive reasons.[421] Rome feared the Carthaginians would take over all of Sicily and dominate the Italian coastline. Punic attempts to annex the island in the fifth and fourth centuries BCE certainly fed these fears, but treaties with Carthage and the presence of a powerful Hellenistic city-state in Syracuse, provided a counterweight to Punic expansion in Sicily in the mid-third century. Despite Polybius' assertion of self-defence, Rome saw the plea for assistance from Messana as a way of continuing their expansionist policies into Sicily.

But Rome's Sicilian campaign illustrated a lack of coherent strategy and the dangers of what modern historians call 'mission creep'. Initially, the Roman Senate regarded the seizure of Messana as a limited undertaking, though when Punic resistance proved light, the Romans decided to seize the rest of Carthaginian Sicily. To meet this objective, Roman generals dispersed their legionaries across the island, only to be bogged down in ineffective sieges against well-defended Punic cities like Lilybaeum and Drepana. Unable to secure Sicily, the Romans expanded their objective to the destruction of Carthage itself, sending an expedition to North Africa in 256. Once again, inadequate siege capabilities thwarted their desire to take the Punic capital, while a battlefield defeat at Tunis in 255 forced a reversion back to their original objective, the capture of Sicily.

Although there were numerous opportunities to end the decades' long conflict, Rome would not settle on anything short of victory in the First Punic War. Perhaps nothing illustrates this determination more than Rome's whole-sale construction of a fleet of warships from the keel up to compete directly with Carthage for command of the sea. One historian places the number of ships constructed between 260 and 241 at nearly 1,000, with most of these being the large quinqueremes.[422] Despite setbacks, Rome successfully defeated the North African thalassocracy at Mylae, Ecnomus, and Aegates Islands, and then demanded a harsh peace from the Carthaginians in 241.

The interwar period between the first and second Punic wars witnessed a Roman grab for Sardinia in 237, further straining Romano-Punic relations. Carthage moved to expand in Spain, but recognized future hostilities with Rome were inevitable. As military governor of Spain, Hamilcar Barca prepared a strategy to bring the war directly to the Romans in Italy, and by breaking up the Roman confederation, reduce Roman power in the region. Hamilcar's son, Hannibal, implemented his father's plan in 218 when he crossed the Alps, striking Rome's sensitive northern border. Although Hannibal recorded four significant victories (Ticinus in 218, Trebia in 218, Lake Trasimene in 217, and Cannae in 216) in just three years, the Carthaginian general could not overcome Rome's massive manpower reserves, and more importantly, the Roman civilization's unrelenting desire to win. Rome held its confederation together, contained Hannibal in southern Italy, and sent three Scipios and their legions to Spain to destroy the Carthaginian general's own base of operations. With Spain pacified by 205, Rome took the war directly to North Africa in 204, a campaign which culminated in the Battle of Zama in 202 and a second defeat of Carthage. Rome waged a form of total war in its battle against Hannibal, marshalling its wealth and natural resources to raise, pay, feed, clothe and equip its armies, while simultaneously building and equipping large fleets. And when these armies or ships were lost, Rome built new fleets and raised new armies to replace them, sometimes at the expense of private citizens when public coffers ran low.

While the Romans suffered the depredations of Hannibal and his army marauding through Italy for fifteen years, the Carthaginian elite, safe behind their capital's massive city walls, watched their strategic situation slowly unravel, first in Spain and then in Italy. When Roman armies began ravaging the North African countryside, the Punic leaders called Hannibal back to defend the homeland. After the defeat at Zama, the Carthaginians realized a prolonged siege of their city was not in their best interest, while Rome, fatigued by nearly two decades of warfare, did not relish the prospect of reducing one of the strongest fortifications in the ancient world. Rome forced Carthage to sign another punitive peace treaty, then treated the vanquished North African civilization as a subject people.

It would be another fifty years (201–149) before Rome mustered the political and military will and resources to tackle the daunting task of besieging Carthage. During these years, Carthage met all of its treaty obligations to Rome, and even provided ships and troops for Rome's wars in the east. But Rome, egged on by the sophistry of Cato the Elder, finally dispatched an army to North Africa in 149. The Third Punic War lasted three years (much longer than the Romans originally expected) and culminated in the capture of Carthage and the annihilation of Carthaginian civilization in 146. Once again, Rome showed an unrelenting desire to conquer its enemy, though this campaign took on the complexion of a religious crusade, with the only acceptable outcome being the eradication of a longstanding and mythic adversary.

Although Roman imperialism was not created by the three Punic wars, it was perfected during these conflicts. Before 264, Rome had no history of projecting force overseas, but decades of campaigning in Sicily, Spain, and North Africa taught the Romans how to supply their legions far from home, lessons they would use in their wars against Macedon and Syria in the east. The development of these logistical lines helped Rome secure its growing Mediterranean empire in the second and first centuries BCE.[423] Rome also continued to perfect its art of war during the Punic conflicts. The Romans had always borrowed weapons and tactics from their opponents, often improving upon them to suit their own needs. The Roman legionary adopted and adapted both the *gladius* and *pilum* during these wars, creating a soldier with both missile and shock capabilities and the most lethal fighting man in the classical period. Under the command of capable Roman generals like Gaius Marius and his nephew, Gaius Julius Caesar, these legionaries would routinely defeat foreign armies much larger than their own and become pawns in the civil wars which eventually ended the Republic.

The legacy of the Punic wars is that it transformed Roman civilization forever. When Roman legions crossed the Strait of Messina in 264 BCE, Rome was an Italian power with limited regional aspirations. By the conclusion of the Third Punic War in 146 the Roman state had not only become accustomed to frequent and large-scale foreign wars, it was also becoming accustomed to maintaining a large army and governing foreign provinces. Over the course of these wars Rome was flooded with immense amounts of treasure and slave labour from the conquered regions, transforming the Roman social order. A new class of wealthy plebeians challenged the primacy of the Patrician class, initiating ferocious political competition and the rise of demagoguery. The Roman free farmer, once the backbone of the Roman economy and a traditional source of military manpower, was displaced by the rise of the corporate farm or *latifundia*. Displaced farmers fled to the cities, swelling the ranks of the urban poor and creating a new political class that would influence Roman politics for centuries.

Conquests continued in the first century BCE, with Rome adding provinces in North Africa, the Levant, Transalpine Gaul, and Egypt to its holdings and greatly expanding the wealth of the Roman elite. In the end, Rome's republican system would be unable to manage these problems, initiating a century of civil war, dictatorship, triumvirs, and ultimately, the institution of monarchy under Caesar Augustus in 27 BCE. The future Roman Empire was cast in the crucible of the Punic wars.

Notes

Introduction

1. Victor Davis Hanson, *Carnage and Culture: Landmark Battles in the Rise of Western Power* (New York, 2001), p. 110.
2. Nigel Bagnall, *The Punic Wars, 264–146 BC* (London, 2002), p. 68.
3. Appian, *Libyca*, VII.96.
4. David Soren, Aicha ben Khader, Hedi Slim, *Carthage: Uncovering the Mysteries and Splendors of Ancient Tunisia*, (New York, 1990), p. 86.
5. Ibid., pp. 86–88.
6. Aristotle, *Politics*, 2.2. Aristotle only gave this praise to one non-Greek civilization.
7. Soren, Khader, Slim, *Carthage*, pp. 123–145. This practice was enacted during times of great national crisis.

Chapter 1: The First Punic War

8. Michael Grant, *The Ancient Historians*, (New York, 1970), pp. 144–164.
9. *Ibid.*, pp. 217–242.
10. J. F. Lazenby, *The First Punic War: A Military History*, (Stanford, 1996), p. 26.
11. Polybius, *The Rise of the Roman Empire*, I.33. See Richard A. Gabriel and Donald W. Boose Jr, *The Great Battles of Antiquity: A Strategic and Tactical Guide to the Great Battles that Shaped the Development of War*, (Westport, 1994), p. 290, for the estimate of 1,500 Carthaginian troops.
12. Lazenby, *The First Punic War*, p. 26.
13. *Ibid.*
14. Mark Healy, *Cannae 216 BC: Hannibal Smashes Rome's Army*, (London, 1994), pp. 26–27. Also see Peter Connolly, *Greece and Rome at War*, (London, 1988), p. 150.
15. Gregory Daly, *Cannae: The Experience of Battle in the Second Punic War* (London, 2002), pp. 55–56.
16. The Roman scutum was oval like the Spanish model, though it was concave, rather than flat.

17. Gabriel and Boose, *The Great Battles of Antiquity*, pp. 290–291.
18. Polybius, III.114.
19. Polybius, III.114. Also see Livy, *The War with Hannibal*, 22.46
20. Gabriel and Boose, *The Great Battles of Antiquity*, p. 291.
21. Daly, *Cannae: The Experience of Battle*, pp. 107–108.
22. Gabriel and Boose, *The Great Battles of Antiquity*, p. 291.
23. Healy, *Cannae 216 BC*, p. 24.
24. *Ibid.* Also see Daly, *Cannae: The Experience of Battle*, p. 100.
25. Daly, *Cannae: The Experience of Battle*, p. 92.
26. Healy, *Cannae 216 BC*, p. 24.
27. John Warry, *Warfare in the Classical World: An Illustrated Encyclopedia of Weapons, Warriors and Warfare in the Ancient Civilizations of Greece and Rome* (New York, 1980), p. 94.
28. Warry, *Warfare in the Classical World*, p. 95.
29. Gabriel and Boose, *The Great Battles of Antiquity*, p. 292.
30. Gabriel and Boose, *The Great Battles of Antiquity*, p. 292.
31. Gabriel and Boose, *The Great Battles of Antiquity*, pp. 291–292.
32. Simon Anglim, Phyllis Jestice, Rob Rice, Scott Rusch, John Serrati, *Fighting Techniques of the Ancient World, 3000BC–AD500: Equipment, Combat Skills and* Tactics (New York, 2002), pp. 140–141.
33. Gabriel and Boose, *The Great Battles of Antiquity*, p. 292.
34. Lawrence Keppie, *The Making of the Roman Army from Republic to Empire* (New York: Barnes and Noble Books, 1984), p. 14.
35. *Ibid.*, pp. 14–15. For an outstanding study of the history of Roman cavalry from its origins through the Imperial period, see Karen R. Dixon and Pat Southern's *The Roman Cavalry* (London, 1997).
36. Chester G. Starr, *The Emergence of Rome*, 2nd ed., (Westport, CT, 1982), pp. 9–10.
37. Peter Connolly, *Greece and Rome at War*, p. 95. Also see Connolly's chapter 'The Early Roman Army' in *Warfare in the Ancient World*, ed. John Hackett, (New York, 1989), p. 36.
38. Connolly, *Greece and Rome at War*, p. 95.
39. *Ibid.*, p. 95.
40. Peter Connolly, 'The Early Roman Army', p. 136; John Warry, *Warfare in the Classical World*, p. 109.
41. Connolly, 'The Early Roman Army', p. 136.
42. H. M. D. Parker, *The Roman Legions* (Cambridge, 1958; reprint, New York, 1992), p. 10.
43. Warry, *Warfare in the Classical World*, pp. 109–111; Connolly, 'The Early Roman Army', p. 136.
44. Robert L. O'Connell, *Of Arms and Men: A History of War, Weapons and Aggression*, (New York, 1989), p. 74.
45. Michael Grant, *The Army of the Caesars*, (New York, 1974), p. xxx.

46. Warry, *Warfare in the Classical World*, p. 109.
47. *Ibid.*, p. 113; Connolly, *Greece and Rome at War*, pp. 220–221; Parker, *The Roman Legions*, pp. 199–205.
48. Robert L. O'Connell, 'The Roman Killing Machine', *Military History Quarterly*, Vol. 1, Num. 1, (1988), p. 38.
49. Connolly, 'The Early Roman Army', p. 138.
50. Parker, *The Roman Legions*, 11.
51. Adrian Goldsworthy, *The Complete Roman Army*, (London, 2003), pp. 26–27. Also see Warry, *Warfare in the Classical World*, pp. 112.
52. Goldsworthy, *The Complete Roman Army*, pp. 27. Also see Karen R. Dixon and Pat Southern's *The Roman Cavalry*, pp. 23–25.
53. Warry, *Warfare in the Classical World*, p. 112.
54. Antonio Santosuosso, *Soldiers, Citizens and the Symbols of War From Classical Greece to Republican Rome, 500–167 BC* (Boulder, 1997), p. 157.
55. For excellent illustrated accounts of the organizational changes associated with the reforms of Camillus see the diagrams in Warry, *Warfare in the Classical World*, pp. 110–113; Connolly, *Greece and Rome at War*, pp. 126–128; and Goldsworthy, *The Complete Roman Army*, pp. 26–27.
56. Goldsworthy, *The Complete Roman Army*, p. 27.
57. *Ibid.*
58. See Adrian Goldsworthy's thoughtful defence of the *quincunx* formation in his *Roman Warfare* (London, 2002), pp. 55–60. Goldsworthy maintains the Romans fought in this checkerboard formation because 'the maniples of the line behind covered the intervals in front'.
59. Many scholars believe that the distance between maniples was equal to the frontage of the maniple itself (Keppie, *The Making of the Roman Army*, pp. 33–40; Connolly, *Greece and Rome at War*, p. 128), but Livy states that the maniples were 'a small distance apart' (Livy, *Ab Urbe Condita*, VIII.8.5, (Loeb Classical Library. Cambridge: Harvard University Press, 1919).
60. F. E. Adcock, *The Roman Art of War Under the Republic*, (New York: Barnes and Noble, 1960), 8–13; Gabriel and Metz, *From Sumer to Rome: The Military Capabilities of Ancient Armies* (Westport, CT, 1991), pp. 34–35. For an excellent illustration of these manoeuvres, please see Anglim et al, *Fighting Techniques of the Ancient World*, p. 52.
61. Polybius, 15.15.
62. Warry, *Warfare in the Classical World*, p. 111.
63. Gabriel and Metz, *From Sumer to Rome*, p. 65.
64. Archer Jones, *The Art of War in the Western World* (Urbana, 1986), p. 27.
65. Gabriel and Metz, *From Sumer to Rome*, pp. 34–35. Vegetius tells us that Roman recruits trained both morning and afternoon against wooden posts with shields and swords twice the weight of normal *scuta* and *gladii* in order to build strength and endurance (from Roy Davies, *Service in the Roman Army* (New York, 1989), pp. 77–78).

66. Gabriel and Boose, *The Great Battles of Antiquity,* p. 296.
67. Warry, *Warfare in the Classical World,* pp. 100–108. For a concise treatment of the Tarentine and Punic Wars see John Boardman, Jasper Griffin and Oswyn Murray, *The Roman World: The Oxford History of the Classical World* (New York, 1988), pp. 26–33.
68. Many of these Mamertines once served as mercenaries for the Syracusan tyrant Agathocles.
69. Lazenby, *The First Punic War,* p. 48. Two third century BCE Roman legions plus cavalry amounted to 9,000 men, and there would most likely have been an equal number of auxiliaries.
70. Paul Bentley Kern, *Ancient Siege Warfare* (Bloomington, 1999), p. 256.
71. Polybius, I.20. There is some confusion about when and where this ship ran aground, but Polybius clearly states that one ship was used as a template. The name *quinquereme* probably refers to the five files of rowers from stem to stern, and not the number of banks of rowers.
72. Chester G. Starr, *The Influence of Sea Power on Ancient* History, (Oxford, 1989), pp. 55–56.
73. Polybius, I.21.
74. Starr, *The Influence of Sea Power on Ancient* History, p. 56. Also see Lazenby's *The First Punic War,* pp. 68–72 for a thoughtful discussion on the various theories on the construction of the *corvus* and how it was employed.
75. Polybius, I.26.
76. See John Warry's *Warfare in the Classical World,* pp. 30–31, for an outstanding illustration of various naval tactics utilized by classical navies.
77. Polybius I.23.
78. *Ibid.* Also Lazenby, *The First Punic War,* pp. 71–72. Lazenby puts forth the idea that Polybius' fifty ships may be a rounded figure. Other secondary Roman sources put the number of ships lost closer to forty-five.
79. Polybius, I.26.
80. *Ibid.,* I.32.
81. *Ibid.*
82. *Ibid.,* I.33. Please see both Goldsworthy, *The Punic Wars,* pp. 88–91, and Lazenby, *The First Punic War,* pp. 102–106, for modern reconstructions of the Battle of Adys.
83. Polybius, I.33.
84. *Ibid.*
85. *Ibid.,* I.34.
86. *Ibid.,* I.37. See chapter seven of Lazenby, *The First Punic War* for a detailed discussion on the size of the Roman fleet.
87. Lazenby, *The First Punic War,* p. 110.
88. *Ibid.,* p. 21.
89. Polybius, I.64.

90. *Ibid.*, I.59.
91. Goldsworthy, *The Punic Wars*, pp. 123–124. Polybius gives the number of ships at 200 (I.59), while Diodorus (XXIV.11) gives the number at 300 warships and 700 transports.
92. Goldsworthy, *The Punic Wars*, p. 124.
93. Please see Goldsworthy's discussion of the figures given by both Polybius and Diodorus on the number of ships present at Aegates Islands and the casualty figures in *The Punic Wars*, pp. 124–125.
94. *Ibid.*, p. 126.
95. *Ibid.*, p. 128.
96. *Ibid.*, p. 126.
97. Polybius called this conflict the 'Libyan War' (I.70) because of the central role the Liby-Phoenicians played in the revolt. See Goldsworthy, *The Punic Wars*, pp. 133–136; and Lazenby, *The First Punic War*, pp. 173–175, for more on the origins, course and outcome of the Mercenary War.
98. Polybius, III.10.
99. There is a controversy concerning whether Hamilcar was chosen by the legislative body for this assignment, or by the suffetes. For more on this controversy see Goldsworthy's *Punic Wars*, pp. 136–138.
100. *Ibid.*, p. 137.

Chapter 2: The Early Campaigns of Hannibal
101. Ernle Bradford, *Hannibal*, (New York, 1981), p. 32.
102. Healy, *Cannae 216 BC*, p. 6.
103. Polybius, III.11. Polybius refers to the chief god of the Carthaginian pantheon as Zeus, though it was most probably the god Ba'al Hammon.
104. *Ibid.*, III.13.
105. Soren, Khader, Slim, *Carthage*, p. 103.
106. Daly, *Cannae: The Experience of Battle*, p. 10.
107. Livy, XXI.7.
108. Paul Bentley Kern, *Ancient Siege Warfare* (Bloomington, 1999), p. 272.
109. Livy, XXI.7. Also see Polybius, III.40 and III.41 as well as Livy, XXI.17. The Roman strategy is also discussed by F. E. Adcock, *The Roman Art of War Under the Republic* (New York, 1940), 7p. 9.
110. Livy, XXI.17.
111. Adcock, p. 79.
112. Polybius, VII.9.
113. Daly, *Cannae: The Experience of Battle*, pp. 10–11.
114. Livy, XXXIV.60.
115. Healy, *Cannae 216 BC*, p. 12.
116. N. B. Rankov, 'The Second Punic War at Sea' in T. J. Cornell, N. B. Rankov and P. Sabin, eds, *The Second Punic War: A Reappraisal*

(London, 1996), p. 53. Also see Lazenby, *Hannibal's War: A Military History of the Second Punic War* (Norman, 1998), p. 31, for a detailed discussion on Roman sea power at the beginning of the Second Punic War.

117. Thomas A. Dorey and Donald R. Dudley, *Rome Against Carthage* (London, 1971), pp. 29–30.
118. Livy, XXI.23; Polybius, III.35.
119. Polybius, III.35.
120. Polybius believed the Spanish troops were dismissed as a conciliatory measure (III.35), while Livy maintains that 3,000 deserted and Hannibal released another 7,000 to shed unreliable troops and cover up the desertions (XXI.23).
121. Polybius, III.38.
122. Healy, *Cannae 216 BC*, p. 13.
123. Polybius, III.41. See Lazenby, *Hannibal's War*, pp. 34–40, for a spirited discussion of how and where Hannibal crossed the Rhone. Also see Healy, *Cannae 216* BC, p. 13.
124. Lazenby, *Hannibal's War*, p. 34.
125. *Ibid.*, p. 36.
126. Polybius, III.44.
127. Livy's translation taken from Lazenby, *Hannibal's* War, p. 37.
128. Goldsworthy, *The Punic Wars*, pp. 161–162.
129. Polybius, III.45.
130. Livy, XXI.34.
131. Polybius, III.53.
132. Livy, XXI.34.
133. *Ibid.*
134. Polybius, III.54.
135. *Ibid.*
136. Polybius states that it took Hannibal fifteen days to cross the Alps (III.56). There is a great deal of speculation concerning whether a fifteen-day march across the Alps is possible. Lazenby, *Hannibal's War*, chapter 2, reconstructs the march in great detail and comes up with a twenty-four day crossing, nine for the ascent and fifteen for the descent.
137. Polybius, III.56.
138. Lazenby, *Hannibal's War*, p. 48.
139. Goldsworthy, *The Punic Wars*, p. 168.
140. *Ibid.*
141. Livy, XXI.51.
142. Goldsworthy, *The Punic Wars*, p. 168.
143. For an outstanding reconstruction of the Battle of the Ticinus, see Goldsworthy, *The Punic Wars*, pp. 169–173.
144. Polybius, III.66.

145. Under normal circumstances, a consul would have at his disposal two legions made up of 16,000–20,000 infantry and from 1,500 to 2,500 cavalry. About half of the infantry and one-quarter of the cavalry were made up of Roman citizens, with the rest drawn from Roman allies or auxiliaries. After their election the consuls appointed twenty-four military tribunes, ten of which were senior tribunes with at least ten years of service, while the remainder required only five years of service. But during the manpower shortages of the Second Punic War, tribunes often were placed with less experience. Connolly, *Greece and Rome at War*, p. 129.
146. Polybius, III.69.
147. *Ibid.*
148. *Ibid.*, III.72.
149. *Ibid.*
150. *Ibid.*
151. *Ibid.*, III.73.
152. Livy, XXI.56.
153. Healy, *Cannae 216 BC*, p. 51.
154. Polybius, III.74.
155. Polybius, III.77.
156. Lazenby, *Hannibal's War*, pp. 60–61.   Also see Daly, *Cannae: The Experience of Battle*, p. 15 and Connolly, *Greece and Rome at War*, p. 172.
157. Polybius, III.79 and Livy, XXII.2.
158. Healy, *Cannae 216 BC*, p. 57.
159. Lazenby, *Hannibal's War*, p. 63. Lazenby believes that Hannibal peeled off some elements of his army as they marched in the valley along the coast of Lake Trasimene before setting up the remainder of the ambush that evening.
160. Polybius, III.84.
161. See Lazenby, *Hannibal's War*, pp. 62–66, for a detailed reconstruction of the Battle of Lake Trasimene.
162. Polybius, III.84.
163. *Ibid.*
164. Livy, XXII.6.
165. Polybius, III.84.
166. *Ibid.*, III.85.
167. *Ibid.*, III.86.
168. *Ibid.*
169. Jones, *The Art of War in the Western World*, pp. 65–68. Jones describes the anatomy of the original Fabian strategy and the difficulty faced by the Carthaginian army while operating in Italy.
170. *Ibid.*, p. 67.
171. *Ibid.*

172. Polybius, III.114. There are many fine monographs which concentrate on the battle of Cannae available in print. Please see Healy, *Cannae 216 BC: Hannibal Smashes Rome's Army* (London, 1994), Gregory Daly, *Cannae: The Experience of Battle in the Second Punic War* (London, 2002), and Adrian Goldsworthy, *Cannae* (London, 2001).

173. Victor Davis Hanson, *Carnage and Culture: Landmark Battles in the Rise of Western Power* (New York: Doubleday, 2001), p. 107. Hanson notes that the depth of the Roman infantry formation was the deepest since the Theban victory over the Spartans at Leuctra in 371 BCE.

174. *Ibid.*, p. 108.

175. Polybius, III.115.

176. Polybius, III.117.

177. Lazenby, *Hannibal's War*, p. 85.

178. Connolly, 'The Roman Army in the Age of Polybius', in John Hackett, ed, *Warfare in the Ancient World* (New York: Facts On File, 1989), p. 163. The 'tumbling effect' was coined by the military historian John Keegan.

179. Polybius, III.117. Livy XXII.52.

180. Livy, XXIII.12.

181. Livy, XXII.51.

182. *Ibid.*

183. For a detailed explanation of the problems facing Hannibal had he besieged and invested Rome, please see B. S. Strauss and J. Ober, *The Anatomy of Error: Ancient Military Disasters and their Lessons for Modern Strategists* (New York, 1992), pp. 54–155.

184. Healy, *Cannae 216 BC*, p. 86.

185. J. F. Shean, 'Hannibal's Mules: The Logistical Limitations of Hannibal's Army and the Battle of Cannae, 216 BC', *Historia*, 45.2, pp. 175–185. Also see Jones, *Art of War in the Western World*, p. 68. Also see Duncan B. Campbell's excellent treatment of siege warfare during the Punic wars in his *Besieged: Siege Warfare in the Ancient World* (Oxford, 2006).

186. Hanson, *Carnage and Culture*, p. 110.

187. Livy, XXII. 58–59.

188. Livy, XXII. 58.

189. J. F. C. Fuller, *A Military History of the Western World, Volume I, From the Earliest Times to the Battle of Lepanto* (New York, 1954), pp. 128–129.

190. Livy, XXIII.13. Livy states that when Mago returned to Carthage in 216 to report on his brother's progress, the Carthaginian government unanimously agreed to send Hannibal 4,000 Numidian cavalry and forty elephants from North Africa and 20,000 infantry from Spain to help with his Italian campaign. But most of these troops were never sent.

191. Lazenby, *Hannibal's War*, p. 44.

192. Livy, XXVII.9.

Chapter 3: The Early Campaigns of Scipio

193. Livy, XXI.46.
194. Livy, XXII.54.
195. Livy, XXII.53.
196. Goldsworthy, *The Punic Wars*, p. 224.
197. *Ibid.*, p. 225.
198. Lazenby, *Hannibal's War*, p. 95.
199. P. Brunt, *Italian Manpower*, (Oxford, 1971), pp. 416–422. Also see Goldsworthy, *The Punic Wars*, pp. 226–227.
200. Lazenby, *Hannibal's War*, pp. 9–10, 234.
201. Livy, XXII.22.
202. There is great debate concerning whether the deaths of Gnaeus and Publius happened in 212 or 211. Livy states 212 but most modern historians believe it took place in 211.
203. Livy, XXV.32.
204. Livy, XXVI.18.
205. *Ibid.*
206. Livy, XXVI.19.
207. Bradford, *Hannibal*, pp. 158–159.
208. Polybius, X.9.
209. Livy, XXVI.43.
210. Polybius, X.12.
211. Polybius, X.13.
212. Polybius, X.15.
213. Polybius, X.16.
214. G. Veith and J. Kromayer, *Heerwesen und Kriegfuhrung der Griechen und Romer* (Munich 1928), p. 325.
215. Livy, XXVII.17.
216. Polybius, X, pp. 34–35.
217. Livy, XXVII.18
218. *Ibid.*
219. Lazenby, *Hannibal's War*, p. 141.
220. Polybius, X.38.
221. Polybius, X.39
222. *Ibid.*
223. Livy, XXVII.20.
224. Lazenby, *Hannibal's War*, p. 143.
225. Livy, XXVIII, p. 1–4.
226. Nigel Bagnall, *The Punic Wars: Rome, Carthage and the Struggle for the Mediterranean*, pp. 233–234.
227. Livy, XXVII.43.
228. Livy, XXVII.45
229. Livy, XXVII.46.

230. *Ibid.*
231. Livy, XXVII.47.
232. Livy, XXVII.48.
233. Lazenby, *Hannibal's War*, p. 190.
234. Polybius, XI.1. Appian maintains that there were fifteen elephants fighting for Hasdrubal at Metaurus (*Hannibalic War*, 52).
235. Livy, XXVII.49.
236. Polybius, XI.2.
237. Livy, XXVII.49. This number seems preposterous, especially since it exceeds the total number of Carthaginian forces at the Battle of Metaurus River.
238. Polybius, XI.3.
239. Livy, XXVII.51.
240. Livy, XXVII.51 and XXVIII.9.
241. Goldsworthy, *The Punic Wars*, pp. 242–243.
242. Livy, XXVII.29.
243. Livy, XXVIII. 28.4.
244. Lazenby, *Hannibal's War,* pp. 144–145.
245. Polybius maintains that the Carthaginians had 70,000 infantry and 4,000 cavalry at Ilipa (XI.20), while Livy believes 50,000 infantry and 4,500 cavalry were present (XXVIII.12).
246. Goldsworthy, *The Punic Wars*, p. 279.
247. Polybius, XI.21 and Livy, XXVIII.13.
248. Livy, XXVIII.14.
249. Livy, XXVIII, 15.
250. *Ibid.*
251. Goldsworthy, *The Punic Wars*, p. 283.
252. Lazenby, *Hannibal's War*, p. 50.
253. Goldsworthy, *The Punic Wars*, p. 284.
254. Livy, XXVIII.17.
255. Goldsworthy, *The Punic Wars,* pp. 286–287,
256. *Ibid.*, p. 286.
257. Livy, XXVIII.45.
258. *Ibid.*
259. Lazenby, *Hannibal's War*, p. 195.
260. Livy, XXVIII.46.
261. Goldsworthy, *The Punic Wars*, p. 287.
262. *Ibid.* Also see Lazenby, *Hannibal's War*, p. 203, for a discussion of what Scipio's troop strength was for the African landings.
263. Livy, XXIX.3.
264. Goldsworthy, *The Punic War*, p. 288.
265. *Ibid.*

266. For a detailed account of the Locrian affair and its repercussions in Rome see Livy, chapter XXIX.
267. Livy, XXIX.22.

Chapter 4: The African Landings and the Battle of Zama
268. Livy, XXIX.25.
269. See Lazenby, *Hannibal's War*, for a discussion on the Roman warship strength and theories on why the fleet was so small (pp. 203–204).
270. Livy, XXIX.25.
271. Livy, XXIX.28.
272. Livy XXIX.29
273. Livy XXIX.34. The site of the battle has been identified as being south of the saddle joining the hills southwest of Utica, now called Djebel Menzel Roul, to the Djebel Doumis.
274. Caesar, *Civil Wars*, II.24.
275. Polybius, XIV.1 and Livy, XXIX.35.
276. Livy, XXX.1.
277. Polybius, XIV.2.
278. *Ibid.*
279. Polybius, XIV.4.
280. Polybius, XIV.6. The casualty numbers given by Livy (XXX.6) are farcical (40,000 dead and 5,000 taken prisoner), as are those given by Appian (*Libyca*, 23), who states 30,000 were killed and 2,400 taken prisoner.
281. Polybius, XIV.5.
282. Polybius, XIV.6.
283. Polybius, XIV.2.
284. Polybius, XIV.7.
285. Lazenby, *Hannibal's War*, p. 209.
286. See Polybius, XIV.8 and Livy, XXX.5 for accounts of the Battle of the Great Plains.
287. Lazenby, *Hannibal's War*, p. 210.
288. Polybius, XIV.8.
289. See Lazenby, *Hannibal's War*, p. 210, for a detailed and entertaining discussion of the possible tactical arrays used by the Punic and Roman forces at the Battle of the Great Plains.
290. Goldsworthy, *The Punic Wars*, pp. 295–296.
291. Polybius, XIV.9.
292. Polybius, XIV.9 and Livy, XXX.9.
293. Polybius, XIV.11 and Livy, XXX.10.
294. Livy, XXX.10.
295. Polybius, XIV.11 and Livy, XXX.10. Also see Lazenby, *Hannibal's War*, pp. 209–211.

296. Livy, XXX.11.
297. Livy, XXX.15.
298. Livy, XXX.17.
299. Polybius, XV.1.
300. Livy, XXX.16.
301. *Ibid.*
302. Appian, *Libyca*, 32.
303. Here, Livy and Polybius differ in their interpretation of events. Polybius states that the treaty was ratified by the Roman Senate, while Livy maintains that the treaty disintegrated when the Carthaginian delegation attempted to alter the agreement. The Punic ambassadors were expelled and Scipio given the authority to negotiate new terms or renew hostilities. Please see Livy XXX.17 and Polybius, XV.1 for differing interpretations of what happened to the Punic delegation to the Roman Senate.
304. Livy, XXX.16.
305. Livy, XXIX.36–38.
306. Lazenby, *Hannibal's War*, p. 215. Professor Lazenby makes the point that Hannibal's strategic position was eroding in southern Italy.
307. Livy, XXX.18.
308. Livy, XXX.19.
309. Lazenby, *Hannibal's War*, p. 215.
310. Livy, XXX.20.
311. Appian, *Hannibalic War*, pp. 58–59.
312. Livy, XXX.24.
313. Livy, XXX.25 and Polybius, XV.1.
314. Livy, XXX.27.
315. Polybius, XV.3. Hannibal had abandoned most of his best horses when he left Italy.
316. Polybius, XV.5.
317. Lazenby, *Hannibal's War*, p. 218.
318. *Ibid.*, pp. 218–219.
319. Livy, XXX.29.
320. Livy, XXX.29. Polybius, XV.5.
321. Livy, XXX.29.
322. *Ibid.*
323. Livy, XXX.30.
324. Polybius, XV.6.
325. Polybius, XV.8.
326. Lazenby, *Hannibal's War*, pp. 218–219. See Lazenby for a very detailed discussion of the possible locations of the Battle of Zama.
327. *Ibid.*
328. Polybius, XV.11.
329. *Ibid.*, XV.3.

330. Appian, *Libyca*, 40.
331. *Ibid.*, 41.
332. Please see Lazenby, *Hannibal's War*, pp. 218–219, for a very thoughtful discussion on the troop strength controversy for the Battle of Zama.
333. Polybius, XV.9.
334. Goldsworthy, *The Punic Wars*, p. 302. Also see Lazenby, *Hannibal's War*, p. 222.
335. Polybius, XV.11 and Appian, *Libyca*, p. 40.
336. Lazenby, *Hannibal's War*, p. 222.
337. Livy, XXX.23.
338. Polybius, XV.11.
339. Goldsworthy, *The Punic Wars*, 303.
340. *Ibid.*
341. *Ibid.*
342. Polybius, XV.10.
343. Polybius, XV.11.
344. *Ibid.*
345. Polybius XV.12. It makes the most tactical sense to send the first and second lines immediately after the elephant charge to take advantage of the chaos the pachyderms created.
346. Lazenby, *Hannibal's War*, p. 223.
347. Livy, XXX.34.
348. *Ibid.*
349. Polybius, XV.13.
350. *Ibid.*
351. *Ibid.*
352. Lazenby, *Hannibal's War*, pp. 223–224.
353. Polybius, XV.13.
354. Polybius, XV.14.
355. *Ibid.*
356. *Ibid.* In fact, many of the weapons used by Hannibal's veterans were taken from fallen Roman legionaries in past battles.
357. *Ibid.*
358. Appian, *Libyca*, 41.
359. Livy, XXX.35.
360. Polybius, XV.14.
361. Polybius, XV.16.
362. Polybius, III.40.
363. Livy, XXXV.14. This translation comes from Adrian Goldsworthy's *In the Name of Rome: The Men Who Won the Roman Empire* (London, 2003), p. 77.
364. Livy, XXX.35.
365. Livy, XXX.36.
366. *Ibid.*

367. *Ibid.*
368. Livy, XXX.40. In fact, one of the two consuls of 201 tried to replace Scipio, only to be stopped by a timely intervention by well-placed tribunes in the Roman Assembly and further debate in the Roman Senate.
369. Polybius, XV.18. Also see Livy, XXX.37.
370. Livy, XXX.37.
371. *Ibid.*, XXX.43. Livy's sources state that these 500 ships consisted of all oared vessels of all types and sizes.
372. *Ibid.* By Latins Livy probably meant members of the Roman confederation who deserted to the Punic cause.
373. The historian Appian makes the claim that Rome forced Carthage to accept a subordinate position equivalent to how Rome treated its Italian subjects in the Roman confederation (*Punic Wars*, 54).
374. Livy, XXXIV.60.

Chapter 5: In Zama's Wake and the Third Punic War
375. Livy, XXXIII.4.
376. Livy, XXXIX.51.
377. Livy, XXX.45.
378. *Ibid.* Livy remarks that he was unable to discern who first conferred the name 'Africanus' upon Scipio.
379. Goldsworthy, *In the Name of Rome*, p. 85.
380. *Ibid.*, p. 29.
381. Plutarch, *Cato the Elder*, 27.
382. *Ibid.*
383. Goldsworthy, *The Punic Wars*, p. 336.
384. Appian, *The Punic Wars*, 80. These numbers are exceptionally large, and it is possible that the Romans exaggerated the number of panoplies and siege equipment turned over by the Carthaginians.
385. *Ibid.*, 75.
386. For an outstanding description of the siege of Carthage during the Third Punic War, see the beginning of chapter twelve of Paul Bentley Kern's *Ancient Siege Warfare* (Bloomington, 1999).
387. Appian, *The Punic Wars*, 95.
388. *Ibid.*, 97.
389. *Ibid.*
390. *Ibid.*, 98.
391. Ibid.
392. Goldsworthy, *The Punic Wars*, p. 343. Please see Goldsworthy's chapter 15 for a detailed discussion on the origins and course of the Third Punic War.
393. *Ibid.*
394. Appian, *The Punic Wars*, 99.

395. *Ibid.*
396. *Ibid.*, 101.
397. *Ibid.*, 103.
398. *Ibid.*
399. *Ibid.*, 108.
400. *Ibid.*, 109.
401. *Ibid.*, 112–113.
402. *Ibid.*, 114.
403. *Ibid.*, 116–117.
404. *Ibid.*, 117.
405. *Ibid.*
406. *Ibid.*, 118.
407. *Ibid.*, 119.
408. *Ibid.*, 120.
409. *Ibid.*, 121.
410. *Ibid.*, 122.
411. *Ibid.*, 122–123.
412. *Ibid.*, 124.
413. *Ibid.*, 125.
414. *Ibid.*, 126.
415. *Ibid.*, 127.
416. *Ibid.*
417. Appian describes three boulevards sloping up from the captured Agora to the Byrsa, each flanked by tall buildings, some as high as six stories. Carthage, as a Hellenistic city, was built on a rectangular grid pattern, with each building often possessing a central courtyard and garden. The main streets were twenty-one feet wide, while side streets were narrow, averaging only sixteen feet in width (Appian, 128). For more details on the archaeology of this area of ancient Carthage, see Serge Lancel, *Carthage* (Oxford, 1995), pp. 156–172, 425–426.
418. Appian, pp. 128–129. This translation was taken from Nigel Bagnall's *The Punic Wars, Rome, Carthage, and the Struggle for the Mediterranean*, p. 319.
419. *Ibid.*, pp. 128–130.
420. Goldsworthy, *The Punic Wars*, p. 357.
421. Polybius, I.10.
422. Goldsworthy, *The Punic Wars*, p. 359.
423. For a detailed study on the development of Roman logistics during the republic and imperial periods, see J. Roth, *The Logistics of the Roman Army at War, 264 BC-AD 235* (Leiden, 1999).

Glossary of Important Personalities

Agathocles: Tyrant of Syracuse and later king of Sicily. The son of a potter, Agathocles joined the military and rose through the ranks, seizing control of Syracuse from a ruling oligarchy in 317. He expanded his control over most of the island, initiating a war with Carthage in 311. He eventually settled with Carthage and declared himself king in 304, reigning until his death in 289.

Andriscus: Pretender to the Macedonian throne. After the disbanding of the kingdom of Macedon by the Romans into four republics at the end of the Third Macedonian War in 168, the pretender Andriscus reunited Macedon and defeated a Roman army dispatched to put down the rebellion, initiating the fourth and final Macedonian War in 149. The Roman general Quintus Caecilius Metellus finally chased him from the country. Rome annexed Greece in 146.

Antiochus III ('the Great'): Seleucid king of Syria. Antiochus' campaigns in the Near East earned him the epitaph 'the Great', although he was never able to consolidate these gains. He attempted to fill the vacuum created with the defeat of Philip V in the Second Macedonian War by expanding in the eastern Mediterranean. His actions drew him into a conflict with Rome. The resulting Syrian War forced him to evacuate Asia Minor.

Attalus I: King of the Anatolian kingdom of Pergamum. Attalus secured his position by defeating a Celtic tribe known as the Galatians in the 230s. His opposition to Philip V of Macedon's ambitions made him a natural ally for Rome in the region, though he died shortly before Philip's defeat at Cynoscephalae in 197.

Cato, Marcus Porcius ('the Elder'): Roman consul (195/194) and politician. Cato was a keen politician who attracted broad support in the Senate due to his unwavering integrity and traditional attitudes. Cato's antagonistic relationship with other powerful Romans (Scipio Africanus and Flamininus) solidified his conservative base. For decades he advocated the destruction of Carthage, ending his speeches with the statement 'and Carthage must be destroyed'. His stance became Roman policy with the outbreak of the Third Punic War in 149.

Censorinus, Lucius Marcius: Roman consul (149/148) and general during the Third Punic War. Dispatched along with Manius Manilius to North Africa to initiate hostilities against Carthage, Censorinus was unable to take the city quickly by storm, and the war bogged down into a three year siege.

Camillus, Marcus Furius: Roman dictator (396, 390, 389, 368, 367), general and statesman. Camillus captured the Etruscan city of Veii in 396 after a ten-year siege. He was exiled, but was recalled to Rome after the Gauls sacked the city in 390. He is credited with reforming the Roman army, transforming it from the Greek-styled phalanx-based army into a more flexible, linear system.

Fabius, Quintus (later 'Maximus'): Roman consul (233/232, 228/227, 215/214, 214/213, 209/208), dictator (217) and general. Hannibal's defeat of three Roman armies in two years (Ticinus in 218, Trebia in 218 and Lake Trasimene in 217) caused the Senate to elect Fabius as dictator, and he instituted a policy of harassment rather than pitched battle, earning him the nickname 'Cunctator'or 'the delayer'. His actions helped Rome recover after three battlefield defeats, though he was not popular for his decision. Rome returned to an offensive strategy in 216, but the debacle at Cannae vindicated Fabius' policy, and he was re-elected as consul. By 206 his strategy was considered overly cautious, and despite leading the opposition to Scipio Africanus' plan to invade North Africa, the Senate backed Scipio. He died in 203 before the successful conclusion of the Second Punic War.

Flaminius, Gaius: Roman consul (217/216) and general. Elected as consul in 217, Flaminius brought a Roman army north to meet and defeat Hannibal Barca, but was sucked into an ambush at Lake Trasimene and killed. This Roman defeat opened the way for Hannibal to push southward past Rome and deep into Italy.

Flamininus, Titus Quinctius: Roman consul (198/197) and general during the Second Macedonian War. Elected consul at 30 years of age and sent by the Roman Senate to stop Philip V of Macedon's incursions into Greece, Flamininus defeated the Macedonian king at Cynoscephalae in 197, then championed limited Greek autonomy. He would use his considerable diplomatic skills to keep Greece under Roman suzerainty.

Hamilcar Barca: Carthaginian general and father of Hannibal, Hasdrubal and Mago Barca. A leading military figure in Carthage, Hamilcar commanded Punic forces in the final stages of the First Punic War and suppressed the mutinous mercenaries in the Mercenary War. He was also responsible for building up Carthage's power base in Spain before his death on campaign there in 229.

Hannibal Barca: Carthaginian general and son of Hamilcar Barca. Roman sources indicate a life-long hatred of Rome, inculcated by his father. Born in Carthage but raised on the Spanish frontier, Hannibal showed great military acumen early on. After securing his Spanish base, Hannibal took the Second Punic War to Italian soil, crossing the Alps in 218 BCE and defeating the Romans at Ticinus (218), Trebia (218), Trasimene (217) and Cannae (216). Unable to unravel the Roman Confederation, he spent the next thirteen years fighting in Italy until being called back to defend Carthage from Roman attack in 203. He was defeated at Zama in 202 by Scipio Africanus. He spent the remainder of his life in exile, serving Hellenistic kings (Antiochus III of Syria and Prusias of Bithynia) in the eastern Mediterranean until his suicide in Bithynia in 183. Hannibal is considered a tactical and strategic genius and one of the greatest military minds in history.

Hasbrubal Barca: Carthaginian general and younger brother of Hannibal Barca. Hasdrubal was left in command of the Punic empire in Spain at the beginning of the Second Punic War. He defeated Publius Cornelius and Gnaeus Cornelius Scipio in 211 at the battle of the Upper Baetis. He led a Punic relief army into Italy to assist his brother Hannibal, but was defeated and killed by Gaius Claudius Nero's Roman forces at the Metaurus River in 207.

Hasdrubal Gisgo: Carthaginian general in Italy, Spain and North Africa during the Second Punic War. Gisgo fought alongside Hannibal at Cannae in 216, then returned to Spain, where, along with Hasdrubal and Mago Barca, he was responsible for expanding Punic control in Iberia and fought in most of the major campaigns. After Scipio Africanus' victory at Ilipa (207), he returned to North Africa and married the Numidian king Syphax's daughter. He was defeated at the Battle of the Great Plains in 203.

Hasdrubal (Third Punic War): Carthaginian general and leader of Carthage during the Third Punic War. Hasdrubal initially commanded the field army which threatened the Roman siege, and then took over command of Carthage itself in the last two years of the siege (148–146). Although he offered a spirited defence of the city, his efforts ultimately failed and Carthage was seized and razed in 146.

Himilco Phameas: Carthaginian commander during Third Punic War. Himilco was very active in the defence of Carthage during the first phase of the war, but defected to the Roman side in 148, accompanying Publius Cornelius Aemilianus Scipio to Rome and receiving gifts from the Senate.

Indibilis: Chief of the Ilergetes tribe in southeastern Spain. Indibilis was an ally of Carthage in the wars against Rome in Iberia during the Second Punic

War, participating in the defeat of Scipio the Elder near the city of Castulo in 211. He organized a tribal rebellion after the Roman victory at Ilipa in 207, but his efforts were crushed.

Laelius, Gaius: Roman consul (190/189) and distinguished cavalry and naval commander during the Second Punic War. Laelius served with Scipio Africanus in his Spanish campaign (210–206) and was an important commander at Baecula (208) and Ilipa (206). He raided the coast of North Africa in 205, and then joined Scipio in North Africa where he participated in the battles of the Great Plains (203) and Zama (202).

Laelius, Gaius: Roman commander during the Third Punic War. The son of the vaunted commander of the Second Punic War by the same name, Laelius served Scipio Aemilianus Africanus as a faithful and competent commander in the final year (146) of the siege of Carthage, leading the breach of the harbour which sealed the city's fate.

Laevinus, Marcus Valerius: Roman consul (210/209) and general during the Second Punic War and First Macedonian War. Laevinus was active in the Adriatic against Philip V of Macedon. As commander of the Roman fleet based out of Sicily, he raided the North African coast and defeated the Carthaginian navy at the Battle of Clupea in 208.

Mago Barca: Carthaginian general and younger brother of Hannibal and Hasdrubal Barca. With brother Hasdrubal and Hasdrubal Gisgo, he defended Punic interests in Spain in the Second Punic War. He led a relief army to Italy in 205, but was pinned down near Genua for two years before he was defeated and probably killed by the Romans. His army returned to North Africa and participated in the Battle of Zama.

Maharbal: Senior Numidian cavalry commander who fought with Hannibal Barca in the Second Punic War. Maharbal crossed the Alps with Hannibal in 218 and fought at the battles of Lake Trasimene in 217 and Cannae in 216.

Mancinus, Lucius: Roman general during the Third Punic War. As commander of the Roman navy besieging Carthage in early 147, Mancinus showed great ingenuity, capturing a small corner of the city before being forced out of the city.

Manilius, Manius: Roman consul (149/148) and general during the Third Punic War. Dispatched along with Lucius Marcius Censorinus to North Africa to initiate hostilities against Carthage, Manilius was unable to take the city quickly through storm, and the war bogged down into a three year siege.

Masinissa: Numidian cavalry commander and eventual king of Numidia. Masinissa originally served Carthage as a mercenary commander in Spain, but switched his allegiance to Scipio Africanus and Rome in 206. He became

Rome's principal local ally in North Africa between 204 and 202, consolidating his power base and fighting alongside Scipio at the Battle of Zama in 202. After eliminating his rival Syphax, he ruled as a Numidian king and Roman client for the next half century until his death in 148.

Nero, Gaius Claudius: Roman consul (207/206) and general during the Second Punic War. In 210, Nero was sent to Spain as a temporary commander after the deaths of Gnaeus and Publius Scipio. His success there led to an appointment as consul in 207, where he was given southern Italy and Hannibal Barca as his responsibility. After learning that Hasdrubal Barca was bringing a relief army into Italy, Nero divided his army and quietly slipped off from watching Hannibal and marched north to join Salinator's army shadowing Hasdrubal. Nero and the other consul for the year, Marcus Livius Salinator, decisively defeated Hasdrubal's army at Metaurus River in 207, killing the Carthaginian general.

Paullus, Lucius Aemilius: Roman consul (216) and general during the Second Punic War. Paullus was elected as consul (along with Marcus Terentius Varro) to pursue an aggressive military policy against Hannibal Barca, a policy which led to the Roman debacle and his death at Cannae in 216.

Paullus, Lucius Aemilius ('Macedonicus'): Roman consul (182/181, 168/167) and general. Son of the consul killed at Cannae, Paullus was a member of one of the leading families in Rome who made his military career in Spain in the late 190s before being elected as consul in 182. He served as proconsul during the Third Macedonian War, defeating King Perseus of Macedon at Pydna in 168, then taking him back to Rome as part of his triumph.

Perseus: King of Macedonia and eldest son of Philip V. Perseus inherited his father's expansionist policies, eventually precipitating a Third Macedonian War with Rome in 171. Three years later he was defeated at Pydna by Lucius Aemilius Paullus, accompanying the Roman general back to Rome as part of his triumph. He died in captivity in 165.

Philip V: King of Macedonia. Philip entered into an alliance with Carthage against Rome in 215, initiating the First Macedonian War. Unable to make headway against Italy, he turned his attention towards Greece and became a regional hegemon. He was driven out of Illyria by Rome and finally defeated in the Second Macedonian War in 192.

Prusias I: King of Bithynia. Prusias was a shrewd player in Anatolian politics. His alliance with Philip V of Macedon secured his western front, while he fought wars against Attalus I of Pergamum to expand his power on the peninsula. He stayed neutral in the Roman wars against Antiochus III, though his granting of sanctuary to Hannibal Barca complicated his relations with Rome.

Pyrrhus: King of Epirus. After attempts to secure and expand his position in northern Greece, Pyrrhus responded to a plea from Tarentum in *Magna Graecia* for assistance against the Romans. He defeated the Romans in 280 at Heraclea, though his narrow margin of victory at Asculum led to the term 'pyrrhic victory'. The Romans finally defeated him at Beneventum in 275, taking *Magna Graecia* as their prize. He was killed intervening in Argos in 272.

Regulus, Marcus Atilius: Roman consul (257/256, 256/255) and general during the First Punic War. Regulus defeated the Carthaginians in the naval battle of Ecnomus in 256, and then invaded North Africa where he was conquered and captured at the Battle of Tunis in 255 by the Greek mercenary commander Xanthippus.

Salinator, Marcus Livius: Roman consul (219/218, 207/206) and general during the Second Punic War. In 207, Salinator was dispatched to intercept Hasdrubal Barca's relief army. Along with the other consul of the year, Gaius Claudius Nero, he defeated the Carthaginian general at the Metaurus River, ending any real possibility of a new Punic offensive in Italy.

Scipio, Gnaeus Cornelius: Consul (260/259) and general during the First Punic War. In 260, Scipio directed the construction of the first Roman navy (100 quinqueremes and 20 triremes) from the wreckage of ships on the Italian peninsula, teaching them to row on the shore before sending them to sea against the Carthaginians.

Scipio, Gnaeus Cornelius: Roman general, brother of Publius Cornelius Scipio ('the Elder') and uncle of Publius Cornelius Scipio ('the Younger' and 'Africanus'). Scipio was commander of Roman forces in Spain when the Second Punic War began in 218. A year later he was joined by his brother Scipio the Elder, and together beat back Punic influence on the peninsula until both were killed in separate campaigns a month apart in 211.

Scipio, Publius Cornelius Aemilianus ('Africanus'): Roman consul (147/146, 134/133) and general. Related to Lucius Aemilius Paullus and Publius Cornelius Scipio Africanus, Scipio Aemilianus was destined for political preeminence in Rome. In 151, he volunteered to fight in Spain when Roman reverses had severely impacted recruiting, and distinguished himself there and also in North Africa, where his political skills won him respect with Numidian and Carthaginian commanders. When the Third Punic War was bogged down, he was elected as consul and returned to North Africa to end the siege and oversee the destruction of Carthage in 146.

Scipio, Publius Cornelius ('the Elder'): Roman consul (218/217) and general. Father of Publius Cornelius Scipio ('the Younger' and 'Africanus') and brother of Gnaeus Cornelius Scipio. Unable to intercept Hannibal's army on its way from Spain to Italy, Scipio returned to northern Italy, only to be defeated by the Punic general at the Ticinus in 218. A year later he joined his brother Gnaeus in Spain, and together beat back Punic influence on the peninsula until both were killed in separate campaigns in 211 (the Battle of the Upper Baetis).

Scipio, Publius Cornelius ('the Younger' and later 'Africanus'): Roman consul (205/204, 194/193) and general, and son of Scipio the Elder. Scipio Africanus proved to be one of Rome's greatest statesmen during the mid-Republic and the chief architect of Rome's rise to supremacy in the western Mediterranean. After the death of his father and uncle in Spain in 211, he was elected as proconsul to Spain at the unprecedented age of 26. By 206 he had driven the Carthaginians out of Iberia, winning brilliant battles at Baecula (208) and Ilipa (206). In 205 he was elected consul and prepared to bring the war directly to North Africa, landing there in 204. He defeated Syphax and Hasdrubal Gisgo at the Battle of the Great Plains (203) and Hannibal Barca at Zama (202), ending the Second Punic War. He returned to Rome and took the cognomen 'Africanus'. Over the next two decades he was treated as one of Rome's greatest citizens, rising to the censorship and also assisting his brother Lucius Cornelius Scipio as legate in the eastern campaigns against Antiochus III. His political opponents closed ranks against him at the end of his life, and he died in exile in Campania in 184.

Syphax: King of Numidia. Courted by both Rome and Carthage during the Second Punic War, Syphax sided with Carthage late in the conflict. He was defeated at the Battle of the Great Plains in 203 by Scipio Africanus. He was later captured by a rival Numidian prince, Masinissa, ending his reign.

Varro, Marcus Terentius: Roman consul (216/215) and general during the Second Punic War. Varro was elected consul as a *novus homo*, or 'new man', based on dissatisfaction with the dictatorship of Fabius Maximus. He commanded the Roman forces at the defeat at Cannae in 216 and barely escaped with his life.

Xanthippus: Spartan mercenary general in the service of Carthage during the First Punic War. He was a capable and charismatic leader who was hired to defend Carthage against a Roman invasion of North Africa. In 255, he led his army against the Roman consul Marcus Atilius Regulus and defeated him in the closely fought Battle of Tunis.

Glossary of Military Terms

articulation (tactical): A military term describing the offensive capability of troops. Unarticulated troops usually lacked the drill and discipline to march and fight in close order, and therefore usually fought in static, defensive formations. Well-articulated troops were capable of offensive action in close-order combat.

auxiliaries: Non-citizen troops recruited to serve as valuable extra manpower for the Roman army, as well as specialized tactical roles such as cavalry and light infantry. They were organized into *cohorts* and *alae*.

centurion: A professional class of Roman officers who served for long periods of time and provided the backbone of experience for the Roman army. There were sixty centurions per legion and each commanded a *century* of 60–80 men.

century: The basic subunit of the Roman legion, consisting of between 60 and 80 legionaries. The century was commanded by a centurion and was eventually made up of ten *contubernia* (groups of eight men who shared a tent and messed together).

consilium: A Roman war council held by commanding generals or commanders to seek advice from military legates, tribunes and other officers.

corvus: (Latin for 'crow') A raised gangplank in the bow of the ship with a large spike on the underside. The *corvus* was Rome's secret naval weapon in the First Punic War. To overcome their naval inexperience, the Romans dropped the *corvus* on to one of the more-manoeuvrable Carthaginian ships, and the spike held it in place. The Romans could then board the ship and use their superior marines to take the ship. In effect, they turned naval warfare into land warfare.

decimation: A harsh form of Roman capital punishment administered by legionaries against their own soldiers. It was inflicted on those who had given ground without cause in combat or exposed their neighbours to flank attack. The process of decimation took place after the engagement, when a tenth of the offending unit was chosen by lot, then clubbed to death by their own comrades.

decurion: A Roman cavalry officer who commanded a section of ten horsemen known as a *decuria*. Three *decuriae* formed a *turma*, commanded by the senior *decurion*. See *turma*.

equite: A general term for a Roman soldier wealthy enough to equip himself as a cavalryman. *Equites* date back to the Roman regal period

falcata: A curved, single-edged weapon used by Spanish warriors, derived from the Greek *kopis*. This weapon's single edge is on the concave surface of the blade, providing the wielder with a powerful weapon for cut-and-slash attacks.

gladius hispaniensis: A short stabbing sword originally used by the Celtiberians in Spain which became the standard Roman infantry weapon for close-quarter combat during the Second Punic War. Used in conjunction with the large *scutum*, the *gladius* became the standard sidearm for legionaries well into the Imperial period.

hastati: The first line of heavy infantry in the legion of the mid-Republican era, recruited from younger men and armed with two *pila*, *gladius*, and protected by helmet, body armour and a large, oval *scutum* shield. See 'maniple'.

heavy cavalry: Well-armoured horsemen who use shock combat as their primary way of fighting. Heavy cavalry relied on collective effort to be effective, and collective effort required discipline and training.

heavy infantry: Well-armoured foot soldiers who use shock combat as their primary way of fighting. Heavy infantry relied on collective effort to be effective, and collective effort required discipline and training.

legion: Originally a term meaning levy of troops. The legion was the basic battle group of the Roman army made up predominately of citizen infantry. From the 2nd century BCE it numbered ten cohorts, totalling between 4,000 and 5,000 men.

legionary: The name given to a Roman citizen soldier throughout the entire Roman Republican and Imperial periods. Although his equipment and fighting formation changed over this one thousand year period, he remained the backbone of the Roman fighting force.

light cavalry: Lightly-equipped horsemen who use missile combat as their primary way of fighting. These units were less-heavily armoured than their heavy cavalry counterparts and consequently had greater tactical mobility.

light infantry: Lightly-equipped foot soldiers who use missile combat as their primary way of fighting. These lighter units were less-heavily armoured than their heavier counterparts, and consequently had greater tactical mobility.

maniple: The basic fighting formation of the Republican Roman legion until the end of the Second Punic War. Each *maniple* consisted of two centuries of one of the three classes of heavy infantry – *hastati*, *princeps* or *triarii* – and would be deployed in the first, second or third line of battle accordingly. There were thirty maniples per legion.

missile combat: A form of warfare where participants use ranged weapons (slings, bows, javelins, throwing spears) against the enemy. Such combat is usually performed by light troops (infantry and cavalry).

onager: A type of crew-served Roman torsion siege engine which fired a medium calibre stone projectile. Torsion engines derive their power from the twisting of a spring mechanism, generally made from a combination of animal sinew and hair.

optio: The professional Roman officer second in command of a century. The optio was hand-picked by the commanding centurion and stood at the rear of the century to maintain order.

peltast: Light infantry skirmishers and screening troops, originally from Thrace, who fought with javelins or spears and who protected themselves with a small, crescent-shaped shield or *pelta*. The *pelta* was usually made of wicker and covered with goatskin. Peltasts were used by Greek and Carthaginian commanders to harass enemy heavy infantry or provide protection as their own phalanxes deployed.

pilum: Two different kinds of weighted javelin used by Roman legionaries as a missile weapon designed to break-up enemy formations before shock combat ensued. The light *pilum* was thrown first at around 35 yards, followed quickly by the heavy *pilum*.

phalangite: A specialized heavy infantryman in the Hellenistic period who differed from a hoplite in that he who wore very little armour and wielded a *sarissa* as his main offensive weapon.

phalanx: A close order heavy infantry formation with spearmen arranged in rank and file. This formation was capable of devastating offensive power through the collision and push of its soldiers. There is evidence that this formation dates back to Bronze Age Mesopotamia, though it was certainly perfected by the Greeks and Macedonians during the Archaic, Hellenic and Hellenistic periods.

'Polybian' legion: Another name given to the Roman manipular legion of the middle Republican period. Modern historians call this legion the 'Polybian' legion because the ancient Roman historian Polybius described its workings.

principes: The second line of heavy infantry in the mid-Republican legion, organized into maniples. These units were armed with sword, *pila* and protected by helmet, body armour and *scutum*. They were recruited in the prime of their lives. They fought behind the *hastati*. See maniple.

quincunx: The checkerboard formation used by the mid-Republican legion in which three lines were deployed with wide intervals between the maniples, the gaps being covered by the maniples of the second line. This formation gave the legion great flexibility, especially in combat against the phalangeal formations from the Hellenistic East.

quinquereme: Larger and taller than a *trireme*, the *quinquereme* had a complement of 300 sailors, of which 250 to 270 were rowers and the remainder manned the rigging, masts, and rudders. These vessels could ram enemy ships, but also carried a detachment of between 80 and 120 marines, including archers and catapult operators for offensive missile fire, and swordsmen and spearmen to defend the deck from boarding.

sarissa: A Macedonian pike used by phalangites in a phalanx. Made of cornel wood and tipped with a heavy iron tip and bronze butt-spike, the *sarissa* ranged from 14 feet to 21 feet in length and was ideally suited for frontal assault.

scorpion: A small Roman torsion siege engine which fired a small-calibre javelin. Torsion engines derive their power from the twisting of a spring mechanism, generally made from a combination of animal sinew and hair.

scutarii: A type of Spanish soldier named after the flat oval shield or *scutum* they used in battle. These soldiers were some of Hannibal's best troops in the Second Punic War and a match for Roman infantry.

scutum: A large shield used by Roman legionaries. The early *scutum* was semi-cylindrical and oval in shape. Later, the shape would change to a rectangle, ideal for close formations. The shield was held by a single, transverse handgrip behind a central boss and was ideally suited to protect the Roman soldier as he wielded his *gladius* in battle.

shock combat: A form of fighting where participants use close-quarter weapons (swords, axes, maces, thrusting spears) against the enemy. This combat is usually performed by heavy troops (infantry and cavalry) and most often in *well-articulated* formations.

signifier: The standard bearer for the Roman century. He carried a *signum* or standard into battle.

slinger, Balearic: A type of light infantry from the Balearic Islands which used a sling for offensive action. Armed with different kinds of slings made from black tufted rush, hair or sinew depending on range and target, the Balearic slingers had a fast rate of fire and were extremely accurate even at long range. The heavy sling could fire a stone the size of a tennis ball over three hundred yards.

triarii: The third and senior line of heavy infantry in the mid-Republican legion. This line was recruited from veteran soldiers who were armed with the long *hasta* or thrusting spear and protected by helmet, body armour and oval *scutum*. See maniple.

trireme: A sleek and fast Greek, Phoenician, and later Carthaginian, war galley with a crew of around 200 sailors. Highly manoeuvrable and capable of sinking an enemy vessel with its bronze and wood ram, this type of warship dominated the Mediterranean during the Archaic and Hellenic periods, but was gradually replaced by the larger *quinquereme* in Roman warfare in the third century BCE.

turma: A squadron of approximately thirty Roman cavalrymen commanded by a *decurion*. Ten *turmae* (300 horsemen) made up the normal cavalry contingent for a Roman legion.

velites: Roman light infantry of the early-and mid-Republican legion. These troops were recruited from the *capite censi* (urban poor) or those too young to serve as heavy infantry. Armed with light javelins and swords and unprotected except for helmets and hide-covered wicker shields, these troops acted as a screen for their heavier-armed and less-mobile comrades, the *hastati, principes* and *triarii*.

Glossary of Roman and Carthaginian Government Terms

aedile, curule: An important post in the Roman government held by two men of rank, who, with their two plebeian counter parts, were responsible for care of the streets of Rome, traffic regulations, public order in religious matters and cult practices, and caring for the water supply. They were also in charge of public games, whose expense was usually born by these office holders.

Comitia Centuriata: A Roman legislative body made up of citizens who elected consuls, *praetors* and *censors* and who had the power to declare war and ratify peace treaties. Membership in this body was originally based on owning a standard panoply (arms and armour). The *Comitia Centuriata* had enormous influence in Roman governance by the time of the Punic Wars.

consul: The senior executives of the Roman republic. Every March two men were elected for a one year term to preside over the Senate and assemblies in Rome, govern provinces, and lead armies in war. Initially, only patricians could hold this office, though by the mid-Republic plebeians could also hold one of the two consulships. Minimum age for consul was 41 for patricians and 42 for plebeian candidates. Consecutive consulships were against the law, though in times of war successful past consuls were often reappointed.

Council of Elders: The Carthaginian chief assembly made up of about 100 members of the ruling oligarchy very similar to the Roman Senate. This council appointed the two chief magistrates or suffetes who held executive power, and they also appointed military commanders to command the fleet and the army campaigning abroad.

dictator: In times of extreme crisis the Roman Senate appointed a dictator to replace the two consuls for a six month term. His emergency powers gave him supreme authority over the legislative and judicial arms of the Roman government, as well as complete command of the Roman military and immunity from any prosecution after his term was complete.

Fetial priest: The fetial Priests conducted international relations for the Roman Republic, including treaties and declarations of war. There were twenty priests altogether who formed a *collegium* dating back to Rome's regal period. Later, these men acted as advisors to the Roman Senate in matters of war and peace. Though they did not make policy, they were sent as ambassadors of Rome to sanctify treaties or declare war.

imperium: The authority to rule during the Roman Republic was called *imperium*. The scope of *imperium* granted depended on the office held (dictators held the most, then consuls, proconsuls, etc.). Magistrates with *imperium* also had the authority to command the Roman army, with greater offices holding more power. Traditionally, dictators, consuls, proconsuls, and praetors were the only ones allowed to hold this power.

legate: The senior member of a Roman general's staff of senatorial rank. Legates were often experienced commanders (even ex-consuls) who served less experienced and ambitious colleagues. The legate outranked all military tribunes and often acted as a general's chief of staff. This position was coveted because legates were granted large shares of the war booty.

lictor: A member of a special class of Roman civil servant who attended high-ranking Roman magistrates. These men acted as bodyguards and performed as extensions of their magistrate's power. Dictators were attended by twenty-four lictors, while consuls were given twelve each, proconsuls eleven, and praetors six.

Magister Equitum ('Master of the Horse'): Originally the head of the Roman army's cavalry, this position evolved during the Republic to become a Roman dictator's chief lieutenant. This person was normally chosen by the dictator, though at times he was picked by the Roman Senate to act as a counterweight to the dictator's power.

patrician: The hereditary ruling class of the Roman Republic. Patricians claimed the ability to trace their lineage to the Regal period of Rome (c.750–509 BCE) and only members of this class were eligible to sit in the Senate and the religious colleges. As the Republic wore on, patricians began to share some of the most powerful offices in Rome with the lower plebeian class.

Plebeian: The traditional middle and lower classes of the Roman Republic, distinct from the ruling patrician class. During the Republic, plebeians began to pull some power away from patricians, setting up their own legislative bodies and demanding important positions in the military and the executive branch (consulship).

Pontifex Maximus: The head priest of the Roman state religion, elected annually, who oversaw a college of sixteen priests (*pontifices*). During the Republic, the Pontifex was elected by the *Comitia Tributa* and served for life. He interpreted omens, sometimes through augurs, controlling and keeping the official calendar, and the oversight of funerals.

praetor: Annually-elected magistrates of the Roman government, praetors ranked just below the consuls. By 197, six were elected annually to act as judges and rule Sicily, Sardinia and Spain. Praetors were also allowed to lead armies not led by consuls.

proconsul: Roman governor of a province given supreme authority by the Senate. He was in sole charge of the military, justice, and of the administration in his province and could not be prosecuted for misdeeds until his office expired. Consuls were often given the rank of proconsul after their one-year term had expired in order to continue to command in a theatre of operation.

quaestor: Roman officials responsible for the financial administration of Rome and in the provinces. They collected taxes and tribute and audited other officials. They also served as subordinate officers with limited command responsibilities.

Senate, Roman: The premier ruling body of the Roman republic, the Senate consisted of about 300 men from the patrician class, whose membership was regulated by the two censors and based on property holdings. Although they possessed little formal power, the Senate did exercise great influence over magistrates, especially consuls, proconsuls and praetors.

suffete: One of two senior executives of the Carthaginian state. Two men were elected into this office per year and whose function was very similar to the Roman consuls except that suffetes did not command armies.

tribune, military: A Roman officer, one of six appointed to a legion. Authority was given to two at a time, with command rotated among the six. Tribunes were often young men of the patrician class appointed by the Senate in order to gain military experience.

triumph The Roman *triumph* was a religious celebration and parade which originated with the Etruscans and continued over a thousand years throughout the Republican and Imperial periods. Traditionally, only the Senate could confer a triumph to a magistrate, and only Romans who held *imperium* were eligible for this honour (consuls, proconsuls, praetors and dictators). The parade always followed a proscribed route and ended at the Temple of Jupiter Capitolinus.

Select Bibliography

Ancient Sources

Appian, *Roman History*, 4 volumes, translated by Horace White (Loeb Classical Library, London: Heinemann and New York: Macmillan, 1912–1913).

Caesar, *The Civil Wars*, translated by A. B. Preskett (Loeb Classical Library, Cambridge: Harvard University Press and London: Heinemann, 1961).

Diodorus of Sicily, *Universal History*, translated by C. H. Oldfather, Charles L. Sherman, Bradford Wells, Russel M. Geer, and F. R. Walton (Loeb Classical Library, Cambridge: Harvard University Press and London: Heinemann, 1933–1967).

Livy, *The War with Hannibal*, translated by Aubrey de Selincourt (New York: Penguin Books, 1987).

Livy, *Rome and the Mediterranean*, translated by Henry Bettenson (New York: Penguin Books, 1976).

Plutarch, *Roman Lives*, translated by Robin Waterfield. (Oxford: Oxford University Press, 1999).

Polybius, *The Rise of the Roman Empire*, translated by Ian Scott-Kilvert (New York: Penguin Books, 1979).

Modern Sources

Adcock, F. E., *The Roman Art of War Under the Republic* (New York: Barnes and Noble, 1960).

Anglim, Simon, Phyllis Jestice, Rob Rice, Scott Rusch, John Serrati, *Fighting Techniques of the Ancient World, 3000 BC–AD 500 – Equipment, Combat Skills and Tactics* (New York: Thomas Dunne, 2002).

Bagnell, Nigel, *The Punic Wars, 264–146 BC* (Oxford: Osprey, 2002).

Bagnell, Nigel, *The Punic Wars: Rome, Carthage, and the Struggle for the Mediterranean* (New York: Thomas Dunne Books, 1990).

Boardman, John, Jasper Griffin and Oswyn Murray, *The Roman World: The Oxford History of the Classical World* (Oxford: Oxford University Press, 1988).

Bradford, Ernle, *Hannibal* (New York: Dorset Press, 1981).

Brunt, P., *Italian Manpower* (Oxford: Clarendon Press, 1971).

Campbell, Duncan B., *Besieged: Siege Warfare in the Ancient World* (Oxford: Osprey, 2006).

Connolly, Peter, 'The Early Roman Army', in John Hackett, ed., *Warfare in the Ancient World* (New York: Facts On File, 1989).

Connolly, Peter, *Greece and Rome at War*, revised edition (London: Greenhill, 2006).

Connolly, Peter, 'The Roman Army in the Age of Polybius', in John Hackett, ed., *Warfare in the Ancient World* (New York: Facts On File, 1989).

Daly, Gregory, *Cannae: The Experience of Battle in the Second Punic War* (London: Routledge, 2002).

Davies, Roy, *Service in the Roman Army* (New York: Columbia University Press, 1989).

Dorey, Thomas A., and Donald R. Dudley, *Rome Against Carthage* (London: Secker and W., 1971).

Fuller, J. F. C., *A Military History of the Western World, Volume I: From the Earliest Times to the Battle of Lepanto* (New York: Funk and Wagnalls Company, 1954–1957).

Gabriel, Richard A. and Karen S. Metz, *From Sumer to Rome: The Military Capabilities of Ancient Armies* (Westport, CT: Greenwood Press, 1991).

Gabriel, Richard, Donald W. Boose Jr, *The Great Battles of Antiquity: A Strategic Guide to Great Battles that Shaped the Development of* War (Westport, CT: Greenwood Press, 1994).

Dixon, Karen R. and Pat Southern, *The Roman Cavalry* (London: Routledge, 1997).

Goldsworthy, Adrian, *Cannae* (London: Cassell and Co, 2001).

Goldsworthy, Adrian, *The Complete Roman Army* (London: Thames and Hudson, 2003).

Goldsworthy, Adrian, *In the Name of Rome: The Men Who Won the Roman Empire* (London: Phoenix Press, 2004).

Goldsworthy, Adrian, *The Punic Wars* (London: Cassell and Company, 2000).

Goldsworthy, Adrian, *Roman Warfare* (London: Cassell and Co., 2002).

Grant, Michael, *The Army of the Caesars* (New York: Charles Scribner's Sons, 1975).

Grant, Michael, *The Ancient Historians* (New York, Barnes and Noble Books, 1970).

Hammond, N. G. L., 'The Campaign and the Battle of Cynoscephalae in 197 B.C.', in *The Journal of Hellenistic Studies*, 108, pp. 60–92.

Hanson, Victor Davis, *Carnage and Culture: Landmark Battles in the Rise of Western Power* (New York: Doubleday, 2001).

Healy, Mark, *Cannae 216 BC: Hannibal Smashes Rome's Army* (London: Osprey, 1994).

Jones, Archer, *The Art of War in the Western World* (Urbana and Chicago: University of Illinois Press, 1987).

Keppie, Lawrence, *The Making of the Roman Army: From Republic to Empire* (New York: Barnes and Noble Books, 1994).

Kern, Paul Bentley, *Ancient Siege Warfare* (Bloomington: Indiana University Press, 1999).

Lancel, Serge, *Carthage*, translated by Antonia Nevill (Oxford: Blackwell Publishing, 1995).

Lazenby, John F., *The First Punic War: A Military History* (Stanford: Stanford University Press, 1996).

Lazenby, John F., *Hannibal's War: A Military History of the Second Punic War* (Norman: University of Oklahoma Press, 1998).

O'Connell, Robert L., *Of Arms and Men: A History of War, Weapons and Aggression* (Oxford and New York: Oxford University Press, 1989).

O'Connell, Robert L., 'The Roman Killing Machine', in *Military History Quarterly*, Volume 1, Number 1, Fall 1988.

Parker, H. M. D., *The Roman Legions* (New York: Dorsett Press, 1992).

Rankov, N. B., 'The Second Punic War at Sea', in T. J. Cornell, N. B. Rankov and P. Sabin, eds, *The Second Punic War: A Reappraisal* (London: University of London Institute of Classical Studies, 1996).

Roth, Jonathan, *The Logistics of the Roman Army at War, 264 BC–AD 235* (Leiden: Brill, 1998).

Santosuosso, Antonio, *Soldiers, Citizens and the Symbols of War From Classical Greece to Republican Rome, 500–167 BC* (Boulder: Westview Press, 1997).

Shean, J. F., 'Hannibal's Mules: The Logistical Limitations of Hannibal's Army and the Battle of Cannae, 216 B.C.', *Historia*, 45.2, pp. 175–185.

Soren, David, Aicha ben Khader and Hedi Slim, *Carthage: Uncovering the Mysteries and Splendors of Ancient Tunisia* (New York: Simon and Schuster, 1990).

Starr, Chester G., *The Emergence of Rome*, second edition (Westport, Greenwood Press, 1982).

Starr, Chester G., *The Influence of Sea Power on Ancient History* (Oxford and New York: Oxford University Press, 1989).

Strauss, B. S. and J. Ober, *The Anatomy of Error: Ancient Military Disasters and their Lessons for Modern Strategists* (New York: St Martin's Press, 1992).

Veith, G. and J. Kromayer, *Heerwesen und Kriegführung der Griechen und Romer* (Munich, 1928).

Warry, John, *Warfare in the Classical World: An Illustrated Encyclopedia of Weapons, Warriors, and Warfare in the Ancient Civilizations of Greece and Rome* (London: Salamander Books, 1980).

Index

TRUESIGHT

David Stahler Jr.

An imprint of HarperCollins*Publishers*

Eos is an imprint of HarperCollins Publishers.

Truesight

Copyright © 2004 by David Stahler Jr.

www.harpereos.com

Library of Congress Cataloging-in-Publication Data

Stahler, David.

Truesight / David Stahler Jr.— 1st ed.

p. cm.

Summary: In a distant frontier world, thirteen-year-old Jacob is uncertain of his future in a community that considers blindness a virtue and "Seers" as aberrations.

ISBN 0-06-052285-2 — ISBN 0-06-052286-0 (lib. bdg.)

[1. Blind—Fiction. 2. People with disabilities—Fiction. 3. Science fiction.] I. Title.

PZ7.S78246Tr 2004

[Fic]—dc22

2003011490

Typography by R. Hult

5   6   7   8   9   10

❖

First Edition

To my wife, Erica

PROLOGUE

"There it is."

The floater sped through the early evening along the plains of Nova Campi, rising and falling with the terrain, riding the gentle waves of hills and valleys at an even speed. Clearing a ridge, the two men in the cockpit looked ahead— one with mild interest, the other with open amazement—as the tall sea grasses of the plain parted to reveal a network of fields stretching to the edge of the colony. Large squares of black soil, striped with greens and golds, blues and purples, lay sprinkled with the shapes of men and women bent over the strips of color, pacing slowly up, down, and between the rows with purpose. The floater adjusted to a makeshift road, slowing and lowering closer to the ground.

The two men were computer specialists from the city, from the other colony, from what might as well have been the other side of the world, the other side of the galaxy. Dressed in crisp uniforms, reclining in the shimmering craft, they gazed at the workers in brown smocks who paused in their direction as they passed. The younger technician drove, casually watching the workers as they resumed their chores. He was native to this planet. He had been here before, though not enough times for the sights to become routine. The other, though older, was a newbie, recently shipped to the frontier from older worlds with more established colonies settled by ancient corporations.

"What are they doing?" the newbie asked.

"Farming, agriculture. It's what they do best."

"I know, but I mean, how can they work if they're blind?"

"How should I know? How can they do anything? They just can. They've been doing it their entire lives. They're all blind here in Harmony Station, have been for generations. It's the way they're made—the way they make each other. Christ, didn't you read your colony manual?"

"Look at them turn toward us. It's uncanny, as if they see us but don't."

"Relax. They're only listening. They still have ears, you know. People say their hearing is genetically enhanced, as their blindness is engineered, but I don't believe it. People say a lot of things." He paused, glancing at his partner. "We're coming to the town, so listen—when we arrive, let me do the talking. They're not exactly unfriendly, but they can be touchy."

"How so?"

"Well, they're polite enough, but you get the feeling they really can't stand us. We're just a bunch of Seers to them; they're only Blinders to us. Same old story."

The road—straight, steady—veered toward the settlement, a series of tiered hillsides ringed with streets, punctuated with occasional squares amid squat concrete buildings. In answer to the setting sun, the gleam of metal winked from the tiers—the fronts of homes snuggled into hillsides. The technician eased the floater to a halt at the edge of town, where a half dozen figures stood waiting to receive them. To the newbie, they seemed fairly unremarkable, like any other group of men and women. They wore draping gowns in basic simplicity—no jewelry or headdresses, no images of adornment except for a small broach of gold or silver pinned on each breast. What absorbed him, however, were their eyes. He couldn't stop staring at them—wide open, gazing straight ahead, unmoving, blue green like the strange color of this world's grasses. They seemed to see everything, though he knew they saw nothing. They seemed to see right into his being, to penetrate him with their indifference, like statues of antiquity. He found himself turning his own eyes away, lowering his head, though they certainly could not know he stared.

"Good evening, High Councilor," his partner said.

"Greetings. Jackson, isn't it?" The man in front, his beard long and brown with streaks of gray, his voice gentle, stepped forward as he spoke.

"You remembered."

"Of course. I thought they might send you."

"Councilor, this is my partner, Holman."

"You're new, aren't you? Welcome to Harmony." The councilor bowed in Holman's direction.

"Thanks. Quite a place you have here. Those fields . . . I've never seen anything like them before."

"I suppose I've never seen anything like them before either."

Jackson shot Holman a look. Holman winced and stammered an apology.

"Relax, Holman," the high councilor said. "It was meant to be a joke."

The leader's face passed the slightest smile before returning to blankness. During the entire exchange none of the other residents spoke; they barely moved for that matter. Holman felt a mild urge to bolt, to jump back in the floater and head for civilization, to Melville, the only other colony on this remote planet. Even its small cluster of translucent city towers stretching above the plains and its meager starport—a lightly droning hive with an occasional ship transporting to and from the orbital cruisers like the one that brought him to Nova Campi—were preferable to this place.

"Jackson, tell your partner there is no need to be agitated. We'll soon leave the two of you to your duties."

"How is the ghostbox running? Anything in particular you want us to examine when we do our inspection?"

"The computer has been fine, aside from the usual glitches in our power stream. Nothing we can't tolerate."

"That's right, same problem as last time. We brought a regulator with us. That should help make things somewhat smoother."

"Good. Do you remember the way?"

"Yeah, I can find it. We should be done in a few hours."

"Thank you, Jackson. You can show yourselves out when you've finished, and I'm certain you need no reminders about our rules of contact."

"Not at all. Don't worry, we'll keep to ourselves. Just give us a good review for the bosses, okay?"

"I always do," the councilor murmured as he left. The others followed him, walking slowly, almost symmetrically, down the center of the path. A sullen breeze arose and swished their robes, ushering them away. As they departed, Holman paused. Ever so faintly, he thought he could hear . . . music. Nothing melodic, only the slightest chorus of tones interwoven and shimmering on the breeze. It was simultaneously soothing and unsettling, the soundtrack of a delicate dream.

The sun had nearly vanished; on the horizon it was tiny and pale, its last light thin and obscure. On the opposite horizon, however, the first of Nova Campi's two moons was rising steadily, visibly. Purple and vast, with great rings that glittered at sunset, it seemed to settle and brood over the dusk. It was something, perhaps the only thing, Holman enjoyed about this quiet world. Still, over the last few weeks, he had found himself coming to terms with frontier life. Less and less he missed the continuous dazzle and stimulation of the urbanized worlds closer to Earth.

"Wake up, newbie. Time to work." Jackson interrupted his trance.

"How can they walk so perfectly, so unhindered? It's as if they can see the path."

"They can, in a sense. See those poles that line the walks? Touch one."

"What's it going to do? Shock me?" Holman asked, walking toward the first pole. As he approached, a resistance arose, a mild tingling sensation that was neither painful nor pleasant but simply there, offering greater resistance the closer he got. He moved close enough to touch it, tried extending his hand to grasp the tiny sphere that crowned the rod. His hand shook with the repelling force. It was like trying to join two magnet heads. Impossible.

"Not bad. An invisible fence."

"A corral for everyone."

They skirted the edge of the settlement for several minutes before Jackson steered the two of them to a path, tiled in white stones, stretching to a distant bunker barely visible in the dusk. Holman stopped after only a dozen yards. Something was missing.

"The force poles. There aren't any lining this path."

"I guess they don't need them here," Jackson said. "Or don't want them. There's a lot of sensitive equipment in that building over there."

They continued in silence. It was darker now. The breeze had died, and the grasses, no longer whispering their presence, slipped into the general shadow of the landscape. Only the tiled path, glowing dimly in the faint moonlight, was visible. It penetrated the dusk, dividing the darkness. Jackson stopped and pulled items from his kit. Headlamps. He handed one to Holman. They slipped them around their heads and flipped the switches, flooding each other's faces with light, blinding each other amid sudden apologies. Each turned his gaze away from the other, and soon the world of sight returned to normal, a world reduced to the sphere of illumination their lights provided.

"Jackson, I heard something . . . before. This sounds crazy, but I thought I heard music."

Jackson paused. "Angelic hosts? Don't worry, you're not crazy. Have you noticed the pins?"

"Yeah."

"All the Blinders wear them. I asked about their significance once—their own invention. Each one is tuned to a different frequency, designed to emit a distinct pitch."

"But I didn't hear them at first."

"They usually require a trigger. Like the wands along the street. The closer a Blinder gets, the louder the note. They can also be triggered by another pin; probably so people won't run into one another on the street. They even have a panic function—simply tap it a few times and help is on the way."

"Clever. I wonder if it ever gets annoying, those tones."

"I wouldn't think so. They must be so familiar that they're hardly noticeable, practically subconscious. Still, you never know when it comes to the Blinders. They might want to annoy themselves for the mere pleasure."

"Pleasure?"

"I don't know. They seem to take a measure of pride in their lifestyle, enjoy wearing a badge of adversity. I guess it can't be that terrible. Everyone seems happy enough, and I've never heard of anyone leaving, or even wanting to. And get this, this is really wild: most of the Blinders are born sightless—you know, prenatal genetic modification—but rumor has it that a few had their eyesight deliberately destroyed and joined the colony as adults. Wackos from Earth, most likely. I mean, would you be blind if you didn't have to be? Holman?"

Holman had stopped and then turned, sweeping his light across the path behind him, then scanning the grass on either side. Jackson followed suit. He saw nothing.

"Mind telling me what we're looking for?"

"Did you just hear something? I thought I heard a rustle."

"I didn't hear anything. You're imagining it."

"In the grass. Clear as day. Someone's out here."

"Nobody's out here, Holman. Look, I realize this place is a bit unusual, especially for someone new to the planet, but relax."

"Something's moving! Look!"

Holman grabbed Jackson's arm, shining his light on a section of grass that flittered and rolled in a wave toward them. Something *was* moving. Jackson's heart began to pound as the wave carried itself to the edge of the path. A shape emerged—white, furry, four legged. It turned and stared at them, its eyes suddenly glowing in the beam of their headlamps.

"A cat?" Holman hissed in disbelief. "A cat? What the hell is a cat doing out here?"

Jackson burst out laughing, relief sounding in his voice. "That's right, I forgot. They have cats. Cats to catch the rats, or whatever it is they call the vermin here. Ugly little critters invade the food supply. The cats love 'em, though."

"How low-tech of them."

Holman had only now released his grip. Still chuckling, Jackson shook his arm to restore circulation. "Hey, it works."

They reached the bunker. The squat steel building at the end of the road was a welcome sight, an island in the darkness. They paused, listening to the low throb of generators that seemed to radiate from the walls. Jackson loved the sound; it was the sound of technology, the sound of power. It was his sound. He smiled and looked at Holman, who stood pale and trembling, his headlamp darting amid the grass.

"Don't feel bad. I reacted the same way when I first visited Harmony—which was only last year, by the way—and I was raised on this planet."

"I don't know. I just feel as if I'm being watched."

"Well, that's probably the only thing definitely *not* happening here. Like I said before, relax."

Jackson removed a slim card from his pocket and ran it through the magnetic slot. A large door slid open before them. As they entered, lights came to life, and the technicians winced momentarily.

"Ah, let there be light," Holman said.

"Probably the only building in the entire colony that's wired for it," Jackson replied.

They switched off their headlamps. Holman smiled as he viewed his surroundings, comforted by the familiar shapes of technology: square and rectangular boxes, colored lights that winked, screens that glowed. Alone, in the center of the room, stood a slender gray obelisk, visually barren in contrast to the gaudy panels that lined the walls. It was the ghostbox, a powerful mainframe that controlled most of the technological functions of the colony. It maintained, it monitored, it diagnosed, it repaired. Though no longer state of the art amid the inner worlds, here at the rim it was a computer demigod. Stately. Beautiful.

"Quite an expensive machine for a place like this; I wonder how they can afford it," Holman remarked.

"Their foundation back on Earth shipped it here a few years ago. A gift from Mommy. C'mon, let's get started. If we hurry, I can be home in time for bed."

"The voice of a newly married man, I'm guessing."

Jackson laughed. "Almost a year. Aren't you married?"

"I was."

"What happened?"

"She didn't like the idea of life on the plains. Hightailed it back to civilization."

They opened their kits and went to work. After a few minutes, Holman spoke again. "Funny, all this equipment here. I mean, these people—farmers, essentially. Self-proclaimed pioneers, self-sufficient, yet how would they live without all this technology? They want nothing to do with the outside world, but they sure seem to depend on it."

"Are you detecting hypocrisy at work?"

"I guess. Don't you think so?"

"I try not to get so philosophical. Besides, they keep us in business."

The next hour passed in total, concentrated silence. Systems were analyzed, programs were checked, stray fragments of data were remerged or cut loose. Holman installed the power regulator. Jackson accessed the ghostbox, programmed the necessary updates. Everything was normal. Everything was fine. They were just finishing up, putting everything back in place, when Jackson turned and saw her.

"Holman."

Holman turned and jumped. She was an apparition, standing at the entrance, pale and delicate, a young woman—almost still a girl—beautiful, with dark hair pulled back tightly and full red lips. She simply stood there, a look of fear on her face despite the eyes that held no focus. Though he didn't believe in superstition, for a moment Holman was sure he was seeing a spirit, a projection of the ghostbox, as if she haunted this place and they were the intruders. Her head suddenly cocked. She became aware of some change. Was it their awareness of her? Holman wondered.

"Who . . . who are you?" Jackson stuttered.

She moved toward him so quickly he retreated in surprise. Her face desperate, she extended a hand, bringing the other one to her face, drawing its index finger to her lips, pleading for silence.

"Be quiet." She whispered so faintly it seemed as though she were only mouthing the words. "They can hear you."

"Who can hear us?" Jackson whispered back.

Suddenly the broach on her chest, a silver swirl, began to emit a light pitch, wavering in rapidly increasing strength.

She immediately tapped the pin to deaden the tone and turned to face the door. Holman could hear voices and the sounds of people approaching. He watched her place her arms around Jackson's neck and bring her lips to his ear. He couldn't hear her words, but he saw Jackson's eyes open wide. Before anything else could happen, a group of men entered the room, led by the high councilor. Their broaches toned loudly, suddenly breaking into a pulsing squeal as they entered the room. They, like the girl, tapped the pins. All noise ceased.

"Delaney? Delaney, we know you're in here!" the councilor shouted. No one said a word. Both the technicians and the young woman—everyone in the room, for that matter—became statues. It was as if time had frozen, leaving only the susurrations of the machines to indicate otherwise. The councilor's pin glittered platinum in the light.

"Jackson, give the girl to me." The councilor's voice barely concealed the anger on his face.

"Wait a minute, Councilor. Let's not rush to any conclusions about what's happening here—"

"I'm here, Father," the girl interrupted so suddenly, they all started. She broke away from Jackson and walked toward the men, reaching out her hand until it brushed against the councilor's sleeve. With a sudden jerk, he grabbed her and pulled her to him.

"Take her," he said, handing her off to the two men waiting behind him. They each took a hand and, slowly turning, disappeared into the outer darkness.

"What were you doing with her?" the councilor demanded.

"Honestly, nothing," Jackson replied. His voice was as

calm and neutral as the councilor's. "We turned around and there she was. Then you showed up. That's about it."

"What did she say to you?"

"She didn't say anything. There was no time—like I said, you came in right after her. She seemed confused, as if she were lost or something. I don't know."

"Yes, that's probably it. She has been known to wander." The councilor hesitated. Holman sensed he was trying to decide whether or not to believe Jackson. Either he did or he decided it wasn't worth the trouble, because he suddenly spoke again. "Please excuse us."

"No problem. We were just finishing up anyway."

The high councilor left the room. The pair finished their work, packed their kits, and left. Several times Holman had turned to speak, and each time Jackson had shot him a warning glance for silence. They left the bunker quietly and hurried down the path, their headlamps lighting the way. Holman couldn't wait to return to the floater. Each moment the darkness became more oppressive, smothering him. Even the great ringed moon, now far past its zenith and approaching the western horizon, seemed barely to glow in the night. As they topped a rise not far from the floater, they paused once more. This time Jackson grabbed Holman's arm, though not harshly nor in fear. Instead, he pointed to the eastern horizon, where Nova Campi's other, smaller moon now rested, pink and cratered. Silhouetted against it was a dark mass, which Holman realized was a group of figures standing on the hilltop. He turned off his lamp for a moment, though he didn't quite know the reason why. Jackson did the same.

"Listen," Jackson whispered reflexively. Holman could already hear it.

It was music. Not like the chiming tones from earlier in the evening, not like the glistening hums emitted by some mechanical device, but the sound of voices. They were human voices, coming from the singers standing on the hill, intertwined in a choral melody that rose and fell with dynamic intensity, meandering around intricate patterns of melody. The chanters' song contained no words—it needed none, it seemed so ancient. The two technicians stood transfixed until the song concluded. When it ended, they walked in perfect silence back to where the floater glowed pink under the moon.

Not until they were well away from the colony did Holman break the silence.

"That music was incredible. So beautiful," he said.

"Sad, too," Jackson remarked.

Holman didn't think it was sad, but he didn't say so. Instead he asked the question that had been burning in his brain since they left the bunker: "Back there, right before the men came in. What did she say to you?"

Jackson shivered before speaking.

"She said, 'Help me get out.'"

PART ONE

CHAPTER ONE

"Ow! You're hurting me!"

"Well, hold still, then."

Jacob squirmed one last time on the stool before settling back down. Snipping scissors sounded in his ear. Always, in the past, the noise had soothed him; the quiet moments he and his mother shared during the monthly shearings had been a constant source of comfort for as long as he could remember. Always, he could feel her hands, delicate and sure, as they caressed his hair, gentle touch reinforced by gentle touch, as hair was cut away. A light pull released by the crisp closure of steel was the rhythm she worked to, a rhythm that worked itself into a lull within him. To this rhythm she would hum in breathy notes the songs of his childhood—the nursery rhymes, the play songs—and the songs of Harmony Station, the songs of its traditions. They rarely talked, and Jacob enjoyed that silence the most; no demands were made, no tests given about rules or history, no pestering inquiries about music or lessons, only touch.

His eyes were closed now against the hairs tickling down over his nose and cheeks. He could sense his mother standing there before him, could smell the essence of the flowers she had been picking from their doorstep an hour ago. Not

1

that it mattered—had his eyes been open, Jacob wouldn't have been able to see her anyway. Like everyone in Harmony, Jacob was blind and had been from birth. Everyone born into the community of Harmony Station, along with her sister colonies and mother foundation on Earth, lived without sight. Jacob himself was hardly aware of what his blindness meant, of what sight meant. The darkness wasn't dark; light, colors, the pictures of the world around him, merely formed an absence that was unaware of itself.

All Jacob knew of the world of sight were the lessons he had learned from his parents and teachers—and from the leaders of Harmony, a council composed of representatives from the Foundation. He knew that sight was a deception, a distraction from the inner world that formed the center of one's being. He understood that vision offered little more than the temptation of appearances or, worse, images of suffering and horror, things that human beings should never have to see. Though he was taught that sight had its practical advantages on a more mundane level, he had been educated in the history of the Foundation, of how its members had decided long ago to embrace what was once considered a handicap instead of abandoning it to the medical technologies that could make it obsolete. Instead they had decided to make their blindness a way of life, and in accepting the difficulties it yielded, would become stronger in their adversity.

"Ow! You did it again! That's the second time, Ma." Jacob reached up and felt along the ridge of his ear. It burned a little from the poke, but he couldn't feel any blood.

"I'm sorry, but you keep moving. You act as if you have squeaks running up your legs. Care to tell me what's on your mind?"

2

"No." Jacob shuddered at the thought of the little rodents clinging to his skin. Every three months the native creatures bred in droves that plagued Harmony for at least a week. One of his earliest memories was awakening one night to a swarm of the creatures crawling all over him. He'd screamed, and they had scattered off his back and legs. His parents, terrified, had rushed in to find him sobbing, but otherwise unharmed. They soon located the rodents' source—a mother had built her nest in the narrow space below his mattress and had recently given birth. The next morning they adopted Unger, one of their neighbor's new kittens, who became a competent, if somewhat ambivalent, squeak eater. After that, the problem abated, though for years Jacob relived nightmares of the experience. He still dreamed about them occasionally, though he told his parents he didn't.

"Come on, Jacob. You know you can't hide anything from me. Out with it."

"Nothing is the matter, Ma! Let's just get this over with already."

"Okay. Relax, but remember what you've been learning in school for the past ten years: 'All thoughts are words. All words are shared.'"

It all depends on the thoughts, Jacob said to himself. If it concerned something good—like an abundant harvest or a month without lost power—then everyone spoke up. If it was something bad—like when the water systems malfunctioned for a week or neighbors argued—no one wanted to hear it. Only his mother seemed to be the exception, at least with him at home. He could tell his mother was hurt by his reticence, but in a way, Jacob wasn't lying. There really wasn't anything the matter—at least, nothing he could think of specifically. All

3

he knew was that his thirteenth birthday was next week and that school would be finished in a month. Then he would graduate and the harvest would arrive. After that, the future. As occurred for all his classmates, specialization was looming and no one knew what to expect. Soon, though, he and his peers would know what the rest of their lives would entail. It was a broad leap. Perhaps that's what was eating at the edges. Whatever the reason, Jacob was getting sick of the sudden waves of annoyance and frustration that arrived from nowhere and swept over him. He had explained his symptoms to his father, who told him it was called growing up. "That's life. Get used to it," his father had said.

Interrupting his thoughts, Jacob's mother spoke again. "I know what it is. You're nervous about specialization, aren't you? Go ahead, be nervous. Everyone always is anyway, but remember, it's a matter of trust. The council always does what's best for the people."

"But what if I don't like it?"

"Of course you'll like it. Don't talk that way."

"Father didn't. He wanted to be a teacher."

"How do you know that?" she demanded.

"I heard him say it once. One night, when you were arguing."

"Well, he shouldn't have said that—he didn't really mean it. And you shouldn't have been listening. As for that specialization, the Foundation provides most of our teachers directly from Earth. Besides, his performance levels were low, and I don't think he wanted it badly enough anyway. He knows it was for the best, that it was his place to be a grower." She paused, measuring the hair on either side of his head by running it through two fingers from each hand. "That's not to say that having greater responsibility in order to better serve the community isn't a worthy goal."

"Not to mention more food. Better things."

"That's not the way it is around here, Jacob. You know that everyone gets their due."

"Maybe some are due more, then. All I know is that Egan has nicer things than I do, and bigger lunches."

"Your friend's father is an important person."

"So what?"

"I'm almost finished. Just a few more snips." His mother seemed eager to change the subject. Jacob felt the same way. By now his face was itching. He wanted to reach up from under the sheet fastened around his neck and scratch his nose and chin. He decided this would probably be the last haircut from his mother. Egan was already teasing him about it anyway. Soon both of them would stop getting haircuts altogether and join the adult men in the community, either growing their hair long and keeping it pulled back, or shaving it off altogether. Hair grooming was an indulgence for children and for the Seers, who were obsessed with outer appearances and neglected their inner selves.

"Why do you spend so much time trimming?"

"I just want it to be even."

"Why? Nobody can see it anyway."

"Jacob!" She cupped his chin. "You know you're not supposed to speak that way, even at home. Besides," she said, softening, "I'm a musician. You know what kind of perfectionists we are."

"I hope I get a specialization in music," Jacob wished aloud. She didn't answer him.

"Speaking of music," she said, "Delaney will be here

5

soon, and you have classes to attend."

"She's going to officially become your apprentice, right?"

"Of course. She's the most talented student I've taught in years. And the conductors are pushing me to take one on. Guess they think I'm getting old."

"Well, you are."

"Thanks." She traced her hand across his face and tweaked his nose. They both giggled.

"It doesn't hurt that she's the high councilor's daughter, does it?"

"Since when did you become so savvy? No, I suppose it doesn't. But that ultimately isn't important. She's very talented and works hard." She paused. "Still, I'm a little worried about her. She seems distracted lately. Depressed. I'm worried her music will suffer. I spoke to her father about it, and he didn't seem too concerned. Let me know if you hear anything at school. Or if she says anything to you—after all, you practically spend as much time with her as I do."

Jacob was silent. Should he tell her? For the last few days rumors had been whispered around school about Delaney, about her attempt to run away with the Seers. He hadn't had a chance yet to ask her if they were true. He was unsure if he even should—what if she said yes? Right now at least, rumors were just rumors, and he could go on disbelieving. In the meantime he would say nothing to Delaney and especially nothing to his mother. It would only disturb her even more than it had upset him. Delaney was practically a daughter to her, one of the few people besides Jacob that she had warmed to, that she seemed to care about more than her music.

The rumors, the uncertainty, hurt. For in the same way she had become like a daughter to his mother, Delaney was like a sister to him. She even jokingly called him her little brother whenever she saw him. There were many days when Jacob would arrive home from school and Delaney, having just finished her lessons, would stick around, sometimes for hours, as if she were reluctant to go home. He loved those afternoons when they laughed and joked around, or maybe played a duet together on the piano, something light and funny. Sometimes—usually when his mother left to run errands—they would just talk. Or rather she would talk and he would listen to all the wild things she said.

He smiled now, thinking about the time when, in this very room, she had stood up on a chair before him.

"People of Harmony," she began, her voice dropping an octave as she mimicked her father, assuming a tone of mock solemnity, "though I am pleased to announce that power loss was restricted to only four occasions last week instead of the customary five, I have great concerns about the upcoming harvest. It has been brought to my attention by certain members of the community that too many people are laughing and having fun when they should be busier working to help feed our society. Isn't that right, Councilor Donato?"

"Oh yes, High Councilor," she replied to herself, assuming the higher, sycophantic pitch of the woman who represented Jacob's section of the community, "you are right as always!"

"Therefore," she continued, her voice dropping again, "it is the council's decision that, until after the harvest, there shall be no more laughing in Harmony! More picking, less grinning!

"Yes, High Councilor! I quite agree!" she said again in the woman's voice, sending Jacob into peals of laughter so hard he fell off the couch.

7

"You there," she barked, again taking on the voice of her father, "did you not hear me? Is that laughter I detect? You must be punished for your insubordination!"

She leaped off the chair, pounced on him, and began tickling him all over so that he laughed even harder, all the while begging her to stop. She was laughing now too as she picked him up off the floor and began dancing with him in circles, knocking into furniture as she sang at the top of her voice in wild abandon. Then she left him panting on the couch, banging out an accompaniment on the piano to the song she still sang—a community march, normally slow and proud, now fast and cartoonish under the strains of her voice.

That wasn't the only time she had poked fun at the councilors, especially her own father, and made Jacob laugh with her wicked impersonations. Her boldness awed him. Nor was that all she did. Sometimes she would confess mild transgressions of the rules, and once even wondered aloud what it would be like to see the world with eyes that worked. The fact that she was the high councilor's daughter only made her comments more scandalous, and therefore more captivating.

In this way she reminded him of his best friend, Egan, who was also the child of one of Harmony's leaders. Though Egan never openly questioned the value of the rules or made fun of those in charge, he had a mischievous streak and reveled in stepping out of bounds once in a while—usually trying to drag Jacob with him. He envied the two of them; they were so different from everyone else he knew. Everyone else was like him—passive, respectful, uncomfortable with anything beyond the structure of Truesight, the philosophy that guided their community and their lives. He had always hoped that he could become more like his two friends, that by being around them, their daring might wear off on him. *Maybe someday I'll be different too*, he often thought.

That wasn't to say that he didn't think about things or wonder about life outside Harmony or even question the ways of his community. However, like everyone else, he kept these thoughts to himself and didn't act on them or say them aloud, mostly because he felt guilty for thinking them in the first place. Sure, he had heard people complain before, quietly in private conversations, but no one really dared speak publicly. When they did grumble, it was almost always about minor inconveniences—shortages of certain items or appliances breaking down—certainly never about the leaders of Harmony or their decisions. Maybe that's why he loved the time he spent with Delaney—she said the things he thought, so he didn't have to.

But over the last few months, things had changed. Delaney stayed to visit less frequently, and when she did, her remarks were sharper, her attitude more cynical than usual, sometimes to the point where even he became uncomfortable. At least before he could say it was all just a joke, that it didn't mean anything. Now he wasn't so sure. This change, coupled with the rumor of her attempted escape, bothered him because he couldn't understand it. If anything, her recent displays annoyed him. There seemed to be a certain degree of ingratitude on her part. He couldn't imagine how anyone could think of leaving Harmony, but especially someone like Delaney. She had what Jacob dreamed of having—a specialization in music, a chance to become one of the future premiere performers in the community. Not only that, she was the daughter of the most important person in Harmony, not to mention smart, kind, and talented. Her voice itself was music to his ears. If she couldn't be happy here, what did that say for *his* future?

"There, finished."

"Thanks, Ma. I'll be home by dinner."

"Fine. Laney and I will be working late today; Harvestsong's approaching. No need to hurry—and Jacob, don't ever tell anyone what you heard your father say. And don't forget to activate your sounder. You already got a warning last week; we can't afford any fines, especially now."

"I will."

Jacob flushed in embarrassment at the memory of the warning. It had been an honest mistake; he had rushed to leave for school and had simply forgotten to turn it on, a normally involuntary gesture. Nothing would've happened if he hadn't bumped into one of the listeners—who rarely activated their own sounders—rounding a corner, a mere block from the school. The memory of the man marching him back to his dwelling, holding his hand tight like a little child, made him cringe. His father had been at home, having just gotten off third shift in the fields. The listener literally handed Jacob to his father, who crushed his hand in anger and embarrassment.

"Your child was found in violation of Harmony's sounder policy," the listener stated coldly. "Please remind him that all citizens must have their sounders engaged in public areas unless specifically instructed otherwise."

"I will."

"This is his first offense, so I will only issue a warning. Next time, however, you will be fined."

"I understand. Thank you. It won't happen again."

The listener departed. Jacob's father released his grip. Jacob stepped back.

"Good going, Jacob."

"I'm sorry, Dad. I was in a hurry. I forgot, that's all."

"Well, if you forget again and our rations get cut, you're the one who's going hungry, not me."

After the incident he hadn't forgotten, had double-checked each time he entered the street. Just like now. Stepping out, Jacob reached up and double-tapped his sounder. The pin made its single, bright tone to alert him it was on. Traipsing along, he could feel the warm breeze on his face and smell the fragrance of neighborhood flower gardens. He could hear the voices of people walking by, some laughing, others bickering, most murmuring in quiet tones. He could hear the chords produced by two or more sounders engaging as citizens passed one another or walked together in the street, could hear the single notes sound as some strayed too close to the pathminders. All these sounds flowed together in his mind as he walked, intertwined in a single song that carried him to school.

CHAPTER TWO

Until the last ten minutes, school flowed uneventfully. First session was the usual—citizenship. A mixture of history and civics, citizenship taught students about the origins of the Foundation, about the settlement of the rim worlds and the founding of their own colony of Harmony Station. Over the past week, as school drew to a close, Jacob and his fellow students had presented final projects. Each student was assigned a topic and was required to speak before the class. Jacob had hoped for a topic about the importance of music in the Foundation—he could easily have put something together. He already knew a lot about it from his mother and had listened to many stories on the subject from recordings in the school library. Maybe that's why his teacher didn't assign it to him.

Instead he was given a history topic—the formation of the original community, which led to the Foundation's establishment. Still, the project wasn't that difficult. He and his classmates knew much of the information already. The presentations were more or less recapitulations of the material they had been hearing continually since starting school ten years ago. Their teacher said it was important at the end of their education to bring it all together and commit it to memory. That way it would remain with them always and provide a sense of purpose and community. Jacob understood all that. He was already proud of Harmony and its sister colonies, despite Delaney's jokes and his own questions. He especially admired the first founders, a gathering of blind couples early in the twenty-first century, when bioengineering was first becoming standard practice among expectant parents back on Earth, who decided that their children would be born like them. In Jacob's mind, in all their minds, these couples were pioneers, braving the criticisms of others, of Seers who misunderstood and judged them cruel. What the Seers failed to comprehend, what Jacob and his classmates knew, was that experience was relative. What one person or group thought was important or true wasn't necessarily so.

Jacob had to admit, it was interesting reviewing their lessons on the initial community of the blind. What he didn't understand was why they never really learned anything else about the rest of the world. They were taught little about the Seers. Most of their learning involved the many wars that had occurred among the nations on Earth and later among the corporations in space. Continual battles over territory and trading rights, atrocities committed by one organization against another, betrayals and subterfuge—an enormous catalogue of sin.

Once he'd asked his teacher about the Seers. "They can't all be that bad, Mrs. Lawson. Can they?"

For a moment silence filled the air. Nobody seemed to breathe. They all waited for the answer.

When Mrs. Lawson spoke, her voice was calm but cold. "No, Jacob. You're correct. They're not all that bad. But even the best of them are limited by their arrogance, by their search for ease in life, by their obsession with material things.

They think they know the answers, but in their own way they are the ones who are truly blind."

That was one of the few times, and the last, that Jacob had asked a question. In general, questions were not asked or encouraged. When someone asked one on a rare occasion, that student was usually met with a perfunctory response: "That's not important right now," or "We'll cover that later," or "You don't need to know that."

Yes, Jacob enjoyed history; it was the other aspect of citizenship class that he didn't care for—what Mrs. Lawson called civics, mostly comprised of constant drills in the rituals and rules of the community. It seemed like there were regulations for everything. Where people could go and when. What they could do, who they could talk to, and where. It wasn't that he didn't think it was important; obviously it was—as his recent warning from the listener had reminded him. It was just that it was boring. Over and over again they repeated the same rules, repeated the proper words to speak at the Gatherings, sang the same songs. It was nothing new. They knew all the rules and songs, which their parents had ingrained in them from the time they could utter their first words. They had been attending the weekly Gatherings for just as long. Jacob didn't complain outwardly, though. No one did. It wasn't the way of the community.

Second session was more interesting. The topics varied, depending on the day of the week. Some days it was music, which Jacob loved most of all. Other days it was science, mostly learning about different kinds of plants, their medicinal and nutritional qualities, their growth cycles, and basic genetics. Today they studied orienteering, the essentials of managing in a sightless world. Having spent their entire lives in Harmony, they all had a clear sense of the layout of the community already. Still, they learned many particulars that Jacob liked for their practicality. They learned how to perform household duties, like cooking and cleaning. They learned how to work in a crop and what to do when lost. Their lessons emphasized safety and efficiency.

Jacob also liked orienteering because they played games, such as seeker, a more sophisticated form of hide-and-seek they had been playing since early childhood. They would have team adventures in which they were brought to an unknown area and competed in finding their way back to school. Jacob was amazed at how much he had learned in the past few years, how much more confident he felt moving around the house and around the streets of Harmony on his own. He loved the freedom the knowledge brought him. He loved how in the past two years his parents had allowed him to leave the house alone, no longer having to be accompanied, always holding one of their hands.

Jacob and his classmates also studied technology. Some days they were taught how their sounders worked, or how the pathminders kept them from walking off the streets. Once they were even taken to the computer. Jacob could still remember the hum that permeated the cool chamber. They learned about what Mr. Robison—their orientation teacher— called the ghostbox, the machine that helped Harmony in so many ways, doing everything from serving as community surgeon to processing the food they grew.

Today they were being taught to use a new gadget, a device called a finder. Jacob had heard of it but had never used one, let alone handled one. He and Egan had been waiting all week for this.

"Please remember," Mr. Robison said, distributing several of the devices, "these are expensive instruments. Most of you will never need to use one, but you should learn in case of an emergency."

"Who does use them?" a classmate asked. Unlike Mrs. Lawson in citizenship class, and many of Jacob's other teachers, Mr. Robison didn't mind questions. He actually seemed to like them.

"Well, Fiona, mostly the listeners because they have the burden of protecting us, making sure we follow the rules so we don't hurt ourselves or others. Also, the guardians in the fields use them so they can better manage the growers."

"What do finders do?" asked another student.

Egan, sitting next to Jacob, snorted quietly in disdain. Jacob felt the same way. Everyone knew what a finder was for.

"Egan Spencer—I heard that. Impoliteness is unacceptable. Apologize to Angus."

"I'm sorry, Angus," Egan said flatly.

"I meant, how do they work?" Angus said resentfully.

"I know you did," Mr. Robison reassured him. "Jacob, why don't you and Beth come up here."

Jacob arose from his seat and walked to the front of the class, trailing his fingertips along the right-hand row of desks as he passed. He could hear Bethany do the same, could sense her near him as they approached each other. He inhaled deeply as she moved close to him. She smelled of lilacs. She always smelled of lilacs. Her mother was a scent-maker who grew her own flowers, using them in the soaps and perfumes that made her a popular figure in Harmony.

"A finder is actually easy to use. It's really just a tiny but powerful computer that holds in its memory a perfect map of

16

Harmony, much like you retain at this point in your own minds. It also contains a sensor that can register any person's sounder, and its range is practically unlimited. The listeners could locate you just about anywhere on the planet, I'd imagine—not that they would ever need to. You hold the finder in your hand, point it straight in front of you, speak the person's name into the device, and slowly begin to rotate. You can set the finder to emit a light tone or a silent pulse. For now we'll use the tone. Beth, leave the classroom and stand out in the hall. Walk a few yards in whatever direction you wish, so that you're around the corner."

As Jacob heard her walk out, a small cylinder was placed in his hands. It was relatively short with two buttons near the tip.

"Beth, you can still hear me, can't you?"

"Yes, Mr. Robison."

"Good. Class, two buttons are mounted on the device. The right-hand one alternates between tone and pulse. The left-hand button records. Hold it down as you say the name. Go ahead, Jacob."

Jacob pushed down the left button and said, "Bethany Tyler." Immediately a low beep began to emanate from the finder in his hand.

"Okay, now slowly turn in what you think is the right direction."

Jacob turned left and the beep quickened, rising slightly in pitch.

"Good. Now, Jacob, walk in the direction you think the finder is telling you to go and bring Beth back in here."

Jacob located the point of the sound's greatest intensity and slowly walked in that direction. When the beep slowed or

17

lowered in tone, he stopped to take another reading. Soon he could sense himself out in the hallway. He turned right, in the direction of the lilac scent. The beeping rose frantically in pitch, accelerated until it was nearly a continuous stream of sound. He reached out and felt the smooth skin of her arm, traced his hand down to her hand. Their fingers interlocked. Her hand felt warm, soft.

"Hi, Jacob," she whispered.

"Hi" was all he could manage. Holding hands, they walked back into the room. They rejoined Mr. Robison in front, finally releasing their hold.

"How was it, Jacob?" Mr. Robison asked.

"Fine," he said, hoping the nonchalance of his words might hide the quiver in his voice. "I mean, it was easy."

"All right. You two can return to your seats."

Jacob went to give the finder back to his teacher.

"No, you keep it for now. All right, I want everyone to select a partner. Each pair will be given a finder for practice outside. Once you have a partner and a finder, meet at the fountain in the yard."

As always, Jacob and Egan paired up and walked outside. Soon everyone was gathered by the fountain. For the remainder of the session, they practiced using the finders, taking turns hiding and locating each other. They practiced in silent mode. Jacob found it strange at first to feel the pulsing waves passing from the cylinder into his hand, increasing in speed and intensity as he locked onto and moved toward Egan. Before long it became second nature, almost reassuring to be led with such precision, trusting the senses of the machine.

Class was almost over. Jacob was standing quietly, hiding around the corner of the school, waiting for Egan to come to him with the finder, when the pain began. It started as a dull ache in the back of his head. A wave of nausea swept over him. He reached out and gripped the wall, struggled to remain standing. Soon, however, the pain sharpened as it spread out and around him, a web of fire lacing through his skull and gathering at the front into a cluster that threatened to burst from his forehead. Then, fading like an echo, it disappeared, and he was left shaking. A hand brushed his shoulder and took hold of his arm.

"Jacob! Hey, Jake." It was Egan, shaking him. "I found you. Come on! What's going on? You all right?"

"I don't know. I had a headache, all of a sudden."

"Aw. Maybe little Jakey needs to go home and take a nap."

"Funny. Give me the finder, it's my turn."

"Too late. Time's up. Besides, you're not feeling good, remember?"

"No, I'm okay." It was true; he was feeling better.

"Good. Anyway, Mr. Robison says it's time to go. Told us to put the finders in his desk."

They walked side by side back to class. But before going in, Egan grabbed Jacob gently by the arm and pulled him aside. He placed his hand over Jacob's mouth to signal quiet. Jacob felt uneasy. Such a gesture was considered antisocial and rude. There was even a rule against it. To be silent, either alone or with another, for the express purpose of preventing your fellow citizens from knowing your whereabouts went against the spirit of Harmony.

When the others had gone inside, Egan removed his hand and whispered, "Come on, let's keep it."

"Keep what? The finder?"

"That's right. Take it home with you."

19

"Yeah, right. Do you know what would happen if Robison noticed it was missing?"

"He'll never notice. We'll fool around with it tonight and return it tomorrow."

Jacob paused. Egan waited for him to give in as usual.

"I can't, Egan. I just got a warning last week for not having my sounder on. If I get in trouble again, that's it."

"Don't be a coward, Jacob."

"Why don't you take it home, then? Your father's a councilor. You never get in trouble."

"No. Forget it. If you're not into it, it's not worth it. When are you going to relax and take some chances once in a while?"

"I've got to go. Put the finder back, okay, Egan?"

"Yeah, all right."

"Thanks," Jacob said, but Egan had already disappeared.

CHAPTER THREE

All the way home Jacob thought about his odd experience during the finder session. The headache was unlike any he had suffered before—so violent and sudden. Should he tell someone? He couldn't imagine telling his father, who never wanted to hear anything, especially a complaint. He should probably confide in his mother, but she was already worried about Delaney. Would he have to go to the doctor? Be examined by the ghostbox? Maybe he had imagined the entire episode. It had merely been a bad headache, like the migraines Egan's mother endured from time to time.

Before long he arrived home. So absorbed in thought, he almost missed the turn into his yard, would have missed it had his sounder not buzzed suddenly, matching notes with a familiar pitch that grew louder until their hands clasped.

"Hi, Delaney." Jacob tried to sound as upbeat as he could to avoid revealing in his voice what he now harbored in his mind.

"Hey, Jacob." Delaney sounded flat, tired. Still holding his hand, she pulled him down to sit beside her on the step, putting her arm around him to draw him in the way she always did. The familiarity of the gesture comforted him. Maybe—in spite of her tenor, in spite of the rumors—things weren't so bad.

"How were your lessons? Hope Mother went easy on you today."

"She was fine. I wasn't the best pupil today, however."

"You don't sound too good. Are you sick?"

"Yes, I am sick. Sick of things. Sick of people."

Jacob stiffened at her remark. "Are you sick of me? Of Mother?" he asked softly, pulling away. He didn't know what else to say. The way she spoke made *him* sick. He had never heard her sound this critical, even in the last few months. He had never heard anyone sound so dejected. It scared him. A hand caressed his face.

"'Course not. Don't talk like that. Regina is always kind, and you're my little brother. Remember that."

Her voice had softened, but her words failed to comfort him. The bitterness was gone, but she spoke with a sadness now that somehow seemed far worse.

"Then what's the matter?" It embarrassed him to hear his voice tremble so, to sound so small and far away.

"Don't you ever wonder what's out there, beyond these streets, beyond the fields?"

"No." It wasn't true; he had wondered. But he didn't want to encourage her—he only wanted her to stop talking like this.

"I do."

Uh-oh, Jacob thought, *here we go*. "You're just going through a tough time right now. It'll pass," he said, trying to sound grown up and strong.

She laughed. "You too, huh? You sound just like my father."

"Well, maybe he's right."

She didn't answer. A minute passed, the silence building

22

until, unable to avoid the question in his mind, he blurted out at last, "Are you going to run away again?"

"You heard?" she snorted. "Of course you'd hear. Everybody knows everyone else's life around here, probably better than they know their own. That's what my *father* says, anyway."

"I heard some kids talking in school, but I didn't believe it."

"'Course not," she said. Her voice now slipped low, mimicking her father as she had done so often for Jacob in the past. "No one has ever left Harmony before. No one has ever wanted to." Her impression was savagely perfect, but this time Jacob didn't laugh.

"Mother doesn't know."

"She'll find out. If you don't tell her, someone else will."

Jacob didn't know how to respond. He felt as if there were something he had to say or ask, like the words of a magic spell that would solve everything. Make everything good again. Magic words that could heal Delaney, take away the sickness. All he could do was repeat himself.

"Are you going to run away again?"

She reached down and, cupping his face in her hands, kissed him on the forehead.

"Don't worry about me, Jacob. It's not right that you should, or that I should trouble you."

You can trouble me, he wanted to tell her. He regretted his earlier annoyance at her defiance. He had been selfish to be irritated by her pain.

She released him entirely and stepped down into the street.

"I've got to get home. Father's been a little strict lately

23

about my comings and goings. You can guess the reason why. I practically had to threaten him not to send a bodyguard along—to protect me, of course, mostly from myself. Bye, Jacob. We'll talk later."

And then she was gone. Jacob lingered in the yard, listening to her footsteps fade, thinking about her words and the question she had left unanswered.

"Jacob, what are you doing out here?"

Jacob started. It was his mother. He felt as if he had been caught doing something terrible. Maybe he had been.

"Are you all right? Come in for supper."

Without a word, he turned and walked past his mother.

"Is there any more?" Jacob asked, finishing his plate of mashed turnip and greens, swallowing the last of his bread.

"I'm sorry, Jacob. That's it," his mother said. "Didn't you have enough?"

"No, that's okay. I'm full," he lied. Lately food supplies were running low in Harmony. Last year had been a poorer harvest than expected. On top of that, the cattle—the colony's main source of meat and dairy—had contracted some native strain of virus, and many had died before the computer could diagnose and treat with the proper antibodies. As a result, rations had been reduced. Some in the colony grumbled, but none openly complained. They understood the necessity of rationing. Besides, no one was actually starving; there was sufficient food that the council deemed it unnecessary to import more from the outside or bargain with the Seers. Still, at times Jacob felt like he could eat more. A lot more. His mother said he was growing. He suspected she was giving him some of her share behind her husband's back, but Jacob couldn't prove it.

"No one needs to worry," his father explained. "Harvest is almost ready and we're on track for a record yield. Those new fertilizers we developed did the trick. Everyone's rations will return to normal. I also heard," he said, dropping his fork on the table to signal he was done, "we're getting a new shipment of cattle. Straight from Earth. From the Foundation. They've produced a more disease-resistant strain, I guess."

"It's okay, Dad. I'm not hungry."

"Well, I am, and I have to say, despite your mother's ingenious recipes, I'm getting a little tired of turnips. Not that the turnip isn't a wonderful vegetable"—Jacob's father paused for effect—"right, Jacob?"

Jacob's mother laughed at the joke. Since early childhood Jacob had hated turnip, and for a long time had refused to eat it. Not these days.

"What's wrong, Jacob? Too old to laugh at my jokes anymore?" Jacob was silent. "He's so serious, Gina." Jacob knew his father was trying to draw him out. Referring to him in the third person to his mother always made him speak up.

"You have been a bit quiet since you got home." His mother reached out to touch his arm. "Did something happen at school today?"

Jacob didn't know how to respond. He couldn't tell them the truth, but he didn't want to lie, not about this. "We learned to use finders today—it was interesting. Ma, how were your lessons with Delaney?"

"Did you run into her on her way out? Thought I heard you two talking out there."

"Yeah. She seemed like she wasn't feeling good."

"That's what I thought too. Today was terrible. She couldn't focus; her timing was way off. She even broke down crying at one point. I just backed off—it happens to everyone. It even used to happen to me when I was her age. Still, this has been going on for too many days now. Did you hear anything at school, Jacob? Like we talked about this morning?"

What should he say? He hated to tell on Delaney, but it almost seemed like she wanted him to tell his mother. Maybe it would sound better coming from him.

"Actually, Ma, I did hear something."

"Well, what? Tell me." She seemed eager, but frightened.

"A couple of the kids said she tried to run away."

"What?" He could hear the shock straining her voice as she cried out. She paused to collect herself. "That's impossible. I would've heard that. She would've told me." Jacob was nervous. His mother was upset. "When did she supposedly try it?"

"Last week. I guess a couple of men from the outside came in. She tried to leave with them."

"What were Seers doing here?" she wondered.

"They were probably just some technicians from Melville," his father replied. "They have to be brought in from time to time. Don't be upset, Gina. She's just going through a spell."

"Richard, I should be upset about this. And so should you." Her voice sharpened. "Did you know about this already?"

"I had heard something about it from Anders a couple days ago. I didn't think I should tell you."

"Jacob, go to bed." *Uh-oh.* He knew that sound in his mother's voice. There was going to be a fight. She pulled him to her as he arose. She ran her hands through his hair,

26

inspecting her morning's work, and kissed him on the cheek. "Now go," she said. For once he didn't protest. It had been a long day. He was exhausted.

As soon as he closed his door, he could hear the voices rise. The thick door muffled the words, but he could sense what they were saying from the inflections, the mostly hostile inflections, in their voices. He undressed and fell onto the bed. Reaching up, he took down the music box from his bureau and held the tiny cube. The metal toy felt cool and smooth, heavy in his hand. He had received it as a gift on his fifth birthday. *Eight years ago next week*, he thought. For almost three years he had played the tune every night while falling asleep. Since then, he played it only when they fought. Things had been quiet lately; he hadn't listened to it in a while.

Now he wound the handle, spun it a dozen times, and let it play. The tiny notes plucked in his ear a melody he had learned long ago, the melody all of Harmony's children learned. It was a child's song, about a woman who planted some flower seeds that sprouted into little boys and girls. She watered the seeds, and they grew in the sun, stayed rooted in the earth, and never got picked. He could still remember the words of the refrain:

The maiden came and planted them;
The soil holds them safely.
They don't need eyes to love the sun,
Or flourish in its beauty.

He couldn't recollect the rest of the lyrics, but it didn't matter. It was the melody he loved. Simple. Pure. The box played its song with mechanical precision. As Jacob listened more intensely, he realized something for the first time. It wasn't just the melody that soothed him. Even more than the song, he found he loved the hum that carried underneath, the sound of the little motor as it unwound itself, steadily slowing to a stop. It was the hum he now heard beyond any other sound, even the song of the music box itself. It was the motor's hum that carried him off to sleep.

CHAPTER FOUR

The notes resonated from the piano, rising and falling about him, absorbing every worry, driving away all thinking until they became his only thought, a consciousness of sound. He had run through the piece at least fifteen times in the last hour, struggling to get it right, to make it perfect the way it should be, the way it deserved to be. And now he had almost done it. He was nearly to the end. For months he had been working to master his favorite piece, Chopin's Nocturne in E-flat major, and now . . . he had finally done it. He let the final chord ring, luxuriating in the sustained waver of joy.

"You were a little fast on the crescendo in the sixth measure," his mother said casually, coming out of the bedroom where Jacob thought she'd been napping.

"Thanks," he snapped, clapping the cover down over the keys. She came up behind him and ran her fingers across his hair. *Probably checking her haircut again*, he thought. She kissed him on the head.

"Don't be upset," she said. "You almost had it."

"You never encourage me," he muttered.

"I'm sorry, sweetie. You played it beautifully, and with feeling."

"That's not what I mean. You know I want to be a musician—like you and Delaney."

29

She sat down beside him now on the bench. He could hear the hesitancy in her voice as she spoke.

"Jacob, I love that you love music, that it means so much to you. No matter what happens in the future, it will always be a part of your life."

"So you don't think they'll choose me for a music specialization?" He felt a sinking feeling down in his stomach. What did she know?

"That's not what I'm saying, Jacob. I don't know what they're going to decide."

"But you must have some say. . . ."

"Not really. You would think I do, but I don't. All I'm saying, sweetie, is that I don't want you to be disappointed if you don't get the choice you want. Being a musician is a tough specialization. It takes a lot of hard work and skill. You are a good player, Jacob, but it may not be your greatest talent. Who knows? Maybe the council has something even better in store for you. The high councilor has mentioned to me on more than one occasion how well you do in school, how highly your teachers speak of you."

"So you don't think I have what it takes."

"I think you're a smart, sensitive, and obedient boy, the way I raised you to be. I know that no matter what happens, you'll do something special. You *are* special."

"Thanks," he mumbled. He slid around and stood up from the bench.

"Jacob, do me a favor—run over to the Corrows' and tell Delaney that I have to reschedule tomorrow's lesson. The caller's on the blink again. I forgot to tell her I have to play at a luncheon in the South Tier tomorrow. Besides, you haven't been out of the house today. Be good for you to get some air."

"Fine," he said. After this conversation he was eager enough to leave the house anyway.

"Don't stay too long," she called out as he opened the front door. "There's a Gathering tonight, in a couple hours, and I want you to come with me."

"Okay."

"And Jacob," she called out again. She waited, as if unsure he still remained.

"Yes?" he said, pausing in the threshold.

"Say hello to Delaney's father for me."

"Right." He closed the door and left.

Jacob walked through the streets in silence, ignoring the greetings of passersby. The antisocial gesture was a violation of the rules, but compared with everything else right now, it wasn't a major concern. Rubbing his forehead, he even forgot for the moment what his mother had said. Last night, for the third time since the initial attack in the school yard, he had awoken to pain. The first two headaches had roused him from sleep but had been less severe than the one at school. He didn't have any headaches at all for three nights after that and assumed that whatever caused them had disappeared. He had almost forgotten all about them until last night, when he suddenly found himself awake in bed, convulsing from a pain so severe he could only whimper through clenched teeth. Its intensity, far greater and longer lasting than the initial attack, frightened him. Even now the memory of it seemed to linger on his brow as his fingers pushed back along the skin of his forehead, as if he could rub it away for good.

He turned in to the home of the high councilor and

passed up the ramp that led to their door. Theirs was not a simple hillhouse like the others in the colony, but a stone bunker, large and square, not far from the council chamber in the heart of the community. Going to knock, he realized the door was open. He could hear muffled voices coming from inside. Without thinking, he passed into the entryway and started down the hall that led to the living room, from where the voices seemed to come. As he got closer, though, he suddenly realized the tone of the conversation sounded angry. He paused in the hallway, not sure what to do. He felt guilty for listening—eavesdropping was a major offense—but something compelled him to stay, to move in closer to the doorway until he could hear what was being said. He could perceive the sharp voice of Delaney but couldn't quite make out her words. He moved closer still.

"No one leaves Harmony," said the deep voice of the high councilor. "No one's ever left." There was a pause. "Why do you want to leave, Delaney? You have everything here. People who love you, a promising career. You know what's out there? Nothing. Garbage, violence, hate, shallow people leading shallow lives, never knowing their depths."

"How do you know? You've never been outside Harmony; you've hardly spoken to anyone except the few who have to come here. You don't know a single Seer, I mean really know any one of them. All you know is what you've been told. That's all anyone here knows. It's us versus them. Right? Blind or not, it's pretty easy that way."

"And you? You know nothing. How do you know it's *not* that way? Why risk what you have, what I've given you?"

"You're right. I don't know about the world out there. But I want to find out for myself."

32

Jacob could hear the councilor wait, resisting her defiance. When he spoke again, his voice sounded gentler. "Come now, Delaney. There's something else behind all this. Tell me the truth. I suppose it's my fault, right? I'm too harsh. I'm mean, as you used to tell me. On the contrary—if anything, I've spoiled you. So why do you want to run away from me?" She didn't answer. "Delaney, I don't like saying this, but you're ill. You're depressed, desperate. We'll take care of you. Maybe the ghostbox can help you, prescribe something so you'll feel better. You're sick, Delaney, that's all."

"Stop telling me what I am." She was crying now. Jacob could hear her sobbing quietly. After a moment she whispered, "Father, I want to see."

Jacob heard a slap, heard Delaney cry out. The sounds stirred him from where he stood transfixed in the hall. In a panic he turned and fled down the hallway, out through the door, running as quietly as he could, trying not to give himself away, trying to forget what he'd just heard. Which was worse— Delaney's shocking admission or her father's reaction? He wanted to keep on running, but he stopped in the dooryard. He still had to deliver his message. Besides, his interruption would stop the fight, wouldn't it? For now, at least.

He returned to the door, closed it, and knocked loudly. When the door opened a moment later, the proximity of their sounders set his to ringing against Delaney's.

"Jacob," she cried. She sounded relieved.

"Who is it?" her father called out from the hallway behind her.

"Jacob Manford," she snapped back.

"Jacob!" the high councilor said. His voice had completely changed, returning to its normal smooth sincerity. There was

33

no sign of anger. "Come in, young man."

Jacob stepped back into the hall for the second time. Delaney reached out and pulled him to her, draping her arms over his shoulders so that he stood between her and her father.

"What brings you here, son?" the man asked.

"Yes, what brings you to our happy home?" Delaney added sarcastically. Jacob could feel the tension hanging in the air.

"My mother sent me over to tell you, Delaney, that she has to cancel tomorrow's lesson."

"Great!" said Delaney with mock enthusiasm. "I have a lot of other work to do tomorrow anyway. Don't I, Father?"

The high councilor chuckled nervously. "Don't be silly, Delaney. I'm sure you've got plenty of practicing you can do on your own."

"Oh really? Is that what you want?" she retorted. From behind him, Jacob could feel the rising intensity of her voice.

"Is everything okay?" Jacob asked tentatively.

"Of course. Of course it is," the high councilor broke in. "Don't mind her, Jacob. She's just in one of her moods today. Everything's fine."

"Oh yes. Everything's fine," she mocked. "As if anything could possibly be wrong in Harmony. In sweet, sweet Harmony—"

"Enough!" The high councilor's roar startled all of them. For a moment no one spoke. Finally Martin Corrow laughed again. "I'm sorry, Jacob. You've caught us on a bad day. If you'll excuse me, I have to go prepare for the Gathering. Delaney, I'll return shortly. I'll expect you to be ready."

34

When he had left, Delaney grabbed Jacob and headed outdoors.

"Where are we going?" Jacob asked as they walked along the street. She was leading him by the hand, nearly pulling him as she marched along with a rapid stride, so that he had to trot to keep up.

"Nowhere, apparently," she replied. "I just need to get out of that house for a minute," she added, slowing her pace.

"He seemed mad."

"Oh, he's mad, all right. He's always mad," she snorted.

"He's never seemed that way before to me," Jacob offered. He didn't know why, but he felt the need to rationalize the high councilor's anger. "He seems to really care about you."

She suddenly stopped, and he bumped up against her. "About me? I'm an embarrassment, that's what I am. He cares about how things seem. That's all that really matters to him. There's a lot about him you don't know, Jacob."

Maybe that was true, but he didn't want to hear it now. A bell sounded from the square not far away. It rang three times, signaling one hour to the Gathering. The afternoon was coming to an end—Jacob could feel a cooler breeze coming in off the plain and the birds began their evening song. He suddenly felt tired.

"Can't we just pretend everything's okay? Like it used to be? We used to have fun. Just for now, let's pretend," he pleaded.

He could sense her hesitation. Then she sighed and squeezed his hand. "All right," she said. "I'll pretend. For you."

She squeezed his hand again, and they turned around and headed back to her house. They took their time, walking slowly, deliberately. But though they were together, though he could feel the warmth of her hand, the beating of her pulse within his hand, she seemed more distant than ever, withdrawn into her silence, both further in and farther away.

They had reached her yard again. She took a step toward the house but still held his hand.

"I better go in," she said.

"Okay."

She let go her grip, and he let his hand drop, but neither of them moved.

"I don't know," she said slowly. "Maybe he's right about me. Maybe I am just depressed. Sick."

"Of course you're not. Don't say that."

She didn't reply at first. For a moment neither of them spoke. When she did speak again, her voice was quieter, and he could tell her back was to him.

"Thanks, Jacob," she said. He listened to her steps all the way up the ramp, listened to the door open and close. Only then did he turn to go.

"Come on, Jacob! We'll be late for the Gathering."

"Here I am, Ma. I'm ready," Jacob said, coming into the kitchen. His mother took his hand and they left the house. "Where's Dad?" he said as they entered the street. It wasn't unusual that he had missed dinner, but they always attended Gatherings as a family.

"In the fields."

"Still? Nobody works during a Gathering."

"He said his shift would probably have to go a little late. They've got a lot of preparations to make for harvest. Don't worry, he'll be there."

36

They were walking for less than a minute when his mother suddenly stopped and drew him aside. He could feel her breath as she leaned down to his ear.

"Jacob," his mother whispered, "you forgot to activate your sounder again." She reached over and tapped the pin on his chest. He suddenly realized that he had been silent, that only his mother's note, a perfect high C, was quivering in the air. His D-sharp in a lower register sounded subdued and quiet as their tones mingled. He could hear other notes begin to chime as they came up behind a crowd, and they all moved toward the central square where every Gathering was held. He felt annoyed at having forgotten again. On the other hand, he was still rattled by the scene at Delaney's house. The words of her upsetting admission to her father continued to echo in his memory as they had all the way home. She had joked about seeing once or twice in the past to Jacob, had wondered what it would be like, but this was different. Jacob shivered now, remembering her voice in the house barely an hour ago as she confessed her desire. It was devoid of humor, of even her characteristic defiance—an utterance of quiet desperation.

They turned onto a wider street. No one spoke. All that could be heard was the chord of sounders woven together, growing louder as more and more citizens merged into the broad avenue that led to the square, until even the muffled steps of shoes scuffing the stones beneath their feet were lost in the music.

They were in the square now. Jacob could no longer feel the mild resistance of the pathminders to his right. Instead he felt the touch of hands from the crowd around him on his back, shoulders, and arms. He, in turn, reached before him to

37

touch the back of another in front. He wondered who it was. Could it be one of his teachers? A neighbor? His own father? Maybe it was Beth. Maybe it was a stranger. His mother held his left hand and they pressed forward, moving deeper into the square, into the mass of bodies. Now the combined sounders of virtually everyone in the colony blended into a single chord of myriad notes, rising to a fevered intensity, creating overtones that seemed to hover in the air above them like insects.

This part of the Gathering Jacob had always loved. He found comfort in the anonymous bodies of those around him, in the loss of self that accompanied his own anonymity. He liked being part of something bigger than himself, adding his own sound to the music of the hive. But today the single sustained chord overwhelmed him; it sounded dissonant and oppressive in his ears, and the bodies around him seemed to be smothering him. The realization crept up on him slowly, a deep and hidden awareness that flirted beneath his consciousness before bursting to the surface. Now his anonymity terrified him, as if he were slipping away from himself, losing himself within the single mass that surrounded him like the grasses of the plain. He felt trapped and had to fight the urge to bolt, had to resist the waves of nausea that were rising at the corners of his consciousness.

Again, as last night, a wave of pain overtook him and he stiffened, bracing himself as the sounders shrieked around him. They pierced his eardrums with their quavering overtones. Now the pain became localized, erupting from its deepest recesses into his eyes. He gasped at its intensity and closed his lids against the pins that pierced the delicate membrane of his eyeballs. Closing them seemed to offer relief, as

38

if someone had poured water on the fire in his brow.

"Ow, Jacob, you're hurting me." His mother was yelling in his ear, though she was barely audible against the sounders. She was trying to pull her hand away from his grasp, and he realized he had been gripping her so tightly that his hand was beginning to cramp and his nails were digging into her knuckles. He relaxed his grip and swallowed. His mouth was dry and had a sour taste. He had to be careful of her hands—she was a musician, her hands were precious. A cymbal crashed and then crashed again. The signal for silence. Simultaneously hands touched sounders, and the chord abruptly ceased. Jacob breathed a sigh of relief. The silence relaxed him, and the impulse to flee receded.

"Welcome, citizens of Harmony!" a man said into the silence. It was the high councilor. His voice surrounded them, amplified by speakers that bordered the square. Jacob listened to the voice that only a few hours ago had been fuming with rage. It was hard to believe it was the same. This voice was the normal voice, the one he'd heard the second time he went into the hallway, the one he'd always heard before. He suddenly realized there was no differentiation in tone between the voice that had spoken to him then and the one that spoke now to a crowd of several hundred. In the house, though they had been only feet apart, Jacob had still felt as though he were being addressed from afar, amidst a crowd like the one in which he was now entangled.

"We have come together to renew our bonds of community, to strengthen our chosen path to Truesight," the voice resonated.

The crowd responded to the familiar prompt, chanting in

unison, "Blindness is purity. Blindness is unity. Blindness is freedom."

Jacob recited the Foundation's motto with the others, but his words were mumbled, his voice low.

The councilor spoke again from the platform at the far end of the square. "For today's Gathering, the East Tier chorus will perform a song recently composed by the musicians of our sister colony on Pollard. It is extraordinary."

A moment of silence elapsed. Then the group on the platform began to sing. The small chorus, five women and five men, sounded much larger, their voices magnified by the speakers in the square. As the music washed over them, the crowd gasped at its beauty. Even Jacob's mother, who was often critical of others' performances, drew in her breath and squeezed his hand as the music surrounded them. Words were sung, but Jacob wasn't listening to them. They were just beautiful sounds that absorbed his earlier unease and carried it away. Though the rhythm and dynamics varied, the song's tempo was quick and light, an intricate dance of notes. There was no instrumental accompaniment; none was needed. Instead the voices themselves seemed to assume the timbre of strings and horns.

The song ended and Harmony exploded in applause. Jacob joined in. He felt whole again, connected to the mass of people expressing their appreciation to the chorus. The feeling of peace lingered, leaving him dazed and barely listening to the high councilor's speech to the community. It didn't matter, though. The brief sermon was usually a variation on a single theme—Harmony Station and the Foundation represented the pinnacle of human virtue and self-fulfillment, a model for the rest of humanity. Occasionally a diatribe would be vented against the Seers, a reference to a recent tragedy somewhere among the settled worlds. The speech usually concluded with a list of Harmony's recent accomplishments—which team of growers had gathered the highest yield that week, a sculptor who had created a new fountain in the South Tier square, a particular student who had been chosen to visit Earth for advanced study with the Foundation. On occasion, before everyone left, there were announcements. Sometimes these took the form of chastisements, such as a warning to conserve food or water or a reminder about a rule. Today an announcement was made, and Jacob tuned back in as the high councilor concluded.

"Citizens of Harmony: tomorrow evening there will be a delivery. Growers will remain in the fields at their stations as usual. All others will observe the curfew and remain at home after the dinner hour. This delivery is important. I've arranged for Harmony to receive a shipment of food supplies to supplement our own stores until the harvest. That is all."

The four horns sounded at each corner of the square, their different pitches guiding citizens in the proper direction toward home. The crowd began to dissemble, sorting themselves toward various exits, quietly seeping out of the square like an evaporating mist. Once back on the avenues, sounders rang once again, growing quieter as people separated into smaller groups along the side streets. Jacob walked with his mother, listening to the excited voices talking about tomorrow's delivery and its promise of better meals. People always became excited when there was a delivery, no matter what its contents. Once they were home, he asked his mother the reason why.

"I don't know. Something different, I suppose. A break from routine."

41

"Have you ever been to one?" he asked.

"Of course not. Everyone's at home during a curfew," she reminded him. "Who cares, anyway? I'm sure it's quite boring. The Seers come in with their haulers, drop off a bunch of crates, and go home. That's it." She sounded impatient, as though she was waiting for something.

"Then, why do we have to stay indoors?"

"For our own protection, probably. It's unsafe to have people on the street with a bunch of vehicles, men, and boxes moving in every direction."

Suddenly realizing his father hadn't joined them after the Gathering, Jacob asked, "Where's Dad?"

"He'll be home soon." It occurred to Jacob that maybe she didn't know. "In the meantime I'm tired. You should go to bed too. You have to deliver your report tomorrow, don't you?"

That's right, he did. He had nearly forgotten about it. Fortunately he'd finished it a week ago. He had practiced with his mother and his father at different times until it was firmly committed to memory. Tomorrow he would repeat the same words, only in front of the class. Since he was scheduled last, he had already heard everyone else's speeches and knew he could do as good a job. He would simply stand in front and press the play button in his memory, like the lesson players in the library. No, he wasn't worried about the report; it was something else that kept him from leaving the room.

"Ma, I haven't been feeling good the last few days. I keep getting headaches."

"So what? My head aches all the time. Take one of my pills if you want." She sounded like his father all of a sudden.

"I was going to, but the headaches don't stay long enough

to bother; they go as quickly as they come."

"Come here," she said. She put her cheek against his forehead. "You don't feel feverish. I'm sure you're fine. Just growing pains, that's all. If you're still having them next week, I'll try to arrange a visit to the infirmary. Wait a minute"—she stopped him as he turned to go—"this is about tomorrow, isn't it? You're trying to weasel out of giving your report."

"No, I'm not," he said. He knew she was teasing him, but it irritated him anyway. He went to his room, got ready for bed, and crawled under the covers. He heard his father come home just as he was falling asleep. He drifted off to the sound of his parents' subdued, angry voices muffled through the door.

CHAPTER FIVE

"Okay, Jacob. Time for your report," Mrs. Lawson prompted. Jacob stood before the class, swaying slightly in the midday sun. As they did on occasion, the students were sitting on the lawn behind the school, a level plane of grass thirty yards square. "Some fresh air today," the teacher had said.

"We've saved Jacob's report for last because, in many ways, his is the most important," Mrs. Lawson continued. "We will end our presentations by going back to the beginning. Jacob will speak on the origins of the Foundation."

The obligatory applause sounded from the class, and Jacob prepared to speak. He found it difficult to concentrate. A haze had been crowding into his brain all morning, gathering like a heavy storm, punctuated by distant lightning flares of pain. Upon standing, the aching intensified, concentrating in his brow. He was sure that insects were crawling along his face, stinging at the edges of his eyes. He closed them and the burning subsided noticeably, dwindling to almost nothing. With reluctance, he opened them. Again, the pain resurfaced, but not as intensely. In its place a brightness so faint it was merely a gray glow hung before him. He blinked several times. He didn't know what brightness was; he only knew that when he closed his eyes, that which was before him changed, and changed again when he raised his lids.

44

"Jacob, let's go. We're waiting," Mrs. Lawson stated impatiently.

I can do this, Jacob told himself. He pushed aside the bizarre sensation flooding his consciousness, let go the words he had heard and spoken so many times.

"The Foundation was created in 2102 by Francis and Jean Aldrich from the city of Toronto in a nation known as Canada. Prior to its creation, many parents had been selecting the characteristics of their children for several decades—everything from gender to eye and hair color—through genetic engineering. Both Francis and Jean had been born blind. They wanted their children to be a part of their way of life, so they decided that their children would share this trait, creating the first generation of children intentionally born with what some considered a disability. The publicity generated by the event persuaded several other couples in Canada and the United States to do the same."

Now the dim gray glow grew to ash, trembled and surged, flirted with silver before finally receding to black. Again the wave passed through him as he stood paralyzed. A voice, sounding small and distant, asked what was happening. He realized it was his own voice, the voice inside his head asking a question for which he had no answer. He realized he had stopped speaking, that everyone waited. How long had he been standing in silence?

Jacob cleared his throat and continued, his voice weaker. "Many people criticized the Aldriches and other parents for the choice they made. They argued that these parents were saddling their children with a burden, that they were doing no less than inflicting cruelty on them. Other, good people, however, hailed the Aldriches for their brave decision. They

45

denounced the critics for their bigotry, for attempting to impose their own cultural prejudices. Heartened by their supporters and aided by an endowment from the Robertson Corporation—an aeronautics company whose founder, Lowell Robertson, was himself blind—the Aldriches and several other sightless families purchased a thousand acres of land and organized the first community on the continent of Australia. Soon blind people from all over Earth began to settle in the community, now named Robertson. Inspired by Eastern spiritualism and a seventeenth-century group called the Puritans, Francis, Jean, and their friends formulated the philosophy they called Truesight."

Jacob stopped. A new wave was approaching; he could feel it. He braced himself as it flared brighter and brighter, this time not fading to black, but holding steady. The light, incredible in the midday sun, penetrated his being. It shone around him as he turned his head—brighter in some places, darker in others, but ever present. Even when he closed his eyes, a part of the brightness remained, though it was a different shade when filtered through the membrane of his eyelids. He opened his eyes again. Now the light was fragmented, brighter above, darker below. In the darker area lighter patches, round in shape, floated before him. He felt dizzy.

"Go on, Jacob, you're doing a fine job," Mrs. Lawson encouraged.

Jacob took several deep breaths and closed his eyes again. Still the light burned before him. "I don't feel good," he murmured. A couple of students giggled. He brought both hands up and covered his eyes, pressing hard against his face to smother the fire. It worked; the brightness was gone. He kept his hands in place. As long as he didn't remove them, every-

46

thing would be all right, the way it was before.

"You're only nervous, Jacob. Now please, finish your report, and afterward I'll send you to the infirmary."

The darkness of the cool hands calmed him. He continued. "By the time Francis Aldrich died, at the turn of the century, the Foundation was firmly established and Robertson had grown to a sizable and thriving community, branching out to form a sister community in New Zealand named after Aldrich. Truesight became a more widely respected philosophy. Some even voluntarily became blind through surgery and moved to Robertson. These people were called Oedipi, named after the ancient hero Oedipus who, in rejecting the evil of the world, bravely chose the path of blindness. To this day Oedipi, like Egan's father"—as he had planned earlier, Jacob paused here to honor his friend—"continue to be among the most respected members of the Foundation, having overcome the limitations of their former sight."

The words now flowed quickly. More than anything, he wanted to be done. He felt self-conscious standing before everyone, hands covering his face; no one knew what he was doing, what lay beneath his hands. Still, it felt like a deceit, though he didn't quite know what he was hiding.

Drops of sweat were forming on his forehead, trickling down behind his ear and onto his neck as he pressed on. "Things were not perfect, however. Over the course of several generations, the Foundation remained the victim of criticism and occasional physical assault. The August Day Massacre— in which four Foundation members were killed and a dozen wounded on August fifth, 2193, by a group of antigenetic terrorists—led the Western Compact to grant the Foundation protected status, which it retains to this day, both on Earth

47

and among the settled worlds. In the centuries since then, the Foundation has spread throughout explored space, free from harassment, and has striven to become a model to humanity. The end."

The abrupt conclusion surprised the class, the teacher, and himself. Finally a smattering of applause sounded from the students. Mrs. Lawson cleared her throat. "You ended a little quickly, Jacob. Did you want to say more?" she asked.

He did have more material, but he just couldn't go on. "No, I'm done," he answered weakly. He sat down and uncovered his face. The brightness remained. When he opened his eyes, he felt a little dizzier. He just wanted to go home.

"Well," she said, "unfortunately, your grade will suffer for ending so abruptly, but what you did say was excellent. You certainly know the history."

Did he? he wondered. As if inflamed by the stinging light, he grew annoyed at the patronizing tone of the teacher's last remark. He had said what he was supposed to say, but the more he thought about it, the less he was sure what much of it meant. What was "Eastern philosophy" or "aeronautics"? Who were the Puritans? He didn't know much about Oedipus, beyond his brief remark. A pulsating tone sounded in the background, the sound of a finder. The students began to whisper to one another, wondering who was carrying the rare device. The sound grew louder and faster as it approached, then stopped. A male voice unfamiliar to Jacob called for the teacher, who left the group and went off to the side for a hushed discussion.

Jacob could sense the other children around him creep forward slowly, quietly, in the direction of the voices. They were eager to find out about the surprise visit and had forgotten about him. He didn't join them. He sat and blinked his eyes. Off and on, off and on, the light before him flashed. Undistracted by having to perform before the class, he turned his head slowly as the sensation of light altered, shifting with the movement of his head from up to down and side to side. It suddenly occurred to him, deep inside, so slightly he could hardly grasp it, what could be happening to him. What shouldn't be happening to him. He knew but was unable to say it, unable to admit it to himself. But he knew.

The voice disappeared, the finder slowly beeping after a new target, and Mrs. Lawson addressed the class. "I have just been told that the delivery will occur earlier than scheduled. Therefore your afternoon session is canceled. Everyone in Harmony is to report home immediately. Curfew will commence in one hour." She dismissed the students and everyone parted for home. Though no one said a word around Mrs. Lawson, Jacob could sense their elation. He wondered why this dismissal couldn't have happened ten minutes ago and saved him the embarrassment of curtailing his report. Still, the idea of going home was preferable to sitting through an afternoon of class. Everything that had happened, that was happening right now, overwhelmed and exhausted him, leaving him empty and confused. He was so distracted he barely heard the familiar pitch of Egan's sounder approaching from behind.

"Hey," Egan whispered in his ear, coming up beside him and taking his arm once they were well away from school, "I have an idea." Jacob groaned—he knew what was coming. "Let's check out the delivery."

"And how are we going to do that?" Jacob asked. "Our parents will never let us out during a curfew."

49

"Come on, it'll be easy for you. Your father's out in the fields, so it's only your mother. You just said you felt sick. Tell her you're not feeling good and that you want to go to bed, and then sneak out. Listen, you bailed out on me the last time I asked you to have some fun. I'm starting to wonder about you."

"What about you?" Jacob shot back.

"Don't worry about me; I have my own techniques of escape," Egan assured him.

Jacob hesitated. Maybe he should go. Maybe the adventure would serve as a distraction. Besides, he had refused Egan last week about borrowing the finder; he didn't want to seem too much like a coward. "All right. But how do we avoid getting caught?"

"Okay, I've thought about that. All we do is leave our sounders at home. We'll be totally silent and the listeners won't be able to track us."

"What about the delivery workers? They are Seers, you know."

"True, but the curfew always starts well before they arrive—I heard my father say so once. We simply leave right after it starts and find a hiding place. You know that little rise just above the drop-off point near the storehouses? We'll slip over there and hide in the tall grass. They'll never be able to see us; I'm sure of it."

It was a good plan, Jacob had to agree. Still, it sounded almost too easy, but he couldn't tell Egan that. Egan depended on enthusiasm, and Jacob had always responded in kind. Now, however, his friend's energy and certainty made Jacob more conscious of his own uncertainties, more aware of his own confusion and pain.

"Jake?" Egan shook him. "Are you there? I'm talking to you!"

"Sorry," Jacob said, "I was thinking."

"Of course. Jacob the thinker. Don't think too much, okay? That's what my father says. And you know what—he's right."

"I suppose," Jacob agreed. Nevertheless, the plan sounded too easy.

"When curfew starts, wait ten minutes and then meet me behind the school," Egan said, turning onto his street. "We'll go together from there, and remember to forget your sounder."

Egan took off. Jacob listened to him go, until he disappeared around the bend, before continuing home. He wondered how his friend could break the rules so easily. After all, his father was an Oedipi, sent directly by the Foundation to assist the council. He was an important person. Maybe that's why Egan acted that way—he probably figured he could get away with it, even if he was caught. Would that bubble of safety cover Jacob as well? Probably not. His father wasn't important; he was a grower. His job was important, but he wasn't. His mother was more prominent, but still, several musicians in Harmony were as skilled as she was.

Jacob picked up the pace, walking with abandon, not caring if he ran into anything or anyone. He was angry with himself for thinking those thoughts about his parents, angry with Egan for being both carefree and powerful, and angry at all the circumstances in his life that he couldn't control. He shut his eyes and this time kept them closed, slipped back into the darkness all the way home. Only when he'd shut the door behind him did he dare to open them again,

51

and all remained dark in the underground house.

His mother was there, practicing a new composition on the antique piano. She barely noticed when Jacob told her he wasn't feeling good and was going to bed. He went to his room and shut the door most of the way, being careful not to latch it. He pulled his sounder off his shirt and tossed it on the bureau, where it landed with a metallic thud before clinking off the music box. Flopping onto the bed, he lay back and listened to the notes drifting from the living room, hanging in the dark. The music stopped when his mother went into the kitchen. Then, distant but loud enough to be heard through the earthen walls of his home, a siren wailed. Curfew had begun.

CHAPTER SIX

Why am I here? Jacob thought as he leaned against the back wall of the schoolhouse. *Because it's Egan,* he realized. In another few weeks school would be over. Then they would be busy working in the fields, helping with the harvest for those two weeks of service, like most members of the community. After that, who knew? Whatever the specialization assigned to him, he knew that it would be different from Egan's. Once they began their training, they wouldn't be spending much time together. So here he was, for what would probably be one last adventure, as Egan referred to them. To this point it had been fairly easy. His mother had resumed playing by the time he left, hammering out notes that filled every room of the house, and was so focused on her music she wouldn't have noticed if Jacob had slammed the door on his way out. After that, slipping along the empty streets was simple.

Surveying the brightness around him, he had a difficult time feeling that anything else mattered right now. Even his recent fears for Delaney diminished in the strange glow that engulfed him. When he left the house, the light had relented from earlier in the day and the air had cooled, as if the sun had decided not to burn so hotly. A pressure filled the air now, a heaviness that reminded him of the Gathering last night. He could sense a storm was coming. Again and again he blinked, amazed and frightened at the novelty of the experience. By now the pain had vanished, but the realization of what was happening to him offered its own pain. For the first time he admitted it to himself. He was seeing, or at least starting to. But this unnavigable blur of light and shadows couldn't actually be sight, could it? He suspected he was on his way, however, and could only wonder how far he would go. Until now, he could hold on to a glimmer of doubt that he was beginning to see. He could hope that this changing awareness was not the thing his entire world was structured against. He could hope that it would disappear, along with the memory, and he would be left behind to continue as he was—a boy dealing with the normal fears of a normal life.

But as Jacob had walked through the town on his way to the school, he had known that it was real. He could see the lighter strip above—which he assumed was the sky—stretching all the way across his awareness, slipping down into the middle, where the street ran straight before him. As before, he noticed the darker patch below the horizon, the earth rising up to either side, where he knew the hills and houses lay. He wondered if he should tell Egan about what was happening to him. Or reveal it to anyone. The thought made him queasy. How could he possibly tell anyone he was becoming a Seer? Still, the idea of keeping this terrible secret hidden— pretending everything was normal, everything was fine— seemed much worse. It went against everything he had been taught—that there were no secrets in Harmony.

Where was Egan, anyway? Jacob had been early and lived closer to the school, but Egan should have arrived about five minutes ago. *He better not be bailing out on me*, Jacob thought. No, if Egan hadn't arrived yet, there was a good reason. Maybe his father was being more vigilant than usual. Jacob had known Mr. Spencer for several years and had decided that he was the most suspicious person he had ever met. Perhaps part of it had to do with having a son like Egan, who would give anyone a reason to be suspicious. Still, Egan's father sometimes gave Jacob an uneasy, almost guilty feeling. The man was continually asking him questions whenever he went to visit Egan, wanting to know about Jacob's neighbors, about his teachers—what did they do? Had they ever mentioned this matter or that idea? Jacob didn't like it and felt sorry for Egan, though he probably shouldn't, since Egan himself didn't seem to take his father too seriously.

He waited a few more minutes and then left. Egan would know where to find him; it was his plan, after all. Moving away from the schoolhouse, Jacob walked as quickly as he could, crossing to the more isolated back streets, and then followed the path that led to the storehouses. He began hearing voices. At first he froze instinctively, as if waiting for the inevitable approach and apprehension. He realized, however, that the voices he heard were far away. He relaxed and continued until the storehouses loomed as dark shapes against the brightness of the sky. Though still distant, the voices were closer now and to his left, coming from the other side of the buildings. He hurried to the back of the nearest structure, around the corner from where the workers waited for the arrival of the Seers. He could hear the high councilor's voice among them, issuing orders.

In the distance came a deep rumbling sound, a bass that he seemed to feel as much as hear. Steadily it grew. It must be the haulers. Under cover of the noise they provided, he slipped away from the buildings and in the direction of the hill behind the cluster of storehouses, entering the tall grass. He dropped to his hands and knees and began crawling up the bank; the tall blades of coarse grass scratched his face and hands as he pushed them aside. By now the rumble of the haulers was incredible. They sounded as if they were about to come rolling down right on top of him. For a moment he panicked, wondering if he had put himself directly in their path. But he knew that thought was ridiculous; they were coming from the other side of the buildings, and he was safe. He stopped to listen, hearing them pull closer before coming to a stop. Their engines wound down and the rushing hiss of hydraulics announced their arrival.

Feeling exposed on the hillside, he picked his way through the cover until he could sense that he had gone up and over the rise. He rolled down the back side of the hill a few yards and came to rest in the grass. He stayed motionless for a moment and caught his breath, looking into the sky that was a gray blur, the tall grass a fuzzy dimness at the edges. *Where is Egan?* he wondered again. He couldn't sense anyone nearby, but that meant nothing. He listened to the commotion of the delivery on the other side of the hill so he could tell his friend later, but heard little. A few indistinguishable voices shouted commands back and forth. He also heard the lowing of cattle. They must be the new stock his father had mentioned earlier. The wind, which had started to pick up in the last ten minutes, began to intensify, rustling the grass, making it difficult to hear above the swishing.

He decided to seek a better vantage point and scuttled back toward the crest and along the top. He heard the sudden rustle at his feet but it was too late. Something heavy fell across his shins and instantly he was tumbling through the air and into the grass, letting out a muffled grunt. He had tripped over someone's leg and was scrambling to rise when a foot drove into his back, a blind kick that knocked him down again. He turned over and lunged back toward the assailant, tackling the figure and pinning its arms against the ground.

"Stop it, Egan! It's only me," he hissed.

"Jacob?" a girl's voice cried out in surprise.

"Delaney?" he gasped, equally in shock. He rolled off her and sat in the grass, panting as adrenaline flooded his body.

"What are you doing here?" she demanded, moving away.

"I was meeting Egan here to check out the delivery." He winced, wishing he hadn't mentioned his friend, though he knew she wouldn't tell. "What about you? What are you doing here?" She didn't answer. Suddenly he understood. "You're going to try to leave again, aren't you? You're going to run away."

"I have to go, Jacob. I have to do it this way; I don't have any choice."

"This is crazy. How are you going to get out of here, anyway? They can see you, you know. Maybe not us, but those other men can. Are you just going to walk down there, in front of everyone, and hop in the back of a hauler, no questions asked? You're only going to get in trouble again."

"I have to try it. I have to do something," she whispered.

"Laney," he pleaded, "this is wrong. What makes you think leaving will make everything better?"

"Great. First my father and now you, too?" Her voice simmered with contempt, but he persisted.

"How are they going to react to this? My mother, your father? How is this going to affect *everyone*?"

"Don't think I haven't considered that. I have, over and

over. But even more, I think about what's out there, what it must be like in a different place. Sometimes it's all I can think about, and then I feel I can never be happy here."

Jacob couldn't speak. The whole conversation was too strange to really be happening. He sat there, feeling powerless, feeling the wind against his face, listening to the bang of crates, the calling of men, and the lowing of cattle below.

"I sound desperate, don't I?" She tried to laugh. It came out sounding hollow and forced. "Well, I am. I'm just sad. A sad case."

"If you try to leave, I'll yell. Right now I'll yell and they'll come. I swear I will," he whispered.

"No, you won't. We're friends, aren't we, Jake?" She reached out and brushed his shoulder, held his hand.

Yes, he thought, of course they were. But what was a friend supposed to do in this situation, a situation that was never supposed to happen in the first place? He wasn't sure. What would the rules say? The rules would say he should report her immediately. But the rules also said he should never be here to begin with. When he didn't answer, she spoke again, raising her voice against a gust of wind.

"Jacob, I don't expect you to understand. Just trust me when I say it's too late for me. If I don't get away with this delivery, it's over. My father—"

"We can hear you there!" a voice called from the hillside a dozen yards away. "Stop, both of you, and stand up!" a man ordered, his voice growing louder as he crested the ridge.

"Run!" Delaney screamed.

Without thinking, Jacob raced in the opposite direction of the voice. The wind roared. The only other sound was the beating of blood in his ears and the gasping of his breath as he

58

tore through the grass. He stopped momentarily to listen and catch his breath, panic rising in his chest. Where was Delaney? Where was he? He had to think. He had to listen. He had to be smart and get his bearings. A listener must have heard them and cried out—the Seers wouldn't have been able to see them behind the hilltop, or even care if they had, would they? He thought he could hear shouting in the distance, but the voices didn't sound close. He figured the listeners either weren't chasing him or were moving in the wrong direction. If they used a Seer to help them, he was finished. He could only hope that they wanted to avoid the embarrassment and not call on them, or that the Seers would be too indifferent to interfere.

Bounding through the grass, Jacob rushed in the direction he thought would return him to his home, back to some street where he could at least stop and get his bearings. The ground was level, which made his going easier, but he stumbled several times, distracted by fear and the echo of Delaney's haunted voice. He paused for a moment and wondered what had happened to her. Had she been caught? Did she escape after all? He began running again, this time frantically, lifting his feet high to avoid the tangling grass. The wind changed directions and began blowing in his face. For the first time, he realized he was crying, the breeze accentuating the tears streaked cool across his cheeks. He ran for what seemed like forever, trapped in a dream, in that nightmare where no matter how fast or far he tried to go, he went nowhere.

With a thud, Jacob tripped and fell. The blades of grass scratched him, their fibers biting into his skin. Burying his face in his arms, he began to cry openly and just gave in to it, listening to the long sobs as though it were someone else who was weeping, somebody else's pain that he had nothing to do with. Swallowed by the grass, the wind blowing stronger, blocking the possibility of any other sound, he felt alone, as if he were the only person who existed, as if all life had disappeared beyond this sphere of grass within the plains. He felt so tired. Maybe he could just stay here and rest, sleep in this cocoon and awake to find himself someone else, someone still blind, someone who wasn't confused and powerless, who didn't know that other people struggled unhappily with their reality.

He was ready to drift off when something soft brushed against his face, startling him. He froze in the grass, not certain what to do. Suddenly a gentle purring murmured in his ear, and a scratchy tongue licked at the dampness along the contour of his face. He sighed with relief and brought the cat toward him. It was a big cat, heavy, with a sleek coat that rolled in his hands as he pulled the animal to him. He lay back with the cat upon his chest, scratching its ears and back, listening to it purr. After a minute it tensed to leave, but Jacob held on. It struggled against his hands until, sick of the game, it turned and swatted a paw against his face. He winced as the tips of its claws caught his nose, and he let go. The cat disappeared, silent and back on the hunt.

He wiped the tears from his face. The crying had run its course and the universe had returned. Picking himself up again, Jacob continued forward, slower now, trying to estimate the distance toward the settlement. The blur of light and dark between land and sky was no help at all, and the difference was less pronounced as the sky darkened with clouds. Time and space seemed distorted as he worked the riddle of movement in his mind. It seemed like he had traveled too far, that he should have found some path a while ago. On the other hand, it also felt as if he had been running for hours, when it couldn't have been more than ten or fifteen minutes since Delaney screamed for him to escape. After a minute he felt his right hand brush against a pathminder. A step later the gravel crunched beneath his feet, and he could feel the repellent strength of the beam, its semicircle of force focused on the street side only. Not sure which way to go, he chose right, hoping to find some familiar landmark that could lead him home. All he desired now was his own room and his own bed, where he could sleep and forget this entire day.

He finally had a bit of luck. After walking only a few dozen yards, he could hear the North Tier fountain in the distance, one of the many fountains scattered throughout the settlement, each with its own distinctive collection of waterfalls and spraying patterns; this one was Jacob's favorite. It was made of smooth rock, saved from the initial clearing of Harmony's fields. It was also the tallest, with a built-in slide on one side, which Jacob and his friends, as young children, used to slip down on hot summer days. Best of all, it was located in his own section of Harmony, only a three-minute walk down a few streets to home.

He quickened his pace and entered the small square dominated by the fountain. He approached its edge and dipped his hands in, scooping a handful of water to his mouth. It tasted treated, more so than most of the water in Harmony, but it was cool. He drank, scooping several more times, cupping both hands together. He hadn't realized he was so thirsty. The staccato clip of the three spigots spraying in unison from the top of the fountain rained a gentle mist on him. He leaned in and felt the cool spray coating his face. He blinked as the water stung his open eyes and, stepping back, glanced at the sky, dimmer now but bright enough to silhouette the dark fountain rising above him. Splashing more water on his face, he felt the sting of tiny cuts and scratches on his face and arms. He quickly washed himself to remove the film of tears and sweat, gasping at the coldness. He wanted to linger and listen to the clicking jets of water, ticking like his mother's metronome against the rush of tiny waterfalls and gurgling rivulets that cascaded down all sides of the fountain and into its collecting pool, but he had to go. He was already unbelievably lucky to have made it this far; the listeners would certainly scan the entire colony after the incident on the ridge.

He traced his way down the last turn and arrived home. No sound emanated from the street; everyone was subdued by the curfew. He listened at his door, hoping for the sound of his mother's piano that would give him the chance to sneak in undetected, but silence greeted him. He turned the latch gently, making sure there was no click of metal against metal that sounded when he normally opened the door. With even speed and pressure he swung the door open quickly, in a way that avoided the usual squeaks. He listened again. All was quiet. *She must be sleeping*, he thought with relief, closed the door behind him, and made for his room through the dark.

"Jacob, stop." He froze at the sound of his mother's voice. For a moment he thought desperately for an excuse, some lie to prove he had never left, but he figured it would only make matters worse. She would already have checked his room and realized he had left and was returning. "You forgot this," she said. A small metal object bounced off his chest and rattled to the floor. It was his sounder. "Well?"

"Well, what? There's nothing to say," he replied, and immediately cringed at his response. He needed to be conciliatory, make a show of remorse. And it wouldn't be fake—he really was sorry he had ever left to begin with. And now this, the perfect end to a horrible day. No. It could be worse. He could really have been caught. He could be sitting right now with the listeners in detention.

"There's a lot to say, Jake. You idiot!" Jacob felt as though he had been struck. She had never called him names, saving nasty words for his father. She was furious. "I cannot believe you would violate curfew. It's just something that—people don't do it, that's all."

"I'm sorry, Ma. I know. It was stupid."

"Okay, then. Good, Jacob. Everything's suddenly fixed. No problem."

He hated her sarcasm. What did she want him to say? This was almost as bad as the conversation with Delaney. Thinking about Delaney suddenly helped him, made him feel better in a way. It put this whole ugly scene into perspective. What did this matter? Not at all. His mother's anger, which was probably equally mixed with fear, would disappear by tomorrow. It always had in the past.

"Can I go to bed?" he asked, his voice as neutral as possible.

"We're not finished. First you get a warning for not activating your sounder, and now this. I don't want to know what the punishment for this would be. I could be demoted, or your father. You could ruin any chance for a decent specialization. You want to be stuck out in the fields, working with your father?" She sounded so contemptuous.

"Why do you always have to go after him?" he retorted.

"You're talking about me right now. Remember?" What did she know about the future? What could she understand about his problems, about what he was dealing with?

"You want to go to bed?" She was holding back tears. "Fine, go to bed. When Richard gets home, I'm going to tell him about this, and tomorrow we're all going to have a talk. Now go away and leave me alone!" She was practically screaming. He marched quickly to his room and slammed the door.

For a few moments he stood there, his chest heaving. He wanted to punch the door, kick the bed, do *something*. Without thinking, he groped across the bureau top, grabbed his music box, and threw it against the wall. He could hear it smash in the darkness, raining fragments of metal that tinkled as they scattered across the floor. Collapsing onto the bed, he drew the pillow over his face. A moment later he could hear the piano notes sailing down the hall and into his room. His mother was back at it. This time she played furiously, pounding the keys, sending minor chords flying around the house, beating against his door. He listened to her play an entire song, and then another, and another, each song equally intense. Jacob pressed the pillow against his ears, but the sound still penetrated. He couldn't escape its terror or its beauty.

Removing the pillow from his ears, Jacob sat up in bed and listened. She had stopped playing midsong. Getting up from his bed, he crept to the door and opened it a crack. He could hear voices in the foyer—his mother's and a man's. At first he thought his father had returned, and his heartbeat quickened, imagining the conversation that was occurring. He moved silently into the hallway and discovered the man's voice wasn't his father's, but a stranger's. His blood pounded harder now at the realization, and he edged himself closer until he could make out the words.

"You say you never left this evening?"

"That's what I said. I've been practicing all evening. I have an important recital next month, and it's occupied all my time."

"We know your husband is on duty right now. What about your son, Jacob?"

"My son has been with me all night. He wasn't feeling well and went to bed early."

"What's wrong with him?"

Jacob's heart beat louder now. He covered his chest, as if he could muffle the sound he was certain they must be able to hear.

"I don't know. He didn't say. He went straight to bed."

"Maybe you should have him examined by the healer," the man offered.

"Maybe I will," she responded, her voice even and controlled. Jacob marveled at her composure.

The man, probably a listener, continued barraging her with questions. "You were playing unusually loud when I came to the door. Aren't you concerned that the noise might wake him?"

"Jacob's a heavy sleeper. Besides, he's used to my playing." A pause ensued, as if the visitation were a game and they were both trying to determine their next move. She spoke next. "Why did you say you were here again?"

He didn't answer but began moving toward the hallway. "Your son's room is down here?" Most homes in Harmony had the same layout.

"Yes, at the end," she said quietly.

The man paused about ten feet from Jacob. Jacob leaned flat against the wall, frozen in terror.

"Do you mind if I check on him?" he asked. Without waiting for a reply, he continued. Jacob held his breath, feeling the air around him stir as the man passed within a foot of him. In a panic Jacob realized his door was open. The listener was nearly at the bedroom doorway when a knock sounded at the front door. Jacob heard the man stop and turn.

"Shall I get it?" his mother asked.

"That's okay, I will," the man said. He breezed by Jacob as he returned to the foyer and opened the door. Another man, who Jacob guessed was also a listener, called to his partner, and the two had a brief, subdued discussion on the doorstep. Then they disappeared, without another word to Jacob's mother, who quickly closed the door. She didn't move for several moments, and he could hear her breathing with heavy, quick gasps. The calm facade had faded, replaced by a struggle to regain her composure. Jacob returned to his bedroom, quietly closing the door. Part of him wanted to rush out, hug her, and thank her for saving him; after their earlier scene, however, he thought she might not appreciate his thanks, since he was responsible for the encounter.

Instead he removed his clothes and climbed into bed. He thought about what she had just done. She had lied for him. She had broken one of the cardinal rules of the community and lied—to a listener, no less. From the first day of school, Jacob had been taught that in Harmony everyone's first duty was to the community. Truth was the most important virtue, as Delaney's father had stated many times at the Gatherings. He wasn't disappointed in his mother—it would be foolish to feel that way, given the circumstances—but part of him was surprised. She had lied to save him. She had lied to save herself, too, he realized. He wondered which was more important to her. *No, that's unfair,* he thought. She could have reported him. Maybe she would have been rewarded. What bothered him most, though, was how they knew to come here, to his house. Had Delaney been caught? Had she told on him? Maybe they had recognized his voice. Maybe he hadn't been alone at all; they could have followed him home. Maybe they would come again tomorrow, this time for him.

As he lay in bed, his mother resumed her practice. This time the tempo was slow, melancholy, and the notes, sustained by the ancient floor pedal, hovered in the air. He could also hear the wind wheezing through the tiny air vent that led from his room to the outside. He knew that only the strongest gusts could cause the high-pitched whine that rose and fell from the narrow grate near the ceiling, as if crying in accompaniment to the classical étude his mother played on the antique piano.

He fell into a fitful sleep, turning restlessly, until several hours later when he heard his mother's voice calling him, rousing him from slumber. He could tell by her raspy voice that she had been crying, that something was terribly wrong. As he sat up in bed she embraced and held him.

"What's the matter?" he asked, not really wanting her to answer.

"Jake," she whispered in a hoarse voice, "it's Delaney," she said, and began to sob. "She's dead."

CHAPTER SEVEN

"How can that be?" Jacob cried. Delaney couldn't be dead. He had just seen her hours ago, had spoken to her, had touched her. He began to feel sick, as if he was going to throw up. "How do you know?" he asked. "Who told you?"

"Jim Mason just came over from across the street. The news is traveling all over Harmony. He said that Martin found her, but that's all I know." She began to cry again. It took Jacob a moment to remember that Delaney's father was named Martin. He jumped from the bed and, after groping for his clothes, began shakily to dress.

"What are you doing?" his mother asked.

"I have to get Dad," he said, his voice also shaky.

"No, Jacob. His shift is almost over—he'll be home in less than an hour. Besides, Jim said that a storm is moving in. Your father is probably on his way home already."

"He should be here. He needs to be here." Jacob didn't really know what he was saying. He just needed to get out of this room, this house. He had to do something.

"Jacob, don't go. You've already been out once today. Don't go again. I need you here," she cried.

"I can't stay. I'll be back soon," he said, and left, slamming the door behind him.

As soon as he entered the street, a gust struck him full on, thrusting him backward for a moment. It was night and the sky was dark. He could see nothing, but he could hear the rumble of thunder in the distance, far deeper than the noise the haulers had made earlier that evening. Occasionally a brief flash altered his awareness. He remembered learning about the electrical discharges that caused thunder. His teacher had called it lightning and now he knew why. He pushed ahead, the wind roaring in his ears, pushing back tears that he realized were streaming from his eyes. *Twice in one day*, he thought. He hadn't cried in more than two years, had prided himself on that, and here he was, hours later, weeping again. He didn't care, though. Delaney was dead.

No, she's not, he told himself. It was too terrible to be true. *She's not, she's not.* He kept saying it as he ran, began yelling it into the indifferent storm, its wind throwing the words right back in his face. He passed to the outskirts of town, moving as quickly as he could against the wind. Rain was beginning to fall. The thick drops splattered on his face, stinging him and running down his cheeks, mingling with the tears. The thunder was louder now as the storm swept across the plains. The lightning flashes grew brighter and more frequent. By the time he reached the edge of town and had started down the wide lane that led to the fields, he was running with abandon. The brief flashes illuminated the blurry straightness cutting through the dark. He fell more than once on the road, which was slippery with mud. Each time he picked himself up and wiped the mud from his face. He didn't care that he was dirty or wet, or that he was crying, or that his elbow was now throbbing from having hit a rock on the path during the last fall. He didn't even care if he found his father. All he wanted to do was run, to lose himself in the storm, in the wind that seemed to strip away all conscious thought. He wanted to forget the words, the voice that had continued to creep along the edges of his mind from the first moment his mother told him Delaney was dead.

It's your fault, the voice said again. He had been with her. He had talked to her. If he had spoken the right words, this would never have happened. He should have told his mother about the encounter earlier so she could have done something. Or maybe he should have helped Delaney escape; then she would be far away and alive, on her way to what she wanted. He could even have escaped with her, protected her. All these thoughts flew around in his head. He kept throwing them away, but they kept returning as he ran, clutching his elbow. The lightning was flashing all around him now, the thunderclaps piling up and hammering him from all sides. A dark shape appeared before him from nowhere, highlighted by a series of flashes, and he suddenly found himself prostrate, gasping from the collision.

"What the hell?" a man cried out. "Something just hit me!"

"It was me," Jacob hollered, trying to be heard above the wind and thunder. He suddenly felt two strong hands reach out, find his arms, and pull him to his feet. A wet hand moved along his face.

"What's going on here?" another man shouted, joining them.

"It's a kid. I think. He just ran into me," the first man explained.

"Who are you?" the second man yelled.

"Jacob," Jacob screamed. "Jacob Manford."

"Richard's boy?" the first man asked. "Hey, Richard!" the man shouted through the storm. "Get over here! It's your son!"

Lightning pulsed an irregular heartbeat of illumination. Under its flare Jacob could see a bright shape emerge from the storm and approach him. "Jacob?" his father cried. "What are you doing here? We have to get home. The storm rolled in quicker than we thought."

Jacob grabbed him by both arms and leaned his forehead against his father's chest. "Delaney's dead!" he shouted to his father. The thunder was booming, crashing in waves that seemed to drown all noise and feeling.

"What?" his father screamed back, unable to hear above the rolling thunder.

Jacob felt as if he were trapped in a nightmare, the one where no matter how loud he tried to scream, no sound came out, or if it did, it emerged compressed and distorted, a static of meaningless noise. "Delaney!" he screamed, his face now directly before his father's, their dripping noses touching. "Delaney's dead!"

"Oh God!" Jacob heard his father say. "How? When?" he hollered.

"I don't know," Jacob shouted back, and began crying again.

"Come on, Richard! Let's go!" the other growers shouted. "It's getting worse!"

Jacob's father grabbed him by the hand, and as they came up behind the others, the group began moving through the storm. As they hurried, slipping in the mud toward the safety of home, Jacob turned his attention to the sky. The flashes were brighter than any light he had seen; his sight, which before had seemed indistinct, was sharpened by the intensity of the lightning. He winced as thin streaks of brilliance seared across his vision. Peering around him, he saw the backs of the

71

other growers flashing in time with the light in the sky. Though the images remained blurry, he was amazed to discover he could see their heads distinct from their torsos and the movement of arms and legs. They all traveled together in a symmetry of fear. In the brilliant strobe he could see them duck downward in a collective crouch whenever the thunder crashed on them. They seemed to advance slowly, without real progress, as the erratic light revealed only fragments of their motion.

The landscape around him cast an eerie glow in the flashes and spread around him far into the distance, giving him his first visual awareness of the expansiveness of space. For a moment he forgot about death, forgot about danger, and was overwhelmed by the intensity of the experience, by the beauty of even the most awkward human movement, and by the smallness of human beings against the land's breadth. Suddenly a particularly strong bolt struck in front of him, flashed so close the thunder seemed to anticipate the lightning and explode before it was done flashing. The light seared his eyes, and for several seconds he could see nothing but the flash. In that moment he felt more terrified than he had ever felt before. He moved close to his father and clutched his hand tighter. It was only after they arrived home that he realized why he had been so afraid—he thought he had lost his sight for good.

The funeral was held two days later. Normally a funeral was a public event that most of Harmony attended, and it became, more or less, a Gathering. Standing on a small hilltop east of town, with people spread out below, Martin Corrow or some other council member would deliver a speech about the deceased, highlighting his contribution to the community, praising her loyalty to the ideals of Harmony and the Foundation. The deceased's sounder would then be presented to a loved one, its unique pitch forever a reminder of the one who had rejoined the greater darkness from which, Jacob had been taught, all things came. Afterward the citizens of Harmony who wished to do so could pay their last respects. Passing by the body in turn, people would trace their fingers across the face of the deceased to take away one last impression of their spouse, sibling, neighbor, or friend.

Jacob had attended many funerals but had made the final passing only once. Two years ago Delaney's mother, who had been ill for a long time, died, and Jacob made the trek to the body on the hilltop with his mother. At first Jacob was eager to make the passing; he had never touched a dead body before and was curious. As he stood in line, however, moving closer to the corpse of a woman he had met only a half dozen times in his life, he abruptly changed his mind. He quietly told his mother he wanted to leave, but she held him firmly by the shoulder and told him it was too late. "Everyone should experience death firsthand," she whispered. He could feel himself trembling as he approached the body. He reached out and moved his hand along the woman's face. He was surprised at the cold, smooth skin; it didn't feel like skin at all. Plastic and stiff, it left him feeling cold as well.

This funeral was different, however. Only a few people had been invited, and many in the community wondered at the high councilor's unusual decision. Yesterday many friends and neighbors of Jacob's family had stopped by to console his mother. She had hardly spoken since waking him with the news the previous night, and when she did speak, her voice

73

sounded distant, so husky and strained that she seemed like a stranger to him. For a while he remained in the house with his parents as small groups arrived, speaking to her in hushed, sympathetic tones. Soon the ordeal became too much, and he felt like an intruder in the blackness of the underground home, an unwelcome witness to his mother's grief, which seemed to overwhelm his own.

He went outdoors to where a crowd gathered in the brightness of the street. It was a rest day—most people, aside from the growers, had no work—but the normal, relaxed tone that a rest day brought had disappeared. Everyone seemed tense and uneasy, and speculations whirled within the conversations. He listened to the people as they threw questions about, troubled by the mystery of the entire affair. Martin Corrow's announcement that morning that it would be a private ceremony—and that there would be no presentation of the body—puzzled many. Other questions surfaced too. How had she died? people wondered. Many thought suicide, but the idea of such an act was so disturbing that no one wanted to consider it, and Jacob knew no one in Harmony would dare ask. It seemed to be the only possibility to him, and he continued to feel a guilt so powerful that he couldn't begin to mention it to anyone, especially his parents.

Now gathered on the hill with his parents, Martin Corrow, and a few council members, Jacob relived, as he had repeatedly done in the last day and a half, his final conversation with the young woman, in which she had called him her friend. It seemed impossible that she could be gone. Without her here now, even in death, the ceremony seemed empty. It was as if they were saying good-bye to a stranger, as if someone else had died and Delaney had simply forgotten to join them in saying farewell. Her father recited a brief eulogy, praising his daughter's talent and her spirit, reminding them of their love for her.

"Though we will always remember her," he concluded, "we must all strive to continue our lives and forget the loss for the good of the community. I know Delaney would want that for us."

Jacob thought the farewell, in contrast to his usual eloquence, sounded hollow and didn't do justice to the truth of her life or death. Worse, it made *him* feel hollow, and that bothered him. Shouldn't he feel more? Funerals were common enough and had never affected him much before, but wasn't this different? Shouldn't he feel more sorrow? No. How could he? Why should he? She wasn't dead. He couldn't— wouldn't—accept it, and it made him angry to think that the others had, that her own father could so easily say good-bye.

When the high councilor had concluded, Jacob's mother played a song—one of her student's favorites—on the small harp she had brought. It was evening now, and as the notes from the harp lingered on the fading breeze, Jacob cast his eyes from the small crowd across to the horizon. He squinted into the distance. Though his vision was blurry, he discovered that with concentration, shapes consolidated and became more distinct. As he strained with the effort to gain control, contrasts in light and dark assumed a different tone as well. In addition to the globular light of the setting sun, he slowly found variations within the lighted forms about him. The rounded plains, no longer an undifferentiated dark mass, became a mixture of green and gold, colors that Jacob was seeing for the first time but could not name. And in the distance, against the dark trace of skyline, he could see a large

75

mass rise up to brood on the horizon—his introduction to purple. He had learned about Nova Campi's two moons at school, as he had learned about the sun, and realized the blurry sphere must be one of them.

His eyes ached, but he didn't want to close them. These incredible differences in light added a whole new dimension to the vista, gave each component its own distinctiveness. Though the scene was still blurred, the richness of color endowed all parts with a depth so intense he could barely breathe at its splendor. He was shaking now. Was it from the pain of concentrated exertion or the power of the image? He held on, resisting the return to the moment. Was it the pulling away or the turning back that he hated most?

His strength gave out, and as the song continued, he closed his eyes to restrain the tears that welled up inside him. Though his eyes were closed to darkness once again, the landscape lingered in his awareness, and he resented himself for the awe he felt at its beauty. How could he feel that way about a world in which people failed one another constantly in large and little ways, a world in which Delaney was dead?

PART TWO

CHAPTER EIGHT

"Happy birthday, Jacob," his mother said, shaking him awake. It had been five days since the funeral, and things were returning to normal. This morning Jacob could hear a glimmer of his mother's former self in her voice. He knew she was making an effort to sound cheerful, perhaps against her own desire, but he was glad for the change anyway. Opening his eyes to utter blackness in the windowless underground house, Jacob stretched and sat up. His mother remained seated near the foot of his bed.

"Morning, Ma," he said.

"Thirteen. Hard to believe. How does it feel?"

"The same, I guess." Actually, it didn't, at least not when he considered how things had changed over the past few days. He recalled that morning, not even two weeks ago, when she had cut his hair. It seemed as if years had passed. Then he was still blind. Delaney was alive and still his mother's star pupil. Now he felt older. Not a better older, just older, waiting for further changes, more of the uncertainty that seemed to color every aspect of growing up.

"I remember when I turned thirteen," she said. "I don't know if I really felt older. Maybe fresher, like I was starting over, as though everything that had happened until that moment was part of somebody else's life, and now I was

79

taking over. It was exciting. I had my music ahead of me, your father, you, but it was still out there, just waiting, and I didn't know anything about it. For the moment I was just fresh and in between." She finished talking and sat silently for a moment, reflecting.

Jacob understood what she was talking about in some ways but felt almost envious. He wished he could feel as if the past were another's life and that he was starting over. He didn't feel fresh. If anything, he felt stained, unclean from the accumulation of time.

"Your father told me to wish you happy birthday for him. His shift got switched to first, so he had to leave earlier than expected. But he'll join us tonight to celebrate. He was going to wake you up, but I insisted on letting you sleep in. After everything that's happened, you deserve a rest."

"You mean I'm not going to school today?" he asked.

"You can afford to miss a day. Did you want to go?"

"No, that's okay. I can stay home." He was too surprised to really be happy. After all, he had never missed a day of school.

"Good. Now, get dressed and come eat breakfast. I saved the last of the blackberry syrup for this morning. The flour's almost gone, but there should be enough for a few decent pancakes."

He arose, lingering in his room, taking time to dress. He listened to her making pancakes in the kitchen, listened to the clanging pans, the whisking of tin on tin. Entering the kitchen at last, he took his seat and found she had already set the dishes. A cloth placemat, used for special occasions, lay beneath the chipped plate. The fork and knife, slightly warped by use, lay next to it, wrapped also in cloth—one of the good napkins.

"Quite the royal treatment this morning, Ma," he commented.

"You deserve it, Jake," she said, then hesitated. "I know it's been tough these last few days, but things will improve. You'll see."

He gasped, and a quick surge ran through him at her last words. Such expressions were frowned upon in Harmony, almost heretical, but people still slipped from time to time. But the more personal meaning of her words was what struck him. She couldn't know, could she? Of course not; it was just an innocent slip. "You know what I mean," she added quickly, her voice dropping in embarrassment.

She sighed and slipped the hot pancakes onto his plate. He covered them with syrup and took a mouthful. He ate the entire meal quickly while she sat across from him at the table. They remained silent. He tried to savor the rich sweetness of the syrup, the last of a delicacy that might not be replaced for some time, but he was too nervous to truly enjoy the experience. *Maybe I should tell her,* he thought. No. It wasn't the right time. It was too soon after everything that had happened. She didn't deserve to be hit with this, especially on his birthday and after she had treated him to this special breakfast, had kept him home from school. To say anything else, to initiate the lightest of conversation, however, seemed like just another form of deception, and so he said nothing.

"Finished? So quickly," she said.

"I was hungry," he replied. "I think I'll go outside."

"Oh," she said. He could hear the disappointment. "I was hoping you would stay with me awhile. I thought we might play together. I have a new composition and could use your help. Besides, it wouldn't be a good idea for you to wander too much when you're supposed to be in school. If somebody heard you, there might be questions."

"All right," he agreed, even though he was certain no one would detect him. He hadn't played with her for a while, and perhaps it might lift her spirits.

"Great," she said, brightening. Together they cleaned up the table, washed the dishes, and then sat at the piano. Jacob took the lower keys, while she played the upper registers. To warm up, she picked a song they had played together often— one of her own compositions. Things began well enough, but as they progressed further into the song, Jacob found himself feeling more and more distracted. He kept thinking about the colors and shapes that had been filling his consciousness for the last several days, the deep blue of the sky, the stretching green of the plains, and the dark forms of prairie birds soaring back and forth between these two realms. He began making mistakes, forgetting chords and measures, plunking the wrong keys, creating awkward dissonances that spoiled the song. Try as he might, he couldn't dispel the images from his mind. With each new mistake he began wondering if this was what sight did to a person, if this was why they had turned away from it. His teachers had often referred to the shallow distractions of appearances—maybe this was what they meant. Several times they had to stop altogether and start a section over, much to his frustration and, he could tell, hers too. When they finally reached the end, she didn't hold the sustain pedal as the composition called for, but released it abruptly, cutting off the last chord, leaving a vacuum of sound to match her stillness.

"I'm not feeling very musical today," he told her. "I'm sorry."

She didn't respond. He got up from the piano bench and slipped away, back to his room, guilty for leaving. For the next several hours they avoided each other in the pitch-blackness of the windowless house. He wandered in and out of his room, fighting back the urge to get out, away from the dark and into the light he found himself steadily craving. She, in turn, stayed mostly at the piano, working on a composition. He recognized the piece. It was one she had begun writing with Delaney only a few weeks ago.

Finally he could stand it no longer. He came up behind his mother, now silent at the bench, and tapped her shoulder, feeling her startle at his touch.

"I'm going out," he said. "I promised Egan we'd get together after school today."

"It's early yet," she said. When he didn't answer, she sighed. "Fine, have a nice time. Just stay out of trouble, okay?"

"I will," he said, turning for the door. Before he could get away, she reached out and grabbed his arm in the darkness and pulled him to her. She held him for a moment, her arms tight around his waist, her head against his chest. He stood there with his arms at his sides, allowing her to hold him. After a minute she released him silently. He squeezed her shoulder lightly and left, closing the door quietly behind him.

The day was beautiful. Shining down from a blue, cloudless sky, the sun illuminated the streets and hillsides. He could see more clearly now, more so since the funeral when he had watched the moon rise over the plains. He could navigate almost exclusively by sight and marveled at the freedom it brought him. He wondered if his eyes now showed him what the Seers saw. As he wandered through the Impressionist painting of his vision, avoiding the shadowy figures of the occasional passerby, moving ever faster through the streets, he soon forgot the darkness of the house and the awkward scene with his mother. He forgot about everything—his birthday, specialization, the fight between his parents at dinner yesterday for the second night in a row. Best of all, he forgot about Delaney. Though the reality of her death had steadily begun to sink in, part of him still couldn't believe she was gone, and that same sick feeling rose inside when he remembered her voice, her laugh. By now everyone understood her death to be suicide, though no one wanted to discuss it.

Instead he lingered by the fountains in the squares, watching the sparkles that the water created in the sunlight as it gushed into the pools. He spoke to no one and avoided others by ducking down empty side streets, resting in the shade amid the neighborhood flower beds and herb gardens when the brightness of noon dazzled his vision. Buzzing among the purple and yellow flowers, only the insects that browsed on nectar seemed to notice him. The afternoon passed slowly this way as Jacob explored. It was strange walking by sight through the community. He had grown up in Harmony, had traversed virtually every street and lane, yet it felt like a different place now. Defined by the boundaries of form, it seemed smaller than it had in darkness, where no horizon existed, where distance was measured more in time than space. Perhaps it had shrunk because he could cover ground more quickly, or perhaps it was because the uniformity of gray buildings and identical rows of hillhouses made every part of town seem the same. The symmetry of the settlement that made navigation simple and provided a comforting predictability in blindness had begun, over the last few days, to impose a bland rigidity on Jacob's world.

People were different. The indistinct figures he encountered always gave him pause. Previously, in his blindness, others he passed in the street would come and go, an anonymous part of the environment. Now, however, safe in the knowledge that he couldn't be seen, he became a watcher, wondering about the identity of each person. Who were the indistinguishable shapes that passed him in the street? How were they connected to him? The mystery added a thrill to his voyeurism and provided moving obstacles in his exploration. Though he wore his sounder, he would step out of range before a stranger came too close. He felt as if he were playing the hider in a child's game of seeker that no one around him knew they played.

Then, in the middle of his wanderings, he stopped. He thought of his mother sitting alone in the house, playing a song that no one heard but her. A fresh wave of guilt washed over him. He thought of the breakfast she had made him, how she had given him the best of what they had, how she had brightened when he agreed to play piano with her. And how did he repay her? By fleeing as quickly as he could to run around the streets of Harmony, playing games in secret. He suddenly felt selfish. Even if it was his birthday, it was wrong to put his desires before others, especially her. Maybe he was becoming a Seer after all, was becoming everything he had been taught to disdain. Closing his eyes, he wondered, *Am I a bad person?*

His mood darkened, in spite of the sun, as he found his way to school and waited until the students were released. He watched them leave, clusters of walking figures separating into blurry groups. Homing in on the pitch of his friend's sounder, he intercepted Egan as he left the school yard.

Egan greeted him with his usual humor. "So, you've come, raised up from your deathbed." He paused, suddenly awkward at the mention of death. "I mean, they told us you were sick today."

"Not really. My mother let me stay home from school. It's my birthday, remember?"

"Oh, right," Egan said in mock forgetfulness. "How old are you again?"

"Shut up," Jacob said, pushing him. They both laughed. It felt good to laugh with his friend again. The last few days had been dulled not only by Delaney's death, but also by Egan's uncharacteristic silence. Jacob's suspicions about Mr. Spencer had been correct. Egan had been forced to stay by his father's side during the delivery and listen to an old recording of a Francis Aldrich lecture on Truesight. Jacob knew Egan felt guilty about not meeting him and tried repeatedly to counter Egan's apologies. He said nothing to his friend about what really happened. Instead he told Egan that he had waited for him at school for a while and then returned home. In fact, Jacob felt relieved that his friend hadn't shown up. Things might have been worse than they were.

"I figured you weren't really sick anyway—your mother's a softy. I hope you appreciate how lucky you are. My parents made me go to school on my thirteenth birthday last month." Jacob didn't respond to his friend's joking play for sympathy. Though neither one fully acknowledged it, they both knew Egan, with his father's connections, had it easier.

"What do you want to do?" Jacob said instead. "I don't

86

have to be home until dinner."

"I know—let's head over to the north field and go for a run."

"Sounds good to me. You know I'm just going to beat you again."

"Doubt it. I've been practicing."

They headed toward the outskirts of Harmony through the north end of town, where the settlement ended abruptly. Unlike the southern end of the colony, which was developed into large squares of cultivated earth for crops, and the eastern edge, where cattle and sheep grazed, the north end was just a broad expanse of grass. Originating behind the last tier of hillhouses, the field extended several hundred yards to the perimeter of the colony, where a line of pathminders circled the outer edge, curving around to create a border no one ever crossed. The council had erected the perimeter several years ago after a child wandered off while playing and disappeared into the plains. Though her sounder was found not far from Harmony, the girl was never heard from again. With the pathminders in place—the only outer section of the colony to be so enclosed—the area was designated for recreation and had since become popular with the colony's children. It was a nice spot to get away from their parents and neighbors, and the two boys sometimes went there to play.

Starting from the hilltop, they would have a race, plowing blindly into the tall grass and running as fast as they could to hear whose sounder would be triggered by the bordering pathminders first. Jacob sometimes wondered what would happen if they continued to the other side, into the open plains, but he had never dared find out, and even Egan never raised the possibility of committing such a bold transgression.

Instead they always stopped short and quickly moved back until their sounders were silent again, as if the guilty noise itself would give them away. A little larger than his friend, Jacob usually won these races, but not always; part of the challenge was moving as quickly as possible without tripping in the tall grass, because one fall could mean victory for the other. Still, it wasn't really winning that was important about these races, at least not to Jacob—Egan was more competitive and took defeat closer to heart—it was really about the freedom that came with running, of being able to hurl yourself into the unknown and not care about what happened. It was the only time he ever felt that way.

Now they stood on the grassy roof of the last house in the northern tier, each bracing for the race. Egan, as always, performed the honors.

"Ready. Set." He paused, relishing the suspense. "Go!" he shouted.

They took off down the hill, bounding into the grassy field. Jacob whooped with a joyful cry that caught him by surprise as he plunged into the green expanse dotted with the gold of prairie flowers, aiming for the horizon, where green met the blue of sky. Egan was a dark blur to his right, on the periphery and slowly dropping from sight. He ran faster, his breath coming in quick gasps. The added dimensions of shape and color brought a beauty to the flow of movement and simultaneously removed some of the thrill of the run, a thrill that came from traveling through unknown blackness so carelessly. He closed his eyes and felt the thrill return.

When he opened his eyes again, he saw the blurry figure of Egan now in front of him and moving swiftly ahead. Trying to regain ground, Jacob ran harder, speeding up until he could almost touch the white back of his friend's shirt. Then he was falling into grass, tumbling into blackness as his eyes shut themselves instinctively with the plunge. He hit the ground squarely, rolling over in a tangle of stalks and flowers and coming to a stop. For a while he lay there with his eyes closed, gasping for the breath that had been knocked out of him. Lying on his back, trying to take deep breaths to fill his lungs, he remembered the first time—the only other occasion—he had had the wind knocked out of him. He had fallen down while playing at recess during the first week of school. The suffocating feeling terrified him and he cried for his teacher, convinced he was dying. After the teacher had calmed him and his wind had returned, she chastised him harshly, telling him—and all the other students gathered to listen—that he should have been more careful, that that's what came from rushing, from denying the reality of his blindness and believing he could move so capriciously.

He rolled over and opened his eyes. They opened to a crystal world. His mind exploded at the crispness of everything around him. He could see the texture of every blade of grass, the detail of each flower in front of him. Looking skyward, he could see the perfect blue marred only by the faintest wisp of high cumulus clouds. He closed his eyes once more and took a deep breath. Only then did he realize that he had been waiting for this moment forever, and he knew that this was what it meant to truly see. He dared not open his eyes. What if this perfection had disappeared? Then he couldn't stand the suspense and opened them. Everything was still as it was a moment ago. He looked once more into the grass and saw an insect before him, perched on the thick purple stalk of a flower. No, there were two of them, he noticed as he leaned closer. The larger one, attached to the stalk, glistening yellow and black and measuring the length of his palm, gripped a smaller one between forelegs almost equal in length to its thorax. The spiky black legs securely held the struggling pale green insect, which jerked wildly in a futile attempt to escape. Jacob watched, transfixed, as the larger bug proceeded to bite with giant mandibles into the head of its prey, which quickly stopped thrashing, giving only a few involuntary spasms as it became food for its captor.

The insects, coupled together in a spectacle of predator and prey, disappeared beneath the foot that came crashing down in front of Jacob's face. A pair of legs parted the grass.

"No!" Jacob shouted in horror.

"Jacob?" Egan said wildly. "Are you okay?"

"I'm fine," Jacob blurted out, rising to his feet. He stared at his friend, who now stood before him, marveling at the detail. He had touched the faces of people, including his friend, and had noted the subtle differences in features that identified every individual, but to see the human face in its entirety amazed him. Egan's cropped brown hair, small nose, and thin lips were eerily familiar, yet pulled together and seen as a whole, along with the light green eyes, unsettled Jacob. It was as if his friend had suddenly been transformed into a stranger.

"What's going on? Didn't you hear me calling you?" Egan was worried. Jacob could tell by his voice and now could see it in the narrowed brow, the tightened lips.

"I'm sorry," Jacob said. He wanted to grab his friend and tell him about the miracle, tell him everything that had happened to him, but when he tried, something prevented him. "I just had the wind knocked out of me."

"Oh. That's all? Well, too bad, then, because clearly you were too incapacitated to hear me win." Egan's worried frown now converted to a smile. Jacob realized he was busy watching his friend's face again and barely listening to his words.

"You just got lucky," he finally conceded, hastily trying to cover for the long, awkward pause.

"Are you sure you didn't hit your head also? You sound funny." Egan didn't bother to wait for a response to the rhetorical jab at his friend. "Anyway, I didn't get lucky. I was way ahead of you even before you fell."

"You were," Jacob agreed.

Before his eyes Egan's face, the tall field grass, the clouds, all disappeared, reverting to a blur of color and indistinct shapes. In a moment the clarity was gone, and he was struck by a pang of disappointment. Again, as he had at the funeral, he squinted in concentration, and after several seconds the world responded like the settling of a pool, returning to focus, bringing a rush that set his heart pounding once more. They walked back toward the settlement, where they could hear wind chimes in the distance.

"Egan, do you ever feel different?" he asked tentatively.

"Yes. Earlier today, in school, I was sad because I was bored, and now I'm happy because I'm not." He laughed. Jacob didn't; he was attempting to be serious and grew mildly annoyed at his friend's unwillingness to engage in real conversation.

"No. I mean different from everyone else. Like you're not like other people."

"No one's the same, Jacob."

"I know no one's the same. You like some things; I like other things. But I guess I mean in another way. Like in a bad

91

way. Like you're too different. Like you're only waiting for the time when everyone will suddenly notice, and then it's too late."

"Too late for what?"

"I don't know. Too late to change. Too late to be normal."

"I don't know what you're talking about, Jacob." Egan sounded annoyed, frustrated. "Hey, are you trying to say there's something wrong with me? Is this because you lost the race?"

"No . . . of course not," Jacob stammered. *Typical, Egan,* he thought. *It's always about you.*

"Well, there's nothing wrong with me. I'm fine, okay?" He sounded less angry now and spoke reassuringly.

"I know you are. You always have been. Forget it."

"Is it about her?" Egan asked, as if he were unable to say the name.

"No, it's not about Delaney. Like I said, forget it. I'm not even sure what I'm talking about. I think you're right; I must have hit my head back there." They walked for a while in silence, pausing near the turnoff for Egan's street.

"Just remember, that's why we're here, in Harmony. Everyone is joined together by a single way of life. We aren't that different from one another; we don't have to be. We all have each other and that's what's nice about it," Egan said. Jacob managed to stifle a laugh at his friend's characteristic mock solemnity; he sounded like Mrs. Lawson from civics class. Only after Egan had left did Jacob realize his friend had been totally sincere.

CHAPTER NINE

"Why are we eating up here again, Jacob?" Richard Manford asked his son.

"I don't know. I just felt like it," Jacob said quietly.

"Leave him alone, Richard," Jacob's mother chided. "It's his birthday."

Jacob looked at his mother, marveling at the wholeness of her face. Her long hair, so blond it was almost white, was pulled tightly into a long ponytail, held in place by a piece of frayed string. The hair cascaded down her back all the way to her waist, fanning out into strands that were picked up and floated by the evening breeze from time to time. Though dressed in a simple robe, its tan folds gathered around her as she sat cross-legged on the grass, she nonetheless exuded a lightness, from the delicacy of her small features all the way to the tips of her long, thin fingers. He had always known she was a small woman, but to see her clearly to such a degree, down to the individual eyelashes, so light they were almost transparent, unsettled him. Though Jacob found her face, her entire body, pleasing in its delicate symmetry, he also found that it seemed to diminish her, to reduce her to this physical form that wasn't much larger than he was.

Looking at his father, he was startled by the contrast. He was as large as he'd seemed the few times Jacob had felt the muscular arms and back, perhaps even larger. He was a man shaped by labor. Jacob could see the hands, hardened, covered with little scars, still darkened with soil and machine oil that never completely washed away but lingered in the crevices, highlighting fingernails and knuckles. Though not unhandsome, his facial features were rough and craggy, with a large nose and deep-set eyes. His entire head, including his shaved scalp, was a uniform tan from days spent in the fields, unlike his willowy mother, who spent most of her time indoors. They were night and day, these two people who had given him life, though both seemed much thinner than Egan, despite his father's wiry bulk. Their faces conveyed a leanness in the slightly sunken cheekbones that Jacob found mildly disturbing.

He looked beyond both of them and at the ground in front of him. The cloth that normally covered the dinner table now lay spread across the short grass that doubled as the roof of their home. It was weighted down with plates, flatware, and bowls of food, and its edges flapped in the breeze in time with his mother's hair. The meal before them was a veritable feast. His father had smuggled some fresh beans from one of the fields he worked in—desperately warning Jacob not to tell anyone, even Egan, especially Egan—and his mother had managed to acquire some meat, several scrawny but still delicious chicken legs. She wouldn't say where she'd gotten them.

Turning his gaze up and away, he looked beyond his parents. The grassy ridge that covered his house, and the houses of everyone on his street, was one of the highest in the colony. Right in the middle of the North Tier, not far from the fountain in the square, it afforded him a broad view of Harmony. Aside from a few of the larger structures—some of which

Jacob guessed to be the school, the council house, and the larger storehouses in the western area of the settlement—much of the town seemed indistinguishable from the surrounding plains. The homes, camouflaged beneath the grassy waves of ridges and hills, were nearly invisible, aside from a few western-facing metallic house fronts in the eastern tier that glittered as they reflected light from the setting sun. Otherwise, it was hard to tell where Harmony began and where the outside world took over, stretching out to the horizon in layer upon layer of grasslands.

Jacob scanned the entire horizon, absorbing the clarity, not knowing how long it would last. Several times after he'd left Egan, his vision had blurred, but he found that with blinking and concentrated squinting, he could refocus, each time more quickly and with greater ease, until finally his vision seemed to hold and hadn't wavered. The sun sat low in the west, reduced from the blinding spot above him in the heat of noon to a small white disk that seemed tired and sullen, having spent its daily quota of energy and light. In the south the fields formed dark squares, covering an area almost as large as the rest of the settlement itself. But Jacob found his gaze hurrying past them to the east, where the real spectacle was unfolding. He had seen the moon rise five days before at the funeral. Then it had been a blob of dim purple light. Now it stood in high definition, halfway over the plains and so vast it seemed to fill the entire eastern sky. What struck him most were the rings. Rising at a forty-five-degree angle to the horizon, the multicolored bands formed a sliver that sliced the purple of the moon itself and formed a thin, oblong disk that seemed to bisect the sphere it contained. Along this sliver Jacob could see clusters of sparkles scattered across the velvet circle of rings.

Jacob found himself overwhelmed. He didn't know which way to gaze, what to watch—the splendor of the vista or the intricacies of detail immediately surrounding him? It was almost too much. Too much beauty, too much stimulation. He wanted to close his eyes but was afraid he might lose clarity. He craved the clear sight that seemed so long in coming. He wanted it to remain, in spite of the pangs of guilt that gnawed at the edges of his desire. *How can this be wrong?* he wondered, thinking back to his earlier doubts. All his life he had been told that what he was doing now was wrong, corrupt, led to pain and suffering. But it seemed like all he had been feeling for the last two weeks was suffering, and now the only anodyne was the moon, the horizon, and the forms of his mother and father, even the chipped plates and dull knives on the frayed tablecloth. On the other hand, these past two weeks had coincided with the arrival of his sight, and with each passing day, with every hour since clarity had come, he could feel himself pulling away, pulling away, like the rounded corner of the moon now severing itself from the horizon's edge.

"Well, I like it up here," his mother chirped. "The breeze is lovely, and listen to those birds. Their music is as beautiful as any of ours." Her blue eyes, as pale as her blond hair, stared blankly ahead as she spoke, but her lips worked into a smile, though the smile faded as soon as she stopped talking. He tuned his ears to where a pair of prairie birds sang on the ridge below and across from them. He watched them flutter in an intricate dance as their cries intertwined, a series of dramatic staccato peeps that rose and sank quickly into the low wail of a drawn-out coo. He wondered why they were dancing.

"I didn't say I didn't like it," his father responded. "I was just curious why Jacob wanted to eat outside. Not that I don't mind it out here. After all, I spend all day outside, rain or shine, hot or cold. I've grown quite used to it." Jacob watched his father's face contort, accentuating only the slightest sarcasm in his voice that Jacob might otherwise have missed. The raised eyebrows and tight smile transformed him, made him a stranger to his son.

His mother didn't respond, though she must have sensed his tone, since Jacob observed the anger in her face. The drawn eyebrows and pursed lips created as startling an image as his father's sarcastic face had, and a visible coldness seemed to wash over her, not dousing the anger, but enhancing its power. Then it passed and a quick smile returned.

"This reminds me of when you were younger, Jacob. We used to have picnics all the time. Remember, Richard?" Her voice retained its sweetness, but her smile, like his father's before, became a sneer.

What does she mean? Jacob wondered. His father didn't answer but scowled.

"I remember, Ma," Jacob said softly. The unfolding spectacle unnerved him. It was as if there were two conversations occurring. He would never have guessed how much people communicated through their faces and bodies. He was both repulsed by and curious at his parents' behavior. "This is good chicken, Ma. Where'd you say you got it again?" He could see her stiffen at the question. A look of concern crossed her face.

"Didn't we already discuss this? It's a secret, a special arrangement for your birthday." Jacob watched her head tilt down and her eyes blink as she spoke. Her thin smile came and went almost as quickly.

97

"Jacob, stop teasing your mother," his father put in. "She obviously doesn't want to ruin the surprise. Just enjoy the chicken, and those beans I risked my neck to get for you."

Jacob had no idea what was transpiring. *Why is he defending her all of a sudden?* Jacob wondered. This entire drama that neither of them knew he could see both baffled and angered him. He felt like a fool. Was every meal this way? He suddenly didn't want to know. Instead he watched their faces—his mother's cold and angry, his father's cautious and sad. Jacob's eyes lowered, following his father's rough hand as it reached over and touched his mother's leg. She quickly grabbed his hand and pushed it away. Jacob watched her turn her head away from her husband, almost as if her blank eyes could see.

"By the way, Jake," she said, "your father and I have a present for you."

Jacob saw her remove a small object from the pocket of her robe. She moved in his direction, reaching her hand out tentatively in an effort to find him. He intercepted her, taking the gift from her hand. It was a small metallic cube with a tiny handle attached to its side. He immediately knew what it was—another music box to replace the one he had destroyed. But this one was different: it was larger, heavier, and engraved with intricate designs pleasing to the touch, a more sophisticated version of the unadorned toy he had been given eight years ago. When he opened the lid, however, the same familiar tune began to play—a child's song about planted children who were never plucked from their flower beds. He closed the lid quickly, cutting off the tune midnote.

CHAPTER TEN

Jacob looked below at the storage houses. The half dozen structures sat in a neat block at the western edge of town. Square and squat, nearly perfect cubes of steel, they contrasted with the random assortment of hills behind them that comprised most of the town. On the outer perimeter of the buildings the land flattened, easing into gentle rises that formed a great plain, before rising up into a disappearing sequence of hilly ridges in the distance. It was midafternoon, and the students had been dismissed an hour ago in preparation for a Gathering. It was the second day after his birthday, and for the second day Jacob did not go home after school. Instead he went exploring.

Yesterday, before Egan had a chance to talk to him, Jacob had immediately left and struck out by himself. He had wandered around the eastern tier of Harmony, meandering through the streets that lay between the rows of hillhouses until reaching the edge of town. There, the terrain flattened—as on the western and southern sides, though not as much—into pastureland, where he watched the animals graze. Cattle were in one field. He had visited the small barns nearby when he was younger, listening then as the cattle tenders acquainted him and his father with the work of feeding and milking the cows, and the challenge of slaughtering the bulls and the occasional older cow when beef was needed. He had also met the sheep tenders, who allowed him to feel the woolly backs of the animals that provided much of the community's clothing, and meat as well. He remembered being frightened of the animals, especially the larger cattle, whose massive sides disappeared above his highest reach and whose heavy, snorting breath felt hot against his face. One of the cows had knocked him down, leaning over him with a wet muzzle to lick his face. He was shaken but determined not to cry, and his father praised him for his composure.

Yesterday, however, returning to the edge of the pasture, he had been surprised at how different the cattle appeared. They still seemed large, especially in comparison with the people he had seen, but in the field they seemed less intimidating, tranquilly grazing or lying about. They had no cares or worries. They watched him, too, as he approached. He felt uneasy for a moment and conspicuous, as if the staring animals possessed some secret power to tell their human masters his secret. But their empty stares, devoid of interest, soon made him feel foolish at the thought.

One of the cows that grazed nearby eventually approached him as he stood silently. He retreated as she moved to the edge of the pathminders, her signal collar preventing her from moving any farther. For a moment they stared at each other. He was amazed at the size of the docile eyes; they were huge, reflective, almost kind. It felt good to see a creature that saw him back, and at that moment he felt closer to the animal than to any human being; at least the cow saw the world the way he saw it, shared with him the consciousness of light. She bent down and pulled a tuft of grass, chewing it with enormous molars, crunching it with a grinding sound pleasant to his ears. Then she sauntered away, left him standing there alone.

He went over to the sheep pasture. The scene was more or less identical, though the sheep were huddled together more closely, moving as a single unit as they browsed among the grass. Several of them were softly lowing as they grazed, their bleating forming a disjointed melody, and he was reminded for a moment of the weekly Gatherings in the main square.

There was a Gathering today—right now, in fact—but he was not present. Instead he found himself back on that hilltop behind the storage houses, where only a week ago he had encountered Delaney for the last time. He wasn't certain why he had returned, but he had. It felt strange not to be at a Gathering and to stare at the deserted paths and buildings while everyone was collected in the middle of Harmony. But it would have felt stranger to be there, surrounded by every person in the colony, blindly herded together in the square, and he remembered the claustrophobic panic that had paralyzed him at the last one.

He pulled up a tuft of grass and examined it, looking at the purple stems and green blades. The tips were seeded, each one encased in hairy fibers and gathered into sheaths. He stripped one of the sheaths away, pulling against the grain until all the seeds were collected in his cupped palm. Each one lay separate and distinct, little tear-shaped pods of life all from a single stem. He blew into his hand and the seeds scattered, jumping out, then disappearing into the covered ground. He tore the empty stem in half, threw it away, and closed his eyes against his sight. Why had it happened to him? What was he supposed to do with it? How long would he, or could he, live alone with the secret, and what would happen to him once it was discovered? There had to be some meaning behind what was happening, but he couldn't figure out what it was. That was why he'd come to this spot, he realized. He hoped that coming here might allow him time to think, that by returning to the place where he'd left Delaney, he might find her here again, or at least a part of her spirit that could give him the strength to make sense of it all. He hoped that as the outer world was made clear, some inner truth might be revealed. But returning revealed nothing but an awareness of his own futility.

He pulled another tuft, listening to the ripping sound made by the fibers as he tore the grass away. It reminded him of the cow he had seen yesterday. He remembered the connection he had felt with the animals. He was one of them, dull, passive, just a watcher standing back against the current of the world. No, they were better. At least they lived their days in relative peace, unconcerned with the future, oblivious to time. They had no secrets or lies. He had lied to his mother this morning in the lightless house, telling her he was attending the Gathering with Egan. She had accepted his lie without a word, and he had fled the darkness with a mixture of relief and shame.

Maybe Egan was right. Maybe I do think too much, he told himself. A quiet voice spoke up, told him he must worry less and enjoy the gift of his sight. The thought startled him. Then another voice chastised him. *It is not a gift*, it said. *It is a curse. You are cursed.* He lay back in the cushion of grass and stared at the clouds that had been rolling in over the last hour, covering up the sun and darkening the plains. Which voice was really his?

A loud bang and the sound of creaking metal made him sit up. He crawled forward a few yards and looked below through the parted grass. The door of the storehouse closest to him was open, the padlock broken. A steel rod leaned against the wall next to the door. Watching carefully, Jacob made his way down the hill, remaining in the deep grass at the edge of the clearing, now only a dozen yards from the building. A minute passed, and then another. He watched, scarcely moving, hardly breathing.

A third minute passed before a man appeared in the doorway. Jacob instinctively crouched to hide before realizing the man couldn't see him. He stood up to get a better look. The man, tall with graying hair, his face gaunt with hollow cheeks and eyes, hurried from the building, stopping briefly to cock his head and listen for any sounds that might indicate a threat. Jacob noticed he was carrying an armful of food—several loaves of bread and some other, unknown packages of foodstuffs. Without thinking, Jacob followed the man to town along the main road. Soon they were back in the settlement proper, hurrying among streets. The man evaded the main avenue that led to the central square where everyone had convened. At one point he stopped and turned, his wide eyes pointing in Jacob's direction. The boy froze immediately, his heart pounding at the thought of discovery. After several seconds of silence, the man continued.

As he followed the man through a maze of streets, Jacob's body trembled at the sight. He was now not only witnessing a crime—perhaps one of the most serious crimes possible in Harmony—but was actually following the thief home. True, his father had stolen some beans from the field, but a handful of smuggled vegetables seemed a far cry from the bounty this man carried in his arms, a bounty taken directly from the storehouse that held the community's dwindling food supply. The armful seemed the equivalent of an entire week's worth of rations. He had never heard of such a theft occurring. An alarming thought struck him: Was he seeing something occurring for the first time, or had such crimes happened before? Maybe he should report the man, cry out and reveal him. But that would also mean revealing himself. Besides, no one was nearby, the streets were empty. Jacob decided to follow the thief home, find out who he was, and then decide.

The man stopped one more time. He seemed to be slowing his pace and breathing heavily. Jacob watched as he set the armful down. The man removed a folded piece of gray cloth from his shirt and held it against his mouth and nose, as if he were about to smother himself. Then, bending over, he coughed sporadically into the cloth. Jacob saw his back heave as spasms shook his body. The man made hardly a sound, however, carefully muffling the noise in his rag. Jacob then knew his identity, who the man must be. He knew only one man who coughed like that, who made that terrible sound— Tobin Fletcher, who lived at the end of Jacob's street and who worked as one of the storehouse keepers.

When his coughing spasm subsided, Tobin placed the cloth in his pocket and, hastily gathering the food, scurried down the street. Jacob resumed following him, but as he passed the spot where the man had paused, he noticed a cardboard box on the ground. It had fallen away from the pile, and Tobin hadn't missed it. Jacob picked it up. The box was small—about six by ten inches—but heavy. He wondered what was in it, but there was no time to open it now. He needed to follow the man home, to make certain it was really him. Sure enough, they passed through the western tier and into the northern section of town. They crossed the fountain square and soon came to the street they shared. Jacob stopped before his own door, following the thief with his eyes until he disappeared inside his neighboring house.

Jacob entered and took the box to his room. He hesitated before opening it. Wouldn't that make him an accomplice to the crime? Could he reveal it to anyone without having to explain himself? Jacob wasn't certain that he should. Though he was horrified by the blatant theft he had witnessed, an act that went against everything he had been taught, he actually liked Tobin. He also felt sorry for the poor man. Both he and his wife, Penny, had been ill for some time. Several of the people in their tier, including his parents once or twice, had helped them on occasion, covering for Tobin when he was unable to work his shift, or helping Penny with work when she was too weak to get out of bed. The Fletchers' next-door neighbor had even discreetly taken up a collection last week, going door to door for any extra food they might spare (which was little) in the hopes that it might improve Penny's strength and, ultimately, her health. Now, with the recently reduced rations, maybe they really needed the food. Maybe their lives depended on it. Did that make what he saw wrong? Did that make it right?

Either way, he decided he couldn't reveal his neighbor's theft. He opened the box carefully. His mother wasn't home, probably at the Gathering, but he still felt the need to be quiet, as if she could hear him across town. Reaching in the carton, he fumbled in the darkness. The box was packed with a dozen small cans. He removed one of the cool, smooth cylinders and, pulling the tab, opened the lid. He sniffed its contents, and a familiar smell struck him. Pears. He had had the fruit only a couple times in his life, on special occasions, but their taste had left an impression on him. He hurried to the kitchen for a spoon and headed back to his room. Then he dove into the can, gobbling down the sweet, slippery fruit neatly sliced into halves. When he had finished, he drank the light syrup until nothing remained. He replaced the cover and put the empty can in the box, resisting the urge to eat every single container of fruit, deciding to save them for later.

That evening, at dinner, his parents talked about the Gathering.

"I think the high councilor gave a particularly good speech today, don't you, Richard?" she said.

"Absolutely. People need to be reassured about the harvest," Richard said. "Tomorrow we'll be able to start processing the crops for storage, and in a week or two things should be back to normal. I've heard too much grumbling lately, and frankly, I'm starting to get tired of it."

"But people are hungry, aren't they?" Jacob asked him.

"Of course. We all are, a little. The last month has been hard; we all realize that, but people aren't starving, are they? Are you starving, Jacob?"

"I guess not," he answered.

"Of course not. Nobody's ever starved, and nobody ever will. That's why it bothers me so much, the quiet complaining. That's not in the spirit of Harmony, like the high councilor said today."

"Maybe it's harder on some people than on others," Jacob said.

"Why should it be? Everyone gets the same amount of food," his father said.

106

"How do you know they do?" Jacob asked.

"How do I know? Because that's the way things are around here. How do you know they don't? That's the real question, Jacob."

"Egan told me his family had a roast the other night. How did they get that?" he challenged.

"Egan's family is bigger than ours. Besides, maybe they didn't accept their meat ration last month. They might have been saving it for this month. Did you ask him?"

"No, I didn't."

"There you go. Jacob, everyone knows that some people in Harmony get special privileges once in a while, councilors and such. It's no secret. But they have greater responsibilities. It's only fair. But when it comes to food, everyone is treated the same. Didn't they teach you that in school?"

"Yes," Jacob answered weakly.

"I know they did. I learned the same things when I went to school. Hey, all I'm trying to say is that we take care of one another. Except for a very few things, we don't depend on the Seers for our sustenance. That's what makes us unique. It's what makes us pure. Hardship is good for the soul. It keeps us honest."

Jacob asked to be excused and went to his room. He opened another can of pears and ate them before going to bed. They were delicious but not quite as wonderful as before; their sweetness seemed diminished after the conversation with his father, their flavor tinged with a mixture of guilt and cynicism. He had always believed his father's words, his teachers' comments. But today he hadn't seen much honesty or, remembering the lean image of the hunched and coughing Tobin, much purity either.

CHAPTER ELEVEN

The next morning, on a rise at the edge of the fields, Jacob sat and watched the growers, busy with the work of harvesting. He glanced nervously as men and women moved about, calling instructions to one another, wheeling carts of newly harvested vegetables from the edges of the crops to the great bins that would carry them to the storehouses for processing. It was late morning, and the sun shone hot. He could see the sweat on the workers as they passed him, drops running off their brows and staining their tunics in dark patches. Occasionally they stopped for water, but for the most part they worked steadily, moving back and forth along the rows, feeling for ripeness, filling their baskets.

He was supposed to be in school, but that morning, right before he entered the dark building, he had paused and stepped aside as the others moved ahead. Nobody noticed. Since leaving the house that morning, he had debated whether or not to skip. At the last moment, the idea of spending the next four hours in the darkness of the classroom seemed too dismal, especially after yesterday's events. The theft continued to bother him, as did his father's words at dinner. He decided instead to go to the fields where his father worked. His father had mentioned they would begin harvesting today, and he wanted to see it happen. He figured it would be as educational as anything he would learn that day, especially in Mrs. Lawson's class. Besides, school was nearing the end, and in a few more days everyone would be joining the growers in the fields, carefully combing the crops to make sure nothing was wasted. Tomorrow and the next day he would have final tests, which he dare not miss; today would be his last and only chance to skip out. He figured he would probably get in trouble, but he didn't care.

When he first arrived at the fields, he walked around, quietly shadowing the growers as they engaged in their separate tasks. Soon he spotted his father—who was now assigned to first shift—and watched him work. He was in a field of tomatoes. Jacob watched him as he carefully passed from plant to plant. At each one he stopped and groped among the leaves, testing each round fruit for the tenderness that revealed its ripeness. Jacob observed that he selected only the brilliant red ones, leaving the green ones on the vine. Sometimes he selected an orange one, other times he didn't, and Jacob wondered what that meant. He also watched his father stop from time to time and quickly stuff a smaller one in his mouth, chew rapidly, and swallow before moving on. Jacob thought about his father's words the night before. Everyone got their fair share, he had said. After the third time his father ate a tomato, Jacob had to leave. But it wasn't only his father who was cheating—virtually all the workers could be seen popping fruits and vegetables into their mouths from time to time, always when no one else was nearby.

Seeing the workers together in the field, each oblivious to the others' illicit pickings, made him bitter. As with yesterday's theft, his sight made him a guilty witness, complicit in crimes that weren't his own. Today would be different, though. Today he would take no food. He wouldn't be like his father and the others. He remembered what Delaney had told him about her father the day before her death. *There's a lot about him you don't know*, she had said. From what he'd seen so far, this seemed to be true of everybody.

Jacob moved deeper into the fields. The whole area was carefully sectioned into grids and lined with modified path-minders to assist the growers in their work. The cultivated sections of land were enormous, and he walked for some time before approaching the periphery. There crops of wheat and corn alternated, creating beautiful patterns of green and gold, all at the peak of harvest. Here the workers used machines to help them collect the crops. He paused near a field to watch. In each plot two workers stood at either end of a tall row of corn, while a harvesting machine hummed its way down the row. He was fascinated by the large steel device that gleamed in the sun, thumping away in a steady rhythm as it crawled forward. The long, heavy arms of the harvester pulled the stalks of corn, drawing them into its belly, where the ears were separated and dropped into a bin that followed behind. The remaining plant material was then chopped into another bin as cattle feed. When the machine reached the end of a row, the worker removed its bins, dumped their contents into wagons, and replaced them. The machine automatically aligned itself at the next row and headed back to where the other worker waited to repeat the procedure.

He watched the harvester thread its way back and forth, leaving behind empty land dotted only by the stubble of corn-stalks. Several pairs of large birds with bright red and blue feathers and broad, wedge-shaped beaks flew down and set-tled in the stubbled patch of field. They passed along the

110

freshly cultivated earth, picking the ground for leftover kernels. He sat near them and lost himself in the crop gathering, relishing the aroma of freshly cut vegetation and the hypnotic hum of the harvester.

The machine moved to the end of the row closest to where Jacob sat. Before the grower had finished replacing a bin, the machine lurched rapidly, swinging itself in a ninety-degree arc. One of its arms swung as well, catching the confused worker in the side of the head. The man dropped to the ground instantly, not moving even when one of his legs came under the harvester as it shifted to the next row. It continued toward the other grower, spraying chopped cornstalks on the ground in the absence of the missing bin.

Jacob's heart pounded as he looked from the machine—slowly making its way down the row—back to the fallen worker. He had to do something. The man's partner stood at the far end of the field, oblivious to what had just occurred. It would be ten minutes before he had any idea that something was wrong. Who knew how much longer it would take to discover the accident; by then, it could be too late. Jacob sprang up and sprinted to the injured grower. He knelt down next to the man, feeling helpless, shocked by the bright red blood that flowed from the corners of the man's mouth. The man lay unconscious, and already a vicious purple bruise was forming along the right side of his face. And then there was the leg. Unable to close his eyes, he glanced at the mangled foot crushed into the ground, blood soaking into the pant cuff around it.

Jacob's first impulse was to scream for help, to alert the partner or anyone else nearby to rush the man to the infirmary, but he checked himself. To yell would mean discovery.

He would have to explain not only why he was out here, but how he had managed to discover the fallen worker. He racked his brain to find a way out for both of them. The man's breathing was shallow and he moaned softly, as if he were simply wrestling with a bad dream and nothing more. But it was Jacob who felt as if he were trapped in a nightmare, agonizing as every second passed. Then his eyes fixed on the polished sounder pinned to the man's chest, and a solution appeared. He remembered learning that every sounder contained a panic function for use in emergencies. Jacob pounded the sounder three times in quick succession. Immediately a high pulsing tone rose and fell in a rapid beat. The piercing noise, which would last only a few minutes before draining the battery, stabbed into Jacob's ears, and he retreated. The pathminders closest to them began to wail in response, and the pitch of alarm transcended everything, even the sound of the harvester.

Jacob searched the far end of the row. The other grower emerged, paused, and began moving down the line, tracing along the edge of the corn with his left hand. As the man reached the harvester, he leaned over and, after a second of groping, flipped a switch. The engine died; the arms froze in midair and its spiked wheels stopped turning. The wailing calls seemed louder without the engine running. *Hurry, hurry!* Jacob thought, resisting the urge to scream out loud as the grower continued toward Jacob and the injured man, moving into a trot. Looking around, Jacob could see other workers coming toward him on the paths as well, emerging from the other fields with concern and curiosity on their faces. He realized he was about to be surrounded and ran to where he had been watching before, turning to see men and women gather around their fallen comrade. They carefully placed him in an empty wagon and began running the cart toward the settlement.

Looking down, Jacob saw wet blood on his hands. Feeling shaky and weak, he ran to catch up with the wagon and followed it to the infirmary, which was fortunately in the southern tier, close to the fields. For a half hour he sat like a statue on a bench outside the infirmary door, hoping to hear some news about the injured worker, but no one came out after the initial group of growers returned to the fields. After a while, having heard nothing and wanting to prevent suspicion by asking, he returned home.

It was only on the way home that Jacob realized he was walking into trouble. He opened the front door and, standing on the threshold, recognized the shape of his mother in the shadows. She was waiting. She knew that he had skipped school; the only question was what she had done about it and what she would do now. He debated whether to ignore her and head directly to his room or remain and call her name, as if he were unaware of her presence. Before he could decide, she spoke.

"Did you have a good day, Jacob?" she asked.

Jacob didn't want to lie, but he couldn't tell her. "It was fine," he mumbled.

"Aren't you going to ask me about my day?" she asked. Her voice was hollow and hoarse.

Here we go, Jacob thought. He could tell from the forced neutrality of her voice what was coming. "How was your day?" he asked.

"Wonderful. For the second time in two weeks I've had to

113

lie for my son." Jacob inwardly breathed a sigh of relief. She had covered for him. "Care to tell me where you were?"

"I wasn't feeling good," he stated. "I needed to get some fresh air, so I went out to the north field." It was only a half-truth, but it was the best he could muster.

"Fresh air? All day? Come on, Jacob, I know you can do better than that."

"I fell asleep," he answered. An image of blood flashed through his mind.

"Fell asleep," she echoed in disbelief.

"Is that all?" he asked, wanting to leave.

"No, actually, it isn't. I've saved the best for last." Her voice sounded strangled now, as if someone else were speaking through her. Jacob's pulse quickened. What could it be? Did she know? How could she? "I was talking to some of the neighbors this morning," she said. "There's a rumor going around that there was a theft yesterday. Somebody broke into the storehouse and stole some food while everyone was at the Gathering."

"Really?" he said. He saw the hunched shape slipping through the streets in his mind's eye. He saw the dropped package in his hands. Suddenly her words coalesced and he realized what was about to happen.

"And behold," she continued, ignoring his response, "what do I find in my son's room this morning, but this"—an empty can bounced noisily on the ground before him—"and this"—another can. "There's more where this came from. Would you care to check?"

"No," he whispered.

"How could you?" she demanded with dismay.

"I'm not a thief," he said. He had to tell her. The theft, the

114

accident . . . everything. He wasn't a thief; he wasn't bad. He had saved a man's life, and he could bring a thief to justice. Weren't those good things? Wouldn't they be enough to offset the sin of the vision that had brought these things about? She would have to accept him, no matter her belief, no matter what they both had always been taught.

Before he could tell her, she broke in. "What hurts, Jacob, is that you don't even seem to care about how this affects me. I know how much Delaney's death disturbed you, but it's been twice as devastating for me. She was my student. We worked together every day. She was like a daughter." She was crying now. "And now this. I don't know whether to believe you or not. You go off every day. Spend hours alone. Egan came by today to check on you. He said he's barely heard from you the last few days, that you've been keeping to yourself. This antisocial behavior, it's not like you. You never used to lie."

He didn't say a word. He was tempted to shout, *What about you?* and point out her hypocrisy. She had lied to the authorities twice. True, her lies had saved him, but all the more reason to be ashamed—they had all been taught that Harmony came first, that truth came first. Family came second. Maybe that was a lie; maybe in reality, truth didn't come first. Maybe the bonds of family were too difficult to break. He would never reveal those thoughts to her, though. He would appear ungrateful. Besides, she was right in a way—it had never truly occurred to him how difficult Delaney's death must've been, and must still be, for his mother. He couldn't tell her about his vision now; it would only make matters worse. She would lose another child. Better that she suspected him a thief, a loner. At least those things weren't permanent.

They could be rationalized as simply a phase, the angst of a thirteen-year-old. He had had a chance to help Delaney and hadn't said the right thing; the only chance to help his mother now was to say nothing at all.

"All I know, Jake," she said, her voice groping for strength, reaching out through the darkness before his eyes, "is that this is the last time. I will never lie for you again. The next time something like this happens, you will have to leave our house and go to the fixers."

Jacob gasped. The fixers took in people who were having trouble with life in Harmony. Sometimes it was because they couldn't follow the rules; others went because they suffered from depression or anxiety. The fixers lived with them in seclusion, worked with them, and counseled them daily until they were cured and ready to resume life in the community. It was usually the last resort, and the people who were cured never acted quite the same after release. Jacob met one once when he was young. A woman in their tier had spent a year with the fixers, though he never found out why. Before she left, Jacob remembered her as loud and chatty. He remembered she would often corner his mother in the street and gossip or complain. He was too young to really know what she was talking about, but he remained fascinated by this bold and animated woman. Upon finally returning, she rarely spoke, and when she did, her words were slow and strangely muted. She died a few years later.

"I'll be good, Ma," he said softly, and went to his room.

Shortly afterward, Jacob heard his father come home. He opened the bedroom door and eavesdropped on his parents' conversation.

"It was pretty bad," his father said. "Thank God they got him to the infirmary in time."

"Is Mitchell going to be okay?" his mother asked.

"He lost a lot of blood, got a nasty concussion. Worst of all, the ghostbox had to amputate his foot, but he'll live." He paused. "It's strange, though. His sounder alerted everyone so quickly. But when they got there, he was unconscious. Nobody can figure out how he activated it."

"Maybe it went off on its own."

"They just don't do that, Gina. They should, but they don't."

"Maybe he activated it before passing out."

"Maybe. But when he came to, he couldn't remember doing it. The last thing he remembers is replacing the chopping bin. That's it."

"Well, he probably can't remember because of the concussion. Besides, who cares, Richard? He's alive, isn't he?"

"I guess. Talk about lucky; it could have been worse—he could have bled to death in the field before anyone noticed, or been dragged by that thing, or even sucked up into it—"

"Okay, I get it," his mother interrupted.

Jacob could hear his father's voice sharpen. "It pisses me off. This is the third time one of those pieces of garbage has malfunctioned this month. I warned Norris that someone was going to get hurt."

"No point getting upset. They'll get some new harvesters eventually."

"Right," he said sarcastically. "Where's Jake? It's almost time for dinner."

"He's in his room" was all she said. Her voice revealed none of the anger Jacob knew was there. "Why don't *you* get him."

117

Jacob heard the heavy steps coming down the hall toward his room. He quietly closed the door and waited for his father, breathing a sigh of relief. The injured man would live.

Dinner was a silent affair, in itself not unusual, but in the stifling darkness of the house it seemed more strained than usual to Jacob. He could sense his mother's anger in every grating of the knife and fork against her plate, a cold anger that set him on edge. His father soon gave up making small talk but didn't seem to notice anything was amiss between wife and son. Jacob figured he was probably too tired to care after the long day of harvest. The image of his father gulping down tomatoes on the sly rose up in his mind as he listened to the man grunt and chew. He didn't seem any less hungry than usual. Then again, his father was always hungry.

"I can help do dishes, Ma," Jacob offered after dinner.

"Don't bother," she snapped. He backed off, not wanting to rekindle her earlier rage.

He went to his room and lay back on the bed. He wasn't tired, but he didn't dare go back out to where his mother and father now sat listening to a Foundation broadcast. Still, just sitting in the blackness of his room had no appeal. He wished he could do something to ease the boredom or, better yet, make things right with his mother.

Suddenly he had an idea. Maybe he could do something to make up for all the pain he'd caused her lately. He got up and went out to the living room.

"I've got to go over to Egan's," he told his parents.

"Why?" his father asked.

"I told him I'd help him study for a test tomorrow. We're having final tests in school."

"You didn't mention it earlier," his father said.

"I forgot."

"I guess it's still early. I don't know, Gina, what do you think?"

"I don't care. He can do whatever he wants. He's good at that these days, isn't that right, Jacob?"

There was an awkward silence for a moment as Jacob hesitated, not wanting to engage her. Finally his father broke in.

"Go ahead, then. Just don't stay too late."

"It won't take long," Jacob replied, heading out. He could already hear an argument starting as he closed the door behind him.

He knocked for the second time, but still there was no response. *Come on*, he thought. *He has to be home.* Jacob knocked a third time, louder now, but still all was quiet. He turned away from the high councilor's door and looked out. The sun had nearly reached the horizon, and the shadows in the street below were long. A pair of wind chimes rang faintly from a neighboring house in the evening breeze. With a sigh, he started down the ramp. All the way over he had been brimming with excitement at the idea of the gift, but now it looked like it would have to wait.

A sudden tone behind him stopped him and he turned back toward the door.

"Who is it?" the high councilor's voice said, sounding tinny and faint through the small speaker by the door, not at all the normal commanding boom Jacob was used to. Intercoms were installed in most of the common buildings, but few residences had them. Egan's house had one, but it had long since stopped working.

119

"It's me. Jacob Manford."

"Jacob?" The man sounded puzzled.

"I needed to ask you something," he replied. Jacob began to worry that he'd disturbed him from something important.

"Yes. Come in."

Jacob opened the door and stepped into the hallway. A familiar smell flooded his senses as he entered. Delaney's scent still lingered in the house, and for a second he half expected to see her waltz into view. Here, though, his memory failed him; he realized he had no idea what she looked like. The impression faded as a figure appeared. Although the door was half open, the light outside was dim enough now that he could barely see. The high councilor was nothing more than a tall, dark shape enveloped in shadow at the opposite end of the hall.

"This is an unexpected pleasure, Jacob," the high councilor purred. "To what do I owe the honor?"

Jacob paused for a moment, gathering his courage. "I have a favor to ask. I know that when people die, their sounder is given away. I was just wondering if"—he hesitated—"maybe I could have Delaney's. To give to my mother," he added.

There was a long pause. As each second passed, Jacob's heart began to pound. Had he insulted the man? When the high councilor finally replied, his voice sounded strange, higher in pitch, tentative.

"That's a kind gesture, Jacob," he said, clearing his throat. "Unfortunately, even if I wanted to, I couldn't let you have it, as I don't have it myself."

Jacob's heart sank at the man's words. "Who did you give it to?" he blurted out, too disappointed to realize the temerity of questioning Harmony's leader.

Again there was a pause. "I buried it with her."

"Oh," Jacob said, puzzled. He had never heard of that before.

"It was too painful for me to keep," the man added quickly. "I felt that the memory of its sound would be too much of a burden. As leader of the community, I carry enough burdens already."

"Oh," Jacob said again, trying to sort out the high councilor's words.

"I fault myself, now, for not having thought of giving it to Regina. She certainly would deserve it. But it is buried with the girl and there it will remain," he said, then added, as if to change the subject, "Your mother really misses her, doesn't she?"

"Yes," Jacob replied.

"And you too, I'm sure."

"Yes."

"Come here, Jacob," the high councilor commanded. Jacob stepped into the shadows until he felt the man's hand on his shoulder. "I know this has been a struggle, young man, but as time passes you will learn to accept what happened. Acceptance is perhaps the greatest virtue. It is what our Truesight is based on. I know it seems heartless to say, but Delaney's death has no meaning in the larger scheme of things. One person, even myself, has no meaning other than that he or she is part of the larger whole, the community. Our community. Do you understand that?"

"Yes," Jacob replied faintly, feeling the firm grip on his shoulder.

"Of course you do. You're a smart young man. Everyone

121

says so. Besides," he said, "Delaney is much better off now. She has gone deep into the darkness, far beyond the reaches of even our own meager attempts. She understands Truesight in a way that neither of us fully can until the day we join her. In life she struggled with it, as I think both you and I know, but in the end she embraced it. I am so proud of her."

Jacob didn't know what to say. He had struggled to accept that Delaney was gone, and felt that he had nearly done it, but somehow the high councilor's words chilled him. If what the man said was true, then Jacob's time in the light was only pushing him farther away from Delaney. But if anything, he now realized, his vision only made him feel closer to her, to what she had struggled with in life. He remembered again what she had confessed to her father the last time he had come into this house. Detaching himself from the councilor's grip, he turned back toward the door.

"Jacob," the high councilor said, and Jacob paused. "You need to help your mother understand this also. If your father cannot, you must. She'll come around. Your mother is a very special woman, very special. I feel fortunate that Delaney was able to have her in her life. We all are."

"Thanks," Jacob said. "I know."

He hurried from the house and ran home through the empty streets. He had come with high hopes and left feeling disappointed and confused. By the time he got home, the sun had long since set, there were no moons yet in the sky, and darkness had settled over the land.

CHAPTER TWELVE

The next day Jacob went to school. All morning he had been having trouble concentrating, and now, sitting in orienteering class, he felt agitated and barely listened as Mr. Robison lectured. It wasn't just the conversation last night with Delaney's father that bothered him. Neither he nor his mother had spoken to each other during breakfast, and Jacob hoped her silence meant her anger was dissipating. However, it could also mean that it was still there, building beneath the surface, intensifying. He recalled the birthday picnic on the hill a few nights ago; in his mind he saw once again the coldness in her face. Then it had been directed toward his father. Had she been wearing the same face this morning toward him? He hadn't been able to tell in the dark.

All Jacob knew was that the more he saw of people's behavior, the less he understood. The last few days had been both exhilarating and bewildering. Last night, as he lay in bed, he began thinking about how his vision might impact his life permanently. It had been less than three weeks since his sight had slowly surfaced, and it was only the fourth day since he had begun seeing clearly. In that time so much had happened. He felt like he was being swung around, faster and faster, through a cycle of ecstasy and guilt, a circle that went nowhere. Would it always be this way? The prospect seemed exhausting.

"Is everyone ready?" Mr. Robison asked. Jacob pushed the thoughts of this morning aside and joined the class as they answered yes. "Okay, let's head outside."

They left the building and entered the school yard. Jacob blinked at the brightness, shielding his eyes from the sun. The students gathered near the mellow tone of the teacher's sounder. Mr. Robison tapped the pin on his chest and it went silent.

"Last week you were tested with the finders. Everyone did well, as they should—finders are easy to use. Today, however, you're going to be tested on finding someone without the help of a device. You've been playing seeker for fun ever since you were little. This time, it's for a grade."

Jacob looked at his classmates. Aside from Egan, he didn't know who belonged to which face; he had been away from school two of the last three days and had been indoors nearly the entire time he was there. They all stared blankly forward, heads turned in the teacher's direction.

"Remember the sweeping techniques you've learned. Use your sounders and your knowledge of Harmony to assist you. As I mentioned earlier, the class will be divided into two groups. Each person will be matched with someone from the other group and will be required to find him or her as quickly as possible. I'll assign a specific place to each hider. Seekers, you'll be told only which tier your partner is in—after that, you're on your own. When you find your partner, return here, and when everyone is finished, we'll rotate so that the hiders become the seekers. Hiders, when you reach your assigned spot, wait in the open—no hiding behind bushes or buildings or in doorways. Right, Egan?"

"I wouldn't dream of it!" Egan said, and the students giggled.

Mr. Robison divided the class into two groups and assigned partners. Jacob was paired with Parker, a boy from the South Tier. He didn't know Parker well, but he had always gotten along with him. Parker's dark eyes pointed straight at Jacob. Jacob found the blank gaze disquieting. He felt vulnerable, though he knew the boy's eyes saw nothing. *It should be the other way around*, he thought. *He's the vulnerable one.* He fought the desire to look away and forced himself to return the stare, to absorb every feature of this person he had barely known over the years. The boy was taller than Jacob, with a dark complexion that matched his eyes. His black hair was longer than most of the others', falling down over his forehead and almost covering his eyes. Parker was quiet by nature. When he did speak, he did so slowly and thoughtfully. Like Jacob's mother, Parker's father was a musician. Jacob wondered why he had never tried to befriend the boy. After all, he had much more in common with him than Egan.

Mr. Robison walked down the row of hiders, assigning each to a spot in one of the four tiers. Before they left, the hiders briefly activated their sounders to remind the seekers of their identity. Parker was last in line. Jacob watched Mr. Robison lean down and whisper instructions in his ear. Parker nodded his head and moved away. Jacob's eyes followed him as he exited the school yard and headed toward the southern tier, eventually disappearing around the corner. Mr. Robison waited so the hiders would have enough time to reach their spots. While they were waiting, he told each of the seekers which tier to search in and reviewed their instructions.

"Remember, you'll be timed. When you hear your partner's

sounder, move in and tap it silent. Then the two of you can come back here."

The seekers were finally cleared to leave, and one at a time they headed out in the same order in which their partners had left. Like Parker, Jacob was last. Leaving the school yard, he headed toward the South Tier. He considered closing his eyes; it would probably be fairer to the others. But whenever he tried, it felt too uncomfortable to move so blindly through the imposed darkness. Eventually he surrendered and kept his eyes open. The streets were quiet, as they usually were this time of day, but Jacob still observed people from time to time moving about their business. Weaving around them, he searched the eastern part, quickly moving down the main avenues between the hills, looking left and right into the side streets, where the houses lay. He saw no sign of Parker, so he headed to the western section.

On his way there, he stopped after rounding a corner. A girl stood in the middle of the street, her arms at her sides. He recognized her from his class; she had been one of the first to be sent away, and he had caught only a brief glimpse before she left. Now she stood alone, waiting to be found. Jacob moved closer, taking slow, quiet steps. He studied her face as he approached. She had black hair, loosely tied back, that fell in curls around her face and onto her neck and shoulders. Thin, arched eyebrows seemed to pull up the corners of her eyes, giving her a regal, almost feline appearance. Jacob was transfixed. He could feel his heart pound as he moved closer. He noticed how her robe gathered tightly at her waist and how she stood so still with a patient look, her lips moist and slightly parted, forming a slight smile in repose. She was beautiful.

126

Jacob tried to be quiet. He was fifteen feet away and moving, but she hadn't seemed to notice him. He felt as if he were being drawn in to the girl, closer and closer, by an invisible cord. He paused only when a breeze suddenly arose and wafted her scent toward him. Lilacs. It was Beth, the girl he had been sent out into the hall to locate with the finder that day in school. He thought about that day, remembering the touch of her soft hand, warm but not sweaty. He wanted to touch her now, to confirm that it was really Beth, that she was really alive and not some statue or vision. He reached out his hand as he continued toward her, breathing quickly. A chord began to ring as their sounders moved within range. Both of them jumped back a step, startled, and the chord ceased. Jacob watched her as a look of confusion and perhaps fear disturbed the calmness of her face. She froze, listening for any noise.

"Susan?" she said.

Susan must be her partner. What should he say? He almost ran without uttering a word, but somehow it felt wrong not to say something.

"It's me—Jacob. Is that you, Beth?"

"Jacob!" she said, and the concerned look vanished. "Yes, it's me. You had me scared for a minute there; I didn't hear you approach."

"I can be pretty invisible when I want to be," he joked, and she laughed.

"Who are you searching for?" she asked.

"Parker. He's around here somewhere." He felt like an idiot. He should say something else, something clever, as Egan would, but he could only stare at the high cheekbones that were now flushed a light crimson. "Well, I better go" was all that came out.

"Good luck," she said. She was smiling; the corners of her mouth seemed to dance. Then, as Jacob moved forward to go around her, she moved too, going in his direction. He didn't prevent the collision, but reached his hands forward as they gently bumped, and steadied her. He pulled his hands away quickly, as if he were touching a plate from the oven. They exchanged mumbled apologies and he left her standing there. As he walked away he could feel the blood pumping through his entire body, and he felt mildly light-headed. He broke into a run, slowing only when he encountered someone briefly in the street, and moved rapidly through the section. He soon found Parker. The boy was sitting outside the infirmary, right where Jacob had sat yesterday. He approached Parker and tapped his pin, and the two of them headed to the school yard.

"That was fast," Parker commented. "I feel like I barely got there before you showed up."

Jacob didn't reply, and for the rest of the way back neither of them spoke. When they entered the school yard, Mr. Robison was amazed.

"Jacob! My God, this is a record," the teacher said. "How did you do it?"

"I was lucky, I guess" was all Jacob said.

It took more than half an hour before everyone was finally back. When they had gathered, Mr. Robison praised Jacob in front of everyone, and they applauded. Suddenly he felt ashamed. He didn't deserve any of it and wished he had waited longer before finding Parker or, better yet, had closed his eyes and searched for his partner the way he was supposed to.

Mr. Robison divided them again. This time it was Jacob's turn to hide. He stood in line, waiting for his teacher's instructions, and stared at Beth in the row across from him.

He watched her as she talked quietly with the girl next to her. He wondered what Beth was saying to her friend. Maybe she was talking about him. A hand shook his shoulder, and he started.

"Hello, Jacob. Wake up." It was Mr. Robison.

"What?" he answered confusedly. He looked around. Everyone in his row had left for a hiding place. Only the students across from him remained.

"I don't know what to make of you these days, Jacob," the teacher remarked. "Either you're doing something amazing, or you act as if you're deaf as well as blind." The students giggled at the joke, all except Parker, who remained as placidly stoic as he had earlier.

"Sorry," Jacob muttered.

Mr. Robison bent over and cupped his hands around Jacob's ear.

"Auckland End," he whispered.

"Okay," Jacob said, and left the yard in the direction of his own North Tier. Auckland End was a cul-de-sac only a couple streets past his own. He paused at the fountain in his district's little square and splashed cool water on his face and neck. Looking around, he saw some flowers in a nearby bed. He was drawn to the yellow ones, each with more than a dozen thin petals around a black center. He picked five, breathing in their delicate scent. He decided he would pass his own street on his way to the assigned spot and stop at home. If he couldn't give her Delaney's sounder, then maybe the bouquet would placate his mother. He used to gather flowers for her all the time when he was younger, and she'd always loved it.

Jacob turned onto his street. He was at the door, reaching for the handle, when suddenly he heard voices coming directly from the other side. Just as he began wondering what his father was doing home in the middle of his shift, he heard the latch begin to turn. He decided to play a joke and surprise them, and leaped to the side and crouched down behind the flowering shrub that grew beside the doorway, deactivating his sounder to avoid discovery. A man stepped into the light, followed by his mother, but it wasn't his father. Through the leaves Jacob caught a glimpse of the man's face before he turned around. He didn't recognize the man with eyes so pale they seemed almost white and a long, dark beard streaked with gray. The pair lingered in the doorway, facing each other. Jacob's eyes widened as he watched them embrace. They didn't speak, only kissed, their arms wrapped around each other, her hand on the back of his neck. Then they parted, and his mother went inside and closed the door, leaving Jacob frozen behind the bush.

It was a long time before Jacob moved. He was stunned by what he had just seen. For the second time that day his heart pounded and his stomach fluttered, but whereas he had felt exhilarated before, he now felt confused and sick. He threw the flowers aside and returned to the square. When Parker appeared, Jacob quietly moved to intercept him, and they headed back to the school. When the exercise was over and the students were released for the day, Jacob approached Egan.

"Can I stay at your house tonight?" he asked, trying not to sound desperate.

"Why?" Egan demanded, his face cold and neutral.

"Please, Egan. I just need to."

"I don't know," Egan said. "You've practically ignored me for the last three days. I was beginning to think you'd found another best friend."

"Of course not," Jacob said. "I've had a lot on my mind."

"Fine, come over if you want," Egan said before breaking into a smile. "After all, it would be an honor to have the king of seekers grace my humble abode." Egan laughed. Jacob tried to laugh too, but the teasing compliment rekindled the feeling of shame.

When he got to Egan's house, Jacob called his mother and told her where he was. It felt strange talking to her—he couldn't get the image of the kiss out of his mind—and he hung up as quickly as possible. That night, he hardly slept. When he did manage to drift off, he had horrible dreams. Images of the last few days rose up and blended together. Beth, his mother and her lover, the blood-soaked grower, the thieving neighbor—all of them seemed to form some insidious drama against him. He fled, struggling into a distorted landscape in which the moon kept rising over and over again, pulling the grass up into the sky until it collapsed and smothered him with a blanket of darkness.

As Jacob awoke, the smothering sensation lingered with him in the utter blackness of the subterranean house. It was morning, but everyone still slept; he could hear Egan nearby, his slow breathing rhythmic and relaxed. Jacob rose silently and left without saying good-bye. The morning surrounded him with sharpness and detail; every leaf, every door, every stone in the street, was perfect in its clarity. Everything was perfect—everything except people like his mother, his father, his neighbors, the workers, and himself. *We are all deceiving one another,* he thought, looking down. His long shadow preceded him as he walked in the early-morning sun. *I am the greatest deceiver of all.* He could stand it no longer. He knew he had to tell someone his secret.

131

CHAPTER THIRTEEN

The next day Jacob decided to reveal his secret to Egan. He felt he should probably tell his parents, but he just couldn't do it. These days his father was busy with the harvest, laboring long hours in the fields and storehouses, and when he was home, he was so irritable from exhaustion that Jacob stayed out of his way, as he always did each year during harvest. Besides, he had never been close with his father, at least when it came to talking about real things. As for his mother, he had been avoiding her as much as possible these last two days since seeing her with the other man. When they were together, they barely spoke.

It wasn't the illegality of his mother's behavior that really bothered him. Adultery was strictly forbidden, but rarely was anyone accused of it. Before these past few weeks Jacob would have believed that meant it never happened, but now he wasn't sure. Maybe it happened a lot; after all, most of the marriages in Harmony were arranged by the council and representatives of the Foundation. The more he witnessed, the more he realized that people probably broke the rules all the time. If so, then what good were the rules? Why bother to pay lip service to principles and then do the opposite? Jacob couldn't figure it out. *Maybe that's the way it's supposed to be*, he thought. Maybe it was better to have rules, even if people failed to obey them, than to have none at all. Maybe it was better for people to do so and feel civilized, even if they weren't, than to give in to any impulse freely without guilt.

Besides, wasn't he a walking, talking, *seeing* violation of the most sacred tenet of Harmony and its Foundation? He was as bad as any of them, worse than any of them, including his mother. No, it didn't bother him that she had committed a significant crime; it was more visceral than that. It was the image in his mind of the caress, of the kiss he had witnessed, that repulsed him every time it surfaced in his memory. Maybe it was the betrayal, but the betrayal was more against his father than him. All he knew was that it filled him with a cold anger, just like the look he had seen on his mother's face the night of his birthday. He probably bore that look now. How long had the affair been going on? A week? A month? A year or more? Maybe his father was aware, but it seemed unlikely. That left it to Jacob to tell. But he realized he never could. Instead, he had another secret to tell, a far more ominous one that trivialized all the darker things he had seen.

Someone had to be told. And so it fell to Egan. They had shared secrets before, about the small things they felt or did, and Egan had never told anyone the thoughts that Jacob shared. He could count on him now to do the same—even with a secret like this one. He needed to unburden himself before things got out of control, and because he didn't trust himself, he would have to trust somebody else, an ally who could help him sort everything out. Egan sometimes lacked gravity and sincerity, but he also possessed a boldness, a clarity that Jacob felt he himself lacked, no matter how clearly he saw the world. For Egan, life was simple and defined.

The two of them were in the main square, returning home

from school—the next to the last day—having paused near the north exit, where they usually parted. Jacob would head north and Egan would go east. The square was almost empty as Jacob looked beyond Egan and surveyed the area. The afternoon sun was cooler now and cast shadows along the western edge, leaving that part of the square bathed in blue. A few old men occupied benches in the shadows, lined up as if waiting for something to come take them someplace else. They hardly spoke; they sat silently, blind eyes pointed straight ahead, moving only to brush the flies away. Whatever they were saying, Jacob couldn't hear; as always, soft music played over the speakers that lined the square, the same speakers that projected the voice of the high councilor at each Gathering. Bouncing off the emptiness of the open space, the music sounded hollow and lonely, as if it sensed nobody listened.

Jacob and Egan were discussing school, anticipating their last day tomorrow, wondering how things would change. Over and over Jacob tried to say the words that kept rising to his mouth like dry heaves. He felt detached, pushed out of himself, watching from the outside as this stranger refused to tell his secret. Now Egan was telling him about his special-ization, about the news his father had told him last night. None of them were supposed to find out until after the harvest, when the work was done, but his father had told him; they shared secrets too. Egan would be leaving, going on a starship to Earth, back to the Foundation with his father and mother to be trained—for what, he didn't really know.

As they stood side by side facing the edge of the square, Egan quietly revealing the news, Jacob stared straight ahead at the wall. Like many of the buildings in Harmony, it was covered with burnished steel sheets that mirrored a warped

134

reflection. He looked at the two of them standing together, his friend not as tall but standing squarely, while he slouched next to him. He couldn't see either of their faces; the mirroring sheets blurred their features, reminding him of his foggy sight before the clarity. He realized that he had never seen his own face. What did he look like?

"Maybe it won't be so bad," Egan was saying. "Besides, I'm sure I'll be back. I'll probably be a councilor someday, like my father. At least that's what he says. Maybe you will too. You're smart. Smarter than I am, probably. I asked my father about your specialization, but he wouldn't tell me. Still, I'm sure it'll be something good. What do you think?"

"I don't know," Jacob replied. He wasn't even sure he cared anymore. Just a few weeks ago it had been all he could think about, a source of subtle but constant anxiety. Now it seemed a trivial concern.

"Oh!" Egan burst out, startling Jacob. "I almost forgot." He dug into his pocket and produced a small black box. He reached out and took Jacob's arm, placing the box in his hand. It was a finder.

"Where did you get this?" Jacob asked.

"I took it from school, stupid. I figured we could have at least one last adventure before I leave."

"Why are you giving it to me?" Jacob asked, tucking it away in his bag. The whole thing irritated him. He needed to tell Egan now before he lost every bit of courage, and this was a distraction.

"You know my father. Mr. Suspicious. If he caught me with it, he'd kill me. You don't mind hanging on to it for me, do you? After all, you've said yourself that your parents—"

"Egan, I can see," he said. There—it was out. For a

moment the world stopped. Even the music ceased briefly as one song ended and another began. Jacob watched Egan's reflection as the figure shifted uncomfortably.

"Yeah . . . right. Anyway, I know we can have some fun with this before anyone notices it's missing. So hang on to it, just for tonight. And whatever you do, don't tell anyone," Egan said.

"I can see," Jacob said again, so quietly this time that even he had trouble hearing himself above the music that wheedled in the background.

"Yeah, Jacob. You said that before," Egan replied, practically shouting in contrast. "I don't get it. What are you saying?"

"I'm saying," Jacob hissed, pulling his friend closer, "that I can see. Literally, with my eyes." He scanned the area nervously. No one was nearby. The square was vacant except for the old men and three women who had just entered from the southern tier. He stared at Egan, who now faced him. His brow was crinkled and a slight frown formed along his pressed lips. Suddenly his eyebrows reversed themselves into an arch, and the lips curled back to reveal his teeth.

"I get it!" Egan said. He tilted back his head and laughed. His howls bounced around the square like an echo and seemed to drown out the music. The sound terrified Jacob; he wanted to cover the laughing mouth with his hands, anything to quiet the reverberating noise. The women halted at the echoes, and the old men suddenly cocked their heads in unison. Finally Egan stopped laughing enough to speak through gasping breaths. "Jacob, you never cease to amaze me. I realize I've made plenty of off-color comments and bad jokes, but I've never heard anything so obscene, and with such perfect timing. Bravo!" he said, and briskly applauded.

This is it, Jacob thought. *All I have to do is go along, and it'll be as if I never said anything.* He was tempted for a second to recover himself, to admit to the tasteless comment, but he suddenly didn't want to. He was an obscenity, sight and all. Why not admit it?

"I'm serious," Jacob said quietly, so no one else could possibly hear. "I can see. Totally. Clearly. I can see you right now." And he could; he could see the look of shock and horror creeping over his friend's face, deeper with every word he spoke. Egan stepped backward, away from him and toward the wall, touching it, as if desperate for something solid in order to orient himself.

"I don't understand," Egan finally said. "How did this happen? . . . For how long?" he stammered.

"I don't know how, but it happened. It started only a couple weeks ago. At first it was just a light, and then blurry shapes and hazy colors. Last week I started seeing clearly. The race—in the north field, remember?"

Egan nodded. "Your birthday," he said. "And you've been able to see since then? You've been walking among us, staring at us, at me, the entire time? So that's how you did so well on the test the other day."

"That's not important. Egan, I don't know what to do." Jacob watched as Egan took another step backward. The expression remained on his friend's face, the look he had never expected to see. This wasn't going well. "It just happened," he said pleadingly.

"I can't imagine. What's it like?" Egan asked. Jacob could hear the wavering in his voice. The look of horror was fading. In its place, Jacob could see anguish and confusion. Anything was better than fear. If Egan was afraid, what did that mean for him?

137

"I don't know how to explain it," he said. "It's as if everything about yourself is suddenly bigger and smaller at the same time. The whole world is bigger because you can see the distances. You can see the sky and watch the grass move and people walk. The sun rises and sets, and the moon climbs too, across your eyes. And all the time the outside edge is pushed farther back, you're pushed farther in, growing less and less. You realize you're nothing in the midst of the world out there. When I was blind, I had only myself, no matter who or what was around me. Nothing distracted me from myself, not even the sounds that defined the space around me. I was inside. Now I'm still in there, but I'm surrounded by everything I've seen. Images emerge without my even thinking about them."

He realized he'd closed his eyes while he was talking, trying to explain the inexplicable. Now, as he opened them, he saw that Egan had turned his back on him, was leaning against the wall.

"What are you going to do?" Egan asked in a strained whisper.

"I don't know," Jacob said, "but you can't tell anyone."

"I can't? Maybe not, but you should. Tell the council what you told me. They'll know what to do."

"I can't do that. What if they do something to me?"

"That's good, isn't it? They can fix you. It's not your fault."

"Why do we have to tell anyone? Just keep it between ourselves."

"Jacob, this isn't some prank, or even like sneaking out during a curfew. This is big—bigger than you or me. Anyway, people deserve to know you can see them, because otherwise . . . I don't know, it's creepy."

"Is that what I am? Creepy?" The words rushed from his mouth before he could think. "Let me tell you, Egan, you're creepy. You and everyone else. Your eyes are open but they see nothing. All around you people are doing things you don't know about, things you don't want to know about. You live in a small world. You live in a tiny place where you're taken care of. You look healthy, your cheeks are full, but most of the others don't look so good. Half of them are skin and bones. Their faces are thin. *That's* creepy, Egan. Not me." Jacob trembled as he spoke. He knew he shouldn't be saying these things, but he blurted them out regardless.

"Maybe I do live in a small world, but not for long. Soon I'll be far away on Earth, and you'll still be stuck here, watching everyone with your creepy eyesight, if you're lucky."

Lucky? What does he mean by that? Jacob wondered. He became scared.

"Egan, I'm sorry. I didn't mean what I said before," he apologized.

"Don't worry about it," Egan said, turning away to hide the tears welling up in his eyes. Jacob had never known his friend to cry before—except the few times he was hurt during a fall—and he didn't want to now.

"I'm only telling you my secret because you're my best friend and I can trust you."

"I know," Egan said, turning away again, this time to leave. "Hey, I have to go."

"Don't tell anyone," Jacob pleaded. "Promise me."

"I won't," Egan said, walking away, "I promise. We'll talk more tomorrow."

Jacob watched him leave. Then he was out of sight, and Jacob realized he was alone in the square. The women had left through the east or west exits, unaware of the boys' conversation; even the old men had disappeared—whatever they

139

were waiting for must have come and gone. All that remained was himself and the music. A melodramatic march, some Foundation standard, was droning weakly through the speakers. As Jacob listened, the player began to skip, causing the same hysterical measure to repeat itself over and over and over. Nobody noticed to fix it.

They came for him the next day. It was the last day of school, and everyone was outside enjoying lunch in the sun. Several times that morning Jacob had tried to talk to Egan, but the opportunity for a private moment never arose. Egan had also failed to appear at their usual meeting place in the square before heading to school.

"I missed you this morning," Jacob said, approaching him before Mrs. Lawson's class.

"I woke up late. I barely made it here on time" was all Egan said. His voice sounded distant, and Jacob became nervous. It wasn't the fear of being discovered that gripped him initially, it was the fear of rejection. All last night he had chastised himself for revealing his secret to Egan, for telling anyone. He had become so accustomed to his sight in the short time since its arrival that it hadn't occurred to him just how outrageous the news might be to anyone. All their lives they had been taught to think of sight as an anathema. Of course Egan would react the way he did. Why hadn't Jacob thought of that ahead of time? Why would he think anyone would understand?

Still, he didn't believe that Egan would tell anyone else. But as soon as the two men appeared at the entrance of the school yard, calling several teachers over, Jacob knew that they had come for him. He watched as the men whispered to his teachers, who physically recoiled at the words spoken to them, the words of his secret. Mr. Robison was now approaching him where he sat among his classmates, eating a piece of bread and a tomato. Jacob stared down at the half-eaten fruit, at its cluster of seeds and the brilliance of its red skin, torn along the edges. He watched the other students, laughing and talking to one another. They were beautiful, the girls and the boys, and he did his best to savor these last few seconds when he was still one of them, another child content to live in darkness.

Coming to the edge of the group, Mr. Robison called to him. "Jacob, come here, please. The listeners want to speak to you."

Immediately all conversation halted. If the listeners wanted someone, it was never good. Jacob looked around him. The students now began whispering to one another, and he could hear the quiet questions buzzing like newly hatched flies. Only Egan, who sat nearby, said nothing; his head was bent, his hands covered his ears. Jacob rose and walked through the clusters of students on the grass to where Mr. Robison waited. He could see the struggle on the man's face, the attempt to be neutral, to hide the fear or repulsion that wanted to show itself. Whether he was trying to hide it from Jacob or himself, Jacob wasn't sure. Mr. Robison slowly offered his hand to lead Jacob away, as was the custom. His arm was trembling.

"That's okay, you don't have to bother," Jacob said. The teacher dropped his arm, and Jacob thought he saw relief on the man's face. They walked side by side to the street.

"You know why they're here, then?" Mr. Robison asked.

"Yes," Jacob answered.

"Is it true?"

"Yes."

141

"Don't be scared. Tell the truth. It'll be easier on everyone."

Jacob knew Mr. Robison was doing his best to be nice, but it only made him feel worse. He felt like a criminal, as if he had just killed someone. They reached the listeners, who stood composed and impassive. They were businesslike and spoke in an abrupt, formal manner that implied the weight of authority.

"Jacob, the council wishes to meet with you about your sight. We're escorting you there now," one of them said, an older man with gray hair shorn close.

"Will anyone else be there with him? What about his parents?" Mr. Robison asked.

"It's none of your concern," the other listener barked.

"I want to know," Jacob said.

"We spoke to them this morning. Your parents will meet you at the council house."

"Come on, Maury," Mrs. Lawson said. "Let's get back to the students." She had been standing to the side when Jacob arrived. Now she stepped in and took Mr. Robison's arm to lead him away.

"She's right. Return to the children. We have everything under control here," the older man assured them.

Under control? Jacob thought. What did they think he might do?

"Good luck," Mr. Robison called behind him as he and Mrs. Lawson walked away. The students in the yard had finished eating and were now grouped together along the fence that separated the school yard from the street, straining to hear any part of the conversation. Jacob heard the teachers order them inside. He wondered what they would tell them.

142

The two men came over and stood on either side of him. Each one took a hand, keeping Jacob firmly between them.

"Don't try to run away," the younger listener warned.

"Why would I?" Jacob asked. He tried to sound calm, but he could hear the quaking in his voice.

"Do you realize your transgression? How serious it is?" the man asked.

"Lay off," the older man ordered. "He's just a kid."

"He's a Seer," the other sneered. Jacob closed his eyes; it was the first time he'd been called that.

"I guess you've heard," Jacob said.

"We hear everything," the younger listener replied with a grin.

CHAPTER FOURTEEN

The council house wasn't far from the school. They journeyed in silence; the listeners remained mute the rest of the way, and Jacob wasn't particularly interested in talking to them, either. Instead he thought about what the council might ask him and what he would say. They passed quickly into the southern tier and up the rise to the council house, set into the hillside. It was one of the largest hills in Harmony. A wide entrance with double doors propped open on either side gaped from the earth. The opening that led into the hall was black, a giant mouth waiting to swallow and consume him. Walking up the straight road lined with pathminders, Jacob avoided looking at that dark hole. Instead he looked beyond where the elevation revealed the landscape to the south. He could see the fields, could make out the growers moving around the vast square patches of crops, dark little shapes scurrying to and fro. Everyone was doing his job, oblivious to what was happening here on the hill.

A breeze picked up and the sound of wind chimes broke the silence. Jacob turned his head to discover they were standing before the entrance. Two large sets of chimes, each a cluster of silver pipes waving and singing, hung from the doors. Above the entrance a large striped cat lay stretched on top of the frame, staring down at him with yellow eyes. The eyes were beautiful the way they set upon him, locking themselves with his own gaze. They were different from the cow's eyes he'd seen earlier. Those alien eyes had taken him in and then left him, disinterested and dull. These eyes penetrated him, remained fixed and knowing, as if a moment of understanding and solidarity now passed between them, a secret shared.

Don't worry. Don't be afraid, they said. *You are not alone.*

I feel like it, he replied silently. *What do I tell them?* he asked, but the spell was broken as the cat severed its gaze and stared away with an indifferent flick of the tail.

"Come on," the older listener said, "it's time." They both tugged him from where he had paused.

As soon as he passed through the chamber doors, the darkness enveloped him. Coming from the bright sun into the cool chamber felt as if someone had suddenly placed a blindfold over his eyes. After a few seconds, however, the light filtering in from outside, faint as it was, brought out shapes before his adjusting eyes. He could see his parents off to the right, silent and still. He couldn't distinguish their faces and wondered what they were feeling right now.

"Hi, Ma. Hi, Dad," he said, trying not to sound scared.

"Hello, Jake," his father said quietly. His voice didn't sound angry, the way Jacob thought it might. His mother said nothing.

"Come here, Jacob," the familiar voice of the high councilor called out. Jacob walked farther into the hall and approached the council. They sat along the far end of the room, six figures in chairs against the wall. They were barely visible at this end of the chamber, and aside from the white folds of their gowns, which draped to the floor, he could only see their general shapes.

145

"We're sorry to have pulled you away from your last day of school, Jacob," the high councilor said, seated in the middle of the group, "but we didn't want to delay any further. We've already spoken to your parents. Unfortunately they were unable to be helpful, though I know they tried. It seems you've done a good job keeping this change a secret—until yesterday, that is."

"Did Egan tell on me?"

"Egan did what he was supposed to do," Egan's father, sitting next to the high councilor, broke in. "If it makes you feel any better, he clearly didn't want to tell me. However, I know my son. I know when something is bothering him. He was disturbed by your revelation yesterday, Jacob."

"So was I," Jacob countered.

"Of course you were, Jacob," the high councilor said. "You should know from the outset that you're not in trouble."

"Just tell us what happened," said a woman's voice on the far left of the shapes. He recognized it as Sonya Donato's. She lived the next street over from Jacob and his parents. "We can't help you if you don't help us."

Jacob wondered what that help would be. He said nothing at first. Fingers of light curled around his legs, casting shadows along the swirling stone of the floor tiles at his feet. For several moments the only sound was the muted tone of the chimes blowing softly from the doorway. Then even that stopped, and there was silence.

"Go on, Jacob. Tell them," his father urged from the corner.

Jacob finally told them. He recounted the last three weeks, about the headaches, the brightening, the colors, the blurry shapes, and the clarity. He left out some of the details, such as his neighbor's theft, and mentioned nothing about what he had witnessed that day his father was working in the fields, leaving his mother alone with the man he had seen outside his door. He was tempted to mention saving the grower's life, but he was certain they wouldn't want to hear it.

"What do you think of all this, Jacob? Do you like having sight?" the high councilor asked when Jacob finished his story.

Jacob wasn't sure what to say. "It's interesting. It makes things easier," he said finally.

"Easier is not always better, Jacob," another councilor said. "The challenges posed by our blindness strengthen us, make us a better people. Surely you know this from school."

"Jacob," the high councilor said, "long ago we abandoned the world of Seers because we understood that appearances can mislead. Vision corrupts the mind with its distractions."

Yes, of course. He had heard all these things many times at school and at the Gatherings. They had always made sense. Now, after everything, they still made sense in some ways, maybe even more so. He had certainly been distracted these past few weeks and had witnessed plenty of corruption, including his own dishonesty, but there was more to it than that.

"I've seen a lot of beautiful things," he said. "The plains, the moons, birds, flowers. Aren't those things important?"

"What is beauty, Jacob?" Egan's father said. "Isn't it all relative? Isn't there beauty in the songs your mother makes, and even those of the birds? The flower's scent is its true essence, what it is within. Those sights you've seen, those pictures that you find so pretty, are merely superficial."

147

"Beauty is beauty," Jacob replied. He didn't believe a word Mr. Spencer said, but he didn't know what else to say.

"If you'd never seen them, you wouldn't miss them," Mr. Spencer continued, ignoring him. "You know, Jacob, as one of the Oedipi, I used to see, back home on Earth. When I joined the Foundation, I relinquished my sight. It was the best thing I ever did. Of course those things you mention have a certain appeal to the average person, but I don't miss them. You don't realize how lucky you are to be raised in a community that is willing to penetrate deeper, to turn inward and have the courage to take what an ignorant person would find a weakness and make it their greatest strength."

"I'm sure these last few weeks have been terrible for you," the high councilor sympathized. "You never asked for any of this to happen. We feel nothing but sympathy for your ordeal."

"How *could* this have happened?" his father asked.

The high councilor answered, "There have been only a few other cases like this in the history of the colony. Once in a great while, a reversion in the genetic code of a fetus seems to occur. It usually manifests itself immediately at birth, when it can be corrected without surgery by covering the infant's eyes at the earliest stages of development. Deprived of visual stimulation, the neural pathways are soon dissolved. In general, the process is too tedious and unreliable to use on a regular basis, but it becomes an effective remedy in those rare situations."

Jacob remained silent. He didn't understand all of the high councilor's words, but the matter-of-fact way the man spoke about these matters chilled Jacob the same way it had when he'd spoken of his daughter a few days ago.

148

"What's unusual with Jacob's case is that it happened so late in life," Mrs. Donato said. "We've contacted the Foundation about the situation. Perhaps they'll have some information on how this could have happened. For now think of it simply as an oversight on nature's part. In the meantime we'll have to decide what to do with your son. Trust us to do what's best for Harmony."

The council asked no more questions and told Jacob and his parents to return home; a judgment would be forthcoming. As they were leaving, Jacob looked back at the council. They remained silent and unmoved.

"Remember, Jacob," the high councilor said, "justice is blind."

None of them spoke on the way home. Jacob wanted to say something to break the awkwardness of the moment, but the day's events hung over them, looming and oppressive. He walked behind his parents, watching the two of them as they reached out to each other and clasped hands. The intimacy of their touch, as surprising as it was, should have warmed him. Instead the sign of closeness made him feel more alone than ever. They turned the corner to their street. Jacob could see some of the neighbors standing or sitting on their doorsteps. Obviously the news had spread over the course of the afternoon. As his mother passed near a pathminder, the tone of her sounder called out. The lingerers quickly scuttled into their houses; the street echoed with the clap of closing doors. His parents flinched at the sound.

Jacob went to bed immediately after dinner. He couldn't wait to steal away from his parents, who said little to him and seemed not to know how to deal with the change in their son.

His father made small talk, mostly about work, and avoided anything that might touch on the day's events. Since the meeting at the council house, his mother had uttered few words. He wished she would scream at him, call him names, anything but give him the silent treatment, which in the total darkness of the house was depressing. She was like a ghost; he could feel her presence, but nothing more. He suspected she was probably considering his change. First Delaney, and now her own son. Before leaving the table, he moved tentatively to her chair. He touched her shoulder, the way he had the morning of his birthday when he left her to roam on his own.

"I'm sorry, Ma," he said.

She didn't answer but pulled him to her lap. She squeezed him hard, and he let her, shaking as her sobs racked her body. He wished he too could cry, but after today's events, he felt too numbed, too frightened, to give anything away. She held him as if he were a baby again, held him for a while, then let go.

Around eleven Jacob, unable to sleep, heard a knock at the front door. He maneuvered quickly to his bedroom door and opened it a crack. It was Mrs. Donato. He listened as she gave his parents the news.

"The council has decided that Jacob will be submitted to the ghostbox tomorrow for surgery to remove his eyesight."

"Is that necessary?" his mother asked. Fear sounded in her voice.

"Word's spread. The news of your son's difference has already created a significant disturbance among the people. Many are uncomfortable with the idea of living with a Seer in their midst. If Jacob is to remain in the colony, his sight must be corrected."

"It might as well be sooner than later," his father responded.

"We agree," the councilor said. "There's going to be a special midday Gathering tomorrow. Bring your son. And one more thing," she added before leaving, "we have decided that when the ghostbox operates, it will also be programmed to wipe Jacob's memory of the last few weeks. As far as your son is concerned, he'll never have seen a thing."

Jacob pretended to be asleep when his parents came in. They woke him up and told him the council's decision; they didn't speak of the memory wipe.

"Are you really going to let them do this to me?" he asked.

In the dark he could hear the awkwardness in his father's voice. "Jacob, we're not happy about the situation, but it's the council's order. We all have to do our best to go along."

"Think about your fellow citizens. You'll be setting a good example for the community," his mother assured him. "This wasn't meant to happen to you. In the end, you'll have lost nothing."

When they left, he lay there stunned. *Who are those people?* he asked himself. These strangers couldn't be his parents. Maybe his father could say those things, but certainly not his mother. She had come to his aid, covered for him several times—why not now? Maybe she was making good on her threat. She had warned him that she was finished helping him. These past few days, and especially today, he could sense the struggle within her, the detachment, the withdrawal; overwhelmed by the loss of one child, perhaps she had no other way to cope with what was happening to her son. Most likely, she and his father had no choice and were simply following orders. Where convenience and necessity met, what else could result but complicity?

Of course they had no choice. He had no choice. It was the will of Harmony—hadn't he always known that that's what set them apart? They didn't choose the selfishness of individual needs or wants. That was left to the Seers, who allowed themselves the indulgence of personal will and who suffered for it, living lives of chaos, each pursuing individual desires, oblivious to the good of others. He tried to relax in the darkness, to reconcile himself to the inevitable future of tomorrow. The councilors had inferred that his vision was an illness. Maybe he *was* sick. They were going to operate on him, after all. Didn't they do something like that only when someone was ill? Tomorrow the computer would make him well; the machine would repair the oversight, would correct nature's interference in the higher aims of humankind. And it would do more. It would ease the soul with forgetfulness, would take away those sights that had disturbed him and erase his crimes. He would be remade back into what he was—a boy who couldn't hurt anyone, who could again be a part of the community that had cared for him and raised him. He could be innocent again. It didn't matter whether he wanted it or not.

Fumbling in the dark, he picked up the new music box from his bureau. He hadn't played it once since his parents gave him the gift; the few times he'd tried, he found himself resisting. It didn't feel right somehow. It was no longer a part of him, and thinking about the song aroused a sadness in him that he had never felt before. The same thing happened now. His hand refused to open the lid, so instead he held it tightly, felt its weight in his palm, its textured metal surface and sharp corners.

Most people would consider me lucky, he thought. *Your life changes. You lose your innocence and it's gone forever; no choice there, either.* He tried telling himself this, but somehow it wasn't enough. There was that other voice there too, the one he had heard before, underneath and rising. It told him that he was different, not only from everyone else but also from himself. That person he once was, that he was sentenced to become again, had disappeared. It could never return, no matter what a computer did to him. Besides, even if he no longer remembered what he had become, everyone else would; he would always stand apart from them, never knowing why.

His mother had told him that in the end he'd have lost nothing. The voice warned him he would, in fact, lose everything. The images—the calm beauty of the skyline, the faces of his family and friends, even the bright blood of a wounded grower—would disappear, as would the freedom to move unhindered through the world, able to focus on richness beyond the self. Most of all, he would lose knowledge—of the inadequacies of human nature, of all the lies that penetrated Harmony like cracks in a foundation, of all the truths that his sight had shown him. All these things were now a part of who he was. In losing them, he would lose himself.

Memories of Delaney flooded his mind, leaving a hollow aching in their wake. He missed her now more than he ever had before. She would have understood him; she wouldn't have abandoned him like Egan, like his mother, like everybody else. He smiled grimly thinking back to all the cutting jokes and criticisms, the impersonations, even the sadder moments of alienation. Her words and deeds that had irritated him with their outrageousness no longer seemed beyond the pale. He understood her now, when it was too late. Most of all, he thought back to her desperate plea to her father the day before her death. *I want to see*, she had said. Jacob had received her wish instead. It had come to him unasked and changed him in ways he had never hoped for, yet wouldn't hope now to be without. It should have come to her. She would have had the strength to yield it. He yearned to be close to her now. Then it dawned on him. Maybe he could.

The house was quiet; his parents had gone to bed. Grabbing the finder Egan had asked him to hold on to, Jacob crept from his room and down the hall, then slipped outside. He headed toward the cemetery. He had never visited the burial grounds before—no one ever did—but he had a rough idea where they lay, just beyond the perimeter of the settlement, north of the grazing pastures, east of the field he'd raced in with Egan. The streets were dead as he made his way to the edge of town in the bright moonlight. He felt like a ghost, haunting the pathways and lanes, wandering through a world he no longer felt a part of. Where the last street ended, he could see a line of pathminders spaced distantly from one another, but tracing a clear line before disappearing over a nearby hill. It must be the way, he decided, and followed them through the night.

It didn't take long to reach the hill. Cresting the top, he gasped at the scene on the other side. A wide depression extended below; stretching across its expanse stood what seemed like hundreds of pathminders laid out in a symmetrical grid, bathed in the purple glow of the ringed moon, bright against the plain. He stared in awe at the collection of those who had lived in Harmony, a vast gathering of dead. Normally he would have been frightened at the idea of going down there, but now, standing alone on the hill, he found he wasn't. Delaney was down there and her sounder was with her. He was eager to seek her out and hoped that in reaching her, in singling her out from the unnamed and unremembered dead, he could find some sort of inspiration, some strength to get him through. At the very least, he could say good-bye.

He made his way down the hill, following the path into the valley, and soon reached the edge where the evenly spaced markers began. Taking the finder out of his pocket, he held the device before him, pressed a button, and spoke into it softly.

"Delaney Corrow," he said.

His pulse quickened as a faint tone began to beat its steady rhythm. Starting from his left, he swept the finder across the entire field in a slow arc, waiting for the telltale change in tempo and pitch to point him in the right direction. But something was wrong. As he passed the finder across the middle of the valley, its pitch lowered and the pulsing slowed. Only at the edges did it quicken again, seeming to point him in two directions at once.

It must be broken, he thought. Speaking her name a second time, he tried again with the same result. This time, however, he didn't stop at the edge of the cemetery but continued in a circle, and as he rotated to face the other way, the tone, though still faint, grew louder and steadier. Puzzled, he followed its direction as it led him back toward town, switching it to pulse mode, feeling it throb lightly in his hand. As he made his way back into Harmony he realized that the high councilor must have lied. He must still be holding on to her sounder. Why hadn't he just told Jacob the truth? He would have understood.

155

But the finder didn't bring him back to her father's house. It steered north and continued west past the center of town, leaving Jacob more and more confused. A half hour later he had reached the storehouses at the edge of Harmony, and still the finder pointed west, drawing him away from the buildings. He stopped a hundred yards out, holding the finder before him, where it continued to throb steadily, leading off into the distance. His heart began to pound so hard he could barely distinguish the finder's throb from his own beating pulse. There was only one explanation. Delaney's father had lied, all right, but not how Jacob had thought. The man had been right in saying he didn't have her sounder, but it wasn't buried in the earth. She had taken it with her. Delaney had run away.

He dropped down into the grass and fell back, his mind spinning with the realization. He could hardly believe it. She had done it, just like she said she would. How did it happen? Had the Seers taken her off? Had she run away like he had upon discovery, only plunging blindly out onto the plains without aid or comfort? Had her father let her go after all? The questions flooded his mind, but in the end they didn't matter. What was important was that she had left, that she was out there somewhere. Best of all, there was the chance that she was still alive.

He sat upright. Maybe *he* should escape, leave now while he still could. Maybe he could find her. If she could do it, why couldn't he? He jumped to his feet and stared out through the moonlight to where the land stretched into nothingness. He hesitated. How could he leave? He had no food, no water, nothing to help him face what was out there. What *was* out there? He had no idea. His entire world was right here, confined to this tiny sphere he'd never traveled more than a few hundred yards beyond, even with his sight. Besides, he wouldn't just be leaving a place. He'd be leaving his family, his community, and his only chance to return to oneness with the collective. Delaney could leave, but she was Delaney. She was strong willed and sure; he wasn't. No matter how well he understood her now, he couldn't make himself be like her. He could only be himself.

Resisting the impulse to hurl the finder far into the grass so that it might be lost forever, he turned his back on the west, full of anguish. She would forgive him. She would understand.

Arriving home, he couldn't bring himself to go back inside. Instead he climbed onto the roof of their dwelling and lay on the damp grass. The great ringed moon was setting, purple against the dark plains. Its smaller sister sat on the other side of the horizon, glowing pink, its craters shadowed. He stared at the zenith and watched the stars drift along. Far above, along the surface of the atmosphere, the dark shadow of a ship punctuated with lights lazily crawled across the sky. Occasionally its jets flared, and the pink moon illuminated its trail of vapor. Jacob watched it for an hour before it disappeared, heading for deeper space. He wondered where it was going.

CHAPTER FIFTEEN

Jacob lay in bed. He could hear the clattering of plates and silverware filtering through the half-open door and the hushed tones of his parents' conversation. He had closed the door last night after returning to bed; one of them must have opened it this morning. Normally they would have long since awakened him, but today was unlike any other day. This was his last morning as a Seer, his last morning as the boy his parents had just yesterday discovered they had been living with. They now knew him in a way that they would have preferred not to know, just as he knew things about them he'd rather not know. He still loved them. Did they feel the same? It seemed to him that that's what the pain of growing had to offer—you saw things you'd rather not see, you learned things about people that surprised and hurt you, but in the end you still loved them. That's what his sight had taught him. It was a lesson he would soon forget, a lesson Harmony would never know.

Jacob waited, lingering in bed until his father finally came in and asked him to get up. By now an incredible and vaguely familiar aroma had wafted its way to his room. It was the smell of bacon and eggs frying on the stove; the last time he had enjoyed the delicious odor was more than a year ago at Egan's house. He got out of bed, dressed slowly, and went into the kitchen. His mother greeted him warmly, as if he were a guest who had popped in for an overnight visit. Both of his parents seemed cheerful, or tried to, anyway, joking with each other as they used to do when he was younger. He walked through the darkness to the front door and opened it; morning sunlight cascaded in, illuminating the kitchen. His parents, unaware of the change, continued moving about, and as he watched them, Jacob felt invisible, as if he had lifted up a rock to reveal a colony of ants that went about their business, oblivious to a spectator.

"Mind if I leave the door open?" he asked.

"What for?" his mother asked, turning in his direction. "Oh," she realized suddenly, and walked to the stove.

"I like the light," he said. They ignored him; he left it open. The way they pretended to be happy, pretended that nothing was wrong, that nothing important was about to occur, irritated him. Maybe they were happy. After all, they weren't the ones about to undergo surgery, to have their memory erased. As far as they were concerned, they would deliver this strange boy and have their old son returned, brand new.

He stared into the street, watching the morning activities. Cats wandered the lane, sniffing plants. One of them hissed at another over the body of a squeak that still twitched between its paws. People were emerging from their homes, leaving for their work duties. One at a time, as they passed by his yard, they stopped and turned in his direction, tilting their heads to catch a scent of the cooking bacon. He watched their nostrils flare, their throats constrict as they swallowed the saliva that he knew flooded their mouths in response to the aroma. Occasionally two or three gathered and whispered to one another, and he knew their conversation, though he couldn't hear the words. One pair, so distracted by the smells that they failed to hear their sounders chime in proximity, ran into each other. One of them lost balance and tumbled; both cried out in surprise.

"Better watch where you're going," Jacob cried, and laughed as they jumped at his voice, guiltily hurrying away.

"Time to eat, Jake," his mother called from inside. Leaving the door ajar, he went in and sat down. He served them all, spooning the scrambled eggs and bacon onto three chipped plates. He spotted an open can on the table with a spoon sticking out.

"What's in the can?" he asked, though he knew the contents.

"We still have some of the pears," his mother said. "I thought you might like some."

"I'm surprised they didn't take them," he noted.

"I guess I forgot to tell them," she said softly.

"This is quite a breakfast," Jacob said brightly. "Bacon, eggs—"

"The high councilor stopped by this morning and brought them," his father broke in. "I thought it was nice of him. He's a good man."

"One last meal?" Jacob asked. Neither of them answered. He could see their bowed heads in the half-light of the kitchen.

"Would you like some pears?" he asked, taking the can.

"No, thank you," they said in unison.

At noon Jacob's parents accompanied him to the common, where the council and most of the settlement had convened for the Gathering. The three of them were escorted by a pair of listeners who had shown up at his house, the same men who had escorted him from school. Nobody spoke en route to the common. As they approached the main square he could hear the chorus of hundreds of sounders hovering in the air above the crowd. The buzzing tone grew louder as he approached. He hadn't attended a Gathering since gaining his sight, and as he came around the corner into the common, the sight of the multitude gave him pause. They stood sideways to him, facing the stage in the northeast corner of the square. Waves of pale heads, lined up in rows, filled the entire space; hands on backs linked each row, creating a symmetry of human shapes almost identical in their coarse brown garments. Their stillness startled him most, however. He expected a crowd this size to appear as a rippling mass of bobbing heads and reaching arms. These figures, however, could easily be mistaken for statues. All that betrayed them as living beings was the occasional blinking of their eyes and the overwhelming hum of their collective sounders. He could hardly remember being one of them.

A man with a shaved head swung an immense mallet against the hanging gong at the edge of the platform. As its reverberations shivered through the crowd, hands reflexively went to pins and the overtone stopped. The square was silent. Jacob felt his heart pounding in his chest, heard the blood pulsing in his ears.

"Come on, Jacob. The high councilor is waiting for you," one of the listeners said.

They separated him from his parents and led him along the edge of the crowd to the stage. He was ordered onto the platform and climbed the stairs with trembling legs. As he reached the top a single man walked to the middle of the stage and stood facing the crowd. It was the high councilor. Not knowing what else to do, Jacob walked over, then froze as the man turned in his direction. His heart leaped into his throat and he gasped for air. Those pale, inhuman eyes, the long, dark beard streaked with gray. He had seen this face before—it had been burned into his memory three days ago at his doorstep. This was the man his mother had embraced. Seeing his mother with her lover had been terrible enough, but knowing it was *him* was far worse. A bitter tang gathered in Jacob's throat.

The high councilor seemed to sense Jacob's hesitation, oblivious to its cause. "Come here, son. Don't be frightened," the man coaxed.

Jacob slowly walked over, full of regret. *I should've run*, he thought. *I shouldn't be here.* Despite his loathing for Delaney's father for all his betrayals, he felt more contempt for himself at his own weakness. The high councilor placed his hands on Jacob's shoulders; Jacob cringed at the man's touch. The crowd, which had begun shifting and murmuring, aware of Jacob's arrival, settled now into silence as the leader addressed them.

"You are all aware of Jacob's peculiar situation. By now you are also aware of the council's decision. We must all remember that our young friend is not at fault. A mistake occurred, and we will fix it, as we do all mistakes in the community. Jacob will soon be one of us again. We know you will all support Jacob and his family in this ordeal."

Jacob stared at the quiet crowd. They were the people he had grown up with, had learned from, had even admired. Now all he could see were faces that reflected a variety of expressions—sympathy, fear, contempt, blankness. And because he knew most of them only by the sound of their voice, their silence made them strangers to him.

"In a sense, we are fortunate," the high councilor continued, "for this incident provides us an opportunity to realize our good fortune and strengthen our bonds. Jacob's bravery in willingly submitting himself for correction serves as a reaffirmation of our own faith in Truesight. He is an inspiration to us all and reminds us of our duty."

"Blindness is purity. Blindness is unity. Blindness is freedom," the crowd chanted in response.

"The council will now escort Jacob to the ghostbox. You may return to your duties, safe in the knowledge that soon all will once again be normal."

The crowd applauded and music blared from the speakers as Jacob was escorted offstage by the high councilor, who held his hand firmly. They left the square, surrounded by a squad of listeners, with the dozen men and women of the council following behind. The blare of music and clapping hands faded as they paraded through the quiet streets. Everyone remained silent; even their sounders had been deactivated, but for two listeners who marched ahead of them. They headed southeast to the edge of the settlement before following a path away from town toward a dark bunker. Jacob had noticed that building from a distance several times and wondered what it contained, for he had never seen anyone coming from or going to it. Now he knew.

The shaking in his legs renewed as they neared the structure. He took deep breaths to calm himself, not to betray his fright. He wouldn't give them that.

The great doors opened with a loud hydraulic hiss. Martin Corrow ushered Jacob along, and they stepped into a chamber. Everyone else remained outside. Except for the dim glow of computer screens and blinking data banks, the room was unlit. But enough light shone from the open doors that Jacob could survey the scene. The room was mostly empty. To his right he observed two figures silhouetted against the wall, waiting patiently in their long white robes. Between them, a table with straps emerged from the wall; above it hovered several robotic arms like those he had seen on the harvesters in the fields, though these pieces of jointed metal protruding from the wall were much smaller and more delicate.

He gazed toward the center of the room, where the only other object stood before him—a tall, dark obelisk, perfectly rectangular and bare but for a single yellow light shining behind a glass lens. The glowing eye met his gaze, burning into him with cold indifference. He closed his eyes and pictured the first clear image that had greeted him a week ago. In his mind, one black-and-yellow insect bit into the head of its smaller prey.

"Leave us for a moment," the high councilor ordered. As the robed figures left, he turned to Jacob, keeping a firm grip on Jacob's shoulder.

"You've viewed the world through a Seer's eyes. You've seen quite a bit, I'm sure—much more, I suspect, than what you've told us. But it's over, Jacob. Any last words? Any final confessions?" he asked, a hint of humor in his voice that froze Jacob's blood.

"I know," Jacob replied softly but with conviction. As frightened as he was by the room and his purpose there, he no longer felt scared of the man. A glimmer of Delaney's defiance rose up within him as he confronted him with the truth.

"Know what? What are you talking about?" the high councilor demanded.

"I know about Delaney. I know you lied—she's not dead. She ran away."

There was a long pause as the high councilor processed Jacob's words. "You're a clever boy, Jacob. However you found out, it doesn't surprise me. Yes, she ran away, but I doubt she survived."

"You mean she didn't leave with the Seers?" Jacob asked in dismay.

"No. I would never allow that. She wanted independence and I gave it to her. I'm sure she discovered for herself just how far it got her."

"How could you? She was your daughter." He couldn't believe what he was hearing.

The high councilor responded defensively. "She gave me no choice. I tried to change her mind, get her to stay, but she threatened to make our lives intolerable."

"You mean intolerable for *you*."

"For us all. I did what I had to do for the good of the community. She was a blight, an anomaly. Just like you. You, however, are easier to fix."

His words stung Jacob. "You're a liar. Everything about you is a lie. I know."

"You know? You know nothing. You're a boy, and a Seer. Sometimes, Jacob, we have to lie to serve a greater truth. Regardless, you will soon forget all this and Delaney will be dead to you once again, as she is to me and everyone else." Jacob could hear the fury rising in his voice. "I didn't enjoy cutting her out, and it saddens me that it had to be my own daughter, but it was a price I was willing to pay. Now it's time for you to pay yours." He leaned down so that his face was even with Jacob's, and tightened his grip. The eye of the ghostbox cast a yellow pall across his face. "Let's just hope the surgery goes well, Jacob. The ghostbox makes mistakes from time to time."

His lips curled back the slightest bit and his left eye blinked, a slow and knowing wink. Jacob recoiled in shock at the gesture, at what it could only mean. One final, dreadful secret revealed, a secret that enveloped all the others, wrapping them in darkness. *He can see!* he thought in horror.

With a sudden jerk Jacob twisted away from the high councilor's grasp and darted through the doors. After a second of stunned hesitation the high councilor rushed to the doorway, crying for him to stop as the small crowd outside turned in confusion. A squad of listeners, alarmed by the cry, jumped onto the path ahead of Jacob, forming a chain in the hope of catching him. Jacob leaped to one side and, bounding through the tall grass, ran toward the colony.

As he fled he heard the high councilor's voice calling out above the confused clamor: "If you leave, you can never return!"

He kept on running.

He darted through the streets toward home, gasping for air, feeling both terrified and exhilarated from the escape. It had happened so fast, had caught him unaware. The wink had done it, a sly and snide revelation of the man's utter corruption that had broken the spell and set him free. In the end, after everything that had happened, everything he'd learned, it was a single, simple gesture that had enraged him and sent him flying through this long, dark tunnel toward the light. But he had to hurry. It wouldn't take them long to figure out where he had gone and where he might be heading. Reaching his house, he threw open the door and ran inside, searching in the meager light. He opened cupboards and drawers until he spotted the glint of metal cylinders. Three cans of pears remained. He took all three, a block of cheese, and a couple loaves of bread and placed them on the table. Then he grabbed a sharp knife, a cup, a bowl, and an electric lighter and put those on the table as well. Snatching a canvas bag from the closet, he dashed into his room and stuffed his blanket into the satchel along with an extra shirt and towel. He grabbed the finder last, tucked it between the folds of his blanket, and raced back down the hall into the kitchen. He stuffed the food and supplies into the bag, zipped it closed, and slipped the carrying strap over his shoulder. Breathing heavily, he gazed around one last time, took the silver pin from his chest, and placed it on the table. Then he left.

He could hear shouts one street over and the sound of running feet approaching the corner. He quickly crossed the lane and climbed the side of the house opposite his onto the grassy roof, and peered down as a group of five men turned onto the street below him. They immediately headed to his house and burst down the door, disappearing inside. He headed in the opposite direction, running along the ridge of the hill until he reached the end and scrambled down to the street. He hurried through the North Tier, stopping in the small square to drink from the fountain. The square was vacant. Dunking his sweaty head into the pool, he sucked in the cool water with long gulps and then was off again, quickly to the north field, where the faint trails of playful children meandered through the waist-high grass.

He could see the line of pathminders standing tall in the distance, tracing the northern perimeter of the colony. Turning around, he glanced back at the colony that stretched below him. No one was nearby; the streets were empty. Either they were concentrated along the southern gate of the colony or had given up, realizing the futility of the search. He turned back and surveyed the field. Beyond the pathminders the plains stretched to the horizon, row after row of hills disappearing into haze. He would cross that northern line, veer left, and head west, where the transports came from, the large haulers driven by Seers. There were people there, he guessed; how far, he had no idea. Among them, hopefully, was Delaney—if she was still alive, he would find her.

He resisted the urge to turn around, to run home, back into the arms of his mother, back into the cool darkness beneath the earth. Instead he ran down the back side of the hill and into the field, leaping through the grass that separated before him and closed behind, swallowing him up. He broke the line, the pathminders wailed, and the screeching in his ears was almost unbearable. Before long, however, he was far enough away that the noise didn't bother him. *Let them wail*, he thought. He didn't stop running until he reached the top of the first set of hills nearly a quarter mile away. There he turned around one last time and scanned the edge of the colony that was the only place he had ever known. He thought he saw dark figures standing on the top of the hill. He reached out as if to touch them, then dropped his arm and turned away for good.

ACKNOWLEDGMENTS

I would first like to thank author Craig Nova—a man writer Garret Keizer once called "the novelist's novelist"—for his considerable advice, wisdom, and warm support throughout the original writing of *Truesight* and beyond. Thanks also to Professor Judy Worman at Dartmouth College for her careful reading and thoughtful line edits during revision, and to Professor Barbara Kreiger for her feedback and support as well.

Thanks are also due to my agent, George Nicholson at Sterling Lord Literistic, for taking an interest in my work and for his skill in finding me a publisher, and to my editor, Susan Rich, at HarperCollins, for her enthusiasm and her great talent in helping me make this a much better book than it might have been otherwise.

I would also like to thank my colleagues at Lyndon Institute for their support throughout this project, in particular English department chair Gerry Stork and headmaster Rick Hilton. Special thanks goes to English teacher John Barksdale for his helpful feedback and suggestions (and even more importantly for his excellent driving skills, which got me to the hospital in time to see the birth of my son).

Finally, I would like to thank my family and friends for their love and encouragement. Most of all, I'd like to thank my wife, Erica, a brilliant freelance editor in her own right, not only for her love and companionship but for her thoughtful ideas and edits throughout the writing of this book.